CANADA AND THE BLACKFACE ATLANTIC

CANADA AND THE BLACKFACE ATLANTIC

PERFORMING SLAVERY,
CONFLICT,
AND FREEDOM,
1812 – 1897

CHERYL THOMPSON

WILFRID LAURIER
UNIVERSITY PRESS

Wilfrid Laurier University Press acknowledges the support of the Canada Council for the Arts for our publishing program. We acknowledge the financial support of the Government of Canada through the Canada Book Fund for our publishing activities. Funding provided by the Government of Ontario and the Ontario Arts Council. This work was supported by the Research Support Fund.

LIBRARY AND ARCHIVES CANADA CATALOGUING IN PUBLICATION

Title: Canada and the blackface Atlantic : performing slavery, conflict, and freedom, 1812–1897 / Cheryl Thompson.
Names: Thompson, Cheryl, 1977– author
Description: Includes bibliographical references and index.
Identifiers: Canadiana (print) 20240465806 | Canadiana (ebook) 20240465830 | ISBN 9781771126540 (softcover) | ISBN 9781771126557 (EPUB) | ISBN 9781771126564 (PDF)
Subjects: LCSH: Blackface—Atlantic Provinces—History—19th century. | LCSH: Blackface entertainers—Atlantic Provinces—History—19th century. | LCSH: Black people in the performing arts—Atlantic Provinces—History—19th century.
Classification: LCC PN2071.B58 T46 2025 | DDC 792.02/8—dc23

Cover and interior design by Lara Minja, Lime Design.
Front cover image: "James Sutherland costumed as 'Civil Rights'" by Willliam Notman, 1875, from the Notman Collection, The McCord Stewart Museum, Montreal. For more on this image, see pages 152–53.

© 2025 Wilfrid Laurier University Press
Waterloo, Ontario, Canada
www.wlupress.wlu.ca

Every reasonable effort has been made to acquire permission for copyrighted material used in this text, and to acknowledge all such indebtedness accurately. Any errors and omissions called to the publisher's attention will be corrected in future printings.

No part of this publication may be reproduced, stored in a retrieval system, or transmitted, in any form or by any means, without the prior written consent of the publisher or a licence from the Canadian Copyright Licensing Agency (Access Copyright). For an Access Copyright licence, visit http://www.accesscopyright.ca or call toll-free to 1-800-893-5777.

Wilfrid Laurier University Press is located on the Haldimand Tract, part of the traditional territories of the Haudenosaunee, Anishnaabe, and Neutral Peoples. This land is part of the Dish with One Spoon Treaty between the Haudenosaunee and Anishnaabe Peoples and symbolizes the agreement to share, to protect our resources, and not to engage in conflict. We are grateful to the Indigenous Peoples who continue to care for and remain interconnected with this land. Through the work we publish in partnership with our authors, we seek to honour our local and larger community relationships, and to engage with the diversity of collective knowledge integral to responsible scholarly and cultural exchange.

CONTENTS

INTRODUCTION • 3

1
Canada and the Emergence of the Blackface Atlantic, 1812–39 • 25

2
Performing Conflict in Blackface, Antislavery Movements, and the First Black Dancers, 1840–57 • 57

3
Newspapers, Railways, Theatre Expansion, and Homegrown Blackface Minstrels, 1858–61 • 88

4
Canada's Civil War Sympathizers and the Rise of *Black* Minstrelsy, 1862–66 • 119

5
The *New* Plantation Minstrelsy, Blackface Political Cartoons, and Choral Songs of Freedom, 1867–86 • 141

6
White Women Minstrels, *Darkest America*, and Black Singers on Canadian Stages, 1887–97 • 184

CONCLUSION • 219

Appendices • 225
Notes • 235
Selected Bibliography • 275
Index • 295

CANADA AND THE BLACKFACE ATLANTIC

❧ INTRODUCTION ❧

In the introduction to *Burnt Cork: Traditions and Legacies of Blackface Minstrelsy* (2012), Stephen Johnson describes being "repeatedly confronted" by the persistence of blackface "in almost every 'walk' of his life as a spectator." Johnson, who is professor emeritus at the University of Toronto's (UofT) Centre for Drama, Theatre, and Performance Studies, spent a career writing about blackface in Canada West (1841 to 1867; also known as Upper Canada from 1791 to 1841) and engaging in archival work related to early British minstrelsy. From that work, he created two digital databases: Canada West: Performance Culture in Southern Ontario, a site that charts performance culture in the region from non-Indigenous settlement to the mid-twentieth century, and The Juba Project site, which contains a geospatial map and theatre details about minstrelsy in Britain from 1842 to 1852. On February 4, 2016, I won a Banting Postdoctoral Fellowship and began working with Stephen. Over the next two years, with a corpus of over 1,100 newspaper articles (including advertisements and editorials) documenting blackface at theatres, performance halls, retail, schools, churches, parks, hospitals, and community centres, 168 images of blackface performers, troupes, characters, and caricatures collected between 2012 and 2020, and a ten-year-plus collection of books, journal articles, book chapters and dissertations on blackface theatre and the sites of performance in the nineteenth century, I was finally able to write this book.[1]

Within these pages, I have engaged in visual analysis, historiographies of Black Canada, media, theatre, music, dance, and performance. I am also responding to Stephen's observation over a decade ago, after being approached by the Canadian Broadcasting Corporation in Toronto to be

∾ INTRODUCTION ∾

interviewed on a radio talk show, that the question, "why has there been a resurgence in the use of blackface in contemporary society?" remains unanswered.[2] *Canada and the Blackface Atlantic* aims to explain the persistence of blackface by moving the topic beyond the limits of opinion-editorial blogs, a specific discipline, or walled garden of academic discourse into an accessible tome that addresses the origins of blackface in the British and American theatres, and its arrival in Canada. I argue that performative *Blackness* was appealing, and in some ways, it was a catharsis for White peoples' anxieties. By caricaturing Black men and women as diminutive fools rather than the absconding and militant Black folks of the nineteenth century who increasingly sought freedom in Canada and elsewhere, the blackface minstrel stage became a powerful socializing agent by the 1830s.

American minstrel companies first began coming to Canada in the 1840s, with the peak years spanning from the 1850s to 1890s. Touring theatrical minstrel productions of Harriet Beecher Stowe's *Uncle Tom's Cabin* headed to Canada West in the 1850s.[3] Like in the US and Britain, these so-called "Tom Shows" attracted large crowds.[4] Robin Winks found that Callender's Colored Minstrels filled every seat in Academy Hall in Halifax in 1884, when J.W. McAndrew, the Watermelon Man, Haverly's Mastodon Minstrels, A.G. Field's troupe, and Jack Diamond, the dancer, toured Canada; "they purported to speak for [blacks]—on occasion with compassion and even affection, but usually with ridicule and low humor," he observed.[5] Winks's *The Blacks in Canada* (1971) is still identified as the first book-length history of Black Canadians (a fact that has been challenged in recent years),[6] but what his text, albeit missing many details, also marks is one of the first moments where blackface is identified as part of the cultural fabric of nineteenth-century Canada. By identifying omissions in the Canadian historical record, my intention is not to shame authors who ignored Black people in their work; instead, my aim is to implore future generations to stop doing so. There exists a record of publication pinpointing blackface as originating and professionalizing in the US, troupes and actors who toured Britain, and a Canadian market for theatrical productions,

∾ INTRODUCTION ∾

songs, and dances. This book centres blackface in Canada, while connecting its origins to those in the US and Britain.

First, I position blackface minstrelsy's development not singularly through the lens of stages and repertoires, but as a sociocultural, political phenomenon that coincided with the growth of theatres, professional companies, and other ancillary industries like the railway, manufacturing, national government, the building of concert halls, and growth of newspaper editorial and advertising. I argue they all played a role in creating public desire for blackface entertainment across Canada. For example, as the electric telegraph expanded into Canada in the late 1840s, bringing news from Montreal and New York to Toronto and beyond, literacy rates grew, and because of the provincial public school system, universities like King's College, which became the University of Toronto in 1849, emerged.[7] That same year, on September 25, Toronto's first professional theatre house, the Royal Lyceum Theatre, opened to the public. Located behind a row of buildings on the south side of Adelaide Street West, between Bay and York Streets, the theatre was managed by John Nickinson (b. unknown), an English actor-manager with much American experience. Nickinson took over the theatre in 1853 (and ran it until 1859), and it garnered a reputation for establishing successful theatre in the city.[8] Not only did the Royal Lyceum become home to the first known Black Canadian theatrical performance, held there in 1849 by the Toronto Coloured Young Men's Amateur Theatrical Society,[9] it was also the place where Toronto-born Colin "Cool" Burgess (1840–1905) performed in blackface before appearing on stages across the US and Britain.

Second, I locate where homegrown amateur blackface has been identified in the writings of other Canadian historians. Jonathan Vance's *A History of Canadian Culture* (2009) describes one of the first cultural events to take place at the barracks of the North-West Mounted Police (NWMP) near Battleford, Saskatchewan in 1879 was a minstrel show, which included such songs as "Massa in de Cold" and "N---er on the Fence."[10] The NWMP, the forerunner of the Royal Canadian Mounted Police (also known as the Mounties) was a frontier police force created by the federal government in 1873 to "keep the peace between Native Indians and white intruders in the area now comprising Alberta and Saskatchewan…. The job of the police was to make sure that a new society replaced the old with as little

5

upset as possible."¹¹ In other words, the NWMP played a pivotal role in the commandeering of Indigenous lands. The clearing of western Canada took place at a time when there was no population to support it. Indigenous people had lived on the land for millennia, and in this era of westward expansion sweeping across the North American continent, the Canadian government saw the clearing—and the dispossession of Indigenous people—as a means to make way for railroads and to remain competitive in an increasingly networked system of capital that had, by the second half of the nineteenth century, become dependent upon railway transportation for growth and development. The Fraser Canyon Gold Rush in 1858, the establishment of the NWMP, and the building of the Canadian Pacific Railway (CPR) in 1881 linked British Columbia with the Maritimes, establishing a transcontinental railway system connecting all provinces; what it also did was create an environment where White immigrants became the "stewards" of the national project of expansion at the expense of Indigenous people, Black people, and Chinese people (whose labour would be depended upon to lay down the CPR's tracks).

One of the questions this book answers is how an organization like the NWMP knew about a song like "Massa in de Cold" (1852), which was written by Pennsylvania-born Stephen Foster (1826–64), the major White creator of minstrel music. How did his music travel to Canada's west at a time when there was no popular radio or reliable communication networks? Not only are many of Foster's songs still known today, but they are also songs many people of a certain age grew up singing. Foster, who is also known as "the founder of American minstrel music," composed a string of popular songs in the late 1840s and early 1850s such as "Oh! Susanna" (1848), "Old Uncle Ned" (1848), "Camptown Races" (1850), "Old Folks at Home," also known as "Swanee River" (1851), and "My Old Kentucky Home, Good Night" (1853). Two of the first songs I learned to play on the piano were "Oh! Susanna" and "Swanee River." Thinking of these songs as a product of history helps to explain (and deepen our contemporary understanding about why) they were performed by organizations like the NWMP. They sang them because they were the popular songs of the day.

Significantly, the American canon on minstrelsy is the most extensive and represents much of the contextual background I used to write this book. Robert Toll's *Blacking Up: The Minstrel Show in Nineteenth-Century*

America (1974) is one of the first texts on American blackface, but since the 1990s, authors such as Eric Lott, William Mahar, Robert Nowatzki, David Roediger, Annemarie Bean, Yuval Taylor, Jake Austen, Bob Carlin, and many others have told this complicated story. US minstrelsy began in the late 1820s and early 1830s, reaching its highest point in the 1840s through the 1890s when it had overt political partisanship linking its White and working-class male originators in the North to the Democratic party, but also to sectional conflicts, slavery, abolitionism, and the expansion of the union westward.[12] As Roediger explains, "the Democratic party reinvented whiteness.... This sense of white unity and white entitlement—of white 'blood'—served to bind together in Democratic slaveholders and the masses of non-slaveholding whites in the South. It further connected the Southern and Northern wings of the Democracy."[13] Blackface began as the performative manifestation of the politization of White men's agency during a period in American history of significant conflict and change. By the 1870s, minstrel troupes toured extensively on three main circuits distributing the musical and theatrical contents of variety shows widely throughout the American South, midwest, west, and north.[14] At the same time, there were parallels, alliances, differences, conflicts, and influences between American and British abolitionism and minstrelsy.[15] Nowatzki observes that the meanings of blackface were influenced by the travels of abolitionists and minstrel performers between the US and Britain and were linked to different nationalisms, to the cultural relations between the two nations, and to ideologies of class in both nations.[16]

Unlike White Americans who "reviled Britain as an oppressive monarchy," many African Americans believed Britain was more democratic than America. Britain abolished the Atlantic slave trade in 1807, which led to the eradication of slavery across its colonies, including Canada on August 1, 1834. As a result, many formerly enslaved people and abolitionists believed that Britain, and by extension Canada, was different from America; Canada offered the promise of freedom and the lure of emancipation not possible in the context of an American society that still prioritized slave labour. In this context, blackface minstrelsy emerged as America's first form of popular entertainment, the sociocultural relations of its "racial" production, and the structural and emotional pressures of the period helped to produce "blackness" as a commodity.[17]

∾ INTRODUCTION ∾

Male actors dressing as female characters dates to the time of Shakespeare in sixteenth-century Britain, when women were not permitted to take part in the theatre—not as playwrights, shareholders, or actresses. The roles of women or girls were all played by adolescent boys whose voices had not yet changed, or young men who could do a convincing job sounding like women. When the British pantomime Dame arrived in the nineteenth century, this cross-dressed character had developed partly from the sixteenth-century commedia dell'arte tradition of Italy and other stage traditions, such as the seventeenth-century Harlequin (comic fool). The Dame, as historian David Mayer notes, was a stereotypical aging female in which "ugliness allied to misplaced vanity, sexual voracity paired with squeamishness, assertiveness, slovenly housekeeping, appalling taste in clothes, excessive curiosity, and chronic and indiscriminate gossiping."[18] While American minstrelsy transformed cross-dressed characters on stage, its masking and cross-dressing traditions were rooted in those that came before. In its first few decades, the *wench* act was a specialty piece featuring at least three of the players and, sometimes, the entire ensemble, which numbered from five to a dozen male performers. The wench dancer usually impersonated a Black woman by parodying both slavery and prostitution as fodder for the audience's fun.

The minstrel stage was not singularly an arena for White working-class men to thwart Black progress in America; it was also the outward manifestation of the "White *man's* burden" that became, as Sander Gilman explains, "[about] his sexuality and its control, and it is this which is transferred into the need to control the sexuality of the Other, the Other as sexualized female."[19] Three of the first actors to gain success as minstrel *wenches*—E.P. (Edwin Pearce) Christy's (1815–62) stepson George Christy (1827–68), Irish actor Barney Williams (1823–76), and English American actor George Holland (1791–1870)—also had minor stardom as pantomime Dames in their careers, and they continued to perform Dame roles in pantomime pieces and Shakespearean burlesques during the antebellum years.[20] American minstrelsy delineated the boundaries of a performative "drag" femininity that aimed to ridicule all women—White women's burgeoning suffragette movement, and Black women's presumed licentious sexuality.[21] Ultimately, the American scholarship has theorized about the complex relationship between racial caricature, gender symbolism, and cultural hierarchy in audiences and performers, especially during the rise of the Jewish blackface performer in the 1870s through 1890s, a period known as vaudeville, when women and men—Black and White—took to stages across North America to perform in and out of blackface as circus and comedy acts, and everything in between.[22]

This book locates, describes, and pinpoints American blackface performers and productions that caricatured the Black body and misrepresented authentic Blackness while also unpacking, probing, and elucidating those narratives in relation to Black acts of resistance that took place in Canada and the US. To understand the import of Toronto's Black community petitioning the city in the early 1840s to ban licences to circuses and menageries that allowed "certain acts, and songs" that depicted "Negro Characters,"[23] one also needs to understand the rise of African American concert singers such as soprano Elizabeth Taylor Greenfield (1809–76) who toured the US-Canadian border cities, including Toronto and towns in and around Chatham in the 1850s. The mere presence of singers like Greenfield, and others like the Hyers Sisters, Anna Madah (1855–1929), Emma Louise (1857–1901), and Matilda Sissieretta Jones (1868–1933) who were some of the first Black women to perform opera on stages around the globe, presented a counternarrative to blackface, as performed by both White and Black troupes.

The emergence of concert singers took place at the same time Black choral groups appeared, like the Fisk Jubilee Singers, an a cappella group founded at Fisk University in Nashville, Tennessee in 1871. During the 1880s and 1890s, multiple African American Jubilee singing groups toured Canada (and the globe). Their songs challenged the "happy" themes of the Southern plantation that had been central to the minstrel show. As educated and trained singers of Negro spirituals, also known as "Sorrow Songs," as coined by the great African American intellectual W.E.B. Du Bois (1868–1963), the Fisk Jubilee Singers sang the songs that helped African Americans not only endure slavery but, in some cases, find their way to freedom. Their acts were in direct opposition to *Black* and White minstrelsy's emphasis on the "good ol' days" of Black servitude. The Fisk Jubilee Singers and other American jubilee singing troupes not only toured Canada, but they inspired Canadian acts like the Canadian Jubilee Singers and Imperial Orchestra, established in Hamilton in 1879, and the

∽ INTRODUCTION ∽

O'Banyoun Jubilee Singers, founded by Brantford, Ontario-born Reverend Josephus O'Banyoun. The O'Banyoun Singers featured members from the Hamilton British Methodist Episcopal Church who also toured successfully into the 1880s. Just as the Fisk Jubilee travelled North America, Canadian Jubilee Singers and O'Banyoun Singers also toured England, Ireland, Wales, and Scotland.[24]

This book traces the rise of blackface minstrelsy in tandem with Black choral groups and Black concert singers to pinpoint when and where White audiences were exposed to competing narratives about Black enslavement and emancipation. It also attends to an existing contention in the US scholarship regarding how to write about Black people in tandem with blackface. In Lott's frequently cited text from 1993, *Love and Theft: Blackface Minstrelsy and the American Working Class*, he articulates how minstrelsy allowed White working-class men in the urban North to manufacture a sense of power over Black people.[25] On one hand, White working-class men in the urban North feared and loathed Black presence, the idea of Black rights, and Black freedoms; on the other, through the performance of blackface minstrelsy, they also acknowledged the ingenuity of Black cultural practices. Importantly, Douglas A. Jones, Jr. argues that much of the literature on early minstrelsy follows the example laid by Lott, where he "hardly attends to black responses to the form, not to mention wider, concurrent black social and political formations that also framed minstrelsy's inception." In Douglas Jr.'s view, this "unfortunate instance of historical continuity in which scholars borrow the model of those who crafted minstrelsy itself" has helped to remove Black people from the historiographic frame and the spaces and places of minstrelsy.[26] This book contends that blackface minstrelsy was a response to Black agency and freedom, a response that was met at the time with a counterresponse via Black actors, dancers, singers, and managers, in addition to newspapers and activism within Black communities. While the theatrical practices, performative texts, representational modes, discursive regimes, and literary genres of White minstrelsy have been the dominant focus of scholars and historians, there has been little attention given to Black performative modes that, while not wholly preserved within a theatre archive or performative collection, can be traced through newspaper discourses, histographies of nineteenth-century Canada, and a reservoir of images that reveal

∾ INTRODUCTION ∾

both the aesthetic choices of minstrel performers as well as minstrelsy's codes and conventions.

From the 1810s onward, enslaved and freeborn Black people from the US, but also the Caribbean, immigrated to Quebec, the Maritimes, Ontario, and Western Canada. (During this same period, White people immigrated to Canada in search of a new life in the aftermath of disease outbreaks, overpopulation, and extreme poverty in Europe.) They came because of the promise of work, building a new life, and (so many thought) the chance to break the shackles of disenfranchisement that had defined the Black experience in the previous three centuries of life across the Atlantic world. Black people followed the "North Star" to Canada with the wind, and the promise of freedom, beneath their wings. One of the first groups of Black immigrants, known as Black Loyalists, arrived in Nova Scotia (some headed to Upper Canada) in the wake of the American Revolutionary War in 1775. By the late eighteenth century, Canada's growth was shaped by these divergent developments: Upper/Lower Canada (present-day Quebec, renamed Canada East in 1841) became the most northern outposts of British colonialism, Indigenous Nations lost control of preserving their lands amid British and American expansion, and Black people, enslaved and free, increased their presence in emergent cities and towns. During the War of 1812, thousands of enslaved Black Americans fled to Nova Scotia, encouraged by a promise of emancipation and settlement on British land. Known as Black Refugees, this group arrived in Halifax in 1813, and they were immediately regarded as a valuable addition to the province's labour force.[27] As Montreal became the national hub for rail transportation in the 1890s, Black men moved there to work primarily as railway sleeping car porters. The service relied exclusively on Black men to work in those roles, and as they headed North, the St. Antoine District, colloquially known as Little Burgundy, became an established Black community.[28]

In addition to Montreal, Quebec City became a place where Black people lived and comingled with White people—Anglophones and Francophones. These cities became home to touring blackface troupes from the US such as Duprez and Green's Minstrels, an American company that travelled across North America, but which specifically recruited French-speaking performers like Verchères, Quebec-born Calixa Lavallée

∽ INTRODUCTION ∽

(1842–91), who would become best known as the composer of "Chant national" ("O Canada"), a song he penned after performing across the US, and as a blackface minstrel musician for the Union Army during the Civil War. Born in France, Charles Duprez (1833–1902) was a minstrel performer and manager who, in addition to Duprez and Green's Minstrels which he had been part of until J.E. Green retired in 1865, also managed The New Orleans and Metropolitan Burlesque Opera Troupe and Brass Band (hereafter the New Orleans Minstrels) troupe throughout its twenty-five year existence.[29] "Cool" Burgess also toured with Duprez and Green in 1862 when they played Toronto (they also toured Nova Scotia and New Brunswick).[30] Duprez had spent time in Quebec as a child where his father worked grain shipping and river navigation between Montreal and Quebec City, and then he moved to the US where he apprenticed as a tailor before entering show business.[31]

What this suggests is that homegrown blackface performers like Burgess and Lavallée cannot be removed from the racial implications of blackface minstrelsy. They may have achieved stardom in the US, but they learned about and were exposed to blackface long before they reached American soil. With a shared history of slavery devoid of a plantation culture, Canadian curiosities and fears about a Black presence allowed for the American South to become a symbolic palimpsest of sorts. In other words, if White audiences did not know real Black people, they were still inundated with a racist visual culture of images and lithographic prints rooted in Black caricature, not to mention a burgeoning literary culture fuelled by slavery narratives like *Uncle Tom's Cabin*. Rather than focusing on a mobile and enfranchised Black subject, this staging of Blackness, predicated as it was on a past of Black servitude, gave blackface minstrelsy significant sociocultural import beyond being mere entertainment.

The name of this book borrows from Black British scholar Paul Gilroy's term the *Black Atlantic*, which speaks not only to a geographic place at the nexus of European colonization and Black servitude, but as an ideological concept that pinpoints how Black people, through acts of disidentifying with Western discourses about nation, citizenship, and freedom, were able

∽ INTRODUCTION ∽

to articulate new ways of understanding who they were and the possibilities for their lives. Where Jones Jr. writes that "For African Americans living in the wake of the nation's founding, they lacked the *security* of being an American and the *surety* of being a non-American; instead, they were at once both, existing in what [he] would call the state of black exception,"[32] Gilroy, writing from a point of view that considered the Caribbean and Britain, similarly articulated a sense of in-betweenness, creolization, and hybridity. This created what he called, "the stereophonic, bilingual, or bifocal cultural forms" that were "originated by, but no longer the exclusive property of, blacks dispersed within the structures of feeling, producing, communicating, and remembering what [he…] heuristically called the black Atlantic world."[33] Gilroy described the Black Atlantic as a conceptual framework for understanding the movement of Black people across geographies of space and place, but also in relation to the formation of hybrid identities and modalities. He writes that people of African descent, and their repeated crossings of the Atlantic Ocean (both forced and voluntary) was a disorienting displacement in which national cultures became insignificant to Black identity.

In *Representing African Americans in Transatlantic Abolitionism and Blackface Minstrelsy* (2010), Nowatzki complicated Gilroy's term by using the concept of the blackface Atlantic to explore representations of Black people in American/British abolitionism and American/British minstrelsy in tandem with the movement of Black people and their representation within creolized spaces.[34] The meaning of the blackface Atlantic was "influenced by the travels of abolitionists and minstrel performers between the United States and the United Kingdom and were linked to British and American nationalisms, to the cultural relations between the two nations, and to ideologies of class in both nations,"[35] Nowatzki explained. Canada has been absent in historical accounts of both the Black Atlantic and the blackface Atlantic. This book borrows Gilroy's and Nowatzki's concepts to explain both the sociocultural conditions that made minstrelsy popular in Canada and the crisscrossing that also occurred at the precise moments when national discourses begin to take on considerable importance across Canada. As a result, "regardless of their affiliation to the right, left, or centre," asserted Gilroy, "groups have fallen back on the idea of cultural nationalism, on the overintegrated conceptions of culture which present immutable, ethnic differences as an absolute break in the histories and experiences of 'black' and 'white' people. Against this choice stands another, more difficult option: the theorisation of creolisation...and hybridity."[36] Canada, like Britain, was positioned within the Black Atlantic world, "standing at the apex of the semi-triangular structure which saw commodities and people shipped to and from across the ocean."[37] At the same time, the blackface Atlantic did not just follow a triangular system of capitalist exchange; instead of trading real Black people as a prized commodity, *Black* caricature was traded, sold, and exchanged for the entertainment of primarily White audiences in the Atlantic world. I italicize *Black* to distinguish the genre that featured Black actors exclusively in blackface from White minstrelsy or "Negro" minstrelsy, which was the exclusive domain of White actors in blackface. By the mid-to late nineteenth century, the memory of transatlantic slavery may have been gone from the public's imagination, but blackface still travelled to places within the triangular trade pathways of the Atlantic Ocean with the same frequency that enslaved Africans had.

Canada and the Blackface Atlantic pinpoints how and where Canadians upheld worldviews about Black people that were connected to southern slavery, despite either having no connection to the South or experiential knowledge of it. A robust Atlantic visual culture industry was one sector responsible for the northern fascination with the South. As Marcus Wood explains, by the seventeenth and eighteenth centuries, Britain had a well-established tradition of representing Black people through visual codes and convention. "By the middle of the nineteenth century the mass publishing industry had the power to absorb and to reinvent it on its own, or its audience's terms,"[38] Wood writes, adding "For a music hall audience in the mid-nineteenth century blackness was almost inevitably associated with slavery."[39] In the context of transatlantic slavery, a *creolized* (a concept that reflects a relationship between time and space—the erasure of a past, replaced by a hybridized present) culture emerged where select elements from the enslaved within multiple sites of enslavement were mixed, intertwined, and reframed with different sets of meanings, such that new identities, realities, and sensibilities emerged across a number of geographies. Blackface minstrelsy, as the dominant entertainment industry by the mid-nineteenth century, played a vital role in creating the cultural conditions for

∽ INTRODUCTION ∾

the public's obsession with Black bodies—enslaved or free. As a creolized form of mass entertainment, blackface minstrelsy was neither one thing nor another but stood as an ever-changing mélange of everything the culture had to offer. It borrowed from the British stage, Irish folk culture, the songs and movements of Africans (enslaved and free), and culture that was born out of multiple sites of transatlantic slavery, from the Caribbean to the North American colonies. As Black people circulated the Atlantic world as both fact and fiction, real and imagined, corporeal and emotional, mass conceptions of Blackness became divorced from actual Black life.

I never set out to write a book about blackface that would span the nineteenth century. As I engaged with the British theatrical repertoire and began to understand how centuries-old theatrical forms became archetypes for American minstrelsy throughout the nineteenth century, I realized that this book had to extend beyond the stages of American minstrelsy to the sociocultural and economic origins of the Atlantic world. I had to contend with the history of transatlantic slavery as it happened, and then, minstrelsy's reproduction of it on stages across the Atlantic world. In the six chapters that follow, I make the case that Canada not only participated in the formation of blackface minstrelsy, but that the genre thrived, multiplied, and diversified over the nineteenth century, and it did so from coast to coast, in and outside the professional theatre, with and without American and British influence. Chapter 1 begins with the two major conflicts that shaped the development of North America—the American Revolutionary War, and the War of 1812. I assert that while the British and French battled for control of Canada, with the British ultimately assuming colonial rule over not only the land, but also slavery, America won the war on the importation of culture, for which theatre was front and centre. The first decades of the nineteenth century were the moments when American popular entertainment fundamentally changed Canadian culture; first, with the arrival of the circus, then, in the 1830s, with the errand slave character "Jim Crow." This chapter locates Canada in a burgeoning "New World" popular culture predicated on the racial caricature and ridicule of Black people. This chapter also provides a historiography of the first White

∾ INTRODUCTION ∾

men to popularize blackface minstrelsy, and the ways the genre's first songs were intimately tied to political conflict and the Black experience in plantation slavery.

Thomas Dartmouth (T.D.) "Daddy" Rice (1808–60), commonly referred to as the "father of minstrelsy," became the first *true* blackface performer whose act transcended the circus. Born and raised in New York's ethnically mixed neighbourhood the Seventh Ward (located along the East River), after spending time working as a carpenter's apprentice, Rice turned to acting. He appeared in "supernumerary roles" in plays mostly, and by 1828 he was on the road full-time with a performance troupe, where he acted in bit-parts in various plays.[40] While Rice had tried unsuccessfully for many years to break into the theatre scene in New York, he eventually drifted west and found himself working as a stagehand and bit player throughout the Mississippi Valley.[41] In this chapter, I explain how Rice, after observing the movements of a disabled Black stable hand in 1830, took to the stage in a mimetic performance of what he saw. His song and dance, which would be called "Jump, Jim Crow," launched an Atlantic world sensation for not only blackface as a desired theatrical repertoire, but songs and dances that harkened back literally to the Southern plantation and slavery, as interpreted by White male actors. This chapter charts the moment Jim Crow comes to Canada, but it also pinpoints earlier blackface performers, such as Richmond, Virginia-born George Washington Dixon (1801–61) who created songs and dances in the late 1820s that became the foundation for American blackface minstrelsy. Dixon was part of a string of White male acts like Pennsylvania-born John Durang (1768–1822), who introduced a hornpipe dance while performing in blackface in the early 1800s.

Both Dixon and Durang were circus performers, and in chapter 1 I discuss the rise of the North American circus and the dances of the circus connected to British folk traditions like the jig, which was often featured in Elizabethan finales in the sixteenth century. Nearly a century before White men in America "blacked up" to mimic African Americans, the act of blackening and comic forms of dancing were also part of British theatrical repertoire. One popular jig, *The Black Man*, performed by Robert Cox in the 1650s featured a character "disguised as a ghost or devil, aiming to deceive the superstitious."[42] The dancing blackface clown was also a fixture in the sixteenth-century British musical drama; by the

∾ INTRODUCTION ∾

seventeenth century, the dancing clown in blackface lived on through "drolls," performances similar to full-length plays often inserted into performances of rope dances and country dances, which were sometimes permitted entertainment when plays were not.[43] Drolls such as *Swabber*, performed in the 1650s, is one of the first examples of blackfaced characters outside the Shakespearean theatre.[44] Blackface minstrelsy was influenced by "Old World" traditions, customs, and racism, but was born of the "New World" and through immigration, ethnic, and racial groups in cities like New York, Philadelphia, Toronto, and Montreal that comingled, co-created, and cross-fertilized in ways that ultimately created a form of popular culture that had never existed before. Chapter 1 situates the birth of blackface in North America as an outgrowth of centuries-old British and Western European theatrical cultures.

By the first decades of the nineteenth century, audiences across the Atlantic world were already well-versed on blackening, Moorish dance, and Black characters depicting degraded social positions on the stage.[45] The Morris dance, for example, was a folk theatrical practice that David Wiles has called "the center-piece of Elizabethan folk culture" for the ways it symbolized the sense of community that supposedly existed in some past golden age.[46] In addition to blackened Morris dancers, Robert Hornback found "the vestiges of early traditions of blackness, blackface, and the black mask [that] can be located in depictions of English drama. Such examples include 'foolish black devils' that appeared in English Renaissance theatre (1558 to 1642), 'devil' plays with blackface and plays with Moors like sixteenth-century jigs."[47] The popularity of blackfaced characters harkened back to "Old World" traditions as it also bespoke the *newness* of North America. The continued presence of these figures ensured that White audiences paid more attention to the exploits of White entertainers, rather than actual Black men and women who became fodder for mass entertainment.

Chapter 2 situates the decades of the 1840s and 1850s as pivotal moments in blackface minstrelsy's expansion into Canada, as the genre morphed from the eccentric expressions of a solo White male actor dancing Jim Crow into a form of entertainment with a format ushered into prominence in 1843, with the Virginia Minstrels and others who travelled the English-speaking world as the first popular blackface minstrel troupes. At the same

∽ INTRODUCTION ∽

time, Black people were becoming more visible in Canada, establishing settlements including schools and businesses. This chapter argues that blackface continued to challenge Black freedoms by reproducing caricatures of Black bodies—in and out of freedom—in addition to captivating set designs that (re)imagined the Southern plantation as nostalgic palimpsest. This chapter centres the first stage productions of *Uncle Tom's Cabin* that toured Canada West in the 1850s as significant to the reframing of slavery's realities. The "Tom Shows" challenged the abolitionist cause by focusing not only on the caricaturing of Black bodies—through dress, expressions, appearances, and adornments—but also on sentimentalizing the plantation itself, the very thing the Atlantic world was economically wedded to.

With its two intersecting narratives about slavery—escape versus servitude—as Canadian theatre historian James Maurice Stockford (J.M.S.) Careless writes, *Uncle Tom's Cabin* was a perennial favourite in Toronto as "the strong abolitionist sympathies among Upper Canadians of the period...were expressed in institutions such as the Toronto Anti-Slavery Society and philanthropic schemes to aid and settle fugitive American slaves."[48] Simultaneously, as Nowatzki observes, "minstrel shows that encouraged antislavery sentiments in their audiences were influenced by abolitionism, though perhaps only temporarily and superficially."[49] Chapter 2 explains the duality that played out on stages across Canada at a time when Black immigration spurred on by antislavery movements was at its peak. I challenge the assertion that blackface held no political import in Canada. In addition to locating some of the first Black protests of minstrel acts in Toronto, and the country's first Black theatrical company, I also examine the first Black actor and dancer to achieve Atlantic world success. New York-born Ira Aldridge (1807–67), who often performed in his "natural skin" on some of the same stages on the same night as White minstrel acts, challenged White audiences' perceptions about Blackness and notions of freedom.[50] Similarly, Providence, Rhode Island-born William Henry Lane (1825–52/53), also known as "Master Juba," was the first Black dancer to perform in blackface on White stages, and he became known for his innovations and competitions against White dancers, most notably, John (Jack) Diamond (1823–57), an Irish American dancer and minstrel performer that became famous in the 1840s for a series of dance challenges against Lane in New York City.

◡ INTRODUCTION ◡

This chapter explains how Durang became a popular solo act in the 1780s, and why he is often credited as one of the first American prototypes for early minstrelsy.[51] While Durang, British-born John Ricketts (1769–1802), who was a trick horseback rider, and Diamond all brought their acts to Canada, once Aldridge left for England in the 1820s he never returned to America. After Lane joined some of the first blackface troupes such as the Virginia Minstrels and the Ethiopian Serenaders, both of which emerged in the 1840s, he would also remain in Britain until his death. The Virginia Minstrels were not the first documented blackface minstrel troupe to create a set format and standard repertoire that other minstrel groups could replicate. In its first decade, minstrel repertoire was not fixed, it did not have specific instrumentation, nor was the format static—it did not yet have an *interlocutor* or *endmen*.[52] The *endmen* assumed chief importance when engaging in dialogue with a genteel, smartly dressed White man, known as the *interlocutor*, commanding centre stage. As Sarah Meer aptly observes, the Virginia Minstrels formalized the fantasy of plantations as "ethnographic glimpse[s] of real slave life."[53] The term "Ethiopian" or "Ethiopian delineator" was made up; it was used interchangeably with "minstrels" to connote White blackface troupes who sang and danced as they imagined African Americans did, and who had not been trained in British theatrical conventions. The presence of Durang, Ricketts, and Diamond in Canada as early as the 1790s means we can locate the formalized plantation fantasy honed on the minstrel stage, and the singing and dance of a mimetic African American as being part of Canadian culture.

Chapter 3 elucidates how and why blackface minstrel shows continued to thrive into the 1860s, not as passing entertainments and menageries but as some of the first forms of cultural productions in remote outposts in Western Canada to multi-night events in theatres in Canada West/East, and the Maritimes. This chapter charts the building of theatres and performance halls as well as the expansion of English-language newspapers and railroads. I situate Black community in relation to this infrastructure building, arguing that such growth not only linked the country but also enabled the expansion of touring American minstrelsy across it. The Great Western Railway, opened in 1854, was the first significant railroad built in Canada. It created new transportation and distribution routes from the

∽ INTRODUCTION ∽

Niagara River below the escarpment, through to Hamilton, London, and Windsor. It was followed in 1856 with the Grand Trunk Railway, which extended this network to Montreal along Lake Ontario's north shore through Toronto and Stratford to Sarnia. The building of railways meant that theatrical acts could travel between Hamilton and Toronto, Montreal and London with larger casts and productions.

These railway lines, after all, were built strategically not only to connect Canada, but to target American seaports such as Portland, Boston, and New York. It is here I unpack the careers of Burgess and Lavallée, Canada's most known blackface performers at midcentury, who achieved fame and celebrity stateside through their *Black* caricature and also helped establish an audience for blackface north of the border. This chapter problematizes Canadian blackface performers as not singularly participating in an American form of popular culture that they were distanced from, as if devoid of racial politics and racist ideology, but as active participants in the development of *Black* caricature that both had nothing to do with Black people in Canada—as the caricatures were of African Americans—and everything to do with Black people in Canada, as *Black* was devoid of nationhood, citizenship, and agency.

Chapter 4 examines how the US Civil War (1861–65) had profound impact on Canada, especially as reported in Toronto's and Montreal's newspapers. This newspaper discourse paints a very descriptive picture about the conflicting loyalties in Canada as it related to the US conflict. Those in Canada West who had taken up the abolitionists' cause sympathized with the Union Army and its aims to eradicate slavery; but, especially in the Maritimes and Quebec, there were southern sympathizers who were financially connected to cotton and tobacco production, and who had long provided economic (and in some cases, personal) support to Confederate soldiers. This support is significant because in the aftermath of the Civil War, as an estimated four million formerly enslaved African Americans were freed, some Black men went to work for railway companies, which brought the American-style Pullman Palace Sleeping Car service north of the border, while others entered theatrical stages for the first time, performing in *Black* minstrelsy across the US and Canada. *Black* in this case is not a racial identifier but a performative artifice interconnected with racial caricature, stereotypes, and denigrated depictions of Black people as performed by Black people.⁵⁴ This dichotomy, if understood within the context of the nineteenth-century racial logic, is a useful way to delineate the sociocultural shifts and changes during the century that are reflected in minstrel discourse.

Black minstrelsy became a viable employment opportunity for Black men and as these acts hits stages as early as 1865, dancing and singing songs about the "good ol' days" on the plantation, the theatrical stage changed. No longer the exclusive domain of White actors and managers, the *Black* theatrical circuit offered these men a chance to cultivate degrees of agency, albeit it performative, which unequivocally helped to ease the financial struggles of the post–Civil War years while also creating racial stereotypes that, in some cases, were more enduring than the ones that had been created by White men in blackface. Charles Callender (b. unknown) was one of the first White managers of *Black* minstrelsy. J.H. (Christopher) Haverly's (1837–1901) "Mastodon Minstrels," and Alfred Griffin (or Griffith) Hatfield, often known as Al G. Field's (1848–1921) troupe, are examples of blackface performance that toured Canada. Their presence in the newspaper discourse reflects the complex intersections of race and of racialized performance that dominated minstrelsy in the late nineteenth century. When Haverly noticed that popular entertainments had "increased and enlarged their dimensions" after the US Civil War, he devised what some historians describe as a "lunatic transmogrification" of a minstrel company.⁵⁵ His Mastodon Minstrels included forty White performers, a brass band, and drum corps.⁵⁶ Meanwhile, Field was a White manager of both *Black* and White minstrel companies, and his most notorious troupe, *Darkest America*, which toured in 1894 and 1896, was distinct because it was the first *Black* minstrel show to centre plantation life in ways that White minstrels could not.

Chapter 5 explores how jubilee singers crisscrossed stages with *Black* minstrelsy, which became more elaborate in its production with large casts and themes that emphasized the plantation context as the *authentic* site of Black life. Jubilee singers changed the American stage by reimagining the parameters of their own sense of freedom. As these choral groups toured Canada with the same frequency as White and *Black* minstrelsy, the cultural landscape was dynamic, always changing, and filled with multiple representations of Blackness. In the wake of Confederation, Canada evolved into a sovereign dominion. This new sense of nationalism led to the establishment of political newspapers such as the satirical weekly *Grip* (1873–94), which played a role in shaping public opinion through its printing of cartoons, such as *The National Policy Minstrels. Brudder Tambo's Astounding Financial Conundrum* (hereafter *National Policy Minstrels*) in 1879 and *The Bill Board Re-Decorated* in 1886. Drawn by Toronto-born cartoonist John Wilson (J.W.) Bengough (1851–1923),[57] *Grip* was modelled after the UK's *Punch*; it represents one of the first examples of a Canadian political print culture.[58] *Grip* also followed the short-lived *Punch in Canada*, launched on January 1, 1849 by John Henry Walker (1831–99) that ceased publication in 1850. This chapter ultimately contends with dualling representations of Blackness that emerged in the last decades of the nineteenth century, from (re)productions of an imagined slavery in *Black* and White minstrelsy, to presentations of the African American experience in slavery as sung by jubilee choral groups, to an emergent Canadian cartoon culture that relied on themes and aesthetics from the American minstrel show to lampoon partisan political figures.

Chapter 6 continues the discussion about jubilee singing, *Black* and White minstrelsy, and Canada's political cartoons, but it contextualizes these developments as part of vaudeville, the new theatrical form that appeared in the 1870s. Vaudeville became a venue for immigrant women, especially Jewish women from Eastern Europe, who brought their gender identities, racial sensibilities, and sexuality to the forefront on the stage for the first time. As they did, they also appropriated many of the forms and modes that White men had originated in the early days of minstrelsy. The irony of the vaudeville stage during its first few decades was that it seemed to democratize the theatre, as audiences became more diverse and varied; so too did the parameters of who could appear on the stage and what they could do on stage. At the same time, a racialized, codified hierarchy remained firmly in place with White men on top, followed closely by White women who replicated many of the same discriminatory practices they had originated. By the 1890s, *coon songs* (which became popular sheet music) as well as minstrel tunes extended the reach of the stage into the realm of the popular culture. Vaudeville might have diversified the theatre's repertoires, but it did not desegregate the stage. This chapter explains how, rather than make room for Black men and women to join them, White women

∽ INTRODUCTION ∾

donned the burnt cork mask of minstrelsy as they performed burlesque acts, "girlie" shows, and transcended White men's hold on gender play. As Canada established its place within the blackface Atlantic, hosting large-scale minstrel troupes at large-scale theatre houses from coast-to-coast and establishing its own local minstrel acts, it also became a destination for a variety of all-female acts from the US and Britain. Most notably, in 1870 Madame Rentz's Female Minstrels was one of the first of these all-female acts to tour the country.

Chapter 6 explains how Black concert singers Taylor Greenfield, the Hyers Sisters, Sissieretta Jones, and many others challenged not only the depiction of plantation Blackness peddled in minstrelsy and vaudeville, but also jubilee singers' songs from the Southern plantation, blending the Black experience in America with highly-trained proficiency in European-style singing and operatic arrangements. The nineteenth-century production of *Darkest America*, which toured Ontario and Quebec, is also examined. During its time, the show was considered one of the most popular *Black* minstrel shows to ever hit the stage. As the production was reviewed by city newspapers, editorials gave readers a vivid glimpse into the extravagance of "big-time" minstrelsy in vaudeville. In this final chapter, I paint a complex picture of theatrical entertainment in the 1890s wherein audiences were exposed to multiple Black narratives, styles, forms, and aesthetics at the exact moment African Americans begin to lose freedoms following the enforcement of a system of segregation in 1896 that would be called Jim Crow—after the minstrel character from the 1830s. I examine the crisscrossing of multiple genres of performance to elucidate the impact of Jim Crow segregation on an entertainment culture not only in the US but also in Canada where White minstrels and *Black* minstrels, all-female vaudeville acts, jubilee choral groups, and concert singers performed to different audiences and in cities and towns that had changed dramatically since the War of 1812. Chapter 6 establishes Canada's role in the blackface Atlantic at the end of the nineteenth century.

This book ultimately argues that the theatre's use of blackening as a rhetorical device predates the Canada we know today, and it also predates the concept of racism itself. But this does not mean that blackface actors, repertoire, and visual culture were not racist by today's sensibilities; rather, it means that when trying to understand blackface—its complexities,

∽ INTRODUCTION ∽

nuances, and contradictions—readers must place it into the context of an Atlantic world where Black people were enslaved by Europeans, but they were also the envy of these same people for their movements, innovations, creativity, and style. To learn about blackface, then, is to (re)learn the story of the Atlantic world and Canada's place within it.

1

CANADA AND THE EMERGENCE OF THE BLACKFACE ATLANTIC, 1812-39

On April 27, 1813, American warships attacked the Town of York (present-day Toronto) in what became the Battle of York. It was one of the many cross-border raids in the War of 1812. York, the capital of then-Upper Canada, stood on the north shore of Lake Ontario. During the War, the lake was the front line between Upper Canada and the US, and also served as the principal British supply line from Quebec (then-Lower Canada) to the various armed forces and outposts to the west. As Olivette Otele explains, beginning in the early nineteenth century, Britain was striving to achieve commercial dominance in North America; in these efforts, it infringed on what the US considered its trading zones. "[In] the Chesapeake Incident of 1807, tensions in Ohio between the United States and Native Americans [were] aided by Britain, and the Royal Navy's habit of 'press-ganging' American sailors all led to a declaration of war in 1812."[1]

Though the April 1813 invasion was short, American soldiers left their mark on the city by looting, vandalizing, stripping homes, and burning structures, including York's parliament buildings.[2] While the War was not the first to impact Canada–US relations, it marked a pivotal moment in North American performance history. The American national anthem, for example, was inspired by the War of 1812. After witnessing an American defence of Fort McHenry, Maryland on September 13, 1814, the young American lawyer Francis Scott Key (1779–1843) wrote a poem about the battle, "Defense of Fort M'Henry," which was put to music and eventually became the "The Star-Spangled Banner."[3] In his initial poem, Key made reference to *hirelings*, a word that connected individuals with the propensity to flee under fire, and more broadly, as David Roediger writes, with behaviour that was "the very opposite of self-sacrificing republican citizens.... Americans by 1814 had substantial doubts, and substantial reasons to doubt, with regard to their nation's ability to preserve a republican vision against 'hireling' corruption."[4] He explains further that "Britain prosecuted that war using hated mercenary or 'hireling' soldiers. Also in the British ranks were about three hundred former slaves, promised freedom and protection by British commanders in exchange for their military service. Some of these ex-slaves helped to burn the White House in 1814."[5]

The War of 1812 has typically been remembered in Canadian history as the conflict that firmly established Canada as part of the British Empire, but it must also be understood as the moment that gave birth to America's popular culture. As the British engaged in battles with Americans over Canada and its contested Indigenous territories, Black bodies became fodder for an emergent musical and sartorial culture. New perceptions were created about their place in the context of North America where people of African descent remained enslaved, but increasingly visible in northern environments as free persons. Just as White American songwriters, playwrights, and dancers had used the African American experience in slavery as their muse, the influx of African Americans into Canada following the War of 1812 also marked a moment when Black people were being constructed, as Russell Sanjek describes of the American context, in "peculiar or eccentric, indulging in odd or whimsical ways."[6] This chapter explores the sociopolitical events and cultural contexts that helped to create blackface minstrelsy in the US, and it explains why, when, and how it arrived in Canada. As one of the first, but not the only, form of imported entertainment, theatrical forms, performative texts, and representational modes circulated Canada's cities and towns, outposts, and trading posts during the eighteenth and nineteenth centuries. Because Canada was still in its infancy as a nation-state prior to the 1840s and 1850s when large-scale transportation and infrastructure growth dramatically changed the country's demographics, most of the performative acts in cities and towns were brought to Canada after wealthy individuals travelled abroad. As John Boyko aptly points out, Canadians "were geographically closer to the North and for years thousands more had travelled to those Northern states for work than to the distant South.... Canadians travelling to Britain often went by way of New York and Boston."[7]

Many immigrants to Canada arrived from the British Isles (England, Scotland, Ireland, and Wales) and they embraced the "New World" ethos of assimilation while also maintaining their traditional cultures such as dances, songs, and theatrical modes of entertainment. Some of North America's earliest dances can be traced back to English folk theatricals such as mummers, callithumpians, and Morris dancers which formed part of a carnivalesque ritual in seventeenth-century Britain, and which allowed for various forms of mimicry not specifically tied to race or racial impersonation, but to the sociocultural milieu of transatlantic slavery.[8] Folk dances were an important part of the Atlantic world culture. In *History of Morris Dancing*, John Forrest cites multiple sixteenth-century examples of blackened figures or Moors in English folk culture. He suggests that Turks, Jews, and Pagans often appeared in similar ceremonies and that the act of masking became commonly "symbolic of the remote and exotic worlds at the fringes of Europe."[9] Thus, blackface minstrelsy's adoption of a racial mask was a mimicry of Black bodies in America, but sartorially also an homage to centuries-long English theatrical traditions. In its early decades, blackface performers, most of whom were northern White men, desired to imagine what their future would look like if African Americans remained in servitude, opposed to, as Douglas A. Jones, Jr. opines, "theatricalize a 'history' of slavery."[10] Stated otherwise, White audiences were fascinated by the idea of an enslaved African American population, even as some were ardent abolitionists. Entertainments that retold the story of slavery, however, were less appealing to audiences who had to confront their own complicity in the degradation of Black people. Thus, as Eric Lott describes, the sociopolitical import of blackface was its lack of consciousness; it was "a socially approved context of institutional control; and, on the other hand, it continually acknowledged and absorbed black culture even while defending white America against it."[11]

Canadians were equally invested in substituting real Blackness for the propagated "blackness" of blackface minstrelsy because, like Northerners in the US, they too felt threatened by the establishment of free Black communities. The growing importation of Africans into the American north in the mid-eighteenth century gave new direction to a previously highly *creolized* African American culture.[12] There was pervasive sentiment that African American arrivals were "rural illiterates with few skills, no moral education, no intelligence, lazy, thieving, incompetent, and, far from being capable of 'passing', quite obviously 'blacker' than the already-settled free black population of Canada."[13] But at the same time, African Americans in New England and New York began to reinvent themselves through public performance by embracing African traditions related to song and dance while adopting elements of the European carnivalesque to create a *creolized* public parade culture. These two traditions, Negro Election Day (dating from about 1750) and Pinkster (early nineteenth century) were born of African origins, and Pinkster in particular was a holiday of Dutch origin that drew on African heritages and ceremonial practices that also featured race and class cross-dressing.[14] These two public performative cultures involving enslaved and free Black people reflected a distinct Black culture that drew on elements of West African culture, but by their very existence also spoke directly to American plantation slavery. These expressions of Black culture influenced the blackface minstrel show as it expanded during the first decades of the nineteenth century.

By explaining the waves of Black migration to Canada before, during, and after the War of 1812 in relation to the development and formation of an American entertainment culture, this chapter charts an early Canadian performative history that is about theatre and its related entertainments (music and dance) but also about migration, infrastructure development, political conflict, and sociocultural change. To tell an Atlantic history of blackface minstrelsy and Canada's place within it, I contend with the origin story of "blackfaced" performance in Britain, the ways histories of transatlantic slavery crisscrossed the Atlantic world, including the Caribbean, influencing early American theatre, dance, and song, and how all these developments intersected with Black migration (forced and voluntary), political conflict, and settlement in Canada. For instance, as thousands of Black Refugees who rebelled against their owners reached British military encampments during the War of 1812, they fled on "a promise of complete freedom and settlement on British land."[15] However, as Harvey Amani Whitfield writes, "The growth and development of the thirteen [American] colonies influenced the so-called Neutral Yankees of Nova Scotia, but not to the point where the colony proved willing to leave the protection of the King's empire." The Black Refugees who arrived in Nova Scotia were largely given land that was in poor condition, and there were many racial hostilities that also made life challenging.[16] In the years following the War of 1812, White Canadians were exposed to multiple waves of free Black people, some of whom had been part of the founding of Quebec; for the English-speaking White settler colonies, like Halifax which was established in 1749, they encountered a Black population that was "a mixture of slaves, ex-slaves, refugees, and loyalists who had fled during the American Revolution or in the wake of the War of 1812."[17]

Historian Richard M. Reid found that Black immigrants to Upper Canada following the War of 1812 also faced challenges. "In Oro Township, northeast of Barrie, a government-sponsored attempt to settle black veterans of the War of 1812 was largely stillborn, and subsequent waves of black migrants who arrived after 1826 failed to establish a more prosperous or larger community," writes Reid, adding "although the Wilberforce settlement north of London and the Dawn settlement near Dresden fell short of their organizers' goals, the efforts to establish a black community at Buxton in Kent County" were successful.[18] In Chapter 2, I discuss the formation of the Wilberforce, Dawn, Dresden, and Buxton settlements in terms of Black community, but also the role these communities played in the development of Upper Canada's entertainment culture. This chapter connects the Revolutionary War and the War of 1812 with the emergence of a "national" performative culture in the US, which spread into Canada from the 1830s onward. I place national in quotation marks to denote that early blackface theatrical entertainment might have been born in the US and was rooted in the cultural context of transatlantic slavery (a southern plantocracy); however, the performative influences from which theatre, music, and other amusements drew their inspiration—drolls, jigs, clog, and hornpipe dances—originated in sixteenth- and seventeenth-century

Britain. By understanding what songs, dances, and theatricals crisscrossed the Atlantic world at the same time images, peoples, and cultures did, this chapter establishes the blackface Atlantic and Canada's place within it.

"Backside of Albany" also known as "The Siege of Plattsburg" was one of the first popular songs inspired by the War of 1812.[19] As music business historian Sanjek writes, "It was sung first to an Albany theater audience in February 1815, and then on the professional stage in New York City by Hopkins Robinson, an actor better known to his fans as Mr. Robertson. The first occasion was Robinson's benefit evening, and, as he did later, the actor appeared in a sailor's costume and blackface to sing the set of four verses to the Irish tune 'Boyne Water.'"[20] After its first performance, "Backside of Albany" was printed in a 180-page songster, *The Columbian Harmonist*, and it appeared in collections up to Civil War.[21] The song retold the story of a Great Lakes battle as sung by a White actor portraying a blackfaced sailor character.[22] The song, written by Michael "Micah" Hawkins, was inspired by Toney Clapp, an African American who was enslaved by Hawkins and who he learned to fiddle from.[23] Based in lower New York City, Hawkins had seen enslaved people dancing and singing in the public market located near his place of business; with this song, he is said to have found his voice, which included subsequent songs that peddled myths of the frontier, plantation, river, and railroad.[24] When actor Andrew Jackson (known as "Dummy") Allen (1788–1853) sang "Backside of Albany," he helped to produce the earliest known "black" dialect song written by an American.[25]

War of 1812 songs illustrate the extent American entertainers not only borrowed from British culture in its early decades, but that American songwriters, especially those writing after the 1810s, consciously derived their material from one of two places—political conflicts that were defining the nation's sense of identity or African Americans, enslaved and free, who were becoming more present everywhere.[26] As Sanjek continues, "White authors and composers had come to see these blacks, as one late-eighteenth century traveler saw them, as 'the greatest humorists in the nation.' The word humorist was not used in its presently preferred definition, as 'an entertainer specializing in humor.'"[27] At the same time, the War of 1812 cultivated a strong sense of distinctiveness among Canadians, and that sense of difference was often manifest in patrons' response to popular entertainments in places like York where disdain for American soldiers still lingered in the years after April 1813.[28] Anti-American sentiment had been growing in the Atlantic Provinces since the latter part of the eighteenth century, but in Ontario (and Quebec) it grew after the War of 1812. As William Baker observes, "By 1812 approximately eighty per cent of the Upper Canadian population was of American origin; only one-quarter of these were Loyalists or their descendants. Active warfare, however, forced the inhabitants to make a decision on the matter of allegiance…the War of 1812 caused a fresh outburst of anti-Americanism which melded with the Loyalist tradition to create an Upper Canada devoted to the task of resisting absorption into the United States."[29] This anti-Americanism also helped to manifest a strong sense of difference that informed Upper Canada's entertainment culture.[30] Some displays of anti-Americanism ignited much vitriol among audiences who did not appreciate the reminder of some Americans' disdain for their British forefathers. Nerves remained raw for decades in Toronto, asserts Jonathan Vance, as the city had been occupied and burned by American soldiers in 1813. "In 1825, a play at Frank's Hotel – the venue for Toronto's first theatrical performance… degenerated into a riot before the actors took the stage, when a member of the company asked crowds to remove their hats as a mark of respect as *Yankee Doodle Dandy* was played."[31] A decade later, a Toronto newspaper also wrote disparagingly of "strolling players from Yankee-land."[32]

The song "Yankee Doodle Dandy" was first popular during the American Revolutionary War of Independence (1775–83), and was originally an insult about Americans; when sung by British soldiers, it told the story of a poorly dressed "Yankee" simpleton, also known as a "doodle." "Yankee Doodle" was so popular with British troops that they played it as they marched to battle; however, at the Revolutionary War's end, it became a symbol of American pride and the new republic's unofficial anthem—until the "Star-Spangled Banner" replaced it.[33] Rebel Americans claimed "Yankee Doodle" as their own, recreating new verses that mocked the British, praised the new Continental Army, and hailed its commander, George Washington (1732–99), as the founding father of a sovereign America.[34] Eventually, British travellers used it indiscriminately to refer to all Americans, and though "the Yankee character was formally associated with New England in literature," the broader use of the word continued, and the American city-dweller also looked at those in rural places with a contempt like that held by the British.³⁵ By the 1860s, Southerners began to attach the label to all Northerners.³⁶

The term "dandy" on the other hand was given to a man who placed particular importance upon physical appearance, refined language, and leisure hobbies. The words "dandy" and "fop" were often used interchangeably but they came into the English language at different times and with slightly different meanings. Anyone could be a fop, but dandies specifically choose the lifestyle, they committed to being a student of the latest fashions that defined them and of the trends around which they could redefine themselves. As Monica Miller describes, "from at least the 1780s, 'dandy' designated a 'swell,' one who *studies* above everything else to dress elegantly and fashionably' (emphasis added)."³⁷ In comparison to the definitive derivation of the fop, which drew some of its meaning from the British "fool," the dandy carefully considered their style and often was more self-conscious and deliberate than that of a fop; this self-consciousness helped to mobilize the figure's currency.³⁸ By the 1820s, the dandy became a caricature of a new social type in the Northern US— the well-dressed, urban, and free Black man.

The Revolutionary War proved a pivotal moment in the development of an American performative culture that was linked to political tensions. At the outbreak of hostilities, the Loyalist governor of Virginia, Lord John Murray Dunmore (1730–1809), offered freedom to the slaves of rebel owners if the enslaved were willing to help return the Old Dominion to "a proper sense" of its duty to the British Crown.³⁹ While American rebel forces were defeated in Canada, they declared victory over the British in 1776, establishing the union as an independent nation—though it would take another five years to completely cut ties with the British. On October 19, 1781, British General Charles Cornwallis (1738–1805) surrendered his troops in Yorktown, Virginia, officially creating the constitutionally sovereign United States of America. Following a wave of Loyalist immigration, the demographics of Canada changed, as well as the Indigenous Nations within it.⁴⁰ Many of the White "settlers" who headed to Canada, including Americans who migrated north and immigrants from the British Isles, expropriated Indigenous people off their lands. Black people who arrived under a system of chattel slavery or those who were newly freed as a result of the war settled on lands in Quebec, Ontario, and the Maritimes, if they were willing to declare themselves Loyalists to the British Crown. Despite the displacement and confusion caused by the Revolutionary War, the other outcome was the evacuation of British Loyalists, Black and White, from Savannah, Boston, Charleston, and New York, writes Whitfield. He adds that "as part of this exodus, approximately 3,500 Black Loyalists migrated to Nova Scotia along with hundreds of Black slaves owned by Loyalist Americans."[41]

After France's defeat with Britain in the Seven Years War (1756–63), and the signing of the *Treaty of Paris*, the French surrendered control of its colonies to Britain.[42] As his first legislative piece of business, John Graves Simcoe (1752–1806), lieutenant governor of Upper Canada, moved the capital from Newark (Niagara-on-the-Lake) to York (Toronto) on the northern shore of Lake Ontario. In 1791 the region previously known as New France (Quebec) was renamed Lower Canada. By the early nineteenth century, Ontario, Quebec, and the Maritime provinces thrived as the sociopolitical centres of Canada. With these changes, the eastern part of the region (which was majority French Catholic) combined with the western area (home to British Loyalists, the majority of whom were Protestant and born in America). By the end of the Revolutionary War a British-centred ideology influenced much of the social and political developments in Canada. For Indigenous Peoples, the *Treaty of Paris* reversed the land rights gains made in the Royal Proclamation of 1763, which had reserved all lands not ceded by or purchased from Indigenous Nations.[43] For Black Loyalists who headed to Upper Canada as "free" subjects, they found themselves in a society where slavery was still practiced; for those brought to Lower Canada and the Maritime colonies they had to adapt to comingling with newly arrived immigrants from Britain, Scotland, and Ireland. Comingling in the Maritimes was often fraught with conflict.

When Black Loyalists arrived in the region during the Revolutionary War, they were among the first settlers in Shelburne, located in the southwest region of Nova Scotia. They helped to build the new settlement and, on its fringes, they established their own community known as Birchtown, west of Shelburne. As many as 10,000 previously enslaved Black people—

approximately one-fifth of the total Black American population in 1783—fought alongside the British in the Revolutionary War in exchange for their freedom and, by the end of that year, almost 1,500 had moved to Shelburne County.[44] However, when hundreds of White, disbanded soldiers were forced to accept work at rates competitive with their Black neighbours, there was ensuing hostility which caused conflict, such as a race rebellion[45] that took place on July 26, 1784.[46] As Jesse Robertson explains, "A group of about 40 white Loyalists demolished the home of Baptist preacher David George. George had chosen to establish his church in Shelburne rather than Birchtown. Moreover, he had challenged the established racial hierarchy by baptizing white Loyalists.... Rioting continued for at least 10 days. Incursions into Birchtown were reported for up to one month."[47] This rebellion marked a significant turning point in Black settlement in Nova Scotia. In its aftermath, many Black Loyalists relocated to other parts of the province, and in 1791–92 some Birchtown residents choose to leave, resettling in the West African colony of Freetown, Sierra Leone.[48]

While the history of the Black Loyalists has not been connected to Canadian performance history by all accounts, performance was used as an act of resistance. There is documented evidence that dances and songs performed by Black Loyalists in places like Birchtown helped to thwart attempts by government officials to restrict the growth of a public culture. For instance, George Elliott Clarke observed that, in 1789, the government of Shelburne passed an ordinance "forbidding Negro Dances & Negro Frolicks," an act that demonstrates the extent Black bodies were restricted in Canada; as Maureen Moynagh describes, "the perceived potency of black communities' expression, even as they supply evidence of the social forces working to contain that expression," existed in Nova Scotia even as the population was considerably smaller than the Black population in New England.[49] Black Loyalists undoubtedly brought Negro dances to Nova Scotia from the northeast where, since the eighteenth century, free African Americans and enslaved people had gathered in taverns and dance houses, engaged in festivals and parades, and generally constituted an acknowledged (and occasionally threatening to the White population) public presence in America.[50] Both Pinkster and Negro Election Day allowed enslaved people to dance, display fancy dress, and highlight oratorical flair to the wider community. However, these public parades were much more than expressive cultures; they were also about the context of plantation slavery.[51]

As early as the 1750s, these parades offered African Americans the opportunity to cultivate a public performative culture rooted in sartorial and corporal formations, but the festivals did little to threaten the institution of slavery itself and in some regard helped to affirm the notion that African Americans enjoyed being enslaved. As Miller asserts, "If what was visible was known to be true, these festivals offered performances in which visibility and spectacle operated to both confirm and challenge social and cultural hierarchies."[52] These festivals were also related to eighteenth-century Christmastime celebrations in the Anglo-Caribbean like Jonkonnu (John Canoe) in Jamaica, J'ouvert in Trinidad and Tobago, and Crop Over in Barbados, festivals that merged cultures—English or French, and West African. Each of these sites carried their own politics, cultures, and responses to Black sartorial and corporal display. In the case of Trinidad these were hotly political affairs. French planters brought elements of Carnival to the island in the eighteenth century when they staged masquerade balls at Christmastime, and during their tradition of a pre-Lenten festival they found it amusing to dress up and dance like their enslaved Africans. Enslaved Africans conversely co-opted these acts, because they found it even more amusing to use the confusion of carnival as an occasion for uprisings.[53] Similarly in early nineteenth-century New Orleans, slave dances at Congo Square drew significant numbers of White onlookers. It is important to remember that Louisiana was colonized by France at a time in the seventeenth century when it still had control of Lower Canada. In the years that followed, additional waves of settlers came from Lower Canada to Louisiana, notably deported Acadians. At least 780 Acadians arrived in the British colonies of Maryland and Pennsylvania and some later migrated to Louisiana between 1766 and 1770. Furthermore, Jean-Baptiste Le Moyne de Bienville (1680–1767), also known as the "Father of New Orleans," was born in Montreal, serving as an early governor of what was then known as French Louisiana (until 1803). Thus, while carnival displays took place in specific areas, they were influenced by a transatlantic migration culture that implicated Canada.

Ira Berlin also notes that an observer of the Negro Election Day festival in Newport, Rhode Island said, "All the various languages of Africa, mixed with broken and ludicrous English, filled the air, accompanied with the music of the fiddle, tambourine, the banjo, [and] drum."[54] Whites undoubtedly indulged and even participated in these festivals because they were perceived as less dangerous; yet, these practices "unsettled even as it fascinated whites."[55] While the emergence of carnival celebrations rooted in the sociocultural conditions of plantation slavery in the Caribbean is widely known, transatlantic slavery as a significant theme in theatrical entertainments in Britain and America has received less attention. On October 3, 1768, a character named "Mungo" hit the stage as one of five roles in *The Padlock, a Comic Opera, in Two Acts* at London's Theatre Royal, Drury Lane (see figure 1.1). Written by Isaac Bickerstaffe (1733–c. 1808) with a libretto composed by author, actor, and theatrical manager Charles Dibdin (1745–1814), *The Padlock* introduced the first blackface comic figure to the London stage; it was one of the most successful theatrical plays of the eighteenth century and specifically connected the British Empire to its Caribbean colonies.[56]

Importantly, Mungo had very little to do with actual Black interiority or subjectivity; "rather, it can be regarded as a particular effect of English participation in the triangular Atlantic slave trade, an element of its growing empire."[57] *The Padlock* remained part of the English repertory at least as late as the 1820s and part of the American theatre repertory at least through the 1830s.[58] By the late eighteenth century, England's exploits in the Caribbean—colonizing Saint Christopher (Saint Kitts) in 1623, Barbados in 1625, and Jamaica in 1655, followed by Nevis, Antigua, and Montserrat—brought people, foods, and items to England, and there was a sense that plays also formed part of the wider sociocultural milieu where "foreign" bodies, accents, and cultures were cast as inferior. By mimicking a so-called "black dialect," *The Padlock* placed Mungo in the Caribbean, speaking patois or, as it was commonly known as in the eighteenth and nineteenth centuries, a lingua franca based on English learned orally in slavery that mixed vocabulary from dialects spoken by West Africans along with German, Dutch, French, and Portuguese. Importantly, *The Padlock* was the second-most frequently produced drama in the eighteenth century, preceded only by another play—*Oroonoko: or, the Royal Slave* (1695), adapted for the stage by Irish dramatist Thomas Southerne (1660–1746) based on Aphra Behn's novella of the same name; it was published in 1688 by William Canning and reissued with two other fictions later that year.[59]

1.1 Illustration of "Mr. Dibdin in the Character of Mungo in the Celebrated Opera of the Padlock," ca. eighteenth century, the Harry Beard Collection at the Victoria and Albert Museum, London, United Kingdom, S.1678-2012.

By all accounts, Behn's novella and Southerne's adaptation revealed a deep sense of ambivalence toward slavery and, more notably, pro-slavery attitudes that caricatured Black people as undeserving of freedom.[60] While other Black characters appeared on the English stage in the eighteenth and early nineteenth centuries, from John Murdock's *The Triumph of Love; or, Happy Reconciliation* (1795) which explored social customs by using a comic Black servant with a Caribbean dialect who danced and sang, to the inclusion of "Negro" types in popular dramatic offerings, like Henry Bate's *The Black-a-moor Wash'd White* (1776), George Colman's *Inkle and Yarico* (1787), and Thomas Morton's *The Slave* (1816),[61] *Oroonoko*, like *The Padlock*, most closely extended the representation of slavery as well as blackfaced characters, making the latter the most direct precursor to American blackface minstrelsy. From the earliest days of White settlement, emigrants to North America from Britain, Ireland, and Western Europe brought with them their songs, dances, folklore, and other vernacular cultural forms, all of which contributed to the creation of local and regional cultures that were interpreted as "new" but were, in fact, a remix or bricolage of forms and movements that had originated in the "Old World." Mungo was one of the first theatrical characters to leap off the stages in England and onto the popular theatre of America.

The year after *The Padlock*'s London premiere, British-born theatre director Lewis Hallam (c. 1714–56) recreated Mungo for audiences in New York City.[62] After its debut in May 1769, *The Padlock* remained part of the American repertory through 1842–43, the same year a troupe calling themselves the Virginia Minstrels developed the minstrel show format that, as explored in Chapter 2, would inaugurate the genre as a uniquely American form of entertainment.[63] By making the leap across the Atlantic, British theatrical productions introduced American audiences to "Negro" characters in blackface. Mungo appeared in nearly all the major stages in cities from New York to Philadelphia to Savannah, Charleston, Richmond, Washington (Kentucky), Baltimore, Newport, and Boston.[64] *The Padlock* was produced even when the theatres were closed during the Revolutionary War as soldiers at Valley Forge were said to have presented the play as a diversion if British forces did not withdraw from Philadelphia.[65] *The Padlock* and Mungo quickly became part of the American repertoire, with the show being printed in Boston in 1795 and New York in 1805 with one of Mungo's songs published in an edition of the *American Songster* in 1788.[66] It is very unlikely that *The Padlock* appeared in Canada given that theatre houses were primarily built in the nineteenth century. However, circus entertainers like American John Durang and John Ricketts were some of the first entertainers to perform in the tradition of English theatre. Ricketts, who established his own circus company in 1791, is credited with bringing the first modern circus to North America.[67] Durang gained

Atlantic fame as a professional dancer after introducing the "Sailor's Hornpipe – Old Style," a clog dance that mixed European ballet steps with African American shuffle-and-wing steps, which were a product of foot-shuffling square dances held on southern plantations during the eighteenth and nineteenth centuries. Durang and Ricketts toured Montreal with six trained houses in 1797, and in the summer of 1798 they took their show to Quebec City.[68]

The "circus" or circular configurations of entertainment were rarely held in fixed structures; instead, touring circuses were normally held outdoors in makeshift venues, in riding arenas or barns, and from the mid-1820s in newly invented canvas tents.[69] Equestrians remained essential to the structure of the circus, but there were a range of other entertainments such as jugglers and acrobats, animals (other than horses), and clowns. In the case of Durang, many credit him as the first American actor to appear on stage in blackface.[70] As Lynn Matluck Brooks explains, "[Durang] appeared as an African in *Robinson Crusoe; or Harlequin Friday*, a pantomime by Richard Brinsley Sheridan, that had been frequently repeated in London and had already played Philadelphia in earlier seasons."[71] The show received fifteen performances between 1787 and 1799, which was a significant amount of stage time for that period.[72] As Brooks notes further, "[he] was one of the few native-born performers with the Old American Company, and the role of Friday, in blackface, was an important step for him toward more prominent pantomime roles."[73] As part of Ricketts's circus company, Durang performed in variety show extravaganzas that had become all the rage in the late eighteenth century. "The show was a mixture of tricks on horseback, clowning, pyrotechnics…Ricketts, the more talented horseman, was known for being able to dance a hornpipe on the back of a horse as it raced at full speed around the ring. Durang, on the other hand, was the comedian," writes Vance.[74] The hornpipe was a popular stage dance in early America. As Philadelphia historian Christian DuComb observes, "it featured the miming of shipboard labour to an up-tempo beat, with the high steps and bent knees and elbows of an Irish jig," and it was also "a movement style that presaged the nineteenth-century Jim Crow dance."[75] Durang performed his hornpipe routine in drag (he cross-dressed as a woman) and blackface, and was the first American to lay the foundation for the minstrelsy craze that would hit America in the 1830s.

As previously noted, "Yankee Doodle" was one of the earliest folk themes associated with two battles between the British and French during the Revolutionary War.[76] The song also directly spoke to events that took place in Cape Breton, Nova Scotia. "The shortest group of stanzas describes the ignorance and cowardice of the American militia at Cape Breton," writes Leo Lemay who studied the song's origins; the verses of the song were "no doubt popular with the British soldiers and probably originally caused them to adopt 'Yankee Doodle' as their anti-American war song of the Revolution."[77] There is documented evidence that Yankee-themed theatre remained popular into the 1830s when Dan Marble (1810–49), a Connecticut-born comedic actor, rose to prominence playing "the Yankee." In 1834, he brought his low-comedy role in a strolling tour through western New York state and Lower Canada.[78] In Upper Canada, a play named *A Yankee Story* also appeared in 1835 at Wellington Inn, in Kingston (Frontenac County).[79] While there is little known about the contents of the play, one of the distinct features of any "Yankee" story was the narrative being prominently centred around issues of liberty and freedom in the context of a newly sovereign America. For example, Marble's most famous character, "Sam Patch" was based on the real-life story of Buffalo, New York-born Sam Patch who became the first famous American daredevil after successfully jumping from a raised platform into the Niagara River near the base of Niagara Falls on October 7, 1829; Patch later garnered nicknames like the "Yankee Leaper" and the "Daring Yankee."[80] After catching the imagination of American audiences of the day, Marble portrayed Patch, or the Daring Yankee, year after year before enthusiastic audiences in western cities, then in New York and Boston.[81] Given the proximity to Lower Canada and the Maritimes, Canadian audiences would have heard of Patch and Marble, and they would have begun to associate "the Yankee" with risk-taking and heroism—two attributes that would come to personify the American ethos. In addition to comedies, when Americans began to write their own dramatic theatre it helped cultivate confidence in their own forms of public culture distinct from English dramas. The origins of an American drama can be traced to *The Disappointment; or the Force of Credulity* (1767), which is widely recognized as "the first American opera."[82]

Composed by Samuel Adler in two acts with a prologue and epilogue, to a text by Thomas Forrest (1747–1825), *The Disappointment* is one of the first productions to include the lyrics of "Yankee Doodle" and is the first play in the history of American drama to feature a Black character—"Raccoon" (performed as a Jamaican Black man).[83] Undoubtedly inspired by Mungo, Raccoon was a prototypical "foolish and ignorant Black character" of the eighteenth century.[84] Additionally, the name "Raccoon" was applied to "a member of the New Jersey militia in the American Revolution" and it carried Black connotations that, according to Carolyn Rabson, might not have existed in the original play; however, the term "coon," which became associated with Black men by the late nineteenth century, likely originated from Raccoon in *The Disappointment*.[85] This play is also connected to *coon songs*, which as explored in Chapter 5 became the first popular form of sheet music in the 1890s.

After the War of 1812, many Americans expressed the need for distinct forms, symbols, and institutions that would assert the nation's cultural uniqueness as clearly and emphatically as the decades between the Revolutionary War and War of 1812 had reaffirmed its political independence.[86] As urban areas grew due to industrialization and cities like New York and Philadelphia drew significant numbers of working-class people from both Europe and rural areas of the US, this influx of people led to socioeconomic disparities. These day-to-day struggles with shelter, food, safe drinking water, and poor sanitation created harsh living conditions. As Dale Cockwell asserts, "it was better to be a landowner than not; it was better to be rich than poor; better to be Protestant than Catholic; English than Irish; white than black; freedman than slave. The Northern, urban American stage vicariously played out these human realities by giving voice to those people with little more than the wherewithal to buy a cheap ticket to the gallery."[87] At the same time, in the thirty years after the War of 1812, the forces demanding a "common man's culture" had transformed American entertainment.[88]

White men had portrayed Black characters in the American theatre well before the Revolutionary War (e.g., Mungo and Raccoon), but until the War of 1812, these characters were depicted in popular songs as either "comic buffoons or romanticized Noble Savages" using dialects that owed more to English traditions (e.g., Caribbean lingua franca) than American "black dialect." After the War of 1812 however, the quest for a distinctly American culture took over the arts, and blackface characters became increasingly caricatures of African Americans—the very people comingling and coexisting in cities in the North where a White majority both feared and loathed their presence.[89] As early as the 1820s, saloons and grocery-grog shops had become the centrepiece of an emergent American culture and racial imagery was typically used to soothe Northern working-class White men's fears.[90] There is evidence promoters with wagonloads of European paintings travelled to Canada in the first decades of the nineteenth century and set up exhibitions in churches or town halls with panorama paintings, a phenomenon that swept North America in the mid-nineteenth century; these panorama displays toured Upper Canada with graphic depictions of British soldiers enduring all manner of agonies.[91] By 1848, huge panorama paintings of the Great Lakes and the St. Lawrence River were on display in Montreal; three years later, a panorama of the Mississippi River came to Quebec, enabling people to travel vicariously from St. Louis to the falls of St. Anthony, Minnesota.[92] The arrival of the American circus in the first decades of the nineteenth century marked the beginning of blackface characters who also performed popular songs and appeared in routines that began to resemble the signature style of the American theatre.

The American circus is believed to have started in 1816 with Nathan Howes (1796–1878), who purchased the second elephant imported into the US from their owner, Hackaliah Bailey, of Somers, New York.[93] By the mid-1820s, thirty circus companies were touring, reaching as far as Detroit in 1830 and largely consisting of a few wagons, four trained horses, and some half-dozen performers, mostly tumblers and vaulters, with the essential trick rider and a singing clown, who often wore blackface.[94] The elements of the circus that became "stock" elements of blackface included songs, dances, jokes, and skits. Ricketts's circus was not the only American circus to visit Canada in the first decades of the nineteenth century. In her novel about life in rural Canada in 1854, Susanna Moodie described the visit of a travelling American circus to Belleville, beginning with the arrival of large posters "containing coarse woodcuts of the most exciting scenes in the performance."[95] While the details of this performance are not fully known, Moodie makes several references to "Negro" men and children in her book, indicating that Black people were in Belleville and surrounding areas at least from the 1850s. Circuses had brought equestrian and hornpipe acts north of the border since the late eighteenth and early nineteenth centuries, but the Royal

Circus, which appeared in Brockville, Kingston, and then York in 1826 was Canada West's first formalized circus.[96]

If circus performers wore blackface from at least the 1770s through 1820s, it is reasonable to assume that as the American circus headed to cities in Upper and Lower Canada, the Maritimes, where in New Brunswick a performance hall was built in 1824 to host travelling circuses but was converted to a theatrical hall in 1828, and in Nova Scotia, where promoter Charles Powell found that crowds at the New Grand Theatre (built in 1789) "demanded impressive shows with spectacular sets, big props, and lots of action," Canadian audiences were exposed to blackface characters and the themes of the American circus early on.[97] Blackface clowns were extremely popular in circuses, almost all of which featured at least one.[98] As Stephen Johnson asserts, "The Clown figure…was permitted to mock everyone in the venue, performers and audience members alike. He wore grotesque makeup, by turns laughable and frightening, and dressed outrageously, in a mockery of the costumes of the equestrian and the acrobat."[99] Circus blackface figures were representative of the blackface Atlantic as they spoke to both a transatlantic slave culture and blackfaced characters of English theatre such as the harlequin of the commedia dell'arte, the clown of English pantomime and the "blackamoor" of English folk theatre.[100] The theatrical Moor was a characterization that developed out of European encounters in Africa. Derived from the Latin word "Maurus," the term Moor was originally used to describe Berbers living in North Africa and those from the ancient Roman province of Mauretania, which would have also been people living in communities across Morocco, Algeria, Tunisia, Libya, Egypt, Mali, Niger, and Mauritania.[101] Over time, it was increasingly applied to Muslims living in Europe and during the Renaissance, as Moor or "blackamoor" were used interchangeably to describe any person with dark skin.[102] The shifting meaning of the term Moor was linked with European conquest when, between 1609 and 1614, almost all of the Muslim population of Spain, known as the *moriscos*, were expelled from the country.[103] By the seventeenth century, Moors lived across Western Europe, including England, which is when they began to appear as characters in English theatre.

The most famous Moor of all-time appeared as the titular character in William Shakespeare's *The Tragedy of Othello, the Moor of Venice* in 1604.[104] Portrayed by a White male actor serving as a general in the Venetian army, there are long-standing debates about whether Shakespeare and other playwrights meant for the Moor to be a Black African or if the Moor was a North African White Moor.[105] However, as Phyllis Natalie Braxton notes, it is through metaphor and dramaturgical devices that we can read Othello as Black. "The play...required a character who would be recognized by the audience as someone out of his native element—a wanderer. Persons with black skin in Elizabethan England could generally be classified as wanderers; Othello is thus depicted with the black skin common to these wanderers."[106] What's more, the Moor was always a racialized Other in the English Tudor theatre, regardless of how dark their hue, as he or she was undeniably Other in religion, culture, temperament, and ethnicity.[107] If, as Dale Cockrell estimates, between the first American performance of *Othello* in 1751 and the first full-fledged minstrel show in 1843, around 20,000 blackface performances were given in American theatres, blackfacing was a comic device that was as common a practice in America as it had been in Europe.[108] By the second decade of the nineteenth century a new generation of American-born performers created an entirely new genre of theatre. Drawing on English traditions of blackening like *Othello*, clog and hornpipe dancing, African American public culture, and transatlantic carnival displays, this new performative culture became known as blackface minstrelsy, and while its formalization would take place in the 1840s, by the late 1820s this genre would change theatrical repertoires on both sides of the Atlantic, including Canada, for its explicit mimicry of Black people in America.

By the 1820s, American performers who acted out supposed "Negro" songs and dances in circuses included the likes of George Nichols, Bob Farrell, Joel Walker Sweeney, John N. Smith, Micah Hawkins, and Thomas Blakeley.[109] The most talented clowns often left the circus because the pay was low. They then set their sights on hitting the "big time" in city theatres like those in New York and Philadelphia. One of the most successful of these new American blackface circus performers was George Washington Dixon. Born to a poor family in Richmond, Virginia, Dixon was discovered by a circus manager who noticed his potential as a vocalist at the age of fifteen; he subsequently apprenticed in a traveling circus as an errand boy

1.2 "My Long Tail Blue" Sheet Music Cover, ca. 1873, Prints and Photographs Division, Library of Congress, LC-USZ62-109816.

where, as Cockrell argues, "it is likely he first used blackface as a clown in the circus."[110] As the first popular blackface actor to give performances of what became known as "plantation melodies," when Dixon stepped on stage in Albany, New York in 1827 and the following year at the Chatham theatre in New York City, singing a mixture of comic English and frontier humour songs, he ushered in a new era in American performance.[111] His singing and dancing has been described as blackface dandyism, a genre of performance he likely first used as a clown performer in the circus.[112] Dixon became known for two popular songs, "My Long Tail Blue" (1827) and "Coal Black Rose" (1829), both of which depicted a minstrel character that became known as "Zip Coon," a northern "dandy" or dapper, posturing, formerly enslaved Black man (see figures 1.2 and 1.3). "My Long Tail

1.3 "Zip Coon, A Favorite Comic Song, Sung by Mr. G.W. Dixon," ca. 1830–38, Butler Collection of Theatrical Illustration, Manuscripts, Archives, and Special Collections, Washington State University Libraries, cg430n1141.

Blue" also referred to the type of tailcoat favoured on Sundays by Black dandies, who are the subject of the lyric, and it depicted a blackface character in fancy evening attire. "As one of the first blackface acts, Long-Tail Blue strutted on stage in 1827, newly free and nattily attired, potently incarnating a question that hovers over the minstrel show generally," writes Miller, adding "What if blacks were free? And not just in the North? What if they had money, access to education, unchecked social, cultural, and economic mobility?"[113]

"Coal Black Rose," first performed by Bob Farrell—sometimes also credited as being the first circus performer to sing in blackface—was appropriated by Dixon as his signature tune and first published in 1829 and 1834.[114] The song gave rise to the blackface character Zip Coon, and became the first commercially successful blackface minstrel song, most identifiable because of its "Sambo" lyrics.¹¹⁵ As DuComb explains, "At the beginning of the song, Sambo, a suitor to Coal Black Rose, calls on his beloved, singing and strumming his banjo. Rose puts him off for four verses, responding to his entreaties with the lines 'yes I cum' and 'I cum soon,' whose sexual connotations landed just as squarely with early nineteenth-century audiences as they do today."¹¹⁶ Dixon's Zip Coon character, which also harkened back to *The Disappointment*'s Raccoon, answered Long Tail Blue's questions as he simultaneously revealed (and helped to repress) Whites' anxieties about race, class, gender, and sexuality. These characters amused at the same time they revealed "the affinity between effeminacy associated with extreme attention to dress and appearance and hypermasculinity linked to a sexual rapacity that exceeds racial boundaries."¹¹⁷ The difference between the blackface depiction of Black dandyism and the dandyism that existed before it is that the latter was a kind of embodied presence that encapsulated the normative categories of valorized identity, especially in the US system of capital (Whiteness, maleness, elitism, heterosexuality, and patriotism); meanwhile, the former was a caricature that struck at the American distaste for pretentiousness, which enhanced the pleasure derived from ridiculing those who claimed to be what they truly were not—gentlemen.¹¹⁸ On May 21, 1830, when T.D. Rice performed "Jump, Jim Crow" for the first time, his comic "plantation darky" slave character, who would be called Jim Crow, was brought into the popular theatre.

As legend has it, Rice got the idea for the song and dance after an experience outside a Louisville, Kentucky theatre where he, and other performers, witnessed an enslaved Black man working in the stable yard in the eyeshot of the theatre doing odd jobs for a White stable owner named Crow. The Black man had a deformity that affected his right shoulder along with his left leg, which was said to be crooked at the knee, leaving him with a limp, and while he did his work, he sang and jumped in the air.¹¹⁹ Rice watched him closely, and when he returned to the theatre he put on an old patchy coat, a pair of shoes composed of patches on his feet, a coarse straw hat in bad condition, and a black wig of matted moss; as he took to the stage, his "Jump, Jim Crow" was little more than an imitation of Crow's movements (see figure 1.4).¹²⁰ "The next day the song Jim Crow was to be heard everywhere in Louisville," observed a 1932 *New York Times* editorial memorializing the one-hundredth anniversary of Rice's New York city debut,

1.4 Sheet music cover featuring "T.D. Rice as The Original Jim Crow," ca. 1885, MS Thr 556 (157), Harvard Theatre Collection, Houghton Library, Harvard University, Cambridge, Massachusetts.

adding, "When Rice moved on to other cities he took his song with him. Rumors of the immense success he was having with it must have reached the New York of 1832...daily advertisements appeared in the New York papers."[121] One of the first evidences of a Jim Crow character (it is unknown whether this was performed by Rice) in Canada appeared in Toronto's *Correspondent and Advocate* in 1836. A promotional advertisement declared, "a touring menagerie carried three American performers 'to sing several comic Negro Songs, among others the celebrated JIM CROW'."[122] By the 1840s, other minstrel stars visited England like Ned Harper, known for his burlesque "Negro" character, and banjo player Joel Sweeney (1813–60), who is often credited for introducing early minstrel forms of the banjo to British audiences.[123]

Not only did Dixon's "My Long Tail Blue" describe a competition between the story's main character Zip Coon and Rice's Jim Crow, an act which paralleled the onstage rivalry between the two performers behind the personages, it also created early minstrelsy's most dominant theme— a wheeling and pretentious free Black male versus a comical and happily enslaved Black male.[124] Dixon's and Rice's songs, dances, and costumes reflected the transnational exchange of the blackface Atlantic. First, these early minstrel songs resembled Irish folk tunes and English stage songs; but more than just being songs, they were meant to be danced to, with the dance as a key component of their staged performance.[125] Second, Rice's rhythm and motion, in particular, with his shuffling, twitching, turning, jumping, and wheeling about was described in a 1928 book about the New York stage as "very much deformed...the right shoulder was drawn up high, and the left leg was stiff and crooked at the knee."[126] This was also referred to as a "kneebone-bent" movement and would have been appropriated from West African dances brought to Europe and America by enslaved Africans. As Robert Hornbeck asserts, "Most telling of a degree of imitation of blackness...are the distinctive 'kneebone-bent,' spread-legged/knees-apart, elbow-bent, over-head hand gestures (either one or both hands) that dance historians associated with African American body movements in New World dance."[127]

In West Africa, straightened knees and elbows and hips were the signs of the corpse: it was the loose, the limber, the bent knee that was the emblem of life.[128] In her examination of the rise of social dance in African American culture, Katrina Hazzard-Gordon explains further that when West African ethnic groups were brought to the Americas, they brought with them the motor-muscle memory of their cultures. West African dances were "characterized by segmentation and delineation of various body parts, including hips, torso, head, arms, hands, and legs... these esthetic and technical commonalities continued to be governing principles as dance moved from its sacred context to the numerous secular uses it acquired under slavery."[129] Further, after watching enslaved African Americans dancing in 1839, British actor and writer Fanny Kemble (1809–93), fascinated by their movement, is said to have described the dancing in contrast to Rice's Jim Crow, an act that speaks to the role European thespians played in validating new American theatrical practices and their acknowledgement that these theatrical practices were rooted in "borrowing" from the Other.[130] Audiences across the blackface Atlantic were familiar with the name Sambo because White actors had been playing the ignorant or comic *Black* character as early as *The Disappointment*'s Raccoon. There were a plethora of "foolish and ignorant black characters with names like...Caesar, and Pompey [that] soon followed in other plays, all in the eighteenth century."[131]

As the likes of Dixon, Rice, and others circulated the blackface Atlantic, by the late 1830s the "trickster" in American folklore (Zip Coon) became entangled with the fool (Jim Crow) who was akin to the English Moor, a figure that came to define American minstrelsy. Rather than interpret the movements of Black men as reflective of cultural traditions, Zip Coon's exaggerated dress came to *represent* (in a distorted and disparaging way) the imagined northern Negro, while Jim Crow's distorted movements became exemplar of the Negro *par excellence* on both sides of the Atlantic. As Michael Pickering notes, "Jim Crow soon became a pervasive presence, and not only on stage. Frenziedly marketed spin-offs, such as Jim Crow hats, pipes, and cigars, sold widely, *Punch* labelled a turn-about politician 'Jim Crow,' a mock autobiography, *The Origin of Jim Crow*, was quickly rushed into print in 1837, a book of children's songs titled *Jim Crow's Alphabet* was published."[132] While Dixon's contributions were significant, Rice's Jim Crow launched an Atlantic craze that fundamentally shifted the role and importance of America in charting a new era in theatrical entertainment. Unlike the English theatre, which centred European themes and British slavery, Jim Crow represented the "New World" and a new style of performance that overtly used the African American body and cultural narrative as its unauthorized muse.

By the end of 1832, as word spread of "Jump, Jim Crow," Rice's legend as the "grandfather of blackface minstrelsy" grew.[133] At the same time, he also assumed roles familiar to Americans like the Black servant Mungo, who he performed in addition to Jim Crow.[134] Importantly, as Benjamin Miller observes, "between 1828 and 1834 the iconography of racism that permeated the popular imagination of working-class Americans amplified subhuman, demonic and grotesque features, and it did so to ease white audiences' concerns about abolition, amalgamation and other discourses of black freedom."[135] It is difficult to say with certainty if Dixon or Rice performed in Canada in the 1830s, but the fact of British immigration meant people would have known of blackfaced theatre and the themes of early minstrelsy. As cities across the country began to grow, the building of theatres was fundamental to that growth. In the Maritimes, theatres were built in cities like Charlottetown in 1800, and by 1809 Saint John had its own professional theatre, which suggests that performance was a significant part of the region's development; like minstrelsy in the northern US, these theatres tended to cater to the desires of a working-class population.[136] New Brunswick theatre historian Mary Elizabeth Smith found the same was true in the Maritimes as in Canada West, where regular and frequent amateur fundraising concerts, occasional amateur readings and dramatic events, touring lectures, professional singers, minstrel troupes, and an occasional circus and theatrical troupe were ever-present. There were also "sporadic professional seasons in the Temperance Hall in Halifax and the regular summer seasons offered by J.W. Lanergan's company in the Saint John Dramatic Lyceum."[137] In Saint John, a new performance hall built in 1824 changed over to theatrical performances in 1828 but was in a part of town that, as Vance writes, "the better class of citizens would never have dreamed of frequenting."[138] Smith writes further that "a larger, less educated and generally less prosperous group, liberally sprinkled with Irishman, formed the bulk of the audience."[139] Like in Saint John where performances changed to suit the differing crowds, it was the same in Halifax where "promoter Charles Powell found that crowds at the New Grand Theatre demanded impressive shows with spectacular sets, big props, and lots of action. In 1798, he bent to the popular will by advertising 'A Representation of the Savages Landing in their Canoes, with the original march from their Landing, and an exact Performance of the War Hoop

Dance and Martial Exercises.'"[140] Maritimers with money and leisure were most connected to Boston and New York, and some, as Smith observes, who rarely travelled to Montreal or Toronto, would cross "the ocean to London, visiting theatre on those occasions."[141]

During the 1830s, due to a significant immigration wave, the demographics of Upper Canada changed drastically. After an outbreak of cholera across Europe (1832), and changes to immigration policy in Britain (beginning in 1815) which forced millions of people to seek refuge in North America, most of these new emigrants were farmers, agricultural labourers or skilled artisans and craftsmen from traditional trades with large families.[142] In the late eighteenth and early nineteenth centuries, waves of cholera—a highly infectious water-borne virus that rapidly brings on intense diarrhea, vomiting, and death by dehydration—had swept out of India into Russia, and eventually through cities of Western Europe. According to John Lorinc, there were hundreds of deaths from a wave of cholera that swept through then-York in 1832, which "prompted colonial administrators to pass legislation the following year allowing for the establishment of local boards of health with mandated powers in all towns."[143] In Britain, some 1,800 men, women, and children were sent by the Petworth Emigration Committee (initiated and organized between 1832 and 1837) from the south of England to Upper Canada.[144] Helen Cowan asserts that three emigrant groups—the Irish, Scottish, and English—had been immigrating to Canada since the eighteenth century, with the vast majority of these emigrants coming from farming areas; the numbers that reached the North American colonial ports tripled in 1839, and following rebellions in Upper Canada, they doubled in 1840.[145] The year 1847 looms particularly when over 100,000 Irish emigrants reached Canadian shores in search of refuge from the poverty, disease, and hunger caused by the Great Potato Famine (1845–52).[146] Toronto, a staunchly Protestant town of around 20,000 at the time, would see over 38,000 Irish, largely Catholics, land on its shores that summer.[147]

The rebellions of 1837 and 1838 were about sovereignty and the question of Canadian nationalism. In Upper Canada, the conflict was led by William Lyon Mackenzie (1795–1861), a Scotland-born newspaper publisher and eventual member of Ontario parliament (after Upper and Lower Canada merged) who challenged the British Crown and the political status quo that maintained a system of land grants that favoured settlers from Britain, as opposed to those with ties to the US.[148] In Lower Canada, Montreal-born Louis-Joseph Papineau (1786–1871) led a group of *Patriotes* and moderate French nationalists in a rebellion against the authority of the Catholic Church with an aim to weaken the powers of the British governor.[149] In the wake of the uprisings, Lord George Lambton Durham (1792–1840) came to Canada to report on the conflict's causes. In what became the first national document, the *Report on the Affairs of British North America* (1839), several recommendations were made, including the unification of Upper and Lower Canada. In 1841, in an act seen as a forerunner to Confederation, the two were brought together as Canada West (Ontario) and Canada East (Quebec).[150] By the end of the early 1840s, Toronto became the largest city in Canada West with a population of nearly 50,000, and it is estimated that 500 to 1,200 of those residents were Black;[151] among the most notable was Wilson Ruffin Abbott (1801–76), a freeborn Virginian businessman who had settled in Toronto with his family in 1835. Thornton Blackburn (1812–90) and his wife Lucie (1803–95), who had escaped from slavery in Kentucky, also lived in Toronto. The couple landed in Detroit, but eventually found their way to the city where they established the first taxi company.[152] With its geographic location, communication, transport, and growing urbanization and industrialization, Toronto developed a theatrical scene.[153] It was third only to Rochester and Buffalo in size and prosperity among the Great Lakes ports of its day.[154] With the building of rail networks connecting Toronto to towns east, west, north, and south, plus the building of large-scale transport systems that expanded capacity for retail stores, printing industries thrived and the financial sector boomed. Toronto quickly evolved into a regional metropolis with distinguished architectural buildings like Osgoode Hall (built in 1832), St. Lawrence Hall (built in 1850), and University College and The Cathedral Church of St. James (both built in 1853).

The multiple waves of White settlement to Upper and Lower Canada and the Maritimes beginning at the end of the Revolutionary War, and new waves of immigrants from the British Isles to Canada West in the 1830s, changed the country. While Canada did not experience widespread racial anxieties and rebellions like in the US northeast, the expansion of British rule also required the expulsion of the land's Indigenous Peoples. Between 1781 and 1830, the Ojibway, Indigenous Anishinaabe people whose homeland covers much of the Great Lakes region and the northern US plains, were forced to gradually cede to the British most of the land north of what is now southern Ontario, and the British presented land treaties as statements of loyalty to the Crown and as guarantees that the lands would be protected from White settlement.[155] Black "settlers" to Ontario were essentially caught between British colonizers and White immigrants on the one hand, and violently displaced and colonized Indigenous Peoples on the other. They had no place to call their own, but they had a strong desire to make a home out of their own forced or voluntary displacement. In this regard, there is a prima facie difference, as Jeff Malpas asserts, between *place* and *placedness*. "'Placedness' or 'being placed' names a characteristic, even if generalizable, of that which is placed, whereas 'place' names that to which what is placed stands in relation. *Placedness* would thus seem, on the face of it, to presuppose *place*. On that basis, there can be no *placedness* without *place*, and the two notions are inextricably bound together even though they are also distinct."[156]

Jennifer Nelson notes that British colonization fundamentally changed the demographics of the Maritimes. "The Acadians lived on Mi'kmaq lands...similarly, the lands allotted to black migrants were neither within the rightful jurisdiction of the British to distribute, nor in possession of the black settlers...the former landed unannounced and forcibly claimed the territory, the latter were, variably, exiled or escaped peoples struggling for survival. Many blacks came unwillingly, and those who selected Nova Scotia as their home did so within a severely limited range of choices."[157] Ultimately, by the 1840s, Zip Coon and Jim Crow were representative of the contradictory nature of race across the blackface Atlantic. There was cultural exchange via minstrelsy between America and Britain, but at the same time and on both sides of the Atlantic, antislavery movements which abhorred the abasement of Black people under systems of bondage were becoming more active, even as antiabolitionist race rebellion threatened to thwart these movements. In 1831, (the same year of the Jim Crow craze) William Lloyd Garrison (1805–79) founded *The Liberator* (1831–65) in Boston, a weekly abolitionist newspaper; by then, a second wave of British antislavery had been active for nearly a decade. When Britain abolished chattel slavery in its Caribbean colonies in 1834 and ended its apprenticeship system four years later, this included Canada. While a transatlantic antislavery movement premised on the emancipation of Black people coincided with a transatlantic entertainment circuit centred on peddling stereotypes of Black people, the concurrent rise of abolitionism and minstrelsy produced innumerable representations, and these images proved to be serviceable in discussing other issues, such as nationalism, labour, and class.

Meanwhile, class sociability in Northern American cities in the first decades of the nineteenth century revealed that there were profound changes in American culture between 1825 and 1835, such as the emergence of a White working-class urban culture that created the cultural conditions for theatrical minstrelsy to thrive. Cities like New York, Boston, and Philadelphia became home to American minstrelsy's first theatres and blackface performers who were also working- or middle-class Whites. As the classes began to forge social lives independent of one another, cheap dance halls, billiard rooms, saloons, and amphitheaters for bare-knuckle prizefights and cockfights, as well as minstrel shows, began to establish themselves by the late 1830s.[158] In 1826, New York's Bowery Theatre opened, and other theatres like the Chatham and Park Theatre established themselves as the primary venues for blackface minstrel shows by the late 1830s. At the same time, race rebellions frequently erupted in New York and Philadelphia, which had a significant impact on minstrelsy's latent meaning for both the White performer and White audience. Philadelphia's first full-blown race rebellion took place on August 12, 1834, and according to John Runcie's study of the event, "The rioters were mostly young and from the bottom rungs of the occupational ladder. Some of them were of Irish origin, some of them had criminal records, and a few of them were skilled craftsmen."[159] Like in New York City where rebellions took over the city for three days in July 1834 in response to economic downturn (which led to social tensions and grievances between newly arrived immigrant ethnic groups and African Americans in the North who were all vying for work, housing, and sociability) the people who participated in the Philadelphia race rebellion were using violence in what Runcie describes as "a rational controlled way for the attainment of specific goals and objectives."[160] Some of these goals and objectives included a desire to remove Black people from their neighbourhoods to increase their own economic opportunities. These rebellions pointed to anxieties—not only fears of Black competition for jobs—in a working-class population that was experiencing new forms of "industrial discipline," wherein race rebellions embodied the traditions and rituals of often new urbanized working-class communities; the ethos of these same communities was ardently anti-Black and antiabolitionist.[161]

The 1840s, however, witnessed a new era in minstrelsy's North American expansion as concert halls and theatres began to feature performances by full-fledged White minstrel troupes in blackface. In 1843, four White men from the northeast formed the Virginia Minstrels who, along with Stephen Foster, the major White creator of minstrel music, would also become known as "the founders of American minstrelsy." At the same time, the first Black dancer of international acclaim, William Henry Lane, would revolutionize minstrel dance, creating "an imitation of *himself* that no one could copy."[162] Chapter 2 explains how, in the 1840s and 1850s, new acts ushered in a surge in popularity of touring circuses and blackface troupes, even as Black community began to protest them. During this period, large theatre houses were also built across Canada to facilitate the arrival of larger American blackface productions.

2

PERFORMING CONFLICT IN BLACKFACE, ANTISLAVERY MOVEMENTS, AND THE FIRST BLACK DANCERS, 1840-57

At the end of the 1830s, the circus (sometimes called a "menagerie") was the first to bring Jim Crow blackface clowns to Canada. A June 1840 article in the *British Colonist*, a short-lived newspaper published out of Toronto, referenced a performer who sang and danced "á la Jim Crow."[1] While "Negro songs and dances" had been performed by White men in blackface at circuses and in variety "olios" since the 1820s, and the circus was where the vast majority of minstrelsy's first popular acts got their start, Canada did not have a circus company; instead, it relied upon travelling circuses, which had been touring the country since the late eighteenth century. By the 1840s, Toronto's Black population was significantly engaged politically, and they demanded these kinds of performances be forbidden in the city. Members of the community petitioned the city's mayors to not grant licences to circuses and menageries: Mayor John Powell (1809–81) in 1840, his successor George Munro (1801–78) in 1841, and Henry Sherwood (1807–55) during his tenure in 1842 and 1843. All failed to take the Black community seriously enough to act on their petition, which decried that "certain acts, and songs, such as Jim Crow and what they call other Negro Characters" be banned from the city's stages.² As Stephen Johnson writes, "[the Black community's] petitions failed in every respect. They failed to stop the entertainments they protested. They failed to convince the broader population of Toronto to turn away from this kind of demeaning, segregationist, racist entertainment. And they failed to make their way into the narrative history of theatre of performance in Canada."³ Ignoring these petitions meant that blackface entertainment had become so important to the city that no amount of protest to ban them was going to succeed in thwarting their popularity.⁴

In his study of Toronto's theatre history, Patrick O'Neill located the decade between 1838 and 1848 as a period of considerable dramatic activity. While the city was not New York or Philadelphia with their Black and immigrant communities geographically separated by racial-ethnic lines further complicated by steep class divisions, in Toronto, as O'Neill observes, "If the upper classes provided a more liberated atmosphere for their young people than they had in the previous years, the influx of labourers working on the railroad which would reach Toronto also brought a rowdier element into the city. In 1848 Toronto claimed a tavern in every block which offered whiskey at twenty-five cents a gallon and provided the chief places of public resort…and many men 'loaded up' every Saturday for an inebriated weekend."⁵ There was a particular class of men in nineteenth-century Toronto who, like in the northern US, resisted the Protestant Anglo-Saxon ideal of manhood and who typically attended the theatre, especially blackface minstrel shows. As Christina Burr describes, "The male 'rowdies' who frequented the street corners of Yonge and King Streets were the antithesis of [this ideal], with its emphasis on self-control, self-discipline, and hard work."⁶ "The notion of masculinity idealized by reformers was constantly challenged. Certain groups of immigrants were blamed for this 'degeneration,'" she writes further.⁷ In the decades after the War of 1812, two political groups emerged in Canada West—Liberals and radical Reformers—and this polarization reflected a sharpening clash between "American and British elements, between advocates of change on conceivably American democratic lines and defenders of British institutions against new Yankee menaces."⁸

For a good part of the nineteenth century, political and popular discourses in Canada were taken up with the supposed threat to the social order posed by "the dangerous classes."[9] In his examination of Toronto's nineteenth-century class divisions, Bryan Hogeveen found that there were two broad groupings. "First, respectable working-class males were industrious, took their role as breadwinners seriously, ensured their children attended school, and followed a sober, law-abiding course of life" but the second grouping were the reverse; "unlike the respectable working class, the dangerous classes lived in abject poverty as a result of their disconnection from the labour market. They dodged domestic obligations, were habitually criminal, fond of alcohol, and flouted what élites considered decent and honest conduct."[10] As British immigrants crossed the Atlantic during the first decades of the nineteenth century, they were already familiar with Jim Crow and Zip Coon, and by extension held attitudes about Black people's sovereignty and supposed rightful place in society. By the early 1840s as blackface minstrelsy formalized and continued to travel the Atlantic world, it increasingly borrowed less from European folk traditions and instead *became* a distinctly American form of entertainment consumed by Canadian, British, and foreign audiences alike.

This chapter examines the 1840s through to the early 1850s, one of the most pivotal periods in blackface minstrelsy's development, when across North America theatrical entertainment began to thrive: specifically burlesque lectures, conundrums, equestrian scenes, comic songs, and formalized blackface minstrelsy as a three-part program with stock characters. Instead of a travelling menagerie consisting of a blackface clown, minstrelsy developed into a first part with sentimental music, a middle or "olio" section containing a variety of acts (such as a stump speech), and a third part comprising a skit situation in the plantation South with a troupe seated in a semicircle with actors playing bones and tambourine at either end of the band, often referred to as *endmen*. For the minstrel show to have an audience in Canada, designated theatres were needed, and they replaced temporary stages and saloons, which housed these acts prior to the 1840s.

As early as 1809, there were performances at York (Toronto) by American companies, but it was not until 1834 that Toronto had its first real theatre, a converted Wesleyan church.[11] In 1846, Toronto's first designated theatre, the Toronto Lyceum, opened, and it attracted both amateur and touring professional groups for two seasons until the government took the building back for other purposes; in 1848, a new permanent theatre, the Royal Lyceum, was built.[12] This theatre was the first in Toronto to be erected for exclusive theatre use, the first proper theatre in town, and, from all accounts, the first proper theatre in Ontario. Histories differ on the matter of an opening date, although according to the *Globe* at the time, the theatre opened on December 28, 1848.[13] A blackface troupe calling itself the Ethiopian Harmonists was the first to draw large crowds at the Royal Lyceum in 1849.[14] As the city's first purpose-built theatre, the Royal Lyceum was financed by wealthy landowner John Ritchey, and it was significant not only because it was Toronto's first opera house, but because it offered more than opera; it featured plays, groups of actors, strolling musicians, soloists, and elocutionists.[15] The theatre also ushered in a new era of professional theatre in the city as programs ranging from Shakespeare to blackface were all staged there with no reports of rebellion or disruptions, "Although [John] Nickinson succeeded in attracting the upper class of Toronto Society to the theatre," writes Patrick O'Neill.[16] Toronto audiences were not yet prepared to support a regular professional theatre, and despite dreams of seeing the city become the centre of a circuit, it remained in its embryonic condition in the 1840s.[17] At the same time, musical and choral societies began to form around the region as well as public and masonic halls.[18]

Significantly, the business and political class in Upper and Lower Canada had long established ties to Atlantic slavery; several prominent leaders owned and sold slaves. Upper Canada-born Samuel Jarvis (1792–1857), for example, was part of a slaveholding family. Jarvis fought in the War of 1812 and was part of Toronto's political class when the city was incorporated alongside his father, American-born William Jarvis (1756–1817), a militiaman and member of early local governments in York. The Jarvises owned at least six Black slaves, even as the law in Upper Canada was decidedly antislavery, according to John Ross Robertson's (1841–1918) book *Landmarks of Toronto*, written in 1894.[19] Peter Russell (1733–1808), an Ireland-born military officer in the Revolutionary War and a government official, politician, and judge in Upper Canada, was also a slaveholder. Of the believed-to-be fifteen enslaved persons living in York in the early nineteenth century, the majority were owned by Russell and Jarvis, who by all accounts were corrupt and unsavoury officials.[20]

Even though a 1793 Act to Limit Slavery in Upper Canada was the first legislation in the British colonies to restrict the slave trade, as a gradual abolition bill it did not end slavery outright.[21] This meant existing slaveholder property rights remained, and children of enslaved women were only free after the age of twenty-five (their own children would then be considered legally born free).[22] According to Adrienne Shadd's findings, American Loyalists and immigrants from the British Isles enslaved Black people; so too did some First Nations in Brantford including Joseph Brant (1743–1807) or Thayendanegea, the Mohawk leader of the Six Nations at Brantford, who was notably said to possess many slaves.[23] Originally from Ohio, Brant relocated to the Mohawk Valley of New York State with his family. While fighting as a British ally in the Indian and Revolutionary Wars, Brant took an estimated upward of forty slaves; after the Wars he kept many of them as his personal servants, such as Sophia Burthen Pooley (1772–1860).[24] Pooley's testimony is documented in American abolitionist Benjamin Drew's *The Refugee: or Narratives of the Fugitive Slaves in Canada* (1856), and is considered to be one of the only first-person narratives regarding slavery in nineteenth-century Canada by an enslaved person.[25]

Brant, the Jarvises, and the Russells rank as some of Upper Canada's most powerful historical figures. They were directly connected to fighting for the British during the Revolutionary War, and later they carried significant weight across the region as political leaders. The fact all three enslaved Black people is also significant to the story of settlement and belonging. Black people lived in Upper Canada at the end of the eighteenth century and they were also part of the region's renaming to become Canada West in the mid-nineteenth century.

Wealthy businessmen in Lower Canada carried out similar actions. McGill University is the most salient example of English Montreal's ties to slavery. Named after James McGill (1744–1813), the Scotland-born merchant bequeathed his intention to found a college that would bear his name to the Royal Institute for the Advancement of Learning (RIAL) in his will. The RIAL became the governing body for McGill College, which was officially established in 1821.[26] In McGill's case, he received rich endowments from Prince Edward Island-born, Montreal-bred William C. Macdonald (1831–1917), a manufacturer and education philanthropist whose tobacco empire drew upon raw material from enslaved African Americans in states like Kentucky, in addition to his own slave ownership.[27] These figures are important to locate in a history of blackface in Canada because they either financed the building of theatre, were patrons of theatre, or had personal ties to southern plantation slavery.

In Quebec, theatrical entertainment can be traced back to the eighteenth century. American circus acts like John Ricketts performed in Montreal and Quebec City in 1797 and 1798, but English-language theatrical performances really began to appear there in the early nineteenth century as a growing Anglophone population attracted American acts.[28] As Elaine Nardocchio found in her study of Quebec theatre, "Most of the productions were in English, and although both French and English attended, it was the English garrison troops and their friends who made up the majority of the spectators. Between 1804 and 1898 at least twenty-five theatres were opened in Montreal for these eager audiences."[29] There were several main venues for theatre, arts, and culture: the Montreal Theatre (1818), which later became a hotel called Mansion House, the Hayes Theatre (1847), which was used for a time as the Parliament Building after the original burned down in 1849, Mechanics' Hall (1854), which hosted operas, the Academie de Musique (1874), an eventual vaudeville house, and Her Majesty's Theatre (1898).[30] The Salle de Concert de l'Hôtel de Ville opened in January 1852, along with several smaller venues such as the 1,200-seat Bonaventure Hall on Craig Street (now Saint-Antoine). By the end of the decade, three venues on Great Saint James Street (now Saint-Jacques), the Odd Fellows' Hall, Mechanics' Hall, and Nordheimer's Hall, were the main centres of entertainment in 1850s Montreal. The 1,500-seat Theatre Royal, centrally located on Côte Street, just north of Place d'Armes, was the city's fourth theatre with this name.[31]

After the opening of the trans-provincial Grand Trunk Railway in 1856, Montreal relied upon New York City for much of its artistic and cultural entertainment, though European theatrical companies also brought their productions there.[32] The Grand Trunk Railway was the world's longest line in its day, extending travel from Toronto to Montreal, and eventually its construction continued westward to Sarnia on Lake Huron. Long before the Canadian Pacific Railway (CPR), the Grand Trunk Railway was the most important railway, and its building not only fostered growth and development across Canada East and West, but it also established the infrastructure for larger scale entertainment. As Brian Christopher Thompson explains, "With its place on the edge of the continent's touring circuit, Montreal enjoyed a wide variety of entertainment. 'Curiosity shows' were highly popular, allowing spectators to view strange or deformed creatures—often human—for a small fee.... Even more popular than circuses were the travelling minstrel shows that frequently appeared at the Theatre Royal and the Mechanics' Hall through the 1850s."[33]

When companies came to Montreal, they then travelled west, playing towns along the north shore of the St. Lawrence River and Lakes Ontario and Erie; the northern route from Montreal passed through cities and towns like Ottawa and Renfrew; to the west and south of Toronto, theatrical stops were very close together as theatres were built at Brantford, Hamilton, Guelph, London, Chatham, Woodstock, and St. Thomas; later, the CPR connected Toronto and the towns around Georgian Bay (Barrie, Collingwood, Orillia, Midland) to towns to the north of Lake Huron (North Bay, Sudbury, and Sault Ste. Marie).[34] In his study of the city's musical theatre, Marc Charpentier found that as early as the 1842–43 theatre season, the Comic Opera Company of Paris came to Montreal after a successful tour of New York City, and during the active 1859 season, Montreal received the Sanford Opera Company in June, the Parodi Italian Opera in July, and the Cooper English Opera in November.[35] Clarence Bayne found that the Odd Fellows Hall (opened in 1846), a social club for prominent elected members of Parliament, and the Garrick Theatre Club (1849) served as venues for blackface shows, including the Ethiopian Serenaders from Philadelphia.[36]

The Ethiopian Serenaders, who were also called the Boston Minstrels, Dumbolton Company or Dumbolton's Serenaders, made their American debut in 1843 and first appeared in Britain in 1846.[37] These troupes combined American blackface with the British blackfaced fool while singing and dancing in patterns originated by Africans who White performers consciously imitated in the staging of their performances.[38] In the 1860s, Wood's Minstrels arrived from New York and proceeded to attract large audiences in Montreal where minstrel shows were extremely popular in 1861 and throughout that year; Christy's Minstrels and Brass Band also presented: "original programmes, descriptive of Darkey Life in the South."[39]

Wood's and Christy's Minstrels toured for many years together before they travelled to Montreal.[40] Although French was the majority language spoken in Canada East, English-language theatre dominated, therefore American minstrel acts were in high demand.[41] While Toronto's first theatre opened in 1849, Montreal's first purpose-built English-language theatre, the Theatre Royal (founded by John Molson to stage plays by Shakespeare and other English playwrights) was originally built in 1825, torn down between 1844 and 1845, and rebuilt in 1851. Thereafter, it became the main theatrical venue for travelling theatre, concerts, circuses, and other burlesque entertainments.[42] By the mid-1840s, Charlottetown and Saint John had purpose-built theatres, and the Theatre Royal at Spring Gardens in Halifax, opened in 1846, even had boxes to accommodate over 160 patrons.[43]

Understanding the timeline for when Canada's theatre houses were built is important to this discussion of blackface. It illustrates the significance of theatre in the country's formidable years of development, and how central racial politics were to entertainment culture in an era of significant change and conflict. As Black people begin to imagine their own emancipation by migrating north to Canada, blackface minstrelsy *reimagined* plantation slavery for popular audiences. While the ruling White political classes and newly arrived White immigrants had the privilege of, and access to, land ownership through the assistance of antislavery societies (the first founded across the Atlantic at the end of the eighteenth century), Black people were able to establish free settlements across Canada West, though few were able to become landowners. This convergence of events, people, and varying degrees of enfranchisement took place at the exact moment blackface minstrelsy, the railway, and newspapers emerged as key institutions in the modernization of cities across North America.

By the 1820s, there were two antislavery societies on both sides of the Atlantic. The Society for the Relief of Free Negroes Unlawfully Held in Bondage formed in Philadelphia in 1775, and in 1823, Britain's Society for the Mitigation and Gradual Abolition of Slavery Throughout the British Dominions was founded. The American abolitionist movements reached new heights in the 1830s with the establishment of antislavery societies in Cleveland (1833), Philadelphia (1833), Vermont (1834); the largest and most influential of these organizations, the American Anti-Slavery Society (AASS), formed in 1833.[44] Free settlements for Black people were also established in Upper Canada beginning in 1829 when Wilberforce, a refugee community located near London, Upper Canada was founded by American freemen James Charles Brown (1800–1859) and Benjamin Lundy (1789–1839), who had been inspired by their attendance at a Philadelphia abolitionist conference the year before.[45] The Dawn Settlement, established in Dresden in 1841 by the British American Institute, became home to one of Canada's first schools to emphasize Black vocational education, and also home to the Reverend Josiah Henson (1789–1883) who had helped establish the settlement. Eight years later, Scottish-born abolitionist and Reverend William King (1812–95), who had experienced slavery in the American South, established the Elgin Settlement at Buxton. King had envisioned a free settlement for African Americans on lands north of Lake Erie near Chatham. In 1850, Kentucky-born abolitionist Henry Bibb (1815–54) and his wife Mary were among some of the first Black people in Sandwich (present-day Windsor), along with Wilmington, Delaware-born Mary Ann Shadd Cary (1823–93), who cofounded two newspapers with her male counterparts—*The Voice of the Fugitive* (1851–53) and *The Provincial Freeman* (1853–57). After settling in the Refugee Home Society in Sandwich on the Detroit frontier, Shadd opened a school for freedom-seeking African Americans. After moving the *Freeman* to Toronto in 1853, Shadd eventually relocated to Chatham and published the paper there from 1855 until it folded.

In her study of Black presence in Canada West at midcentury, Kristin McLaren asserts that many White residents opposed the settlement of Black people in or near their communities and they refused them entry into public schools; one such person was Edwin Larwill (1806–67), school commissioner in Raleigh Township, editor of the *Chatham Journal* and local politician, who led a racist movement in Chatham opposing school aid for Black residents in 1841.[46] On August 24, 1852, Frederick Douglass (1818–95), the most prominent African American antislavery leader of the century, also visited St. Catharines in the aftermath of a devastating race rebellion that destroyed sections of the town's "Colored Village."[47] His presence made it clear that as Black people were becoming more visible in places like Chatham, a backlash against them was just as visible. At the same time, and despite an overwhelming historiographic focus on the Underground Railroad, as Deirdre McCorkindale writes, "Chatham's Black community was made up of more than fugitive slaves. Between 1855 and 1865, Chatham had several practicing Black doctors, including Martin Delany."[48] Delany (1812–85), born free in Virginia, was one of many abolitionists, including Douglass and Massachusetts-born William Lloyd Garrison (co-founder of the abolitionist newspaper *The Liberator* in 1831, and the AASS in 1833), who all used their voices to fight for Black freedom.[49]

However, as Eric Lott aptly notes regarding the striking convergences of this period, "[The] economy...responsible for the first blackface tunes and dances which began to appear after the War of 1812, was played out in somewhat subtler ways in black theatrical performance...the twin births of minstrelsy and Garrison's *Liberator* at the beginning of the 1830s may be added to the demise of black theatrical institutions such as New York's African Grove Theatre," that offered opportunities for Black actors but also to White actors, which sometimes led to race-class conflicts.[50] In Chatham, White abolitionist John Brown (1800–59) held a constitutional convention attended by close to fifty abolitionists; following the Chatham convention, Brown undertook his raid on Harper's Ferry in 1859 and was captured and executed. Freeborn African American Osborne Anderson (1830–72), the only Black person in John Brown's group and one of the few to escape after the failure of the raid, returned to Chatham and published his account of the event. Some of Chatham's other residents included Thomas Joiner White (1827–63), who was also born in Virginia. According to the 1855 census, White was working in New York City but in 1859, with his wife Emma J. Gloucester, they moved to Hamilton and later settled in Chatham where, by the early 1860s, he was practising medicine on King Street, a significant thoroughfare.[51] Several hotels and taverns, including Israel Evans's Cross Keys Tavern in the 1830s, the Royal Exchange (1840), the Rankin Hotel (1852), and the Garner Hotel in the 1870s were all located on King.[52] Flour mills, shipbuilding, tanneries, large lumber merchants, carriage plants, soap shops, saw mills, and ship-plank mills were established along King Street, Wellington Street, and Third Street, as access to the Thames River provided industrialists and merchants access to the city's downtown.[53]

Chatham is the perfect example of the convergence of contradictions related to Black life that defined the nineteenth century. At the same time the town was a place where Black people thrived, it was also a segregated town. The Black community lived on King Street East and the neighbouring streets, while the White community lived on King Street West and beyond. The James Charity Block, Murray Block, and Boyd Block were Black areas that housed commercial and professional businesses and did well over the course of the mid- to late nineteenth century.[54] Importantly, as Adrienne Shadd explains, "One reason that Chatham attracted these people was the considerable employment prospects the town offered, as well as the fact that it was the largest town in Kent County, which held by far the largest population of Blacks in the province, owing to the location of the Black colonies of Buxton and Dawn within its borders."[55] One of the reasons why so many African Americans were heading north in search of freedom in the 1850s is because of the Fugitive Slave Act, passed by the US Congress on September 18, 1850—a few short years after Douglass and Delany cofounded the abolitionist newspaper the *North Star* (1847–51), an outlet created to fight for the emancipation and full citizenship for African Americans. These and other events helped to conjure a belief that Canada represented as the "north star," and that it would function as a guide just as the Star of Bethlehem had led the three wise men to Jesus's birth in the Chistian Bible. As Sharon Hepburn writes, 1850 marks the moment when "slaves incorporated the lore of Canada into their culture, particularly its religious folklore components. Such a strong association between Canada and the promised land developed that a myth arose equating Canada with the biblical land of Canaan."[56]

The Fugitive Slave Act placed the issue of capturing African Americans (both enslaved runaways, those who had manumitted their freedom, and freeborn) under federal jurisdiction, giving citizens the right to aid in the recapture of those persons who reached the US North while also denying African Americans trial by jury or the right to testify on their own behalf.[57] In recognition of the changing political and racial milieu in the US, on February 26, 1851, Toronto newspaper magnate George Brown (1818–80) formed the Anti-Slavery Society of Canada, which sought to make connections with the British Anti-Slavery Society and the AASS.[58] During the first week of April in 1851, British parliamentarian George Thompson

(1804–78) drew 1,200 people to his talk on abolition in Toronto, and Douglass also delivered a rousing speech before a crowd of two thousand where he suggested that some Refugees (freedom-seeking African Americans living in Canada) in the audience might have served the cause better by staying in America and revolting against slaveholders.[59] From September 11 to 13 that same year, hundreds gathered at Toronto's St. Lawrence Hall (opened in 1850) for the North American Convention of Colored Freemen, a three-day event focusing on the fight against slavery in the US and how to assist African Americans fleeing into Canada West.

Many prominent African Americans living in Toronto were in attendance such as Virginia-born Dr. Alexander T. Augusta (1825–90), who had moved to Toronto in 1853 and studied medicine at the University of Toronto's Trinity College, opened a drugstore, had a surgical practice in the city, and was president of the Association for the Education of Coloured People in Canada.[60] Harriet Tubman (1822–1913), who in 1849 had fled to Canada, was also at the Convention.[61] As John Boyko recounts, "Twelve hundred people applauded speaker after speaker, including Brown, who attacked the Fugitive Slave Law, the institution of slavery, and the Southern interests that defended both. Brown promised to urge the Canadian government to do all that could be done to end slavery in the United States."[62]

This short historiography of Black presences in Canada West in the 1850s is significant to this discussion of Canada and the blackface Atlantic because it is usually not discussed in relation to theatre, minstrel shows, and the racial caricatures that circulated during this period. The White population in Canada West (like in Nova Scotia nearly seventy years prior) did not want Black people to become part of their communities. As historian Dorothy Williams writes, "A system of separate schools and separate communities was set up in each province, and 'separate but equal' legislation was used to segregate Canadians of African origin. In other provinces with pockets of blacks, local ordinances kept blacks out of the local and provincial mainstream."[63] There existed a duality in Canada regarding African Americans who headed north. As Johnson writes, "To the extent that residents of Canada West sympathized with black immigrants, they welcomed them. To the extent that they believed them to be an insignificant Other, a lesser kind of human being, they feared and disdained their presence."[64]

There were a range of contradictory cultures and subcultures in the nineteenth century that make it difficult to gauge public opinion on slavery in Canada West (and East) but what is abundantly clear is that White people—whether religious Protestants (English or Scottish), Quakers or Irish Catholics, Anglophones or Francophones—were sympathetic to the cause of Black freedom, but just as many were hostile and belligerent toward Black participation in the social and/or political betterment of cities and towns. As Marcus Wood observes, "Outside the 'educated' responses to blacks evolved by abolitionists and missionary philanthropists, there was a range of popular responses which involved the stereotyping of black sexuality, morality, history and character traits."[65] The sociocultural context of conflict and caricatures gave rise to blackface minstrelsy as a popular form of mass entertainment across the Atlantic world because it helped convince a White majority of why Black residents needed to "stay in their place," that they were inferior, and that keeping Black folks segregated also served a purpose—if you did not know a group of people, ridiculing, lampooning, and caricaturing them would not have caused much debate or disruption to daily life.

The decades of the 1840s and 1850s were pivotal moments in blackface minstrelsy's expansion into Canada as the genre morphed from the eccentric expressions of a sole White male actor dancing Jim Crow or singing "Coal Black Rose," to becoming an Atlantic-based industry with a format and characters that travelled the English-speaking world as popular entertainment. Although the minstrel show underwent many transformations between the 1840s and 1850s, the basic structure of three distinct parts, a semicircle of blackface performers in the first section of the show with *endmen* characters often called *Tambo and Bones*, a second part of the show with a variety of acts, and a final segment that centred on the plantation setting, remained consistent.[66] The geographies of the South and North bifurcated Black representation on stage into mutually exclusive stereotypes most aptly summed up as grotesque portrayals of the Northern Black dandy (Zip Coon) and the happy, Southern errant slave (Jim Crow). British-born White settler author Susanna Moodie (1803–85) recalled the merger of circus sideshow acts featuring wild animals and blackface when writing about Belleville, Ontario in the 1850s, describing "Barnham's traveling menagerie of wild animals, and of tame darkie melodists."[67] "Darkie" was a derogatory term used to refer to White performers *performing* plantation-themed acts and as Robert Winans writes, "minstrel performers sang in dialect, which as written in the song sheets bears little resemblance to actual black American speech patterns. But they sang that way, of course, because they were whites, only parading for a time in blackface, as some of the programs and sheet music covers were careful to point out, showing the troupe both in and out of blackface."[68] As cities began to modernize and urbanize across Canada, there existed a whole generation of residents who did not experience or remember slavery as existing in the region. Slavery remained an American institution that was only recognizable through the clandestine immigration of African Americans to cities and towns across the region but as newspapers, universities, railways, banks, theatres, and music halls were built, part of the "new" of this infrastructure transformation were efforts to forget the past and rewrite the present. These developments contributed to a demand for the theatre; as newspapers began to announce and write reviews, theatrical events could reach a mass audience like never before. At the same time, blackface minstrelsy's racial themes depicting the plantation Jim Crow and Negro dandy made clear that a distinction existed within Black people. Even if White residents did not *know* Black people, they were exposed to imagery via newspapers, lithographic prints, and advertising cards that depicted some Black people as "threatening" and others as "comical," which ultimately meant that most White Canadians *experienced* a commodified Blackness that many, especially in remote areas, interpreted as "real."

The popularization and formalization of blackface minstrelsy can be traced back to political events that took place in 1820, when US House Speaker Henry Clay of Kentucky and Senator Jesse B. Thomas of Illinois led the Congress on an accord between pro-slavery and abolitionist states which allowed Maine and Missouri to join the Union (the former as a free state, the latter as a slave state) while prohibiting slavery in the Louisiana Purchase lands north of the 36°30' parallel.[69] Known as the Missouri Compromise, this bill established a temporary political balance but worsened the realities of life for African Americans, as it created a Union divided along sectional lines with northern states prevented from ever prohibiting slavery's expansion.[70] In 1824, Andrew Jackson won the popular vote but fell short of the required electoral vote majority; the House of Representatives elected John Quincy Adams as president, who placed second in both the electoral and popular vote. However, when Jackson was eventually elected in 1828, most historians pinpoint this moment as the founding formation of the present-day Democratic Party.[71] From its inception, blackface minstrelsy was linked ideologically with Jackson's vision for America, imitating the Democratic Party's class identification and hostility toward abolition and temperance, as well as its embrace of territorial expansion.[72]

By the early 1840s, many White minstrel entertainers were heavily involved in the anti-abolitionist wing of the Democratic Party, composing songs about the unifying ethos of the South.[73] Minstrelsy's major innovators rejected the Protestant ethic and escaped into the latitudes of the entertainment world; they also shared with their families' political ties to the Democratic Party, which was the party of Andrew Jackson, antimonopoly, expansion, and White supremacy.[74] The Democratic Party reinvented Whiteness in a manner that "refurbished their party's traditional links to the People and offered political democracy and an inclusive patriotism to White male Americans."[75] Blackface minstrelsy reflected the ethos of the Democratic party where there was a "sense of White unity and entitlement—of White 'blood'" that "served to bind together the Democratic slaveholders and the masses of non-slaveholding whites in the South."[76] This White comradery and connection to slave culture was infused into minstrelsy's development. The Virginia Minstrels (see figure 2.1) were the first White troupe to inaugurate this new era in minstrelsy's development when, on February 6, 1843 at the Bowery Amphitheatre in New York City, "a novel, grotesque, original and surpassingly melodious Ethiopian band," as described in a *New York Herald* advertisement, hit the stage.[77]

Composed of four young men—Billy Whitlock (1813–78), Dick Pelham (1815–78), Daniel Emmett (1815–1904), and Frank Brower (1823–74)—the quartet's first advertisement took great care to note that they provided "*exclusively musical entertainment.*"[78] The quartet appeared just four months before the debut of the Ethiopian Serenaders. Parts of the show spawned by the Virginia Minstrels in the 1840s were explicitly labeled as "southern darkies" or as "plantation darkies," and the many troupes that followed

2.1 Illustration of the Virginia Minstrels performing "The Celebrated Negro Melodies," ca. 1843, Prints and Photographs Division, Library of Congress, LC-USZ62-42353.

the Virginia Minstrels advertised themselves as performing real "insight[s] into slave life in America," including songs, refrains, and ditties "as sung by the Southern slaves."[79] While blackface clowns had performed on stages in Britain and America prior to the nineteenth century, minstrelsy appeared at a time when America was establishing its own national identity and individual Americans were using their membership in an emergent middle class as a reason to also redefine themselves.

Some of the Virginia Minstrels had performed as dancers and musicians. Pelham, also born in New York City, had been a blackface dancer on the New York stage when he teamed up with Ohio-born Emmett, who had worked as a drummer, fiddler, banjo player, and blackface singer in travelling circuses; Emmett would go on to compose "Dixie's Land" (1859), a song that became popular in the South where it emerged during the Civil War as "Dixie," the de facto Confederate national anthem.[80] Finally, Baltimore, Maryland-born Brower was also a dancer who had toured with Emmett.[81] These four men had spent little time in the South, but they used the name Virginia to enhance claims of southern authenticity, as the state was the first to legalize slavery.[82] Importantly, the term "minstrels" was taken from the Rainer family, a non-blackface Swiss singing group who had successfully toured America calling themselves the Tyrolese Minstrels. According to Hans Nathan's findings, two musical phenomena arose in the US during the early 1840s—the minstrel show was one, "singing families" from Europe was another. The Tyrolese Family Rainer had come to America in 1839 and, before they departed in 1843, they transplanted the idea of "family" performances, establishing the group-arrangement that was adopted by their blackface successors in America, with one or two "sisters" in the middle and men flanking them, each resting his hands on his hips or belt, performing informal "mountain style" ensemble-singing and free harmonizing.[83] After adopting the name, the Virginia Minstrels' success was quickly emulated by numerous other troupes, such as the Ethiopian Serenaders, the Sable Harmonists, and E.P. Christy's Minstrels (see figure 2.2).[84]

As Bob Carlin explains, "In the aftermath of the *Virginia Minstrels*, a multitude of groups with a myriad of names formed to take advantage of the demand for ensembles. Solo performers saw the financial advantages to joining with three or more other like-minded blackface entertainers in the

2.2 Sheet music cover for "Christy's Melodies as Composed and Sung by Them" composed by E. P. Christy, ca. 1847, 07_07_000075, the Music Special Collection, The Arts Department, The Boston Public Library, Boston, Massachusetts.

move toward minstrel bands."[85] In 1844, the Ethiopian Serenaders played at the White House for "Especial Amusement of the President of the United States, His Family and Friends" and in 1846, Christy's took up permanent residence in New York City's Mechanics Hall.[86]

The Virginia Minstrels toured Britain in 1843 and by the late 1840s, minstrelsy's success in both nations "ensured its position in Anglophone transatlantic culture."[87] As Stephanie Dunson aptly observes, "By broadening the venue of blackface, performers such as the *Virginia Minstrels* and other troupes of so-called Ethiopian Delineators provided white audiences with a wide screen for the projection of their wildest fantasies and deepest fears about themselves and, by extension, the black population."[88] These troupes idealized Southern slavery through songs, stump speeches made a mockery of free African Americans in the North, and plantation skits parodied Black family relationships.[89] While it is unclear if the Virginial Minstrels toured Canada during this period, many troupes did tour the country after the passage of the Fugitive Slave Act through to the US Civil War. The question of why audiences were drawn to White performers calling themselves "Ethiopian delineators" or "minstrels" can be best surmised in Wood's articulation of *catch-22 racism* wherein "the qualities which white society legitimates for blacks…physical prowess, suffering and heroism…are instantaneously subsumed into white neurotic laughter."[90] Across the blackface Atlantic, the stereotypes peddled in minstrelsy that became associated with Black people were nothing if not contradictory. White minstrels caricatured Black people for fun and frolic through song, dance, and speech, but conversely, Black people were rendered foolish, hypersexual, and in some instances, dangerous. These themes manifested themselves in makeup and clothing, but also in minstrelsy's instrumentation and song lyrics. The instruments the Virginia Minstrels used on stage—banjo, fiddle, bone castanets, and tambourine—became standard minstrel repertoire, in addition to a dialogue section composed of riddles and conundrums as a stand-up scene between two characters, the giving of a mock scientific lecture, and an "extravaganza" created by acting out the textual implications of the songs.[91] The audiences were told the Virginia Minstrels' songs, refrains, and ditties were "as sung by the southern slaves at all their merry meetings such as the gathering in of the cotton and sugar crops, corn huskings, slave weddings and junketing."[92]

2.3 Illustration of William Henry Lane "Master Juba," ca. 1850, from the New York Public Library Schomburg Center for Research in Black Culture, Photographs and Prints Division, The Dance Collection.

By the late 1840s, the minstrel show's spatialization of race (where caricatured Black bodies lived in southern and northern binaries, and where the racialization of space meant that stage practices such as clothing, speech, makeup, and other repertoire created imaginary racial lines) demarcated who did and did not "fit" within specific and *real* geographies of place. With the arrival of the first Black blackface performer, William Henry Lane briefly challenged White men's superiority on the stage. Lane is often remembered as "the Jackie Robinson of the American stage" for the ways he revolutionized minstrel dance in the 1840s (see figure 2.3).[93] His success followed that of Ira Aldridge (see figure 2.4), who was part of the African Free School established by the New York Manumission Society in 1787, and which not only educated Black children but also became the early manifestation of the Abolitionist movement.[94]

2.4 Ira Aldridge as Othello, oil on canvas painted by James Northcote, ca. 1826, NPG L251, Private Collection; on loan to the National Portrait Gallery, London.

As the first successful Black American to perform Shakespeare—Aldridge is said to have played Mungo and Othello—when he could not fulfill his ambition to become a professional actor in the US he not only emigrated to England, but when he arrived there he secured his first engagement with top billing at London's Royal Coburg Theatre (now the Old Vic) in October 1825.⁹⁵ It is extraordinary to imagine someone like Aldridge beating all odds against him to become an actor in the nineteenth century. The risk to Black life was very real, but so too were the dangers associated with Black theatre companies, many of which were short-lived. Still, reviews at the time were split between celebrating the heightened sympathy and credibility obtained by having a Black person play a Black character on stage and the novelty or curiosity of seeing a "real" African-descendant person on stage.[96] For example, in the role of Mungo (and to lesser extent Othello), Aldridge made room for Black performers to exist, even as he returned precisely to the kind of "inept black man that many in his audience had been expecting to see as an actor when they first entered the theatre."[97]

Lane's life began sometime around 1825 when he was freeborn in Providence, Rhode Island. By 1845, he was "beyond question the very greatest of all dancers," writes Marian Hannah Winter, adding "he was possessed not only of wonderful and unique execution but also of unsurpassed grace and endurance."[98] Lane's fame came so quickly that at one point he achieved the unprecedented distinction of touring with four White minstrels where he received top billing.[99] Throughout the nineteenth century (and for most of the twentieth century), Black performers often did not get work unless they fitted themselves into the mold cast for them by White producers and casting directors. Thus, for Lane to not only determine his billing, but to share the stage with White performers meant that his talents were truly extraordinary. For a moment, White audiences suspended their beliefs in a supposed inferior Black person as they celebrated his talents; however, this suspended reality came with a caveat—Lane was often forced to wear the burnt cork mask of minstrelsy.

Lane's performances, which were original and inventive, also borrowed elements from Moorish and jig dances he was exposed to in the multi-ethnic saloons and dance halls of New York's Five Points neighbourhood, which developed a reputation as a densely populated section of lower Manhattan with high crime, prostitution, and poverty. The Five Points is sometimes considered the original American melting pot, as it was home to newly emancipated Black Americans and ethnic Irish who had lived in the area since the seventeenth century. Lane quickly became "the only black performer in America who could publicly claim superiority over whites, and it was his blackface mask that had enabled him to do so."[100] After touring the New England states with the Georgia Champion Minstrels, Lane began performing alongside John Diamond at the Chatham and Bowery Theatres in New York and his celebrity began to grow.[101] From the very beginning of Lane's career he embodied the double-edged sword of being a Black performer in the nineteenth century—blackface was demeaning for Black performers and Black audiences, but it could also be liberating because it enabled dancers, singers, and the Black consuming public to escape the oppressive reality of White supremacy while on the stage; the Black performer could be *free* to move, act, and sing. Lane's dance competitions against Diamond exemplify his performative *freedom*.

Diamond was an Irish American dancer and minstrel performer who toured with P.T. Barnum in 1840–41, and brought his amalgamated dance style (a merger of elements of English, Irish, and African dance) to the minstrel stage. Barnum was an important part of the collective redefinition of White America because, through his showmanship and ability to create a paying, reliable public, he helped the emerging sphere of American popular entertainment define itself.[102] As Roediger observes, "The substantial sallies of minstrel entertainers engaged popular attention, as did the tendency of some highly successful performers and promoters (including P.T. Barnum) to do blackface for a time as prelude to fame and fortune elsewhere. In a real sense, then…blacking *was* an accumulating capitalist behavior."[103] As American show business historian John Springhall also notes, "the blackface or white 'Negro-dancer' John Diamond…this Irish American dance prodigy specialized in Ethiopian 'break-downs,' during which he 'twisted his feet and legs into fantastic forms.'"[104] Importantly, dance competitions, known as "cutting contests," were a popular form of entertainment in the mid-nineteenth century, providing a showcase for young talent; in the case of Lane, they helped him earn acclaim competing against the best dancers of his day, like Diamond.[105] Some historians have gone so far as to call Diamond "the greatest *white* minstrel dancer" for the ways he emphasized lower-body movements and rapid footwork when dancing.[106]

In part, Lane's success was due to his ability to imitate the steps of famous White minstrel dancers of the day, such as Diamond, then he would execute his own specialty steps, which no one could copy.[107] The juba dance, the etymology of which can be traced to West African Bantu words *juba, diuba, guiba*, which mean "to pat, to beat or count time, the sun, the hour," was a step-dance that resembled an Irish jig with elaborate variations.[108] Lane was such a first-rate singer and a tambourine virtuoso that by 1845, after competing against Diamond in a series of jig dance challenges, he was hailed "King of All Dancers" and that's when the name "Master Juba" became attached to him.[109] In the summer of 1848, Lane headed to Britain where he was often billed as "Boz's Juba," largely due to English novelist Charles Dickens who, in 1842, had made a tour of the US where, while visiting a Five Points dance-hall, he witnessed Lane take part in an African American "break-down."[110] In his book *American Notes*, Dickens subsequently used the name "Boz's Juba" when recounting Lane's movements: "Single shuffle, double shuffle, cut and cross-cut; snapping his fingers, rolling his eyes, turning in his knees, presenting the backs of his legs in front, spinning about on his toes and heels like nothing but the man's fingers on the tambourine; dancing with two left legs, two right legs, two wooden legs, two wire legs, two spring legs – all sorts of legs and no legs – what is this to him?"[111]

There is no question Lane's movements were a cross-fertilized reimagining of the acrobatic clowns of English pantomime, the lowly Irish jig, and highly valorized Italian commedia dell'arte with its masking and improvisational movements. "Jigging" or jigs were frequently mentioned in plays and other documents of the sixteenth-century Elizabethan period into the seventeenth century, but relatively few texts of jigs have survived. As William West observes, "like ballads or similar texts, the jigs that are extant say relatively little about how they were performed."[112] What we do know of surviving texts is that jigs usually were dances in dialogue form, with characters alternating lines or verses and steps.[113] Importantly, British audiences would have interpreted theatrical comic dancing as a form of performative Otherness. "Thematically, jigs were associated with all kinds of disorders and disorderings, sexual, social, and others. The chaotic sounds and movements of jigs seem also to have reminded their audiences of other kinds of confusion. The word jig was frequently associated with the word gig, with its variant *whirligig*, meaning a child's toy spinning top."[114] In the nineteenth century, the term *whirligig* or *whirl-i-gig* would be associated with travelling circuses, and by the end of the century, burlesque shows used low-comedy slapstick techniques while incorporating melodies and songs of minstrel shows into *whirligigs*. "The emphasis on the physicality of the jig and its link to barely contained (or sometimes stoutly resisted) disorder is a recurring feature of discussions of the jig," West writes further, adding "Jigging readily slops over its confines into other areas of physical humour and excess."[115] White viewers of Lane would have recognized his movements as being in conversation with jigs, but they would not have fully appreciated that the juba he performed was an African-infused dance movement.[116]

When Lane travelled to Britain, he performed with the Ethiopian Serenaders, led by Gilbert W. Pell (also known as Pelham).[117] According to British minstrelsy historian Michael Pickering, Lane "stole the show when the troupe appeared at a crowded Vauxhall gardens."[118] Johnson also found that the Ethiopian Serenaders, and Pell specifically, "can be credited with making minstrelsy 'safe' for the British middle class – with a 'cleaned-up' act and dressed in tuxedos, minstrels became fashionable."[119] With Lane as the headliner, Pell's Serenaders toured England and Scotland for eighteen months, playing in legitimate theatres and lecture halls.[120] Significantly, however, Lane worked day and night for eleven years in Britain, and in 1852 he died at the age of 27; as some have observed, "he had quite literally danced himself to death."[121] There is no documented evidence of Lane or Aldridge performing in Canada but we know from the work of Winks that Diamond performed in the Maritimes. Given that both were Atlantic world sensations, like Diamond, their rumoured talents would have travelled the world.

Amateur theatre such as the Gentlemen Amateurs of Toronto, which inaugurated a lengthy season in December 1846, the Amateur Theatre Society who performed in 1843 and then again in 1846, and the Toronto Coloured Young Men's Amateur Theatrical Society, which rented the Royal Lyceum for three nights in 1849, were undoubtedly attuned to Atlantic world theatre.[122] Most notably, the Coloured Young Men's Amateur Theatrical Society performed *Venice Preserved* by Thomas Otway (1652–85) along with selected scenes from Shakespeare, according to an advertisement in the *Toronto-Mirror* on February 9, 1849 that promoted their three-night run (February 20, 21, and 22 of the same year) at the city's only theatre.[123] By all accounts, this is the first known performance by an all-Black theatre company in Canada.[124] There is no question that the Toronto Coloured Young Men's Amateur Theatrical Society's performance was inspired by the city's rejection of the Black community's petition to stop public appearances of blackface menageries a few years prior.[125] It is also possible that they were bolstered by news of Lane's and Aldridge's theatrical success.

At the same time, the style of minstrelsy ushered in by the Ethiopian Serenaders with the assistance of Lane represented "the new vein of 'refined negro music'...[that] was quickly taken up and developed by British minstrel troupes and companies. Much of the original appeal of negro delineators and minstrels had been founded on their singularity and quaintness, the catchiness of their tunes, and the way their odd comicality gave novel features to tomfoolery and clowning."¹²⁶ This new style of minstrelsy also made its way to Canada West in the late 1840s. In the aftermath of Lane's passing, another Black man—though mostly fictionalized—transformed not only the literary world but also Atlantic popular and consumer culture, and eventually minstrelsy. His name was Uncle Tom, a character that first appeared in Harriet Beecher Stowe's *Uncle Tom's Cabin* (1852) that was loosely based on the life of Josiah Henson.¹²⁷ In addition to corresponding with Stowe during the composition of *Uncle Tom's Cabin*, Henson was featured in *A Key to Uncle Tom's Cabin*, a post facto attempt to provide a historical source for every character and event in the novel.

The first stage productions of *Uncle Tom's Cabin* occurred during the novel's serialization. Since copyright laws for fictional material for stage did not yet exist, playwrights and producers were free to adapt the novel as they saw fit. A mere five months after the novel's debut, Nova-Scotia-born George C. Howard (1818–87) premiered his production of *Uncle Tom's Cabin* in New York set to Boston-born writer George Aiken's (1830–76) script.¹²⁸ At the same time British dramatist Charles Western (C.W.) Taylor (1800–74) launched two performances in late August and early September 1852 at New York's Purdy's National Theatre.¹²⁹ The Tom Shows, as they became known, relied on stage conventions such as minstrel songs and blackface makeup, and foregrounded not only sectional conflict but also the blackface forms that had shadowed these developments. For example, in his reading of the Tom Shows that toured Canada West, Johnson notes that "There were no set rules, but in general these were variety shows that mixed the portrayal of southern slaves on their plantation with the portrayal of northern black freemen or fugitives trying (and failing) to behave 'white.' Most performances included at least one narrative sequence, an opera or play burlesqued through its performance by the inept black characters."¹³⁰ He writes further, "There is ample evidence to show that the general citizenry drew an analogy between the Black plantation slave and the working class 'wage slave' – a term coined just at this time. Blackface was a means for vengeful satire."¹³¹

The term "wage slavery" entered political discourse in the US in the 1830s to describe "the condition of at least the artisan portion of the working class."[132] The term drew a metaphorical equation between northern White workers and southern enslaved Black people, and as such, the racial rhetoric of the minstrel show became instrumental to ideas about working people themselves.[133] There appears to have been a growing acceptance of blackface minstrelsy up the ranks of class in Canada West, and while at first it belonged to the circuses and saloons, by the 1850s minstrel shows were "appearing in the best and most polite of venues."[134] Given its geographic location, small-scale productions from New England and New York came across the border with stage adaptations of *Uncle Tom's Cabin*. At the same time, because Henson lived in Canada West, there was some local interest in the topic, asserts Johnson adding, "these so-called 'Tom Shows'...attracted a large segment of the population that otherwise would never expose themselves to the evils of the theatre."[135] As the only theatre with dressing rooms, stage lights, an orchestra pit, and balcony, the Royal Lyceum became the first venue to stage *Uncle Tom's Cabin* in 1853, and again in 1854, 1856, 1857, and 1860.[136] Two panoramas of *Uncle Tom's Cabin* also appeared at St. Lawrence Hall in 1851.[137] More than half a dozen prominent troupes visited Toronto in the early 1850s, including the Nightingale Ethiopian Serenaders and White's Serenaders.[138] St. Lawrence Hall also became home to one of Canada's first "homegrown" blackface performers—Cool Burgess frequented the Hall when visiting blackface troupes, and with American-born Toronto resident Denham Thompson, who spent the better part of twenty years in Toronto, he put on makeshift minstrel concerts in barns and saloons.[139]

By the first half of the nineteenth century, the cities and towns in Upper Canada that once served as battle fronts during the War of 1812 became key locations in the growth of theatre. York, Hamilton, Cobourg, Kingston, Brockville, St. Catharines, Woodstock, and Niagara-on-the-Lake all built professional theatres by the 1860s. Specifically, Toronto had its Royal Lyceum, London (incorporated as a town in 1826 and as a city in 1854) had its Theatre Royal, Hamilton (incorporated as a city in 1846 which grew into a rail and industrial centre) had the Royal Metropolitan Theatre, and in 1854, Ottawa (founded in 1826 and incorporated as a city in 1855) had Her Majesty's Theatre, a one thousand-seat house on Wellington just west of Bank Streets.[140] In 1853, when John Nickinson opened the second season at the Royal Lyceum, his company included appearances from Denham Thompson and T.D. Rice.[141] In 1854, the Royal Lyceum also staged *Yankee Duellist, The; or A Day in Toronto* and when Nickinson returned to Hamilton's Royal Metropolitan Theatre in 1855, T.D. Rice appeared on stage in roles that included Jim Crow and Othello.[142] While the circus was still part of the entertainment circuit, such as Barnum's Menagerie and Museum which was seen in Guelph (incorporated as a town in 1855), as Mary Brown explains, "these peripatetic shows, the garrison theatre tradition, and immigrants' memories of theatrical performances in their homelands were the backdrop for the development of touring theatre companies and the various forms of variety theatre that flourished in Ontario from the mid-nineteenth century to 1914."[143]

In 1857, Burgess sang in the chorus of another production of *Uncle Tom's Cabin* that appeared at the Royal Lyceum, in which Thompson played Uncle Tom and Charlotte Nickinson (1832–1910), John Nickinson's eldest daughter and one of Canada's first female thespians, performed as Eliza, both of whom were in blackface.[144] Importantly, as Brando Simeo Starkey notes, "whereas the stage plays were mainly performed for melodramatic purposes [similar to Stowe's text], the minstrel shows mercilessly mocked blacks."[145] In 1853, for example, the Christy and Wood Minstrels began performing *Life Among the Happy*, a lampoon of the novel's subtitle, "Life Among the Lowly," and in so doing, the duo turned the minstrel adaptation of Stowe's novel into a full-length opera in the spring of 1854 that stripped the horrors of slavery entirely. Instead, the show involved a "grouping of plantation songs and dances loosely connected by a weak plot."[146] While living in Canada, Henson published his self-narrated biography, *The Life of Josiah Henson, Formerly a Slave, Now an Inhabitant of Canada* (1849) but so intertwined was his biography with Uncle Tom that by the time he published additional autobiographies, both of which appeared in 1879 and 1881, he had morphed into both Stowe's Uncle Tom and the Tom Shows' Tom.[147] When Henson toured England for the last time, Wood writes that "he presented himself, and was presented by his escort and biographer John Lobb, *as* 'Uncle Tom'.... Henson was paraded around the country as the living embodiment of the good Christian ex-slave, the show reaching its climax with Uncle Tom's meeting with the Queen."[148]

Thus, by the mid-1850s, Canada West was firmly established as a theatrical centre for minstrel shows. Audiences were well-invested in the stories and caricatures that sought to retell histories of the Atlantic world in ways that did not require Canadians to reflect on their own racial attitudes, even as racial hostilities were on the rise south of the border.

The Astor Place Rebellion in New York City in 1849 was a singular turning point, marking the visibility of class, ethnic, and national conflicts that existed in the middle of the nineteenth century.[149] The rebellions happened because conflict between European elite groups and anti-aristocratic "common people" in antebellum theatre audiences burst into open combat.[150] The rebellion, which has also been called the Shakespeare Riot, was spawned by a bitter rivalry between British Shakespearean actor William Charles Macready (1793–1893) and American actor Edwin Forrest (1806–72) who had portrayed Macbeth in a concurrent New York production, and who were proxies for opposite sides of a growing class division in American urban society.[151] Opened in 1847, Astor Opera House had been designated as a theatre for the upper class who enjoyed "highbrow" theatrical performances like operas, ballets, etc., but an emerging lower class or "lowbrow" street culture embodied by "b'hoys," or "Bowery boys," who enjoyed slapstick and vulgar comedies, threatened its existence.[152] Many scholars of minstrelsy mark the Astor Place Rebellion as a watershed moment in the changing audience composition of the minstrel show. From this point onward, a single theatrical location could not safely house or accommodate various forms of "highbrow" and "lowbrow" entertainment in one package because of increasing divisions and fears that audiences would reject one or the other depending on an individual's level of taste. As Roediger writes, "the minstrel stage became a truly popular form of entertainment able to attract the immigrants, 'b'hoys' and unskilled of the city while also making special appeals to…some in the respectable middle classes and above."[153]

The Compromise of 1850, passed by the US Congress on September 18 and which updated and strengthened the first Fugitive Slave Act, was also a watershed moment in American politics. This Act established California as a free state, making no mention of slavery in the nearly acquired New Mexico and Utah territories, and it "adjusted" the Texas–New Mexico boundary; while it abolished the slave trade in the District of Columbia, it did not prohibit slavery.[154] The establishment of California as a free state was deeply interconnected with the gold rush (1848–55). As the South increasingly became the "preindustrial" enemy of Northern territorial expansion, by the late 1840s agitation around the issue of western lands raised the bitter question whether newly acquired territory would be slave or free, a rather ominous fact given the importance of "Manifest Destiny" to northern social aspiration.[155] Blackface songs, especially those of Stephen Foster, helped create themes that represented the economic possibilities of California gold.[156]

Born and reared in Pittsburgh, Foster played a role in influencing American politics, as his songs constructed a mythology about the republic and the legislative compromises that represented "minstrelsy's mapping of white men's move west."[157] He had been an amateur blackface performer, but after composing songs for the medium he made a name for himself. Among the first of these songs was "Oh! Susanna" (1848). Originally published in 1847, its use of non-narrative, irrational lyrics in a dance-tune based melody, coupled with the song's use of syncopation catapulted it to great popularity.[158] "The fame he garnered from this song and others of the period encouraged Foster to attempt (and succeed at) what no other American had achieved – status as a professional composer of popular songs," writes Dale Cockrell, adding that "against a social and political backdrop in which racism and slavery were hotly debated, Foster's minstrel songs trace a remarkable line. *Susanna* was nearly all idiom and convention, with few indications that the composer...was aware of any political or social message conveyed by the song."[159] One year after "Oh! Susanna" was first published, it became the marching song of the "forty-niners"—White men who left their homes in search of gold in California—and is still considered the theme song of the gold rush and the slogan of pioneers.[160] By seizing upon "Oh! Susanna" as their own, westward migrants used the mask of minstrelsy to celebrate their move west, an act that increasingly connected "the North's westering impulse and its growing distaste for southern slavery."[161] Many of Foster's early songs reached the public via Christy's Minstrels, such as "Old Uncle Ned" (1848), "Camptown

Races" (1850), "Old Folks at Home," also known as "Swanee River" (1851), "Massa's in de Cold Ground" (1852), and "My Old Kentucky Home, Good Night" (1853).[162] With these songs Foster emerged as a composer of popular "Plantation Melodies" and "Ethiopian Melodies."

With Foster's songs creating an enduring national culture rooted in lyrics and melodies connected to the minstrel show and the Virginia Minstrels, Ethiopian Serenaders, Christy's Minstrels, and others spawning a popular theatrical sensation that led to dozens of blackface troupes on both sides of the Atlantic, by the late 1850s, minstrelsy was firmly part of Atlantic entertainment culture. In Britain, Pickering found that "everybody, from Queen Victoria to the chimney-sweep, laughed at minstrel jokes and the antics of blackface performers."[163] In the span of a few years, minstrelsy continued to evolve, becoming entangled in the political cultures of the period. From 1843 to 1848 the minstrel show created and standardized repertoire consisting of comic parodies of Italian opera arias, popular stage burlesques as southern plantation caricatures, and the mimicry of African Americans living in northern urban centres.[164] During its second phase from 1849 to 1857, which also marked the ramping up of the abolitionist movement's expansion, minstrelsy formalized into a three-part program consisting of more elaborate "plantation" elements with shows incorporating longer burlesques of Italian and French opera, choral parodies, Ethiopian sketches, and afterpieces.[165]

Chapter three examines minstrelsy's third phase from 1858 to 1861 when minstrel troupes played on the commercial power of nostalgia with companies becoming some of the first to double back on their own repertories. When sectional conflicts erupted into a Civil War in 1861, the stage became one of the first outlets for a newly emancipated Black population to take up space. While the 1840s and 1850s were decades marked by territorial conflicts over slavery and caricatures of enslaved and free African Americans, the 1860s marked a decade of emancipation not solely in terms of slavery but also performative freedom as Black actors and dancers, typically banned from performing as minstrel troupes before the Civil War (with the exception of Lane and Aldridge), now gained access not only to the minstrel stage but also to concert stages as virtuoso singers. This era in minstrelsy had to contend with Black freedoms in never-before-seen ways not only onstage but across the Atlantic world.

3

NEWSPAPERS, RAILWAYS, THEATRE EXPANSION, AND HOMEGROWN BLACKFACE MINSTRELS, 1858-61

Between the mid-1840s and early 1850s, transportation routes, modes of communication, and newsprint expanded and modernized across Canada. These developments allowed for longer regional travel, diverse outlets of promotion, and the wide circulation of editorial news on the economy, politics, and culture. From the *Globe* (1844–) to the *Kingston Chronicle and Gazette* (1833–47), *Hamilton Spectator* (1846–), *London Free Press* (1849–), and numerous small-town presses in between, Canada was becoming a print nation. At one point the *Globe* claimed the largest circulation in North America after it installed a "giant" steam-drive rotary press in the early 1850s, and another in the early 1860s, to turn out its dailies, weeklies, and farm journals, along with handbills and general job printing.[1] Black newspapers also competed for audiences during this period, and most were directly tied to abolitionism. In Canada West, the *Provincial Freeman*, edited by Ward and Shadd Cary, was particularly instrumental in creating news about African Americans living in Canada. They, along with Mary and Henry Bibb, helped to establish Sandwich's Emancipation Day celebration. In *Emancipation Day: Celebrating Freedom in Canada*, Natasha Henry provides a timeline for locating emancipation festivities that marked the end of slavery across the British colonies, including in Canada, the Caribbean, and beyond. The first such events were held in towns and cities across Canada West and East in 1834, and in British Columbia in 1858.[2] In the Maritimes, Greg Marquis observes that "Before, during and after the Civil War, blacks in Saint John and Halifax gathered to celebrate Emancipation Day, 3 August, the anniversary of the abolition of slavery in the British Empire. The Charitable African Society of Halifax marked the day in 1846 with a parade and picnic and a loyal address to the governor that praised Nova Scotia, 'where all are free to enjoy equal rights.'"[3] These celebrations in Halifax are quite significant considering on July 29, 1847 there was a racial conflict that erupted in the city in which Black and White residents "fought in the streets of the city's downtown core" marking a significant moment primarily because "it demonstrated a determination, emerging within Halifax's Black community, to become involved with mainstream politics."[4] The 1847 conflict was in response to the assertion of collective and public agency by Halifax's Black population in the provincial election, one of the first times the White population was confronted by Black citizens who were exercising their right to express political opinions.

By the 1850s there were very consistent and well-defined practices of commemoration around the international public observances of British emancipation.[5] In places like Chatham, Sandwich, Amherstburg, and surrounding areas, commercial and industrial centres began to emerge at midcentury, and there were many Black-owned businesses such as masonry and carpentry companies, blacksmith shops, tailor shops, grocery and general merchandise stores, and several farms. As Henry explains further, the community began to "organize themselves to protest and challenge many forms of racism they faced on a daily basis.... Blacks in Windsor also sought to secure their rights and freedoms through military service. About two hundred Black men defended the Detroit frontier against attacks from Americans during the Rebellions of 1837/1838."[6] Reporting on Emancipation Day in 1858, the *Globe* detailed not only the Black community's presence in the city but also the role of the church and music at these public events:

At six o'clock in the morning, the members of the Toronto Association, accompanied by the members of the Young Canada Society, met in the Baptist Church, Sayer Street, where fervent prayers were offered up for the total abolition of Slavery throughout the world.... Shortly after ten o'clock, the party were marshalled into procession with flags and banners flying, and, headed by a band of music, marched to St. James' Cathedral, to attend Divine service. Following the band, came the members of the Young Canada Club, who were attired in bright uniforms, and wearing sashes and rosettes.... After parading till nearly three o'clock in the afternoon, the party reached the University grounds, where lunch had been provided.... In the evening a soiree was held in the St. Lawrence Hall, which was well attended.[7]

The following year Toronto's Black community arranged with community members in Hamilton to alternate festivities, so celebrations were held there.[8]

Located between Toronto and Niagara Falls, Hamilton, which was first known as "The Head-of-the-Lake" for its location at the western end of Lake Ontario, consisted of towns and villages like Dundas, Ancaster, and Stoney Creek. Hamilton's Black community held its first Emancipation Day in 1837 and by the 1850s there was a diverse and growing Black community there. Hamilton historian Adrienne Shadd writes that "[In] 1851, one-quarter of men reported that they were labourers. However, there was a sizable number in the skilled/semi-skilled trades and a number who owned their own businesses. Black men held jobs as shoemakers, blacksmiths, carpenters, and barbers. There was also a cooper (barrel maker), a dyer, a gunsmith, saloonkeeper, and bricklayer."[9] In terms of Black women, Shadd found that 73 percent had no occupation listed beside their names in 1851, but there was a schoolteacher, cook, and seamstress, and the remaining Black women residents were listed as servants, housekeepers, domestics, and washerwomen; ten years later, 83 percent of women did not report an occupation, 5 percent held skilled occupations as dressmakers, seamstresses, fancy workers or tailoresses, and cooks, and 12 percent were in the unskilled job category, working as servants, laundresses, or hucksters.[10]

By the 1850s, a small but significant Black community was also established in London, the chief metropolitan city between Toronto and Windsor. London enjoyed moderate growth until the early 1850s when, after the passage of the Fugitive Slave Act and the building of railways connecting Canada West with Canada East and beyond, the city experienced rapid growth and emerged as a major centre for administrative, financial, and manufacturing industries. As tens of thousands of Black people began to settle in Canada West, London historian Tracey Adams points out that it did produce some racial tensions. "White Canadians became less tolerant of African American immigration and began to fear the larger numbers of settlers arriving in their towns,"[11] she writes. In his 1846 book, *The Refugees from Slavery in Canada West: Report to the Freedmen's Inquiry Commission*, educator and abolitionist Samuel Gridley Howe (1801–76) describes the discrimination against Black people in Canada West. "This prejudice exists so generally in Canada, that travellers usually form an unpleasant and unjust opinion of the colored refugees, because it is usually strong and bitter in that class of persons with whom travellers come most in contact," writes Howe, adding "It is not…hotel clerks alone, but grave officials, Mayors and others, who, when first addressed, are apt to speak contemptuously of the colored people."[12]

Thus, in towns and cities across Canada West, the mythology of the "promised land" was just that—a myth that served to "free" African Americans from draconian US federal legislation post-1850 but that was not a promise of complete freedom from racial prejudice and White supremacy. As one African American living in London, A.T. Jones, a proudly self-declared British citizen, confessed to Howe in 1863, "We won't stay here after this [American Civil] war is decided."[13] Alfred T. Jones and his brother, A.B., managed to extricate themselves from slavery in Madison County, Kentucky; they first travelled to St. Catharines but soon after settled in London. According to Adams's findings, "A.T. Jones had established a 'New Fruit Store' by the late 1840s, and in the 1850s, he was the owner of a successful apothecary. Not only was he literate, but one 1850s traveler found him hard at work learning Latin, so that he could fill doctors' prescriptions. He was married and the father of eight children, all of whom attended an integrated school. A.B. Jones also established a family, and he was listed as a 'grocer' in the 1856 London directory."[14] By the 1850s, White entertainers performing in blackface offered "a lively blend of song, dance, jokes, and consistently drew large and enthusiastic audiences" in the Maritimes; the same was true across Canada West and East. As Sutherland explains further, "These productions offered a crude and demeaning caricature of the black personality. White audiences, however, generally came away thinking that what they had witnessed was an accurate portrayal of their black neighbours."[15]

Importantly, in the 1850s, railways emerged as powerful new forms of mass transportation that could not only move people but also expand distribution routes. "At its peak, the sprawl of stations, sidings, depots, and roundhouse would dominate the land south of Front Street," writes Chris Bateman about the construction of Toronto's first railway in 1851. "Before the construction of the railway, Toronto's only links to the outside world were via water or road. Early highways were unpaved and frequently impassable in poor weather; meanwhile, during the winter and spring, ice made the St. Lawrence River and Lake Ontario unnavigable."[16] In 1847, electronic telegraph arrived in the city, enabling Toronto to communicate near-immediately with remote cities using Morse code, which connected the city with Hamilton, St. Catharines, Niagara Falls, Montreal, and parts of Quebec; and, with the building of the first steam locomotive in 1853 (the line reached Allandale later in 1853 and Collingwood in 1855), people could travel much more quickly and easily than ever before.[17] When the Ontario, Simcoe & Huron Union railroad was restructured and renamed the Northern Railway of Canada in 1858 it fell under the ownership of the trans-provincial Grand Trunk Railway. By the late 1850s, railway lines stretched across the western peninsula of Canada West, major urban centres grew, and this boom decreased isolation in the hinterland regions, opened new through routes, and provided year-round transport for heavy goods as well as faster and more secure travel for passengers.[18] Niagara Falls and Windsor grew because of the Great Western Railway line, and smaller cities like Guelph and Kitchener experienced rapid growth and emerged as financial and manufacturing centres.[19] As Mary Brown explains, "early performers who came to Ontario before the completion of the railway from Montreal to Detroit in 1856 depended upon ferries and steamers operating between American and Canadian ports on the Great

Lakes and on stage coaches that travelled daily between most towns."[20] From telegraphs to railways, performers and companies were now able to give early advance notice of their arrival in town, which could be reported in newspapers that began to feature theatrical news, both local and international.[21] Toronto and Montreal became major Canadian centres for large-scale theatre because of their population growth, newspapers, and railway connections.

This chapter examines the role of Canada's newspapers and railway expansion in blackface minstrelsy's growth at the same time Black people across North America acquired levels of sociopolitical agency many had never seen before. Newspapers not only reported on Atlantic news such as slavery and antislavery activities in America, Britain, and the Caribbean, but also propagated rhetoric that contributed to minstrelsy's staying power. On the one hand, these English-language newspapers often reported on the British Crown's continued exploits in cotton and sugar production, but on the other, while thousands of African Americans lived in Canada West, local customs that relegated Black residents to second-class citizenship either through limited employment options, poorly maintained educational facilities, or overt discrimination, did not form part of the dominant culture's news coverage. In the Black press, African Americans like Shadd Cary penned articles such as the pamphlet, "A Plea for Emigration, or Notes on Canada West," in which she promoted Canada West as a prime site for Black resettlement in large part due to the principles of the British Constitution and British rule of law.[22] As the US Civil War approached, however, Shadd Cary became one of the loudest voices loathing the continued separation of Black children from common schools in Canada West. As a result, by the early 1860s there were several factors that contributed to African American movement back to America.

These moves increased rapidly in 1861 because most wanted to fight for their freedom in the Civil War. Second, government policy brought more restrictions on immigration, and greater organization among trades and factory workers brought more formal restrictions against African American workers. Third, rising education requirements for many excluded Black people whose education was negatively affected by educational segregation. Finally, continued prejudice against Black immigrants meant opportunities for Black people were fewer and farther between; as a result, they were restricted in areas of employment where, just a decade prior, they had opportunities.[23] The Common Schools Act of 1850 authorized the creation of separate schools, leading to provincially funded Catholic schools and racially segregated public schools. This development took place under the leadership of Egerton Ryerson (1803–82), who served as the chief superintendent of schools for Canada West from 1844 to 1876. Born of a Loyalist family in Charlotteville Township, Norfolk County, Upper Canada, Ryerson willfully allowed discrimination in schools, claiming there was nothing he could do in his position to stop White residents from preventing Black children from attending common schools.[24] Importantly, as Kristin McLaren explains, "Toronto was perhaps the one place where segregation in public education was never the norm.... In other regions of Canada West, school segregation was the norm. Few influential white leaders in the Western and Niagara peninsulas spoke out against the exclusion of African Canadians from common schools.... In practice, the provincial Board of Education tolerated and even encouraged segregation."[25]

Black resistance to segregation and a culture of exclusion was rampant throughout the 1850s. Frederick Douglass made appearances at three Black settlements in 1854, all of which had established separate schools for Black children.[26] In addition to visiting Buxton to deliver a speech, Douglass also attended an Emancipation Day celebration that drew hundreds from the surrounding area.[27] Douglass had remained vigilant in his mission to spread the message of emancipation throughout Canada West, and on August 3 of that year, he visited Chatham to speak at the local courthouse; while there, he delivered a compelling message explaining his stance against mass migration, noting that "in Canada, as the Black population increased, so too did racial strife…if Canadians want to get rid of us, they must banish slavery from the neighboring Union."[28] Throughout the 1850s, name calling, occasional riots, and public school segregation illustrated the persistence of race prejudice in Canada West and while it did dismay some African Americans who believed Canada to be a haven for the oppressed, many Black people stayed in Canada because "British law protected them from enslavement and ostensibly provided them with legal rights as British citizens."[29]

This chapter also pinpoints how, as the genre's popularity grew in the late 1850s and into the early 1860s in large part due to the expansion of railway lines that made intercontinental travel safer and more reliable, and the growth of an English-language newspaper industry that constructed narratives about slavery, emancipation, and the rightful place for Black people in North America, Canadian troupes, amateur ensembles, and professional companies begin to tour with more frequency. Two homegrown performers—Cool Burgess and Calixa Lavallée—became transnational stars out of this milieu. They established successful touring careers as blackface minstrel performers; in the case of Lavallée, as a highly sought-after minstrel musician who could play violin and cornet, he performed on both sides of the border in English, though his first language was French. One American periodical noted that Canada was "overrun by Negro minstrels and will ballade singers, and other 'artists' of the seventh or eight order" by the 1850s.[30] Meanwhile, in the Maritimes, one of the first minstrel shows took place in Bridgetown, Nova Scotia's Victoria Hall in 1853.[31] Located in north-central Annapolis County, there is not much known about the Colonial Troupe's performance as the Ethiopian Burlesque Minstrels, but it would have been in the same style as other acts that bore a similar name, given that "Ethiopian" was a name that joined forces with "serenaders" and "minstrels" anywhere there was blackface entertainment. In Saint John, New Brunswick, a group calling themselves Carle's Ethiopian Serenaders also played the Mechanics' Institute there in 1853.[32] While it is important to acknowledge not all audiences enjoyed these shows, such as one Halifax newspaper editor who complained about how the "vulgar witticism and distasteful contortions" of the minstrel actors had driven "respectable men and women from the theatre,"[33] it is equally as important to consider the sociocultural context that established these shows as commonplace theatre. These shows appeared in places like Halifax, Saint John, Montreal, and Toronto (and cities and towns in between) at the same time Black communities exercised agency and their political rights. The minstrel show was a vital tool to thwart Black social progress while emboldening Whites and newly arrived immigrant groups to assume their rightful place as legitimate citizens.

By midcentury, the blackface minstrel show began to look back at itself through sentimentality for an era of slavery that appeared to be steadily coming to an end. At the same time, two significant moments—the California gold rush in 1849, which spread out from the original find in

Sutter's Creek up the west coast and into British Columbia, and the Fraser Canyon gold rush in 1858—linked Western Canada and the US as Black emigrants left San Francisco as part of a larger fraction of adventurers who travelled north in search of "the new gold" in Canada.³⁴ A few hundred African Americans settled primarily in the city of Victoria on Vancouver Island.³⁵ Though founded in the eighteenth century, Victoria became a major port, supply base, and outfitting centre for miners on their way to the Fraser Canyon gold fields after it was incorporated in 1867. From 1858 onward, Victoria served a double life in a cultural sense, becoming "amusement for the large floating population of hopeful miners, and another for the sophisticated and conservative circle of British settlers."³⁶ Victoria's Colonial Theatre opened in February 1860, and by 1891 Vancouver had a 1,200-seat opera house.³⁷ British Columbia witnessed a surge of African American immigration throughout the 1860s.³⁸ This chapter ultimately charts the growth of railways and newspapers as central to understanding how and why blackface minstrel shows thrived north of the border; not as passing entertainments and menageries, but as some of the first forms of cultural production in remote outposts in Western Canada and multinight events in the theatres of Canada West, East, and the Maritimes. By the late 1850s, Canada produced and exported its own homegrown minstrel performers who became the first non-American and non-British blackface stars of the stage.

There were dozens of newspapers that began to sprout up in Canada after the 1830s. In Canada West, the *Globe* was perhaps the most influential. It was published by George Brown, who thrived in the newspaper industry and would go on to become leader of the Reform Party and play a significant role as one of "the Fathers of Confederation."³⁹ Brown, who had first emigrated to America in 1837, gained experience working in New York City's established newspaper business with his father, before moving to Toronto in 1843, where he founded the *Globe* one year later.⁴⁰ Because of Brown's involvement with the Anti-Slavery Society of Canada, the *Globe* initially made the antislavery movement part of its editorial focus. For instance, when Texas joined the union as a slave state on December 29, 1845, in a reprint from the *New York Tribune*, an editorial on the newspaper's front page declared, "The deed is done." "Against her slavery we shall continue to war, so far as we constitutionally may, and especially against the admission of new Slave States formed from her territory," the article continued, adding "We hope yet to snatch the fruits if not the laurels of victory from the hands of those who have so greedily, recklessly, obtained it. But enough for the present. Texas is in the Union. Let us see what good may come of it."[41] The *Globe*'s early editorials reflected the contradictory nature of pro-abolitionists in the nineteenth century.

Newspapers were some of the first major businesses to maintain large plants and workforces that could provide editions for both town and country, and their growing readership by midcentury meant that papers began to establish themselves as politically partisan. By the early 1860s, there were 150 weekly newspapers across Canada West, and another seventy-nine throughout the rest of British North America, but few of them, weeklies and dailies alike, had circulations over one thousand readers.[42] Under Brown's tutelage, the *Globe* became more than just another city newspaper; part of its commercial success flowed from its popularity among the wider "rural population, the reading population" beyond the city limits, which means that by the 1850s, it was one of the most read papers and essentially served as a "national" press.[43] As party politics began to play a role in the reporting of weekly and daily news, most papers were established to advance either Conservative or Liberal political ideals, with men moving between journalism and politics with great regularity.[44] For example, Brown helped the Reformers, a group led by several business and political men, including William Lyon Mackenzie. Reformers saw themselves as citizens of Great Britain with all the rights granted by the British Constitution. They would come to power in Canada West in 1848, and in so doing the *Globe* became a vigorous voice for Reformer values.[45] Furthermore, newspapers were also dependent on partisan support.

First, "the role of partisan backers intensified after 1850, as increased capital was required to purchase the new presses and plants," writes Russell Johnston, adding "Under these circumstances, investors had the financial clout to ensure that an editor remained faithful to the party line."[46] The second reason for the partisan support was because local businessmen began to place advertising on a regular basis. While it was a more tenuous form of support than direct backing since advertisers had no stake in a newspaper's finances, as manufacturers, railway lines and steamship companies began to advertise their departure schedules; circuses, theatre companies, and choral shows began to advertise weeks in advance of their performances. This created not only excitement but awareness of the cultural import of the newspapers themselves to disseminate messages. Finally, newspapers were deeply contingent on which political party was in power, as patronage could be sought in the "form of government advertising notices or printing contracts."[47] After reader subscriptions, local advertising, and political patronage, Johnston writes further that "newspapers found their last bit of financing from out-of-town commercial advertisers. Ultimately, this became the most important part of the publishers' revenue."[48] While the first large-scale theatres were not built until the 1870s, the establishment of a transportation network and newspapers with higher circulation runs meant that local and travelling menageries, circuses, and minstrel clowns were steadily replaced by professional minstrel troupes, theatrical productions, and extravaganzas that were double or triple the size of what they were in the early part of the nineteenth century.

Importantly, Brown published articles that ranged from commentaries about the need to eradicate slavery to the need for Negro education. He also published portions of lectures from known eugenicists who believed that people of African descent were the "lesser species," and pro-slavery editorials that warned against abolition sometimes appeared in the *Globe*. As an example of these conflicting editorials, on December 1, 1847, the paper reported on a lecture at the Mechanics Institute delivered by Thomas Henning on "The Natural History of Man" to a "large and respectable audience."[49] Established in Britain, mechanics institutes were designed to provide technical and adult education. By 1834, the Mechanics' Institute (called the York Mechanics' Institute when it opened in Toronto in 1830) served as an educational institution, offering classes on topics from philosophy and music to science, electricity, and architectural drawing; it was also the city's first public library.[50] Henning, husband to Isabella Brown (George Brown's sister), became the first secretary of the Anti-Slavery Society of Canada as well as a member of the *Globe*'s editorial staff until 1854.[51] The paper summarized Henning's lecture as exploring zoology, and racial groups like "Caucasian," "Mongolian," "Ethiopian" (black skin, woolly hair),

"American," and "Malays" (southeast Asia) as separate species. The *Globe*'s editorial reveals that as early as the 1840s even the most ardent abolitionists still believed that people of African descent were intellectually inferior and congenitally defective.[52] In a reprint from the *London Anti-Slavery Reporter* for January, appearing on February 19, 1848, the *Globe* asked readers to think about education in the British colonies. "Wielding the powers of the Government in his capacity of Colonial Secretary, Lord [Earl] Grey decided, in the early part of last year, not only that education in the colonies should be compulsory, but that it should also be religious," the editorial stated, continuing "His Lordship, therefore, in a circular to the several Governors of the colonies intimated his will that schools should be established for the industrial training, the mental improvement, and the spiritual welfare of the negro children."[53] One week later, however, the paper presented Lord Earl Grey's change of mind on the topic of compulsory education for the Black population of the British colonies. "There are peculiarities in the Negro character, which would operate against the success of any such plan, if it would be likely, in the opinion of the local authorities, to generate a feeling of suspicion or irritation in the minds of the Negroes; and tend to defeat rather than promote education, I am far from desiring to oppose to views founded on such local knowledge, my own more general conclusion."[54]

In its first year of publication in 1844, the *Globe* reported on the British House of Commons parliamentary discussions concerning the question of sugar tariffs, specifically free-labour versus slave-labour sugar production. "Lord John Russell was prepared to extend to all Foreign sugar the advantage which Government proposed for free-labour sugar," the paper reported, adding "What was the great argument used in this country against the abolition of the slave-trade? It was said, if we abolish the slave-trade, it would pass into the hands of those nations which would carry it on without regulation, and the evils of slavery would be greatly aggravated."[55] These statements speak to the great investments businessmen had in slavery, which is significant to Canada considering Russell had played a role in creating Durham's *Report on the Affairs of British North America* following the Rebellion of 1837–38 that had attempted to unify the country.[56]

From the earliest days of White settlement, emigrants to North America from the British Isles remained deeply invested in the matters of empire. What has been explored less is their equal investment in maintaining a connection to the song and dance traditions from their homelands. Many took the songs, dances, folklore, and other vernacular cultural forms with them in steerage during their Atlantic crossing. "Fiddle dance tunes central to North American Irish music were adapted for minstrelsy, with jigs, reels and hornpipes being common musical elements in the repertory and the fiddle figuring as a key minstrel instrument. Nineteenth-century minstrel songs imitated the 'Scottish snap' and gapped scale characteristic of traditional Anglo-Celtic tunes,"[57] asserts Michael Pickering. When Lane started dancing in the 1840s, like the *Black* minstrels who would follow him, he was a Black man performing as a White man performing as a Black man. At the same time, while performing uniquely African American dances he also did so while modifying Irish jig steps he learned growing up in New York City's Five Points by adding Black folk elements into them.[58] By all accounts, Lane had an uncanny ability to innovate, mixing and remixing African American dance with European dance, all while cross-dressing and gender-bending like his White male counterparts. The hornpipe, for instance, had been popularized by Durang who, in 1784, won widespread recognition when he introduced to America the "Sailor's Hornpipe – Old Style." By performing the dance in burnt cork makeup, Durang created one of the earliest prototypes of tap dance on the American stage, a prototype Lane more than likely observed and borrowed from to create his unique dance steps.[59] Beyond Lane, there would have been a limited number of real or imagined events in Black life (such as weddings, harvest celebrations, courtship, and familial separations) that White performers, audiences, critics, and observers witnessed and, more importantly, understood.

As cities expanded and transportation improved, spatial segregation became a visible feature of the US northeast. Philadelphia, for example, emerged as an important junction for both abolitionists and free African Americans, and American-born White (Protestant) Philadelphians grew increasingly hostile toward free African Americans and Irish Catholics as more and more migrants crowded into fast-growing ethnic enclaves.[60] After the potato famine created an influx of Irish emigrants to North America in the 1830s, Protestant Americans treasured their Whiteness as entitling them to both political rights and jobs. But what they also cultivated was a shared race-consciousness of associating Blackness with evil. As David Roediger explains, "There is some evidence of [European] folk belief that the devil could turn people black, or turn people inside-out, thus making them black."[61] Because blackface could be everything and nothing at the same time, it was both anti-Black while overtly borrowing from Black expressive culture, just as it was anti-immigrant and deeply rooted in European folklore.

By the late 1850s, America remained a union divided with White men and White women at the top of the hierarchy, and recently arrived immigrants (English and Scottish Protestants and Irish Catholics), African Americans, and Indigenous people at the bottom, vying for rights, lands, access to resources, and most notably, political citizenship. This milieu gave significant power to the donning of blackface as it centred African Americans through mimicry and racial caricature, but also "blacking up" reframed and reimagined space and place as embodied by sets of people who "acted" and "spoke" a certain way based on their level of emancipation. In other words, the minstrel stage became one of the most popular outlets for self-expression and the transgressive display of multiple identities while also the first place to valorize expressions that were deeply rooted in a class-race logic that denigrated persons who were not White, English-speaking, and male. The political milieu in the US also drastically changed following events in the mid-1850s. First, on May 30, 1854, Congress approved the Kansas-Nebraska Act, which allowed voting citizens (White men) of those territories to determine for themselves whether they would enter the Union as a slave or a free state.[62] Following the passage of the Kansas-Nebraska Act, the Whig Party collapsed, with most northern Whigs joining the Republican Party that would be led by Abraham Lincoln (1809–65), and southern Whigs generally supporting the Kansas-Nebraska Act; they either joined the Democrats, supported one or another new party, or remained in doubt as to their political allegiance. Either way, the breakup of the Whig Party created the nascent Republican Party.[63] In addition to the Democratics, the Whigs not only played a role in minstrelsy's development but the conflicts that made Civil War an almost inevitable outcome.[64]

In 1857, the limits of compromises on Black freedoms were put to the test when the US Supreme Court rendered its decision in *Dred Scott v. Sanford*. Scott, an enslaved person in Missouri, travelled with his enslaver, John Emerson, to a free state (Illinois) and a free territory (Minnesota) before he "voluntarily" returned with Emerson to Missouri. On April 6, 1846,

Scott and his wife Harriet sued their enslaver, arguing the time they spent on free soil made them free persons.⁶⁵ Chief Justice Roger B. Taney ruled that because former slaves were not American citizens or citizens of another country, the federal courts did not have to adjudicate their lawsuits; he also declared that Emerson's move to Minnesota was of no legal significance because the Missouri Compromise's ban on slavery north of the 36°30' line was unconstitutional.⁶⁶ While two dissenting judges insisted that free African Americans were citizens, and that the Missouri Compromise was constitutional, seven justices conferred onto the legal precedence two propositions: (1) no Black person could become a citizen of the US; and (2) slavery could not be constitutionally prohibited in any American territory.⁶⁷ In other words, as John Ernest observes, "African Americans had no rights that white Americans were obligated to respect."⁶⁸ The 1820/1850 Compromises were supposed to ease sectional divisions but in practice they only worsened them. As the popular American theatre and penny presses began to play prominent roles in the production of racial discourse, a shifting political climate imbued with racial caricature, slapstick comedy, and sentimental literature created the conditions for Canadians to find their legs south of the border as travelling minstrels, musicians, and actors. They learned the American minstrel tradition by reading newspapers, watching menageries, attending the circus, and studying the novels of the period.

Cool Burgess began performing in blackface in the 1850s, and after years of local success in Toronto, he travelled across the US appearing in minstrel shows for over twenty years. As Gerald Lenton-Young writes, alongside Patrick Redmond and Denham Thompson, two of Toronto's most acclaimed theatre actors in the nineteenth century, Burgess formed the duo "Burgess and Thompson" who billed themselves as "specializing in negro characters."⁶⁹ In an 1858 appearance in Toronto, Burgess and Redmond packed a new theatre house on Adelaide Street, opposite the city's then-courthouse, for a two-night appearance titled, "Fun for the Million," which also included a character named Jim Crow.⁷⁰ At the two-night minstrel show, Burgess changed his name to "Cool" and delivered a monologue on "women's rights" while playing the *endman* character,

Mr. Bones.[71] That same year, he celebrated his eighteenth birthday at the Royal Lyceum as part of Burgess and Redmond's Ethiopian Star Troupe, his first touring company, but when he returned there a year later he appeared as Cool Burgess's Chicago Minstrels, a name that indicated he had catapulted to being front and centre on playbills in the US.[72] Burgess's work with Redman and Thompson was short-lived. Eventually he joined J.H. Haverly to form Haverly-Burgess Minstrels on October 8, 1864 in Toronto, but after they split in 1866 he went on to perform solo in the US and England.[73]

Calixa Lavallée made his debut at Montreal's Theatre Royal in 1859, and at the age of sixteen he set off to join a Providence, Rhode Island-based minstrel show company. He then spent several years travelling the continent as "an itinerant musician, passing through nearly every town and city east of the Rocky Mountains," writes Thompson in his book on the life of Lavallée. "Blackening his face each night, he played the piano, violin, and cornet, and was soon leading the band," he observed further.[74] After the US Civil War began, Lavallée published several pro-Union compositions and then put the theatre behind him to join the Fourth Rhode Island Regiment where, in the fall of 1862, he left the military to rejoin his minstrel troupe.[75] Travelling minstrel productions extended their engagements to multiple nights with advancements in rail travel, especially in the winter season which became less treacherous, particularly up the Hudson River, through Vermont, and into Canada. Railroad construction in the 1850s brought an influx of rural French Canadians and a wave of migrants from Canada West, the US, Britain, and Europe to the province of Quebec.[76] The movement of US minstrels back and forth across the border in the early 1860s was made possible because of a rail network that ran from Newark, New Jersey to Montreal and Quebec City, with other routes through New York, Buffalo, Rochester, Cleveland, Indianapolis, Chicago, Madison, Wisconsin, Detroit to Windsor, Hamilton, London, Toronto, and Ottawa. Minstrelsy's popularity in Canada from the 1860s onward was directly tied to the railway system that linked the two countries.

Burgess and Lavallée are rarely discussed as part of a larger narrative that connects their blackface performances as a form of anti-Blackness. Instead, they are framed as mere "participants" in the most popular theatrical repertoire of their day, a participation often described as devoid of any racial politics. In some cases, they are remembered as sympathizers toward the plight of Black Americans in the South. For example, Thompson describes Lavallée as a defiant and ambitious man, driven more by his own desire to challenge expectations of his Catholic upbringing than as a White man whose participation in blackface minstrel shows reflected his ideological position on race. "Born in a region hit hardest by the effects of the rebellions of 1837 and 1838, its after-effects had formed him," asserts Thompson, adding "His willingness to leave his family at the age of thirteen itself an early sign of his independence...[some] speculated that Lavallée was motivated by the injustice he had witnessed in the American South" when he decided to enlist in the Fourth Rhode Island Regiment of the Union Army during the Civil War.[77] Similarly, in a *Canadian Biography* on Burgess, David Gardner acknowledges that "Burgess was born in the year the black community of Toronto first petitioned against the caricatured depiction of blacks on stage and in circuses...but minstrelsy—America's first indigenous form of entertainment—called."[78] By focusing on the frontiersmanship of these men, an act that was the exclusive domain of White men in the nineteenth century, and downplaying the racial intent of the blackface mask, historians have expunged racism from the Canadian theatrical narrative, ultimately resulting in an amnesia, erasure, and dismissal of the racial import of blackface.

Both Burgess and Lavallée performed in burnt cork blackface makeup, and as the primary convention that identified the minstrel show as entertainment, this makeup was never just an aesthetic choice. As William Mahar has astutely observed, the makeup was a *disguise* for White performers who chose parody and burlesque as techniques to satirize majority values while still reinforcing widely held and fairly conservative beliefs; "burnt cork was a *masking device* allowing professional and amateur entertainers to shield themselves from any direct personal and psychological identification with the material they were performing."[79] As Stephen Johnson noted in his study of the Black community in the 1840s in Toronto and their petitions to the council requesting that blackface performances be forbidden, "The four petitions, taken together, read a desperate warning against an imminent danger. The first alludes to the presentation of 'American' actors that 'ridicule' and 'hold up to contempt' the character of the petitioners, causing, among other things, violence against them."[80] The second petition referred to the way the petitioners' own characters were made "contemptible" and "ridiculous," leading to insults and worse; the third named the offending characters—"Jim Crow" and "Aunt Dinah"—as individual performers in "Yankee" amusements; and the fourth (and last) petition spoke directly to the offence that was being committed: that the Black community was being "taken off," that is, parodied or mocked.[81] Johnson's work has helped challenge the primary narrative of Canadian theatre history that has privileged the presence of purpose-built venues (that is, theatres), and the presentation of dramatic productions.

"Theatres and plays produce the ready-made documentation needed for study—architectural plans, set designs, and play scripts. They are direct and tangible evidence of the event, things we can collect, and from which we can make meaning,"[82] he writes. However, because blackface minstrel shows were often not documented in a way that reflected a traditional performance, their existence has historically not been counted in the establishment of a Canadian theatre history. That Burgess and Lavallée toured with American minstrel companies and performed in blackface means they also participated in dialect humour and aggressive mockery that would have been aimed at reinforcing existing prejudices.

In 1858, Burgess toured with actor Mazzellah Ainsley Scott who joined the New Orleans Opera Troupe; he also performed alongside Montreal-born Hugh Hamall.[83] According to Gerry Boyce, in 1868 "Hamall's Minstrels" went on a tour of Ontario (changed from Canada West after Confederation in 1867). "Their advance agent pasted large, multicolour posters on the blank south wall of Philip Hambly's bakery, confectionary, and saloon at 258 Front Street [in Belleville]."[84] In 1874 Hamall, who is often remembered as "a balladist of the Academy of Music of New Orleans" performed as part of La Rue's Minstrels and Hamall's Serenaders. Created by Hamall, the minstrel troupe formed after other ventures failed. In a wood engraving drawn by John Henry Walker and James Lovell Wiseman (1847–1912) (*La Rue's Minstrels and Hamall's Serenaders*, dated around 1875), the stock characters of the minstrel show are depicted (see figure 3.1). From left to right in the top corner sit two caricatures: one is wearing an elegant suit with a high collar, elongated hat, flamboyant pants, and tailcoat, and the other is wearing an extravagant shirt and fancy breeches. These characters are the uppity northern Black dandy Zip Coon and his

3.1 John Henry Walker's wood engraving titled *La Rue's Minstrels and Hamall's Serenaders*, ca. 1875, M930.50.8.419, McCord Stewart Museum, Montreal.

female counterpart, flamboyantly dressed in a fascinator hat placed atop neatly coiffed hair. Depictions of the Southern Jim Crow and mammy, as denoted by the elongated collar and expanded eyes on the male caricature and "plump" face and headwrap on the female depiction, appear above two *endmen* holding bones and a banjo—the primary instruments of the early minstrel show. In the centre of the print sits an enlarged male character with Afro hair and a deranged expression with bulging eyes, a protruding tongue, and an exceedingly large mouth with several missing teeth.

This grotesque poster speaks to how central these characters were to theatrical culture across the Atlantic world.[85] Lavallée, who in addition to playing several instruments also performed with the New Orleans Minstrels in the early 1860s, is part of this visual history. While we do not have depictions of his blackface repertoire, given the ubiquity of the minstrel shows' stock characters, his performances would have been mimetic of characters depicted in Walker and Wiseman's wood engraving.[86] The New Orleans Minstrels, based in Providence, Rhode Island, formed in the late 1850s, with members drawn mostly from the northeast US and Canada.[87] A troupe calling themselves Sanford's New Orleans Opera Troupe had also played Hamilton in November 1854, and they were described as "The Greatest Novelty of the Age."[88] Thompson makes an important distinction about minstrel companies from the northern US states and the South. "[Charles] Duprez's troupe had a name that evoked images of the South," he writes, adding "If the Virginia Minstrels suggested cotton fields, the New Orleans Minstrels brought to mind the urban South, and Duprez made a point of hiring francophones like Lavallée to help bolster the apparent connection to French-speaking Louisiana."[89]

In the seventeenth century, Louisiana was colonized by French Canadians in the name of the King of France. In the years that followed, additional waves of francophone settlers came from Lower Canada to Louisiana, notably the Acadians who were deported. At least 780 Acadians arrived in the British colonies of Maryland and Pennsylvania and later migrated to Louisiana between 1766 and 1770.[90] Most notably, Jean-Baptiste Le Moyne de Bienville (1680–1767), also known as the "Father of New Orleans," was actually born in Montreal, serving as an early governor of what was then known as French Louisiana (until 1803). If you consider Lavallée's touring schedule—which included stops in Alabama and Savannah, Atlanta, Macon, and Augusta, Georgia, before spending time in Charleston, South Carolina, as well as week-long engagements in Philadelphia, Williamsburg, New York, and Rocky Point, Rhode Island—as part of the New Orleans Minstrels, it is virtually impossible to believe that he (and Burgess) did not view Black people through a lens of deprivation and denigration. After all, this is a period where the dominant Western concept of the "inferior race" was attached to the Ethiopian in that, as Pickering explains, "they were…outsiders—a kind of racial proletariat… unfitted for 'advanced'" Western institutions "such as representative democracy."[91] Thus, the careers of Burgess and Lavallée reflect that blackface minstrelsy was never only one thing, but it was quite clearly about sets of racial relations that helped to justify Black denigration.

Minstrelsy's conflicting meanings and associations were primarily about the South's "peculiar institution," but it also addressed American expansion, sectional politics, and geographics of place. As Dale Cockrell suggests, issues related to slavery and race in nineteenth-century America were central to minstrelsy because they were also crucial parts of the public discourse. While there is no debating whether Black people were misrepresented and viciously stereotyped on the stage, or that White people took pleasure in a spectacle that reflected back to them their own perceived racial superiority to an extent, to declare minstrel repertoire as singularly demeaning of Black people is to "ignore the ambiguous, even paradoxical nature...and to miss the complex constitutions of common audiences."[92] That common audiences could take great pleasure from the song and dance of minstrelsy speaks to the extent blackface offered a little something to everyone; it could appease lower classes while satirizing upper class pretentiousness, just as it could appease White audiences who relished in derogatory depictions of Black people and men who enjoyed ridiculing women. What was on display in American minstrelsy was less Black culture than a structured set of White responses to it, grown out of mostly Northern social rituals and passed through an inevitable filter of racist presuppositions.[93] Minstrelsy was, above all, a commodity and a collection of loosely related genres (the harlequin of the Italian commedia dell'arte, the English pantomime clown, the American circus clown, burlesque, and the "blackamoor" of English folk drama) that reflected frequent content adjustments managers and performers made to meet the expectations of mostly White audiences.[94] Minstrel performers reproduced supposed "authentic" depictions of African Americans; they also provided forums for Black cultural forms like dance, music, and dialect to reach wide audiences.

While Canada had a different narrative (at the height of the Jim Crow craze in the 1830s, for instance, slavery was abolished across the British colonies, including Canada) and its political culture was largely dependent on British parliamentary decisions through the 1860s, what the country shared with the US were myths about its frontier and White settlement. "Frontier masculinity" could be defined as unconventional types noted primarily for their "mock heroic exploits or general belligerence."[95] As previously noted, early minstrel songs like "Backside Albany" (1815) not only mythologized the War of 1812, it also fabled myths of the frontier, plantation, river, and railroad.[96] The mid-nineteenth century, however, was a moment when Anglo-Canadians' sense of their destiny as a northern people took shape as a paradigm based on the exploration, acquisition, and settlement of the west. As Janice Cavell further explains, as a result there was a belief that "Canada had been built by the movement of explorers and fur traders across the continent from east to west, and by the eventual settlement of farmers...the turn northward into areas that could not be farmed was accompanied by a great deal of rhetoric about Canada's northern destiny."[97]

Elizabeth Furniss asserts further that the mythic epistemology around Canada's frontier expansion "consists of a distinctive set of narratives, metaphors and images that permeate the presentation of history in Canadian literature, in the arts and entertainment industries, and in local and national ceremonies celebrating Canada's past."[98] The frontier myth frames how Canadian history is thought about, experienced, and commemorated not through direct ideological statements, but indirectly and intuitively through metaphorical imagery and narrative forms that are deeply embedded in our cultural traditions.[99] At the same time, the erasure of Black presences in Canada is also part of the mythology of the "Great White North," which frames Whiteness as normative and fundamental to systems and symbols of Canadian representation. This racial myth generates a narrative of Canada that idealizes and naturalizes geography, excludes and renders absent Indigenous and Black communities from the land, and disavows Canada's histories of colonialism, conquest, and dispossession.[100] In Montreal, there is no record indicating the size of the Black community on Emancipation Day in 1834, a fact that remains underexplored as a gap in the documentation on its Black community.[101] Meanwhile, in Nova Scotia and New Brunswick, all-Black settlements populated with formerly enslaved African Americans, free Black people (some descendants of Jamaican Maroons), Black Loyalists, and Black Refugees developed self-sufficient communities.[102]

Unlike the Black population in Canada West that was relatively stable in terms of emigration to other sites before the US Civil War, Nova Scotia's

Black population was marked by multiple movements and migrations of Black people of varying origins. As African Nova Scotian historian Harvey Amani Whitfield explains, some migrations were short distance, others spanned the Atlantic world. "Refugee women engaged in regular travel from their rural homes to the local farmer's market in Halifax, while their husbands, brothers, and sons often found work on the high seas, just as free African Americans in Providence, Portsmouth, and Boston did. Other Refugees, dissatisfied with the economic and social conditions, left Nova Scotia for Trinidad, New Brunswick, or Upper Canada in search of better economic opportunities."[103]

While nineteenth-century Maritime history has not historically explored the in-and-out migration of Black people, in part because the "Underground Railroad" mythology of Canada West has often relegated Black Maritime history to the margins, there is an equally important story in the Maritimes as it relates to why Black populations left. Furthermore, Black populations remained relatively low compared to White populations in the region, despite being some of the first established residents on the lands in the wake of the British displacing the Mi'kmaq and transporting a French Acadian population (who refused to swear loyalty to the British Crown) from their lands over the course of the eighteenth and nineteenth centuries.[104] Given the unique migration of people of African descent, Black Canadians are settlers of a different kind compared to White Canadians, who were encouraged by colonial governments to migrate to Canada. Black people's inability to settle on prosperous lands they could then own and pass on to next generations created a population that, while technically "settled" in a place and space, have historically lacked full rights of citizenship. Additionally, they had to contend with a perpetually complicated relationship with lands that were stolen from Indigenous Peoples. Bonita Lawrence writes, "in order to maintain Canadians' self-image as a fundamentally 'decent' people innocent of any wrongdoing, the historical record of how the land was acquired—the forcible and relentless dispossession of Indigenous Peoples, the theft of their territories, and the implementation of legislation and policies designed to effect their total disappearance as peoples—must be erased."[105] This innocent self-image also requires the erasure of Black migration and settlement in the centuries of European arrival and settlement.

The migration of Black people to the Maritime provinces shared much in common with African Americans in New England, especially related to the public culture that developed there. "In both regions, free black communities formed churches, established various organizations, celebrated their own freedom, fought for political inclusion, and promoted abolitionism," explains Whitfield, adding "Black people in New England cities also named many of their community institutions 'African' to memorialize an important part of their identity."[106] While Halifax did not have a Negro Election Day or Pinkster festival like in Providence, Boston, and Portsmouth, Whitfield found that churches and church organizations established by descendants of Black Loyalist and Black Refugee populations played a significant role in Black communities in Halifax and North Preston, Nova Scotia.[107] In cities like Saint John, Fredericton, and St. Andrews, New Brunswick, there were Emancipation freedom festivities but as in Canada West, anti-Black rhetoric and systemic discrimination was rampant. William Spray's *The Blacks in New Brunswick* (1972) and follow-up *Acadiensis* article, "The Settlement of the Black Refugees in New Brunswick, 1815–1836" (1977) stand as two of the first recuperative pieces of writing on Black life in nineteenth-century New Brunswick. In his initial survey of the Maritime province, Spray observed that freedom-seeking African Americans were mostly welcome in the early decades of the nineteenth century; however, by the 1850s "many found they were no longer welcome in certain parts of Canada where large numbers of Black people had already settled."[108]

Following the end of the Civil War, some African Americans in New Brunswick returned to the US because they felt they "could better combat prejudice and discrimination amongst their brethren there rather than remain in Canada where they were legally given the same rights as whites but faced many types of discrimination."[109] Similarly, when introduced in contemporary discussions of Westmorland (southeast county in New Brunswick), Black residents have been dismissed, imagined as anomalous, or as intrusions from Amherst, Nova Scotia, which once boasted a Black population of four hundred to five hundred; further, while histories of the region celebrate founding families, Black families are routinely overlooked. Their status as enslaved persons or descendants of slaves relegates them to an ancillary status, not relations.[110] While the majority of Black Refugees went to Nova Scotia at the end of the War of 1812, those who arrived in

New Brunswick were treated differently than White settlers who had arrived primarily from the British Isles during the same decade.[111] "White settlers could usually depend on some assistance from friends and fellow countrymen and if they still failed, like...Irish immigrants who also settled...on land equally unsuitable for agriculture, they could move to other settlements in the province or to the United States," writes Spray, adding "For the black refugees the alternative of moving to the United States was not appealing."[112] This sense of "having nowhere to go" helps to explain why the majority of New Brunswick's Black community stayed.

Where the American frontier myth is linked with the gold rush and western expansion, Canada's frontier myth is similarly associated with clearing, settling, and braving the wilderness of not only the west but also the north. In addition to a mythological western expansion narrative that erases Indigenous Peoples in favour of a grand narrative of "law and order" that prioritizes authorities like the NWMP, Canada has its "Great White North" mythology that legitimizes White inhibitors of northern regions of the country as *always already* present on the land, but also as rightfully in place. As Michele A. Johnson and Funké Aladejebi write in the introduction to *Unsettling the Great White North: Black Canadian History*, "[this book] grows out of a desire to offer a scholarly intervention into the continual construction of Canada as a (geographically and) demographically 'White' place and space by confirming and theorizing Blackness/es within the country's historical narratives."[113] Just as the authors take aim at the White settler narrative, which has framed the North as "an arctic land unsullied by conquest,"[114] by studying minstrelsy, this book challenges the "Great White North" mythology that has had the effect of expunging histories of blackface from the Canadian grand narrative.

There were songs and dances that originated in Canada which represented an outgrowth of the popular, a sphere characterized by cultural forms of social and political conflict, neither entirely the "social control" of the ruling classes nor the "class expression" of the dominated.[115] Because the popular is always *produced*, it does not arise in some immediate way from collective popular desires but instead "the popular emerges at the intersection of received symbolic forms, audiences' experiences of authority and subordination...and new articulations by various producers of symbolic forms...it is itself a crucial place of contestation, with movements of resistance to the dominant culture as well as moments of supersession."[116] Canadian blackface must be understood as a site of contestation in that it developed at a time when White "settlers" were loyal to the British Crown, but also when America's exported popular culture was the yardstick for how most people *experienced* Black culture. As Adrienne Shadd writes, "the stereotype of the illiterate slave fleeing a large southern plantation, running through the bushes with only the clothes on his or her back, and making it to Canada" was a prevailing view of how African Americans arrived in the North in the nineteenth century—and such images were incredibly powerful in shaping notions of what Black people were like, and what they brought to Canada in terms of skills, education, capital, and such.[117]

If northern people were associated with "strength and liberty," southern people were viewed as the opposite: degenerate, effeminate, and associated with tyranny.[118] The only way the likes of Burgess and Lavallée could have found success in American minstrelsy is if they had some understanding of racial caricature and, by extension, Black people's subjugation. Even as Thompson explains that through the minstrel show, "Lavallée found opportunities to see the world and attain a degree of fame, if not fortune,"[119] it is through that same experience that he would have seen slavery in the American South, and it is where he would have had to reflect on his homeland as a place seemingly absent of such conditions. It is also important to remember that when the Civil War began Canadian public opinion widely favoured the Confederacy. "For some French Canadians, historical links to the South and to Louisiana in particular were a factor. For some, their aversion to slavery was increasingly tempered by their fear of 'Northern aggression'."[120] In this context of an empty, unoccupied Canadian wilderness with resources and land *free* for the taking, the White settler narrative "established by Europeans on non-European soil," was deeply rooted in the "dispossession and near extermination of Indigenous populations by the conquering of Europeans" but it also authorized a narrative of White agency that would have spilled over into the theatre.[121] This is the reason Burgess and Lavallée could take their lives into their own hands and leave Canada for fame and glory in the US. Even though they were descendants of a generation who were not born in Canada, they viewed themselves as the *original* inhabitants and from groups of British and French-ancestry fully entitled to citizenship rights. This also explains why English men and women in the Muskoka, Lake Simcoe, and Peterborough districts in Canada West built cottages and established themselves as "outdoorsmen and outdoorswomen" during this period; Irish men and women in Nova Scotia and New Brunswick settled the backwoods, and Scottish emigrants to the West saw themselves as homesteaders, not immigrants. The "Great White North" mythology infected the national spirit.

As Renisa Mawani writes of British Columbia, "the assertion of racial distinctions was particularly salient…authorities endeavoured to construct a strong white Canada and a *'British* British Columbia'…the Fraser River Gold Rush attracted thousands of unmarried Black, Chinese, and European men to the province, further skewing…proportions, as did the growth of industry and the building of the Canadian Pacific Railway."[122] A quintessential feature of White settler mythologies is "the disavowal of conquest, genocide, slavery, and the exploitation of peoples of colors."[123] These are all central features of Canada's White settler mythology which has created a narrative that reflects the erasure of a White immigrant story; instead, what gets superimposed onto that narrative is a story of frontier exploration and a romanticization of the supposed barrenness of the land prior to European arrival.

Alexander McLachlan's (1818–96) poem, *The Emigrant* (1861) is representative of the "typical settler who came to Canada":

> In Canada arrived at last,
> Pioneers of a mighty nation;
> Soon we entered in the woods,
> On the trackless solitudes,
> Where the spruce and cedar made
> An interminable shade…[124]

Such romanticized visions of Canada have made it historically difficult to recuperate blackface north of the border, specifically the "White obsession with black (male) bodies" as imagined through minstrel caricature, and White disavowal of their own "fleshly investments through ridicule and racist lampoon."[125] For example, despite having no connection to the Underground Railroad or freedom-seeking African Americans who lived in Canada West in the 1850s (at a time when Saskatchewan's biggest city,

Saskatoon, consisted of fourteen log cabins), in nearby Battleford in 1884, "the first cultural events probably took place at the barracks of the North-West Mounted Police, where a minstrel group had been organized."[126] One of their early concerts in 1879 "boasted such enduring songs as Stephen Foster's 'Massa in de Cold,' the blackface song, 'N---er on the Fence,' and the folk song, 'Mother Says I Mustn't.'"[127]

There is a tendency in Canadian historical studies to minimize blackface or position it as something minor compared to its popularity in Britain or America, such as Robin Elliott's assertion that "the exoticism of minstrel performers would have been less marked in Toronto than in Britain, given the closer geographical proximity of America."[128] Pickering makes the claim that the mobilization of racial ideas and imagery in British minstrelsy was successful "because it worked through the form of the clown's mask."[129] There, as in America, the genre offered paradoxical meanings in that "blackface clowns were not merely pretending to be what they were not; they mediated a conception and view of the low black Other through their impersonation. The mask gave them a licence to simulate cultural and racial Otherness."[130] British immigrants to Canada would have brought with them cultural memories about theatrical forms like blackface clowns. Blackening was a common theatrical device in English theatre, and these "blacked up" characters were often negatively associated with traits such as hypersexuality, thievery, guile, and mischievousness. As theatre historian Robert Hornback writes, the comic tradition of blackface was "prevalent in the Renaissance, often involving episodes of on-stage blacking.... Not only did the fool...appear in blackface, but so-called 'natural' fools (mentally defective, rationally-impaired fools who are either idiotic, mad, or ignorant)...are sometimes depicted as inherently black."[131] Thus, as new immigrants found ways to entertain themselves, they confirmed and amplified what had already been documented in British theatre, travel writings, fiction (like *Uncle Tom's Cabin*), school textbooks, and human sciences—that people of African descent were "Other," not fully human, and most certainly not "settlers."

As James Bruce, eighth Earl of Elgin (1811–63), who served as governor of Jamaica before his appointment as the governor general of Canada West in 1847, expressed to the British colonial secretary, "[I worry Canada will be] flooded with blackies who are rushing across the frontier to escape from the bloodhounds whom the Fugitive Slave Bill has let loose on their track."[132] In an April 1855 editorial, Samuel Thompson (1810–86), editor of the *Daily Colonist* also complained, "We fear that they are coming rather too fast for the good of the Province.... People may talk about the horrors of slavery as much as they choose; but fugitive slaves are by no means a desirable class of immigrants for Canada, especially when they come in large numbers."[133] In 1853, Thompson purchased the *British Colonist*, and with the subscription list from the *Toronto Patriot* (1848–53) by 1857 the *Colonist* printed four editions, including the *News of the Week*, or *Weekly Colonist*, and had a total weekly circulation of 30,000.[134] In early 1858 the *Colonist* was sold; in July, Thompson was involved in setting up the *Atlas* in Toronto to compete with the *Colonist* but later that year bought back the *Colonist* and merged the two newspapers.[135] On December 11, 1858, in the midst of the Fraser Canyon Gold Rush, Nova Scotia-born descendant of British Loyalists Amor de Cosmos (1825–97) launched the *British Colonist* (1858–1980), which eventually became the leading newspaper on Vancouver Island and across British Columbia.[136]

It is impossible to fully understand the rise of Canadian minstrelsy as something distinctly political or as mere comedy; its local inflections and meanings were always in dialogue with other sources. As Simon Featherstone writes of the blackface Atlantic in Britain, "It was this fabrication, with its reference points in slavery and emancipation, as well as in the racist deprecations of blackness and the stage conventions of clowning, that made the entertainment at once legitimate, transgressive and safe. Minstrelsy allowed the unexpected contact of bank clerks and paupers, licensed the former's abandonment before social inferiors, and maintained anonymity and decorum behind the mask."[137] The reason why Burgess and Lavallée could be born in Canada but find great success in the US by assuming the burnt cork mask of minstrelsy, and its lampooning of Black people and culture, is because they understood the import of stereotypes and would have had knowledge of slavery, even though Canadian slavery ended before their births. The same ideologies and mythologies that came to define minstrelsy also authorized separate schools in Canada West, residential segregation in the Maritimes, and Black marginalization in British Columbia.

This chapter has examined how minstrelsy's homegrown performers developed alongside the building of cultural infrastructure such as theatres, railway systems, and newspapers, all of which helped to support large-scale entertainment. As Lenton-Young explains, "In sharp contrast to the small fly-by-night companies were the large variety...minstrel show. Most featured a star who would attract audiences and provide respectability. Billy Whitlock, for example, one of the original Virginia Minstrels, called the show he brought to Toronto in 1850, a 'Grand Olio Entertainment.'"[138] The olio developed as a standard element by the late 1850s; it offered a range of individuals acts, including song and dance teams, acrobats, comedians, and novelties—all while set on the Southern plantation.[139] It should not be asked why Canadians participated in American minstrelsy's plantation depictions, nor why homegrown blackface developed in the absence of plantation slavery. Instead, to understand these developments one must connect a pervasive Atlantic world anti-Blackness as a foundational *structure of feeling*. To borrow from British cultural historian Raymond Williams, that feeling circulated across borders and oceans, infecting not only White Canadians' thoughts about Black people, but how they *felt* about them and how they *experienced* their humanity (or perceived lack thereof). Williams describes a structure of feeling as that "particular quality of social experience and relationship, historically distinct from other particular qualities, which gives a sense of a generation or a period—a kind of feeling and thinking that is indeed social and material."[140] John Frick explains further that, "[Williams] is primarily interested in meanings as they are actively *felt* and *experienced*, not in meanings as they are conceived intellectually."[141]

To understand how Canadian blackface grew during the 1860s, a decade flanked by public celebrations of Black (British) emancipation, a Civil War south of the border centred on questions of freedom, and the unification of Canada via Confederation, it is important to contextualize blackface not on an intellectual level, but on the level of affect. We do not know how White Canadians *felt* about Black people, but we do know they enjoyed Black caricatures, even in places where Black people were entirely absent. Western expansion and the building of railways, newspapers, and theatres created an infrastructure to support Canada's inclusion into the blackface Atlantic, a positionality that presented new challenges to Black freedoms while also creating opportunities for Black people to become part of a transcontinental entertainment industry. In the next chapter, the role of the US Civil War in shifting not only the themes of blackface minstrel shows but also Canadian allegiances is explained. In regions such as Canada West and East, and the Maritimes, the business and political classes were split in their support of the Confederate South versus the Northern Union army.

Prior to the Civil War, minstrelsy was primarily concerned with Black people's "rightful" place in the North and the South, and while that narrative continued into the 1860s, during and after the war, as African Americans gained their freedom, the theatrical stage became one of the first outlets where they could exercise their newfound emancipation. Over the course of five years, not only did the minstrel show dramatically change, so too did race relations in North America. As Douglas A. Jones poignantly observes, "despite universal emancipation and the enshrinement of black citizenship in the Fourteenth Amendment to the Constitution [passed in 1866 and ratified by the US Congress in 1868], the dominant imagination still construed Blackness as the mark of subjects who should be most captive, while whiteness marked those who should be most free."[142] As Canada marched closer to its own sovereignty, the themes of slavery and emancipation remained popular not only in the theatre but also within the editorial pages of the country's newspapers. On the stage, a new genre was born; it would become known as *Black* minstrelsy. Black performers, far from providing an immediate corrective to minstrel types, reinforced them. These nearly emancipated minstrel acts lent credibility to slavery in large part because they fit the ideological forms the minstrel show's White *originators* had helped generate, but also because of the impact of slavery on audiences' racial logics.[143]

4

CANADA'S CIVIL WAR SYMPATHIZERS AND THE RISE OF *BLACK* MINSTRELSY, 1862-66

On November 6, 1860, Abraham Lincoln was elected the first-ever Republican president of the United States. Three months later, the Confederate States of America (hereafter the Confederacy) with Jefferson Davis (1808–89), a Southern plantation owner and Mississippi state senator as its first president, demanded that seven states be granted rights toward the continuation of slavery. The seven slave-owning states were Alabama, Florida, Georgia, Louisiana, Mississippi, South Carolina, and Texas. On March 4, 1861, Lincoln was sworn in as the sixteenth president, and almost a month after his election, four additional Southern slave states—Virginia, Arkansas, Tennessee, and North Carolina—joined the Confederacy. On April 12, after Confederate troops fired on a Northern Union fort in the harbour at Fort Sumter, South Carolina, Missouri and Kentucky subsequently joined the Confederacy. With this act the US officially entered a Civil War, and while this was a domestic issue, these events weighed heavily on the mood in Canada.

As Brian Christopher Thompson explains, "As in Britain, when the Civil War began, Canadian public opinion favoured the Confederacy."[1] There existed a pro-slavery lobby that not only supported Southern aggression against the North, but also had found great pleasure in the minstrel show's slavery narratives. "For some French Canadians, historical links to the South and to Louisiana in particularly were a factor," asserts Thompson, "For some, their aversion to slavery was increasingly tempered by their fear of 'Northern aggression.'"[2]

In New Brunswick, Confederate ships were used in the Fundy Bay harbour in Saint John during the Civil War. As John Boyko explains, "its spies and recruiters [were] made to feel at home in the city's hotels and bars. Many rich Southerners who had for years summered nearby moved their families to the fine cottages to escape the ravages of war and they were openly welcomed in the city."[3] Similarly, in Halifax, the city's businesspeople enjoyed "the profit earned by magnanimously welcoming both Northern ships seeking Confederate blockade runners and the elusive Southerners themselves. In allowing Southern ships free access…the city served as an important link in the communication network between the Confederacy and European capitals."[4] Meanwhile, it is estimated that as many as ninety Maritime-born Black men enlisted in the Union Army during the Civil War.[5] They enlisted even as the Black population in New Brunswick, Nova Scotia, and Prince Edward Island (PEI) were primarily descendants of enslaved African Americans who had arrived after the Revolutionary War and the War of 1812; by 1861, many of these people were only one generation out of slavery and a significant number of aging community members had been born into bondage.[6] At least 835 Union soldiers and 352 sailors gave a British colony as their place of birth at the outset of War; the largest number of Black recruits came from Canada West, where the population had the closest ties with the US.[7]

Shortly after war began, Britain declared itself neutral. Canadian officials dutifully echoed that official line and informed citizens that it was against the law to support North or South, and for individuals to join in the fight.[8] However, across the country, men ignored this official line, including African Americans living in Canada West who left to support the Union Army. They also left because of growing economic challenges that were compounded by widespread discrimination. Before the Civil War, Shadd Cary wrote an "Appeal to Canadians" declaring, "It is an indisputable fact that their rights and privileges to which they are legally entitled under the British constitution as it exists here have been very much infringed upon through prejudice of color...the colored people of Jamaica have access to all the Schools established there [but].... Not so with those in Canada West."⁹ Shadd Cary returned to the United States during the Civil War and worked as a recruitment agent for the Union Army. In Quebec, a letter home from a young Quebecois man stationed in the trenches facing the Confederate capital of Richmond, Virginia in 1864, "spoke with surprise of how many of his French-speaking countrymen he had met...[who] joined the fight, and the ratio was approximately fifty Canadians in Union regiments for every one in a Confederate regiment."¹⁰

The Civil War sparked discussions over the future of the British colonies. This became most apparent in June 1864 when Conservatives from Canada East and West (led by John A. Macdonald and George-Étienne Cartier) joined newspaper editor and Reform Party leader George Brown to form a Grand Coalition aimed at achieving a federal union of the British colonies. The Reform Party had been working to change the provincial legislative councils so that they were elective—and by implication even the governors and other officials—and they also proposed the officials and advisers (i.e., the executive council) of the governors be held responsible or accountable to such elective legislative assemblies. By the late 1840s, however, a rising tide of radicalism split the party; by the 1850s, Reformers had divided into a moderate group and a more radical group, the latter of which was known as the Clear Grits. Macdonald won moderate Reformers over to his Liberal-Conservative Party while the Clear Grits provided the nucleus of what became the Liberal Party.¹¹ The Civil War was a catalyst for Canada to reevaluate its political alliance, but on the other hand it also reignited fears of US invasion that would, by the end of the conflict, provide some of the basis for Confederation. "The security issue came to the fore...during the Quebec Conference [in September 1864 when delegates from Canada West and the Maritimes met at Quebec City] when news arrived that Confederate soldiers had entered the US from Canada, robbed three banks in the town of St. Albans, Vermont, and escaped back into Canada," explains Thompson, adding that the "raiders" were arrested but not extradited to America. As such, "the legal standoff increased fear of US retaliation and added a sense of urgency to the negotiations taking place in Quebec City."¹²

This chapter examines how the US Civil War deeply influenced Canadian politics, newspaper coverage, and, by extension, performance culture. Music halls and performance venues suddenly became outlets for partisanship displays of loyalty. For example, after the Confederate Army led by Robert E. Lee surrendered to Union General Ulysses S. Grant on April 9, 1865, and five days later John Wilkes Booth assassinated Lincoln, Montreal Mayor Jean-Louis Beaudry (1809–86) led a vigil at the Mechanics' Hall in the city.[13] Canada did not have its own cotton mills, but many Maritimers and Quebecers supported slavery's most prized export, even as they might not have supported Black enslavement. "Maritimers had prospered indirectly from slavery," asserts Greg Marquis, adding "and there were rumours that certain Nova Scotians derived income from American cotton plantations. By 1860, White Southerners had developed an articulate response to abolitionist critiques. Slavery, once regarded as a 'necessary evil' was now defended as a 'positive good.'"[14] For some Francophones in Canada East, historical links to the South and to the former French colony of Louisiana were a factor; as a result, any aversion to slavery was tempered by a more pronounced fear of Northern aggression. In addition to examining Canada's role in the US Civil War, this chapter also pinpoints the post–Civil War moment when Black men, most of whom had been newly emancipated, entered the theatre as full-fledged troupes, as opposed to a generation before when the like of Aldridge and Lane performed as solo acts.

The post–Civil War era spawned a new genre of theatre known as *Black* minstrelsy, which was distinguished from White minstrelsy not only because performers were Black, but also because the themes of *Black* minstrelsy were almost exclusively centred on "real" stories of the Southern plantation from "real" formerly enslaved performers. *Black* minstrelsy, then, brought a degree of supposed authenticity to the minstrel stage even as Black performers wore blackface and were essentially performing *Blackness* as if they were White actors mimicking Black people. While the artifice of minstrelsy was the same, the performance of that artifice in *Black* minstrelsy was interpreted by White audiences as the "real thing." To understand the "logic" of this form of racialized performance is to, as Robyn Wiegman outlines in *American Anatomies*, centralize the ways that Whiteness was anchored in the visible epistemology of Black skin, such that "an epistemological relationship circumscribes our cultural conception of race, contributing above all to the recurrent and discursively, if not always materially, violent equation between the idea of 'race' and the 'black' body."[15] Stated otherwise, Black skin had historically not been understood in literal terms, but rather as designating discernible divergence from the standard that was White normativity. Blackface minstrelsy helped to affirm the paradoxical notion that Blackness was not real, but that it could be *performed as real* because White skin was the enabling attribute that afforded someone the ability to discern authenticity; by extension, only White men could interpret and *truly* understand Black expressions.

At the same time, racial difference was real. White performers could "naturally" play in *Blackness* to distinguish themselves or to transgress—albeit for a moment—the constraints of Whiteness that designated White men to see themselves as the arbiters of freedom, agency, and authority. When White men "blacked up" as minstrels they forever fused together the visible markers of Blackness (the corporeal) and a supposed Black culture (the ephemeral) that was both rendered real (through artifice) and invisible (through burnt cork). However, as White managers took over successful *Black* troupes following the Civil War, benefiting from the 1866 tour of Sam Hague's (1828–1901) Slave Troupe in Britain that helped *Black* minstrels establish themselves as "bona fide entertainers back home,"[16] minstrelsy fused three centuries of slavery with the simulacra of the stage. This moment gave rise to a new era in the minstrel show.

The US Civil War did not represent a moment of Canadian self-reflection on racial issues; nor was the Thirteenth Amendment, which abolished slavery in 1865, an opportunity for atonement in the US. In some Maritime churches, racial equality was left at the door, "as in neighbouring Maine, the major churches took no stand on the issues of slavery and abolition. Despite their deep roots in the region, blacks were regarded as aliens."[17] The *Borderer and Westmorland and Cumberland Advertiser* (1856–68) in Sackville, New Brunswick, the only newspaper between Saint John and Halifax, regularly featured anecdotes of "negro humour" on the first page where it also relied on racial stereotypes to represent Black people as incompetent.[18] In Nova Scotia, published pamphlets were circulated just before the end of the War, arguing "that complete emancipation was an 'impracticability' because Southern slaves were thriftless, ignorant and numerous."[19] When federal soldier William Drake wrote to his family in PEI late in 1865, he explained to them that Southern African Americans had been better off as slaves, "for the men are too lazy to work, so that I feel you can't trust them any more.... Without a boss over them, they are nowhere."[20] Marquis asserts that one of the reasons Maritimers held such negative views of Black people, despite the fact that in most cases they had no personal interaction with anyone of African descent, was because there was a pervasive lack of understanding of the poor treatment Black people received in their own community. Biased newspaper coverage depicting the Black community was almost "exclusively in terms of derision." White Maritimers (like White planters in the Caribbean), Southerners, and many Northerners, including those in Canada East and West, tended to view Black people as the papers depicted them—ignorant, lazy, childlike, dependent, and immoral.[21]

In *Montreal Secrets: Confederate Operations in Montreal During the American Civil War*, Barry Sheehy asserts that "Most Canadians naively assume Canada was supportive of Lincoln's war because of their collective opposition to slavery. This is simply not true.... There was certainly a committed abolitionist movement in Canada, especially in Southern Ontario, but the general view of slavery was agnostic. Britain had abolished slavery decades earlier and this was now viewed as an American rather than a Canadian problem."[22] The reason why most Canadians ignored Britain's declaration of neutrality was because many recognized both North and South "as legitimate and equal belligerents with whom they could do business"; further, many readily did business with the Confederacy, especially in Montreal, which played host to "blockade running and contraband for cotton trading on an enormous scale."[23] The Confederacy had financial arrangements with multiple Canadian banks, and according to Sheehy's findings, "inside the vaults of the Bank of Montreal, the Ontario Bank, and other Canadian financial institutions as far away as the Niagara and District Bank in St. Catharines, the Confederates kept on deposit a million dollars or more in hard currencies and gold to fund clandestine activities."[24] When Lavallée enlisted in the Fourth Rhode Island Regiment of the

Union Army as a musician, first class[25] his main motivation was not slavery but a desire to preserve the Union, and even yet, he might have been swept up in the "spirit of the times."[26]

Given that Canada West was the place where abolitionism flourished, the White population was mostly pro-North, especially George Brown, who used the platform of the *Globe* to reflect his stance. "The North has a noble cause to fight for as any for which blood has even been shed," wrote Brown in an April 8, 1861 editorial. "Every motive which impels men to do well and bravely is theirs. If they stand as nobly by their cause as their cause is noble, they cannot fail of success."[27] In Canada East, the *Montreal Witness* (1845–1938) was pro-North while the *Montreal Telegraph* and *Gazette* were pro-South.[28] The *Witness*, founded by John Dougall (1810–88) who had emigrated from Scotland in 1826, was a staunchly Protestant newspaper that was often hostile to Catholics.[29] While Dougall believed that newspapers should be politically independent, like other papers, the *Witness* was generally on the side of the Reform Party or Liberals, but the paper's dislike of Catholics, the Irish, and French was so pronounced it directly resulted in the establishment of a rival paper, the *True Witness and Catholic Chronicle* (1850–1910), founded by fellow Scotsman George Edward Clerk (1815–57), as a voice for English-speaking Catholics in Montreal—though the newspaper also took aim at other Scotsmen, such as Brown, who had been known to espouse anti-Catholic sentiments as well.[30]

In the case of the *Gazette* and *Telegraph*, both supported Cartier's Parti Bleu, founded in 1854 by Conservative members of the former Reform movement in Canada East. The Parti Bleu was ideologically on the political right and ardently supported the Catholic Church.[31] Both papers tended to be pro-Southern editorially, especially as the *Gazette* and the *Telegraph* were, as Sheehy found, "always available in the lobby of the St. Lawrence Hall Hotel on Greater St. James Street—a Confederate favorite" in the city.[32] Brian Gabrial also notes that the *Gazette*'s editors, John Lowe and Browne Chamberlin, "leaned toward the Southern cause, believing that the North's increasing economic and political clout had oppressed the Southern economy.... To them, the South's right to secede was no different than the American colonies' right to declare independence from Great Britain in 1776."[33] Thus, the *Gazette*'s support for the Confederacy was not merely ideological; it represented the interests of many Montrealers.[34] During the

Civil War, Confederate Jefferson Davis, for example, chose to send his four children to Montreal for safekeeping, followed soon after by his wife; upon release from his imprisonment after two years, in 1867, he stayed with publishing magnate John Lovell (1810–93), who was also a supporter of the Confederacy because it suited his political and economic interests.[35] Born in Scotland, Lovell worked at the *Montreal Gazette* from 1824 until the 1837/1838 Rebellions broke out, and he closed his office to join the Royal Montreal Cavalry in support of the British nationalist cause.[36]

Like in Montreal, Toronto's newspapers were split between pro-North/Union and pro-South/Confederacy lines. *The Leader* (1852–78), published by James Beaty, an Ireland-born businessman and eventual member of Parliament, was a pro-South newspaper while the *Globe* was pro-North. By 1861, the *Globe* had a circulation of roughly 30,000 subscribers, making it the most influential paper in Canada West during the Civil War. Considered the chief promoter of the "Northern position," Gabrial explains further that the newspaper published items in fifty-five days of coverage, and its coverage was the most extensive. "In the 12 days before the firing on Fort Sumter, *The Globe* consistently headlined news items about impending or actual hostilities as 'The American Revolution.'"[37] A major factor that shaped, shifted, and divided public opinion among Whites in Canada West and East, and the Maritimes was Lincoln's position on slavery.

Abolitionist Canadians and Maritimers suffered widespread disappointment when Lincoln said in his 1861 inaugural address that he would not immediately emancipate American slaves. As Boyko writes, "Even Toronto's pro-North *Globe* reflected disillusion in an editorial: 'At first the sympathies of the British people were unmistakably with the North. They imagined that Mr. Lincoln had determined to wage a war against slavery, and in heart and soul they were with him.'"[38] Opinions shifted even further when, on January 1, 1863, Lincoln issued the Emancipation Proclamation, authorizing the enlistment of Black soldiers as an official part of the Union army. "[This] symbolized the start of a dramatic if uncertain new era, one that was important to all black North Americans. Of course, these momentous changes had an uneven impact. For African Americans, especially black Southerners, emancipation ushered in a transformative phase in which old social relationships were destroyed and new hopes were raised that a more equitable set of racial associations had begun," writes Reid.[39]

For Black Northerners, the destruction of slavery opened the door for them to imagine full citizenship rights they had never enjoyed before, though this door did not stay open for long. The question of freedom was very real when Robert E. Lee surrendered the last major Confederate army to Ulysses S. Grant at Appomattox Courthouse, Virginia on April 9, 1865, freeing millions of African Americans from bondage. This transitional time was the beginning of a White Southern backlash that would not only shift the power relations that had defined the US, but also blackface minstrelsy's content, which defined its first three decades. Minstrel acts exercised a largely unchallengeable White supremacy that was rooted in the representation of a supposed undeniable Black inferiority. This "master/slave" dichotomy was severed following the outcome of the Civil War. Not only did the South have to redefine itself, so too did the dominant form of mass entertainment that had been vested in the narrative of slavery versus abolition. Post–Civil War, the minstrel show became the way to reimagine slavery as if emancipation had never *really* happened at all.

In 1865, African American theatre manager and performer Charles Barney Hicks (1840–1902), commonly viewed as "the father of *Black* minstrelsy," organized and managed the first all-Black minstrel troupe who would be called the Original Georgia Minstrels. The all-Black troupe seemed to defy logic with respect to the boundaries of Black labour. The stage suddenly became a viable option for Black men, in large part because their labour did not seem to usurp opportunities from a White working-class actor; the performative stage afforded some degree of agency and often celebrated Black originality and innovation. From 1865 onward, *Black* minstrels were called "Georgia" or "Slave" minstrels while White minstrels were still known as "Negro" performers. Sometimes "Coloured" was used interchangeably to describe both *Black* and *White* minstrelsy. Hicks, who was born in Baltimore, Maryland, is the only known African American manager of *Black* minstrel troupes.[40] After Hicks created the Original Georgia Minstrels, billed as "The Only Simon Pure Negro Troupe in the World," the troupe of newly freed African Americans became so popular they reportedly outdrew all other minstrel troupes, *Black* or White, in

1866.[41] Hicks first began touring all-Black companies in the northeast and west in 1865, and by 1870 he and some of his Black members joined with Sam Hague's Great American Slave Troupe, formerly called Georgia Slave Troupe Minstrels and managed by W.H. Lee, for a tour of the British Isles.[42] Born in Sheffield, England, Hague was credited with introducing English clog dancing to America in the 1850s.[43] Lee had managed a troupe out of Macon, Georgia called the Georgia Slave Troupe Minstrels that toured the US and Britain during the 1865–66 season.[44]

Many scholars believe Hicks deserves to be treated as the person who introduced African Americans to American show business. As Henry Sampson writes, "Hicks provided costumes and musical instruments, and went on the road with his troupe under the banner Georgia Minstrels."[45] What can be said with some certainty is that Hicks's Georgia Minstrels was likely the first *Black* minstrel troupe to tour Canada when they performed in Ingersoll, Woodstock, Dundee, Hamilton and Kingston, Ontario in the 1870s. There were many distinguishing features of *Black* minstrelsy. In addition to the performers being Black, in the genre's first few decades actors performed in blackface, but by the 1890s some troupes performed without it, especially when they were staging "straight rather than comic roles," a practice that Yuval Taylor and Jake Austen explain, underlined their "authenticity" as real Negroes and "which was the major bases of their appeal to white audiences" as the genre matured.[46] Another distinguishing feature of *Black* minstrel troupes was their significantly larger size to White minstrel acts. Michael Pickering credits Hague for making this change, as he was among the first crop of White minstrel entrepreneurs who began to form large companies of "up to 60 performers, and for extravagant display that moved minstrelsy away from 'negro delineation' towards the variety entertainment that would eventually supersede both minstrelsy and music hall."[47] Ultimately, *Black* minstrelsy cannot be understood without grasping the impact of an estimated four million previously enslaved people being freed from forced labour into a cultural milieu historically resistant to Black agency. The end of the Civil War spawned a new era of anti-Black sentiment.

This discussion would be remiss if it did not acknowledge that the Confederacy's loss in the Civil War gave birth to the vigilante Ku Klux Klan (Klan). Created in December 1865 in Pulaski, Tennessee, the Klan began as little more than a social club for disaffected, wealthy young White men but it turned into something much more ominous. "Donning white robes and rampaging on horseback in the dark of the night, Klansmen became the shock troops of a displaced Southern aristocracy determined to undermine a new popular order and restore the old way of life," writes Julian Sher.[48] Thus, the post–Civil War era initiated three dichotomies in North America that reimagined and reimplemented new sectional divisions: the first was actualized through the rise of *Black* minstrelsy; the second was exercised through a heightened and mobilized White supremacy; the third was institutionalized through a public desire for the minstrel show, which began to reduce its political content and replace it with comic song-and-dance numbers that were more rooted in an intent to purely entertain the masses rather than sway public opinion. For example, when Duprez joined forces with Lew Benedict (who had joined his group in 1861) after buying out J.E. Green's share in Duprez and Green's Minstrels, the duo, which became known as Duprez and Benedict's Minstrels, sometimes performed skits about the Klan. "[B]ut overall, Duprez avoided current events. Extant programs reveal no references to the impeachment proceedings against President Andrew Jackson that coincided with the Duprez & Benedict 1867-68 tour. The failure of Reconstruction policies might have been simply too sensitive an issue to bring to the stage," asserts Brian Christopher Thompson.[49]

At the end of the Civil War *informal* slavery had not been abolished with the Thirteenth Amendment; rather, four million freed Black men and women, most of them on the same plantation, remained doing the same work they did before emancipation, as if their work had only been interrupted and changed by the upheaval of the war.[50] Cotton production based on slave labour ended in 1865, but a system known as sharecropping became the dominant system of labour in the cotton-growing regions of the American South. This created paid employment opportunities for freed people, allowing them to escape the plantation system of labour; however, in this new system where the landlord/planter allowed a tenant to use the land in exchange for a share of the crop, tenants might have been encouraged to work to produce the biggest harvest they could, but they often laboured under conditions no different from what they experienced during slavery. In this system, many Black families who rented land from

White owners and raised cash crops such as cotton, tobacco, and rice were typically paid with a share of the crop. Sharecropping signaled the demise of the plantation as the basic unit of agricultural production, but it created a new form of indenture.[51] "The typical structure of the new plantation during Reconstruction involved a section farmed directly by the owner or manager of the plantation (average 330 acres) and the remainder cultivated by tenants or sharecroppers (average of ten croppers with 39 acres each)," explains Wesley Allen Riddle, adding "Sharecropping spelled the end of plantation economies and transformed the organic plantations into so many small farms and independent production units."[52] The railroad became the other industry at the end of Southern plantation slavery where Black men could find work, an act that established the public perception that Black men also belonged in service to a White public.

The American railways had been financed through bonds from abroad before the Civil War but after its end, large increases in domestic capital investments increased the rail lines from three miles in 1828 to 23,476 miles in 1860, 30,283 miles in 1870, and over 50,000 miles in 1880.[53] On the rails, part of the "civilizing mission" was to create an experience for White passengers that reinforced their supposed superiority not only over the landscape but any peoples who stood in opposition to that expansion. In addition to sharecropping, the arrival of *Black* minstrelsy coincided with the Sleeping Car Pullman service, named after American industrialist George Pullman (1831–97), who introduced the sleeping car to model the relations of slavery in which Black men performed the role of servant and all-round helper. Pullman's model was eventually adopted by all major railway companies across North America. On the rails, the Pullman Palace Car Company ushered in a new era in Black servitude. As the railroad sleeping car was the exclusive domain of Black men, their presence reminded rich White passengers of a bygone antebellum era of slavery. The limited opportunities for Black men in the decades after the end of the Civil War had much to do with public perception during this era.

In April 1854, when the Great Western Railway declared that it urgently needed eight hundred workers to guard its tracks against stray cattle and hog crossings, it placed an advertisement in Canada's most important Black newspaper, the *Provincial Freeman*, alerting readers that it was seeking Black workers for the task.[54] This was the first glimpse of the Canadian railroad's preference for Black male labour on the rails. Beginning in August 1870, the Pullman Palace Car Company introduced sleeping cars to Canada. The first of these Canadian sleepers—the "Portland," "Montreal," "Toronto," and "Quebec"—were built in Montreal's Pointe St. Charles shop.[55] The late 1860s marked the moment when Canada became a sovereign nation, and the image-making that coincided with the expansion of the railway into the western provinces also began at that same time. The initial railway line (1,600 kilometres longer than the first American transcontinental rail) represented an enormous expenditure for a nation that was only 3.5 million people in 1871, compared to the American population that was just shy of thirty-nine million people.[56] Thus, there were many ways the railroad recreated a master-slave relationship wherein White male workers in an industrializing North, forced to compete with an entirely new group of paid workers, felt betrayed by the outcome of the Civil War. As David Roediger writes, race rebellions that anticipated emancipation "expressed white workers' fears of job competition even in cities where it was highly unlikely that an exodus of freed people would quickly swell the population."[57] In cities like Brooklyn, New York City, and Cincinnati, but also Chicago, Detroit, Boston, and St. Paul, Minnesota, even before the end of the Civil War there were a series of pre-emancipation hate strikes against Black employment and physical attacks on Black workers by their White counterparts.[58]

Importantly, the railroad had played a significant role in the project of nation-building. In this system, White, Anglo-Saxon Protestants—many of whom considered themselves "old stock" second- or third-generation Canadians—established the nation's rail companies, institutions, banks, and publishing houses while racialized others were relegated to low-paying, dirty, physically demanding jobs like shoe-shiner, bellhop, cook, cleaner, and railway porter.[59] The new American union had to contend with millions of emancipated African Americans who would be competing with "old stock" Americans and newly arrived Western European immigrants for jobs. Where before the Civil War the Democratic Party had coalesced around a set of antipathies and principles that emphasized expansion (nationalism), anti-monopoly (egalitarianism), and White supremacy after the war's end, a new era of vast economic development and industrial expansion began.[60] This era witnessed the growth of industry in the northeast, agricultural growth in the middle west, the emergence of a cattle industry in the plains, expanded mining enterprises in the Rockies, and a more developed pacific coast. The South, on the other hand, entered a period of Reconstruction (1865–77).

While the modern Republican Party began when Abraham Lincoln "freed" African Americans from slavery, Southern Black residents were abandoned most pronouncedly when Reconstruction abruptly ended in 1877, once again disenfranchising a formerly enslaved Black population. The Compromise of 1877, as it became known, legislated the withdrawal of the federal government's commitment to fully enfranchise and emancipate all freed persons. After the 1877 election, Republican President Rutherford B. Hayes (serving until 1881) reached an agreement with Southern Democrats to leave the South alone so it could govern itself accordingly. Hayes made a deal with the Democrats to eliminate all Reconstruction protections for Black Americans. The rollback of Black rights and freedoms did not happen because of the actions of one person; it was the result of the unanimous efforts of Hayes, the US Congress, and the Supreme Court, which formally ratified *national* White consensus in the Compromise of 1877, granting White Southerners the right to reduce Black Southerners to a state of legislated subordination.[61] The Freedman's Bureau, which had also employed former Union soldiers to redistribute land, built schools for formerly enslaved Black Americans and mobilized Republican voters in support of continued emancipation efforts, it was also abruptly ended. At the same time, Southern Democrats remained steadfast in their desire to "mobilize hostile southern whites, including returning Confederates, to restore the previous order."[62]

In this new era, protecting the rights of White male workers consumed the nation's political efforts. Labour relations took the form of White Southerners embracing Northern industrialization while establishing a "Lost Cause" movement, led by vigilante groups such as the Klan, who viewed their terrorism against Black Americans as a necessary and redemptive act meant to restore the Confederacy but also reframe the White Southern fight in the Civil War not as a loss, but a "noble" and heroic attempt to protect their way of life. As the embodiment of the Lost Cause, the Klan became a pseudo-military force that essentially served the interests of the Democratic Party, the former planter class, and all those who desired a restoration of White supremacy as the dominant force controlling all aspects of African American life, including labour, and the restoration of a system of racial subordination in every aspect of Southern life.[63]

At the same time, Northern industrialists made little direct use of Black labour in manufacturing jobs, relying on (and welcoming with open arms) White immigrants from Western Europe, while Southern industrialists refused to hire Black men outright in developing textile and commodity industries, instead preferring to keep them relegated to working on the same cotton, tobacco, and rice plantations as their ancestors had.[64] Significantly, when Pullman's Sleeping Car expanded into Canada in the 1880s, Canadian railway promoters did not change anything about the service for its liners. As Sarah-Jane Mathieu writes, "Pullman's sleeping cars encapsulated a gendered and racialized mobile beau ideal in which rich, civilized white men were served by black men doing women's work, thereby reinforcing black manhood's incompleteness."[65] She notes further that "within Pullman's sleepers, black manhood posed no threat to white civilization, since porters, uniformly called 'George,' were most often stripped of their individual identities."[66] This period after the Civil War, bookended with the expansion of the Pullman Sleeping Car service in 1865 and the Compromise of 1877, ushered in a new continental economic system that would be reserved for White workers; Black workers were relegated to dirty, low-paying jobs, except for in the railway, theatre, or as singers on stage. Black immigration to Canada and the building of large-scale theatres also greatly impacted the expansion of *Black* minstrelsy and railway travel.

Minstrel clowns and menageries found an audience in cities and towns where there was either a small Black population or no Black residents at all. Between 1861 and 1871, most estimates have the Black population decreasing by about 20 percent in Canada West, remaining a fraction of the White population; rampant anti-Blackness also helped create the conditions for travelling minstrel shows to thrive during the same period.[67] If slavery is imagined not purely as a system of capital bound by place (i.e., disparate labouring sites on leeward islands or isolated, inland plantations) but as a transatlantic capitalist system of exchange wherein White planter classes in the Caribbean, for instance, invested in sugar cane production but also kept relations with businessmen in the Atlantic colonies, or a Southern planter class that produced cotton and tobacco, these two disparate regions helped to fund British and Canadian investments in cotton mills and other forms of industrial production. Cotton production was the dominant commodity (in addition to tobacco) in the nineteenth century, and Canadians, like the British, were deeply invested in its production. In Montreal from 1861 until 1865, "the city was alive with refugees, soldiers-of-fortune, blockade-runners, US army recruiters ('crimps'), and spies; all of them afloat on a sea of illicit money flowing from Confederate bank accounts, cotton trading, blockade running, and the sale of arms, food, and equipment."[68]

As Sven Beckert writes, "when cotton manufacturing exploded in Great Britain [in the late eighteenth century], it was unclear where enough cotton would come from to feed its hungry factories. Yet despite these challenges, never before had an industry grown so large so fast. Indeed, it grew as large as it did, as fast as it did, not despite but because of its peculiar spatial arrangements and its ability to draw on slave labor."[69] For example, in 1857 British economist John T. Danson published an article on the history of the modern cotton textile industry where he noted that "there is not, and never has been, any considerable source of supply for cotton, excepting the East-Indies, which is not obviously and exclusively maintained by slave-labour."[70] Efforts to cultivate cotton with free labour had largely failed, he observed further, concluding that "as far as yet appears, [cotton] must continue to be grown, chiefly by slave-labour." The connection between slave labour in the US and a prospering European cotton industry was such that in Danson's opinion, "any proceedings for modifying the existing system of slave-labour ...[was] superfluous to say one word."[71] Despite their disinvestment from slave labour, Britain maintained its symbiotic relationship with American slave labour as one of its most important benefactors. "All the way to the Civil War, cotton and slavery would expand in lockstep, as Great Britain and the United States had become the twin hubs of the emerging empire of cotton," writes Beckert further.[72]

Additionally, in this milieu, a transatlantic print and visual culture produced narratives about Black people as ignorant, lazy, childlike, dependent, and immoral. In Hamilton, billboard advertisements depicting grotesque Black faces and bodies incensed the Black community. According to Adrienne Shadd's findings, by October 1866, the community had had enough. "Seventy-two people signed a petition to force city council to enact a bylaw that would refuse to grant licenses to any shows or exhibitions that represented the Black race in such a demeaning manner. A few went a step further. They whitewashed over the signs, causing the proprietors of the show to threaten legal action,"[73] she writes. Hamilton's mayor took the same position as Toronto's mayors twenty years before, arguing that local authorities had no power to restrict advertising as they did not feel it crossed the decency and morality line. While minstrelsy was more entrenched in larger cities, the size of the Black population did not matter; if the Black community was sizable enough to engender a culture of exclusion among Whites, the shows tended to thrive.

Into the early 1860s, minstrel shows in Canada West remained primarily circus acts and menageries featuring Jim Crow characters; additionally, Tom Shows and other blackface acts toured the region. The City of Kingston, the region's first capital (located midway between Toronto and Montreal), boasted a population of 15,000 by 1869, and was on the itinerary of the most renowned minstrel companies, including Duprez and Green, Cool Burgess, Jack (J.H.) Haverly (1837–1901), and Sam Sharpley (1831–75), whose Ethiopian Burlesque Troupe often performed "melodies, jokes, witticisms, and Shakespearian readings," in what advertisements called "illustrations of Dark Dandyism."[74] In July 1862, an advertisement in the "Amusements" section of Toronto's *Daily Globe* promoted, "the largest exhibition in the world consisting of a grand consolidation of FIVE DISTINCT EXHIBITIONS" featuring hippopotamuses, elephants, and horses as part of a circus that had travelled to the city from New York, St. Louis, Boston, and London.[75] Included in the act was "THREE GREAT CLOWNS: WM. KENNEDY, GARRY DEMOTT, AND L.N. BURKE. THE EDUCATED MULES. JIM CROW, AND DAN TUCKER." Importantly, "Old Dan Tucker" (like T.D Rice's "Jump Jim Crow" and George Washington Dixon's "My Long Tail Blue," and "Coal Black Rose") was a song from minstrelsy's first phase that remained popular into the 1860s. Written by Dan Emmett of the Virginia Minstrels, "Old Dan Tucker" emphasized wit and melody, performed comically, and these performances would have, as Eric Lott explains, "consisted mainly of ensemble songs interspersed with solo banjo songs, and were strung together with witticisms, ripostes, shouts, puns, and other attempts at black impersonation."[76] The song described the "ups and downs of Negro life," writes Bob Carlin, pointing to lyrics: *Tucker is a nice old man/He use to ride our darby ram/He sent him whizzen down de hill/If he had'nt got up he'd lay dar still.*[77] These song were designed to display specific behavioural traits characteristic of the various male stereotypes that dominated minstrelsy's first decades.[78]

In 1830, when Rice sang and danced Jim Crow for the first time, he presented the character's tricksterism and foolery as though it were an "authentic" imitation of Black life; but what he also did, as Benjamin Miller observes, was pit two blackface characters against one another. "While Dixon had success with 'My Long Tail Blue,' Rice began composing a song and dance about Jim Crow to which Dixon would respond in turn. Rice's 'Jim Crow' displayed a particular brand of animosity toward black dandies that would become a feature of blackface performance for decades to come."[79] These two dueling figures—Jim Crow, the Southern plantation slave with exaggerated physical characteristics (woolly hair, grotesquely large feet, big lips), and his utter lack of urban sophistication versus Zip Coon, a Northern freedman, a so-called "black dandy" from the city who dressed in high hat, yellow waistcoat, light-coloured breeches, and fashionable swallowtail coat, carried a watch, wore jewelry, and appeared to have a high fashion sense of style—attracted working-class audiences because "their acts drew on racial and class hostilities."[80] Where Zip Coon literally embodied the amalgamationist threat of abolitionism, and allegorically represented the class threat of those who were advocating for it,[81] Jim Crow represented an investment in racial caricature as political material for he was meant to depict Black men as inferior and contented in their servitude—a positionality that had long-held resonance across the blackface Atlantic.

In her study of minstrel shows in Canada, Lorraine Le Camp located a performance by Bob Welch's Minstrel, Burlesque Opera Troupe, and Brass Band in Perth, Ontario in 1866.[82] This represents one of the first minstrel performances in Perth, which might seem an unlikely place for blackface given there is little documented Black history in the city, but considering Perth, along with dozens of other Canada West towns, formed part of the George F. Bailey (1818–1903) circus tour because there existed a public demand for not only animal displays but side shows, carnival elements, and blackface performers, such documented performances make sense. In June 1867, for example, Bailey's circus visited the same towns as Lewis (L.B.) Lent's circus, which had toured throughout Ontario with headlines like "L.B. Lent's Mammoth National Circus."[83] In addition to Perth, these two circuses toured Brockville, Prescott, Ottawa, Aylmer, Kingston, Napanee, Belleville, Trenton, Percy, Cobourg, Port Hope, Bowmanville, Port Perry, Whitby, and Markham in June; and Brampton, Guelph, Berlin, Stratford, St. Marys, Woodstock, Paris, Galt, Dundas, Hamilton, Caledonia, St. Catharines, Brantford, Simcoe, St. Thomas, London, and Chatham.[84] This extensive tour was made possible due to expanded rail service throughout the region. In 1859, the Brockville and Ottawa Railway was built in Perth, and with the connection having been made in 1884 west to Toronto on the Ontario and Quebec Railway, a new station would replace the original in 1886.[85]

Through the 1860s and 1870s, Burgess also toured Ontario extensively, returning to most cities and towns every year.[86] In addition to Burgess's Prendergast, Hughes and Donniker Minstrels, the Campbell Minstrels, Cooper's Negro Minstrels, Rivers' Melodeon Troupe of Ethiopian Delineators, Turner and Davis's Minstrels, Duprez and Green's Minstrels, Charley Shay's Quincuplexal Company, and the Morris Minstrels' Cork Opera all toured Canada West with great success into the 1860s.[87] In 1863, Wood's Minstrels played Fredericton, New Brunswick's Masonic Hall, which suggests that American performers brought their act to the Maritimes during the decade; Wood's Minstrels had performed in Montreal just two years prior, and Skiff & Gaylord's Minstrels would appear at Saint John's Mechanics' Institute in 1867.[88] The troupe, organized in Philadelphia in November 1864 by Johnny Steele, was composed of William H. Delehanty (1846–80), an Irish American songwriter who made his first appearance on stage in 1860 before joining Skiff & Gaylord's Minstrels in 1862.[89] Sam Hague also travelled with Skiff & Gaylord's Minstrels.[90]

Despite the lack of reliable records that allow the growth of the Black community in PEI to be tracked, Richard Reid asserts that "the House of Assembly had legally recognized slavery on the island as early as 1781, and some Loyalists who arrived in 1784 brought their slaves with them. Nevertheless, until the island repealed slavery in 1825, it was ill defined there, as it was in the other colonies."[91] Importantly, most Black people in PEI concentrated in a part of Charlottetown, a city that was formerly established in 1855; according to the 1881 census, the province had only 181 reported Black residents.[92] And yet, Le Camp located two blackface performances in Charlottetown in 1863 from the Snowball Minstrels (in June) and Whitney's Minstrels (in August) at unknown venues.[93] From the fall of 1868, the New Orleans Minstrels continued to tour, performing in Montreal and travelling through Ontario, Michigan, upstate New York, Connecticut, Rhode Island, and Massachusetts, in addition to tours of the South and Midwest.[94] J.M.S. Careless found that "'European' circuses with sets of trained lions and a host of glittering attractions were [also] bringing in the town crowds."[95] In Victoria, British Columbia, The Amateur Dramatic Association of Victoria (A.D.A.V.) opened in 1862 by "a number of prominent gentlemen...with His Excellency Governor James Douglas (becoming) the official patron of the association."[96] The city's Theatre Royal (1861–84) became the primary venue for amateur musical concerts, dramas, and fundraisers, and when the A.D.A.V. performed there, their repertoire included putting on plays or skits that were "usually interlarded with songs, glees and sometimes, negro minstrelsy."[97] In pre-Confederation Canada, minstrelsy was just as commonplace as it was in America, Britain, and beyond. While it is true that on the eve of the Civil War the Black population in the Maritimes was less than 10,000, a small fraction of the 663,000 who lived there,[98] in places like Nova Scotia, with a Black population that was four to five times that of New Brunswick, minstrel shows still appeared in New Brunswick and PEI as they did in Canada West and East in the 1860s.

In the next chapter, *Black* minstrelsy's continued growth into the 1870s and 1880s (and how it arguably became the most liberatory industry in post-slavery North America, offering Black men opportunities to labour off the plantation), even though many of these acts were like those of White minstrels, a mimicry of the Southern plantation, is explained. As noted, one significant factor that distinguished *Black* minstrels from White minstrels was that the former really had been enslaved, and thus in their acts, as Taylor and Austen write, they "underlined their 'authenticity,' which was one of the major bases of their appeal to White audiences."[99] As public desire for vignettes of the *new* plantation (a vignette that ignored the realities of Black sharecroppers and the working conditions of Pullman

Sleeping Car porters on the transcontinental railways) was curated with scenes and songs that crisscrossed North America and the Atlantic, the theatrical stage was increasingly integrated. Under the proprietorship of the "big three" White managers of *Black* minstrelsy—Sam Hague, Charles Callender, and J.H. Haverly—a new chapter in the American story was written on the stage.

At the same time in Canada, on October 21, 1880, with bipartisan support, the government signed a contract with the Canadian Pacific Railway (CPR) to begin construction on a national railway. Beginning in 1881 and ending with the "last spike" on November 7, 1885, the first passenger train departed Montreal in June 1886, arriving in Port Moody, British Columbia on July 4 that year. The CPR linked British Columbia with Montreal.[100] In so doing, cities like Toronto and Montreal became ideal destinations for "big-time" American minstrel theatre while the Maritime provinces

4.1 Photograph of the Fisk Jubilee Singers, 1875, NPG.2002.92, National Portrait Gallery, Smithsonian Institution.

of New Brunswick and Nova Scotia remained destinations for touring companies that crossed the American–Canadian border. After British Columbia's Fraser Canyon Gold Rush, a flood of prospectors, primarily from America, and travelling minstrel performers looking to profit from entertaining the would-be-gold miners, headed west.[101] As Canada became a sovereign nation, larger, more extravagant theatres were built. *Black* minstrelsy might have thrived leading up to Confederation but by the 1880s, the Fisk Jubilee Singers (see figure 4.1), an a cappella choral group founded at Fisk University in Nashville, Tennessee in 1871, also headed north; with their arrival, multiple Canadian jubilee groups would hit stages around the world. As these men and women sang songs of freedom, they challenged audiences to imagine a different representation of Blackness—that of the *free* Black person not plucked from slavery.[102]

5

THE *NEW* PLANTATION MINSTRELSY, BLACKFACE POLITICAL CARTOONS, AND CHORAL SONGS OF FREEDOM, 1867-86

With the passage of the British North America (BNA) Act, which brought the Dominion of Canada officially into being on July 1, 1867, the Confederation of four BNA colonies (Ontario, Quebec, Nova Scotia, and New Brunswick—British Columbia joined in 1871) officially created the country of Canada. It also initiated a growth spurt in cultural and political nationalism. The generation that came to maturity in the wake of Confederation saw "the possibility, even the necessity, of going beyond the deal-making of politicians to give the new nation a distinct culture," writes Jonathan Vance.[1] By the late 1860s, a colour line had been established in Canada, identifying all people of African descent as members of a specified class and setting them apart from the dominant culture, which was majority composed of White, English-speaking Anglo-Saxon Protestants and Irish Catholics. Customs rather than laws upheld this de facto colour line. Furthermore, debates had been ongoing in the years leading up to Confederation, reaching their peak in 1864 at the Charlottetown Conference (organized by delegates from New Brunswick,

Nova Scotia and PEI, which aimed to discuss the union of their three provinces); at the Quebec Conference (also in 1864, which helped to create the country's first constitution); and at the London Conference in 1867 (a meeting that finalized the constitutional details of Confederation).[2] Unlike south of the border where a Civil War had to be fought to establish the unification of the federal government, Confederation was in essence an administrative accomplishment; as Daniel Francis explains, it represented "a practical solution to a political problem, not an expression of some great principle.... According to the imperialist view, Confederation did not imply any loosening of the tie with the Mother Country. The new arrangement was another signpost on the road to self-government, but Britain continued to retain ultimate responsibility for foreign relations and constitutional matters."[3]

All the institutions that formed in the decades after Confederation—the NWMP (Mounties), the transcontinental railway, and the mythology of the North—came to embody important cultural values. During its early years, for example, the NWMP acted as arresting officers, judge, and jury, imposing order from the top down, and while mythologized as "western nation-builders" and "protectors of our lands," they were created for similar reasons as the Texas Rangers, which were created to "specifically address the pressing 'native question' confronting Texas...among the few places where bison still roamed after 1870."[4] The Texas Rangers had played a pivotal role during the US-Mexican War (1846–48). In the 1860s and 1870s, they renewed their mission to "drive Native Americans from within the borders of the state beyond the reach of the resources on which their survival depended," writes Andrew Graybill, adding "the Rangers killed half as many Indians as the federal troops did over the same period [between 1865 and 1881]."[5] The building of the CPR also represented a clearing of Indigenous people from their land. As James Daschuk notes, "Acquisition of the west by the Dominion of Canada in December 1869 brought unprecedented changes to inhabitants of the plains. Within a decade, the bison would be gone, and the people who had depended on them would be marginalized by a new political and economic reality."[6] Daschuk writes further, "Management of the increasingly serious food situation and Indian affairs generally shifted from a position of 'relative ignorance' under the Liberals to one of outright malevolence during the

Macdonald regime," he says, adding "'Pacification' of the plains Indians was an integral, if not always explicit, component of the Tory government's program of development. To ensure that the west would be ready for the Canadian Pacific Railway and settlement, Macdonald himself became superintendent general of Indian affairs."[7]

Significantly, the expansion of the West was a huge economic risk for the Canadian government. "The railway preceded settlement, it did not follow it, which meant that once it was completed, there was no one to ride on it," notes Francis.[8] At the same time, as Sarah-Jane Mathieu observes, "Canadians romanticized and co-opted the arduous construction of their transcontinental line into an ethos of survival and national identity, fashioning it into Canada's 'national dream.'" Mathieu writes further that "Advocates of Confederation in the East argued that a national railway line would be a powerful homogenizing national force. They maintained that if the line reached British Columbia, the Prairies would remain under the Union Jack."[9] Much of the uproar over the railway centred on creating an industry that rivalled the American railway, but part of the task of reshaping Canada into a modern technological force involved cultivating an image of having conquered the West. As Canada's modernizing artery, the CPR promised to populate the vast western provinces with "sound European stock," to save British Columbia from a perceived "perilous proximity to Asia," to rescue the Prairies from its "rebellious Indigenous peoples," and to centralize British-style political power in the East."[10] To achieve this modern myth of the West, Canada had to overcome the challenge of ensuring the CPR turned a profit; to do this, the company first developed an immigration campaign for the Prairies that encouraged White settlement, and second it convinced travellers from across the country and abroad that western Canada, particularly the Rocky Mountains, were attractive tourist destinations.[11]

This modernization coincided with organized mythmaking about the North, which provided an identifier for Canadianness that was not just about a place; it represented a promise and a destiny that was made manifest in the short-lived but influential group of young White writers and intellectuals who called themselves "Canada First." When this group formally met in Ottawa in 1868, they realized their shared desire to articulate what Francis has called the "new nationality" they hoped would take shape in

Canada, a nationality which "imparted to the people living [in its northern climate] a strength of character shared by other circumpolar 'races.'"[12] While Canada First did not last long, what the organized movement solidified was that the North was for White people of European descent with supposedly "innate" traits such as self-reliance, physical strength, stamina, and virility that set them apart as a distinct group; this fabricated form of natural selection was reinforced with the lyrics, "true North, strong and free" that became part of "Chant national" ("O Canada"), a song about Canada—sort of.[13]

Initially written in 1880 as a new national song for Quebec composed by Calixa Lavallée with French lyrics by Quebec City Superior Court judge Adolphe-Basile Routhier (1838–1920), 6,000 copies of "Chant national" were printed by musician and music publisher, Arthur Lavigne (1845–1925).[14] "L.-N. Dufresne signed the first edition, illustrating the cover with a portrait of the lieutenant-governor surrounded by such symbols of French-speaking Canada as the maple tree, the Saint Lawrence River, and the ubiquitous beaver," writes Christopher Brian Thompson.[15] The song made its debut at Quebec City's Pavillon des Patineurs on June 24, 1880 becoming a hit with both French and English Canadians (although the official English lyrics were not adopted until 1980 when a parliamentary committee revised Robert Weir's 1908 lyrics).[16] The fact that a former blackface minstrel performer composed "Chant national" in the context of nineteenth-century Quebec is significant. Blackface minstrel shows frequently toured there from the 1860s onward, but as noted, Lavallée performed in these shows in the US. There is no way to know if he made any connection between the racial caricatures he peddled with Duprez's New Orleans Minstrels and Black people who lived in Quebec, but as Duprez's company made a point to hire French-speaking performers like Lavallée—to keep the connection to francophone Louisiana—and they performed across the South, along the Mississippi River, and to New Orleans and Montreal and back, he would have been exposed to the deprivations facing Black Americans in the North and South.

Significantly, New Orleans was unlike any other city in antebellum America. With a population divided among Anglo-Americans, Europeans, free Black people, and those who were enslaved, it was among the most cosmopolitan cities anywhere. Before the Civil War, free Black people and those of mixed ancestry (known as Creoles of Colour), and enslaved

Black people were spatially, politically, and geographically segregated but they comingled in the city's saloons, public squares, and most theatrical events. This living arrangement was fundamentally changed during and after Reconstruction when a racial line was ardently enforced, placing all Black people (including Creoles of Colour) under what Lerone Bennett, Jr. once described as "not a regional but a *national* system of subordination. The system was created in the South by Southerners, but it could not have survived without a national white consensus on the role and status of Southern black workers."[17] Lavallée would have witnessed this two-tiered system first-hand. But what he likely would not have paid attention to is how a similar de facto system existed in Quebec. As Dorothy Williams's *Road to Now: A History of Blacks in Montreal* (1997) explains, Black people lived in Montreal as early as the seventeenth century, and yet, "there is little evidence that they exerted any socio-economic or political influence."[18] There was some official immigration to Quebec, but there was likely much more clandestine immigration and intraregional movement. As such, it is uncertain what the Black population size was in Quebec prior to when census records became more reliable after Confederation in 1867 when Quebec City became the "national capital" and home of the provincial legislature.[19] Given the well-documented histories of Black settlement in Upper Canada and Canada West from at least the 1820s through 1860s, Black presence in nineteenth-century Quebec is a grossly understudied and needs much more attention.

At the same time, starting in 1871 through to the end of the century, the Canadian government made immigration a priority, attracting almost one and a half million new residents from Britain, central and eastern Europe, and the US; Black and Chinese immigrants, on the other hand, faced considerable hostility and the Canadian government ultimately took steps to restrict their numbers. The Quebec government focused its efforts on keeping its population at home rather than attracting newcomers.[20] Thus, by the late nineteenth century French Canada had developed a distinct culture and the "real" Quebec was, for many English Canadians, represented by "the rural French Canadians, the *habitants*."[21] This notion became a stereotype of French Canada that circulated the print-visual culture of politics, and from late 1870s onward it was one of many other racial stereotypes that included Black people and stereotypes of Irish, Chinese, and Jewish immigrants that were depicted in the pages of English-language political magazines.

This chapter examines the popularity of blackface minstrelsy across the newly formed Canadian dominion after Confederation. It contends with the sociocultural changes that happened post-1867, and how emergence of Black choral singing offered a different viewpoint on the Black experience in the aftermath of the end of American plantation slavery, but also the dispossession, removal, and extermination of Indigenous people from their lands. Between Confederation and the late 1880s, Canada witnessed a rapid modernization, urbanization, and industrialization that coincided with the railroads becoming the chief employer of Black men, both Canadian-born and emigrants from the US and beyond. The CPR not only had a profound effect on the settlement of the Prairies, including in cities from Winnipeg to Vancouver that became heavily dependent on the railway, but it also linked large cities to smaller towns that were "strung out along the railway like beads on a string."[22] The nation's viability was essentially hedged on the CPR, which was framed as not only key to building a national economy but also a national culture. Despite hostility toward Black immigration, Black people lived in cities and towns across the country by the time of Confederation. In British Columbia, Black people who had been living there since the Fraser Canyon Gold Rush had, after almost a half a century's contribution to the province, gained little more than tolerance from White residents. By the last years of the nineteenth century, Black immigration to the province continued but it did not do much to change what Crawford Kilian describes as the community's "shrinking minority" status.[23] Like most Canadian cities in the nineteenth century, Victoria had relied on travelling theatrical troupes for its entertainment culture. White Euro-Canadian settlers, townspeople, miners, and labourers who resided there welcomed the production of live shows in their communities by groups of travelling entertainers as a brief relief from their daily hardships; they were highly entertained by the rough and tumble, lowbrow comedy which blackface minstrel shows were based.[24] Even Shakespeare's *Macbeth* was performed in the Victoria Theatre and the entire production had a kind of "Monty-Python-esque charm about it," observes Jonathan Vance, adding that "the set was a cotton plantation being reused from a previous show."[25]

As American themes became part of the theatrical culture of Western Canada, "the shows likely involved the same repertoire that Ricketts and Durang gave to eager Montrealers [a decade earlier]: jugglers, magicians, gymnasts, acrobats, dialecticians, singers, dancers, monologuists, and minstrel shows with blackface performers whose materials parodied the singing and dancing of slaves."[26] Importantly, when the CPR launched an advertising campaign to "fill in the middle," as Laura Detre explains, it aimed to lure "prosperous, white, family farmers."[27] These immigrants began to arrive on the Prairies in the 1870s, and this migration helped to construct a Western society envisioned by Canadian officials—one that excluded Indigenous Peoples, Black immigrants, and by the 1880s, Chinese people. Between 1881 and 1884, more than 17,000 Chinese men arrived to work on the CPR, ten thousand of them arriving on chartered ships straight from China; this immigrant group was never given the opportunity to become citizens like the Scottish, Irish, and British labourers who had arrived in Canada a generation before.[28] For example, British Columbia Premier George Walkem (serving from 1874–76 and 1878–82) was elected for a second term on the promise of introducing a Chinese Tax Act to help keep the province White.[29] That was followed by the federal government's implementation of the Chinese Head Tax in 1885, which imposed a fifty-dollar fee on every Chinese man who wanted to enter Canada, marking a period of several discriminatory legal measures passed against Chinese immigrants until 1923 when the Canadian government enacted an outright ban on all Chinese immigration.[30]

This discussion of Chinese immigration is significant to the expansion of theatre in the nineteenth century. By the end of the decade, one of the first theatrical shows about Chinese people appeared on Broadway; *A Trip to Chinatown*, written by American dramatist and playwright Charles Hale Hoyt (1859–1900) appeared at the Madison Square Theater in 1892. Set in San Francisco, it was a musical centred on a group of White people venturing into Chinatown, a relatively new phenomenon in the 1890s, which became a site that both ignited fascination and fear among White communities. The Chinese community in California had grown because many men worked as labourers and miners in the gold rush of 1849; some of these labourers subsequently headed north during the Fraser Canyon Gold Rush in 1858, and a further wave of immigration occurred when men were brought in from China to work on the CPR. By the 1890s, many Chinese workers were dismissed, and most eventually moved to Calgary, Moose Jaw, Winnipeg, Montreal, Toronto, and even St. John, forming a large reservoir of cheap labour that placed them in potential or actual competition with White residents.[31] As news spread across the country of Chinese immigrants, who made up over 40 percent of the non-Indigenous mainland population in British Columbia at Confederation, stories about them would have appealed to White audiences. As an example, after its Broadway run, Hoyt's *A Trip to Chinatown* subsequently appeared at London, Ontario's Grand Opera House in 1894 and toured other cities across the region.[32] Opened on September 8, 1881, the Opera House sat on the northwest corner of Richmond and King Streets. It eclipsed the city's Mechanics' Institute, providing the first proper theatre in town. With its 1,228-seats and French Renaissance-style auditorium, rooted by an elaborately dormered attic and the building exteriors made primarily of red pressed brick, the lavish theatre was embellished with illuminated tile belts and with band coursing and window labels of Ohio stone.[33]

Enakshi Dua poignantly observes that "despite its claim to whiteness, at Confederation (1867), Canada was far from 'a white man's country,' as it had substantial numbers of Aboriginal, Asian and Black residents."[34] This milieu ultimately meant that when European settlers arrived and the "settler colony" became a nation, another part of the Canadian national story began to be told that did not include everyone. As Sherene Razack describes, it is "the story of the 'empty land' developed by hardy and enterprising European settlers. In our national anthem, Canadians sing about Canada as the 'True North Strong and Free'...the imagined rugged independence and self-reliance of the European settlers are qualities that are considered to give birth to greater commitment to liberty and democracy."[35] This chapter probes how blackface minstrel shows were some of the first forms of culture early White settlers produced on the Prairies, as well as in Ontario, Quebec, and the Maritimes. During British Columbia's Gold Rush, blackface minstrel shows entertained White miners, and shortly after landing in the Prairies, the Mounted Police produced their own minstrel shows, all before American minstrel troupes appeared on theatrical stages in Manitoba in 1873, Saskatchewan in 1882, and in Alberta by 1896.[36] The cultural milieu of the 1870s and 1880s is vital to understanding what Canada was like when the first documented *Black* minstrels, using "Georgia" as part of their name, appeared in 1868 at Saint John's Mechanics' Institute and Fredericton's Temperance Hall.[37]

By the 1880s, Black choral singing, which had largely taken place in churches, also began to appear at newly built concert and performance halls. The first and most prominent of these choirs was the Fisk Jubilee Singers, who started out on a small fundraising tour for their school in 1871. Fisk University was founded as the Fisk Free Colored School on January 9, 1866 during Reconstruction just shortly after the end of the Civil War. Almost immediately, the Fisk Jubilee Singers rose to international prominence, even performing before Queen Victoria of England, as well as at the White House for President Ulysses S. Grant; their success also included multiple tours of Canada.[38] As John Frick explains "it was a group of freed slaves at Fisk University, originally known as the Colored Christian Choir, that initiated the trend.... In an attempt to inspire the company of nine performers, the group's leader, George L. White, renamed them the Jubilee Singers, a biblical reference to the year of Jubilee (the year all the slaves would be freed) mentioned in the Book of Leviticus."[39] As Black men, and later women, donned blackface to perform scenes and vignettes that reproduced the plantation South in minstrelsy, jubilee singers, as an educated class of Black performers, created a new genre of musical performance—Negro spirituals. In his 1903 canonical text *The Souls of Black Folk*, the great African American intellectual W.E.B. Du Bois called the songs of the Fisk Jubilee "Sorrow Songs," noting that "through all the sorrow of the Sorrow Songs there breathes a hope—a faith in the ultimate justice of things. The minor cadences of despair change often to triumph and calm confidence. Sometimes it is faith in life, sometimes a faith in death, sometimes assurance of boundless justice in some fair world beyond. But whichever it is, the meaning is always clear: that sometime, somewhere, men will judge men by their souls and not by their skins."[40]

The Fisk Jubilee Singers' success quickly spread to other newly formed Southern Black colleges such as The Hampton Institute, founded in 1868 as Hampton Agricultural and Industrial School in Hampton, Virginia. Students formed their own jubilee ensemble, the Hampton Jubilee Singers, which also toured North America to raise money for their school; in June 1874, they performed at Toronto's Music Hall.[41] In February 1877, a group billed as the Original Nashville Coloured Jubilee Singers performed at Toronto's Royal Opera House, and on April 27 that same year, another jubilee group sang at the Grand Opera House.[42] The Jubilee's spirituals were literal songs about their lives not performed to singularly entertain White audiences but also to impart hope into their lives, especially as some of these African Americans had either been formerly enslaved or the first of their families to be born free. As choral singing brought a new image of Black life to Canada and beyond, the racial stereotypes of *Black* and White minstrelsy became more aggrandized, almost as a response to jubilee singing. These two genres of Black performance circulated the Atlantic world as a representational bifurcation of Black life.

In Ontario by 1871, 20 percent of the province's population consisted of urban residents, and by 1891 they represented 35 percent of its more than two million inhabitants.[43] Hamilton's population rose from 26,000 to 49,000 in the same period, London's from 16,000 to 32,000, and Ottawa's from 21,000 to 44,000; meanwhile Toronto had grown more than threefold, from 56,000 to 181,000.[44] Ontario was a staunchly Anglo-Saxon Protestant province with a long-standing sentimentality for the antebellum South. As sectors of nation-building developed, especially publishing and culture industries, this sentimentality helped drive the kinds of entertainments that were brought to cities like Toronto, Hamilton, London, and Ottawa. It was also one factor in the building of larger theatre houses, which became a feature of the period, along with music pavilions and performance halls such that by the 1880s, cities like London, Hamilton, and Ottawa each had an opera house, and there were two in Toronto.[45] Ottawa had three public theatres: Her Majesty's Theatre (built in 1854), The Rink Music Hall, Gowan's New Opera House (built in 1875), and a private house, Rideau Hall (built in 1838). London's Theatre Royal (originally named the Garrison Theatre) was built in the 1840s, but the Grand Opera House, built in 1881, was a 1,228-seat theatre on the second and third floors of a masonic temple that would eclipse the city's Theatre Royal and the Mechanics' Institute Hall, providing the city its first legitimate theatre.[46]

The Hamilton Royal Metropolitan was built in 1854, but when it burned down in 1866 it was replaced by the Grand Opera House, an auditorium with 1,169 seats.[47] The *Hamilton Spectator* once described the Grand Opera House as "This first-class theatre building, which opened in 1880...[and] constructed for $25,000. The architect George H. Lalor spared no expense on the building, which drew international stars to its stage. The Opera House attracted such crowds that it underwent several overhauls and expansions in ensuing years."[48] By the 1890s, the theatre needed repairs; after extensive renovations, the Grand Opera House reopened in 1892 with a house of 1,256 seats, and a proscenium arch surmounted by a metal sounding board, which created a technologically advanced theatre sound for its time.[49] Toronto's Grand Opera House, located on Adelaide Street, west of Yonge Street, opened to the public on September 21, 1874. It was managed by actor Charlotte Morrison (née Nickinson), John Nickinson's eldest daughter; she was married to Daniel Morrison, an ex-farmer and Toronto theatre critic for the *Daily Telegraph*, a short-lived Conservative newspaper founded by John Ross Robertson in 1866 (to 1872) after he left the *Globe*.[50] By all accounts, Morrison was one of the first woman theatre owners in Canada, and she brought in her three actress sisters while her brother managed the bookings; like her father years before, she ran her own stock company, acting in and directing many of the plays, and touring when possible.[51] According to the *Canadian Illustrated News* of August 29, 1874, the Grand Opera House had a "seating capacity of 1,323 and campstool and standing room for 500 more."[52] Importantly, by the end of the 1877–78 season salaries were not being paid and Morrison was forced to let her actors go and give up her role as manager. She was succeeded by Augustus Pitou, who had been a member of the company. The Grand Opera House would eventually decline, and on November 29, 1879 it burned down but was quickly reconstructed and reopened on February 9, 1880.[53]

Between 1874 and 1913, Toronto became home to ten large venues, making it the largest urban centre for theatre in the country. It was also home to music halls like Temperance Hall, the Mechanics' Institute, and the Music Hall, in addition to St. Lawrence Hall, the Princes of Wales Music Hall, Palmer's Concert Hall, the Agricultural Hall, and Horticultural Gardens.[54] In terms of theatres, The Royal Lyceum, long past its prime by the time it burned down in 1874 was reconstructed by a new proprietor, James French, to the designs of his architect, Wallace Hume of Chicago; thereafter, the building became known as the Royal Theatre, or the Royal Opera House.[55] That same year, The Grand Theatre (1874–1927) was erected with 1,300 seats (compared to the Lyceum's 600–700) with a big, well-designed stage, and a domed auditorium; the Grand competed for productions with the Royal Opera House until it burned down in 1883.[56] This new theatre helped make Toronto one of the foremost destinations for travelling minstrel shows, comic operas, and burlesque acts. Famed French actress Sarah Bernhardt (1844–1923) gave one of her first Canadian performances in Montreal in 1880 and later at the Grand Opera House in 1881; she returned to cities across Ontario on eight separate tours between 1887 and 1917.[57]

As theatre continued to thrive in Montreal, what also appeared were photographic depictions of minstrel performance, and other racially coded photographs, the majority of which were taken from Scottish-Canadian photographer William Notman's (1826–91) studio at 17 Bleury Street on the eastern end of Old Montreal (or as it is called today, Vieux Port de Montreal). He took thousands of images of touring minstrel acts and actors born and raised in Montreal.[58] Barry Sheehy's research located Notman as "a favorite of the Confederate community in the city. Confederate agents, commissioners, and operatives went to his studio... to have their photographs taken" and as such Notman's collection at Montreal's McCord Museum is also a reservoir of Civil War and post-Civil War images.[59] As an example of Notman's post-Civil War work, in 1875 he took a photograph titled, "James Sutherland, costumed as 'Civil Rights'" (see figure 5.1). In it, Sutherland, who is in blackface, wears a pinstriped suit and Afro wig. He is piggybacked by a mannequin wearing figure skates and dressed as Abraham Lincoln in top hat, bow tie, and pinstripe pants à la the iconographic "Uncle Sam" who first appeared during the War of 1812 as a symbol of American patriotism. The words "Civil Rights" are affixed to the Lincoln mannequin's right sleeve, and Sutherland is holding a circular object in his right hand (unfortunately the text is indiscernible due to the lighting in the image). This image represents civil rights in a way that would have suggested to White Montrealers that Black people were riding on the backs of their White counterparts to obtain their freedom.

In a wood engraving titled *Theatre Comique* (c. 1870s) by cartoonist John Henry Walker, multiple elements of a minstrel show are depicted

5.1 Photograph of "James Sutherland costumed as 'Civil Rights,'" 1875, II-15870.1
The McCord Stewart Museum, Montreal.

5.2 John Henry Walker's wood engraving "Theatre Comique," ca. 1850–85, M930.50.7.572 The McCord Stewart Museum, Montreal.

(see figure 5.2). Two *endmen* appear in the top right corner wearing shirts with elongated collars, one a top hat too small for his head, the other playing a banjo, and both depicted with exaggerated mouths. The engraving also features circus-like characters reflecting Theatre Comique's broad repertoire that included minstrelsy but also comic operas, dramas, and other forms of theatre.[60] This inverted view of slavery parallels American visual culture in the post-Reconstruction period where some paintings and sculptures depicted enslaved and semi-nude Black men exulting their emancipation by holding up broken manacles and kneeling in gratitude before godlike, formally clad White men.[61] The 1876 Emancipation Memorial in Lincoln Park, Washington, DC, for instance, depicts an elegant Lincoln standing over a kneeling and shirtless Archer Alexander, a formerly enslaved African American born into slavery around 1810 in Richmond, Virginia. These depictions intensified the problem of representing formerly enslaved Black men during the Reconstruction period. As argued in *Uncle*, "Once abolished, slavery retreated to the domain of memory. There, those collective memories had to be reckoned with in one way or another: suppressed, integrated, or romanticized. Emancipation, in effect, moved four million formerly enslaved African Americans, with their history of enslavement, into the national memory."[62] The shifting visual culture in 1870s Canada also created the conditions for *Black* minstrelsy to thrive.

Between 1866 and 1877, *Black* minstrelsy ushered in new themes and narratives. To survive as entertainers, these Black actors had to develop masks and facades that allowed White audiences to indulge their racial fantasies, while creating their own performance art whose words and actions could be differently interpreted by audiences composed of either aspiring actors or ordinary working-class people, both Black and White.[63] The presence of *Black* minstrels undoubtedly served to legitimize the racist caricature of "plantation darkies." As John Springhall writes, "lampoons of ungainly black soldiers in uniformed marching units, for example, had been occasional minstrel features since the Civil War and from the mid-1870s they became the standard finale for the first part of the black minstrel show."[64] The idea that African Americans were natural high-stepping "strutters" also painted an image of post-emancipation Blackness that, as David Krasner writes, was created as "the real was commodified in order to lead the challenge against minstrel theater."[65] Stated otherwise, given the few opportunities for Black Americans, *primitive realness* was one of the few commodities available to them. But as the stage became a form of performative authentic-inauthenticity that was not just unique to *Black* minstrelsy but was, as Yuval Taylor and Jake Austen write, a fundamental element of American entertainment, which "has always had a desire to 'keep it real,'...the black minstrel show was...more real than the white minstrel show could be."⁶⁶ As *Black* minstrelsy was billed as "authentic," even though performers were not depicting real life on the plantation as they had lived it but instead were primarily imitating how White Negro minstrel shows had depicted plantation slavery, they appealed to White audiences who had sympathized not only with Southerners but also formerly enslaved African Americans who now were thought to be depicting "real" vignettes of their formerly enslaved lives.

Significantly, it is important to recognize that Black people had been in proximity to blackface theatre almost from the start. They attended minstrel shows, and "must have laughed at...characters for some of the same reasons whites did.... In other words, audiences, black and white, could laugh down at characters who were worse off and/or more ignorant than anyone in the audience."⁶⁷ However, as Douglas A. Jones, Jr. writes, "Perhaps more than any other factor, white actors and managers barred the onstage contributions of actual African Americans, even though their performances usually took place near black communities. Black performance by black people would have subverted the mechanisms of identification and structures of (inter)racial feeling that white audiences (predominantly male) worked out for themselves in minstrelsy."⁶⁸ While Jones, Jr. writes further that "African Americans remained outside the theatrical frame, and blackface minstrelsy emerged as a performance form for, by, and about the white community,"⁶⁹ by the end of the nineteenth century, theatres began to cater to a diverse group of people, even as many theatres restricted Black patrons to the "cheap and less desirable seats up in the gallery."⁷⁰ This suggests that blackface was not singularly a racist form of entertainment that debased Black bodies, but that after the 1870s it was often *the* only mass form of entertainment available to Black people. Across the English-speaking world, *Black* and White minstrelsy was viewed by audiences who were fluent in English, which limited the extent productions could penetrate Europe, but the genre did have an impact in more distant parts of the English-speaking world.⁷¹

In South Africa, John Blair notes that blackface minstrels "who took part in Queen Victoria's Diamond Jubilee in 1887 spawned 'Coon' singers in blackface as an on-going part of the Cape Carnival. Similarly in Australia minstrels were a big hit. Theatre records from Sydney show that in the

1870s hardly a month went by without some blackface performances by British or American groups or their local imitators."[72] In Britain, Michael Pickering found that blackface minstrelsy encouraged all social classes "to think in racial categories, and to rank those categories on the basis of allegedly innate inequalities between races."[73] British audiences were not confined to young working-class males in its early days; from the outset, the genre was "cross-class and cross-gender in its popular attractions."[74] Audiences of minstrel shows in Britain accepted White minstrelsy as authentic because this "authenticity" was defined in contradiction to British cultural identity. Stated otherwise, minstrelsy in Britain—even when performed by White Britons—was interpreted as racial cross-dressing that was not created out of British culture but that had a place in a modernizing British culture. The Slave Troupe of Georgia Minstrels, which came under the management and proprietorship of Sam Hague (a White minstrel performer who left Skiff & Gaylord's Minstrels and changed the troupe's name to Sam Hague's Slave Troupe of Georgia Minstrels) toured England.[75] Hague's Slave Troupe of Georgia Minstrels was composed of twenty-six formerly enslaved African Americans who had been freed from plantation existence only a few months before their first performance in England at the Theatre Royal in Liverpool on July 9, 1866.[76] As Pickering explains further, "Hague hoped to ride the wave of interest in the slavery of the Deep South that had been regenerated by the Civil War. His ragged band, now billed as the Great American Slave Troupe, ...[had] little if any prior experience of the popular stage. They were mainly required to offer a portrait of life on the old plantation, and their only stage costume consisted of garments identical to those worn in their slavery days."[77]

Initially, *Black* minstrelsy in Canada was most popular in the Maritimes. The region had long consumed Southern nostalgia and Lost Cause justifications. In simple terms, many Maritimers were on the side of the Confederacy, and theatrical productions depicting the *new* plantation only reinforced their beliefs that slavery was right and justified. As John Boyko writes, "[in Saint John] in 1862, hundreds of folks gathered to enjoy a large and boisterous parade celebrating a Confederate victory."[78] He further writes, "Its Irish-Catholic majority empathized with Southern nationalism and with fighting a distant government."[79] In 1865, *Montreal Gazette* publisher and Confederate sympathizer John Lovell printed, "In the Land

Where We Were Dreaming," a poem about the South's lost dream of independence; according to Sheehy, "it became part of the South's 'lost cause' mythology."[80] In the decades after US slavery ended, in many parts of Canada the abolitionist cause was replaced with a strong sentimentality for the South and a "happy" return to the plantation. In this context, minstrelsy of all forms flooded Canada with sentimental songs longing for the antebellum past and songs that were coterminous with ideologies of Southern redemption and Lost Cause justification.[81]

The expansion of railroad lines in towns that connected Windsor to London and Hamilton, and Toronto to Ottawa, greatly contributed to *Black* minstrelsy's expansion in Canada. In 1884, the Toronto, Hamilton and Buffalo Railway Company was incorporated to build a track from Toronto via Hamilton to the International Bridge on the Niagara River and Bridgeburg (now Fort Erie), however, no action was taken until 1890 when an act was passed granting authority to lease to the Michigan Central or the Canada Southern; this connected Hamilton with the Brantford, Waterloo, and Lake Erie Railway Company near the City of Brantford.[82] *Black* and White minstrel troupes performed more frequently in Ontario, Quebec, and the Maritimes after the Intercolonial Railway was opened in 1876, which linked the Maritimes and central Canada. Specifically, it connected Halifax to Quebec City, and eventually provided a continuous connection, with branches from Montreal through eastern Quebec and New Brunswick, to North Sydney, Nova Scotia, and later PEI.[83] With the CPR connecting Western Canada to central Canada, minstrel troupes also increased their tours of the Prairies because of the ease of transportation afforded by these interconnected rail lines. The Georgia Minstrels was one of the first to perform at Toronto's Music Hall on November 21, 1868.[84] Also that year, they appeared in Saint John at the Mechanics' Institute, and at Fredericton's Temperance Hall.[85] Haverly's Minstrels appeared at City Hall in Halifax in 1879 before playing Toronto's Grand Opera House in 1879 and again in 1882.[86] On December 6, 1879, Toronto's *Globe* had described the troupe as "Haverly's Splendid Triumph" in its reporting of J.H. Haverly's United Mastodon Minstrels who appeared at the Royal Opera House in the city (see figure 5.3). "Numerically the strongest Company in the world. Original of negro minstrelsy and conceded by the press and public a PARAGON WITHOUT PARALLEL," the *Globe* reported.[87]

5.3 Haverly's United Mastodon Minstrels advertisement, 1878, Jay T. Last Collection of Graphic Arts and Social History | Huntington Library, Art Museum, and Botanical Gardens | San Marino, CA.

Born near Bellefonte, Pennsylvania, Haverly first launched his show business career in 1864 in Toledo, Ohio, where he purchased a variety theatre; he created Haverly's United Mastodon Minstrels in 1877 after amalgamating four of the companies he owned and managed into one. Suddenly, the number of performers multiplied, and Haverly unabashedly boasted "FORTY – 40 – COUNT 'EM – 40 – FORTY" minstrels; as Haverly's company toured the country, it rivaled the size and flamboyance of the likes of the Barnum & Bailey Circus.[88] Charles Callender had become sole proprietor of the Georgia Minstrels in 1872 after Hicks, who worked as the troupe's initial manager, sold the company to Callendar.[89] After several poor attendances, Callender sold the Original Georgia Minstrels to J.H. Haverly who promoted *Black* minstrels by increasing the troupe's size, adding new features, advertising flamboyantly, and completely focusing his shows on plantation material.[90] When Haverly took control of Callender's *Black* minstrel troupe and the Original Georgia Minstrels, which were sometimes called Callender's Colored Minstrels, he renamed them Haverly's Colored Minstrels.[91] Haverly's Georgia Minstrels toured Western Canada in the early 1880s, appearing at the Princess Opera House in Winnipeg and Walker Theatre.[92]

Some of the earliest editorials presenting reviews of minstrel shows, both amateur and professional, appeared in Toronto's the *Globe* in the early 1870s. "This minstrel troupe opened at the St. Lawrence Hall last night before a fair audience. The programme was spicy, and many of the eccentricities performed were well received," the newspaper reported of a minstrel troupe calling itself "St. James Combination" in its frontpage "City News" section on May 10, 1873.[93] Haverly's Georgia Minstrels first appeared in June 1877 at Charlotte Morrison's Grand Opera House, and in February 1881 his "Genuine Colored Minstrels" played the venue again.[94] From Hicks's Original Georgia Minstrels to numerous iterations that followed, as managed by Haverly and Callender, *Black* and White minstrels presented pastoral vignettes of the new plantation, stripped of conflict and reimagined as the "authentic" place for Black people. On March 11, 1882, the Grand Opera House "was crowded in every part last evening to hear [Milt] Barlow, [George] Wilson, [George] Primrose, and [William] West's minstrels. This company of minstrels goes far to revive the regard in which the first-class minstrel companies used to be helped in the early days of minstrelsy," reported the *Globe*, adding "From the opening to the close the audience is allowed only moderate relaxation from a strain of high enjoyment. The singing in the first part comprised several novelties rendered by the vocalists of the troupe in good style. This was followed by a series of specialties, character sketches, and dancing, the performance closing with a musical burlesque."[95] The paper went on to describe the show as "beyond all comparison, the best piece of minstrelsy that has been in Toronto this season." Principal comedian Billy Kersands (1842–1915), who toured North America and Britain as part of Callender's All-Coloured Minstrels (see figure 5.4), was one of the first Black actors to introduce audiences to "feats of dancing with a cup and saucer inside his mouth, or giving a monologue with several billiard balls in his cheeks."[96] In 1878, an advertisement

5.4 "Lithographic Portrait of Billy Kersands promoting Callender's Minstrels," ca. 1880–85, from the New York Public Library Billy Rose Theatre Division, Callender's (Georgia) Minstrels Collection.

for The Georgia Minstrels' performance at Toronto's Royal Opera House alerted readers that Kersands would be appearing as part of the ensemble. He was described as "one of the most famous of all African American minstrel performers."[97]

When Kersands toured with Callender's Georgia Minstrels he became famous for singing songs like "Old Aunt Jemima" and "Mary's Gone with a Coon." As Lynn Abbott and Doug Seroff note, "Kersands' unflagging charisma was an essential factor" in his performances which is why he is "widely heralded during the 1890s and thereafter as an 'unconscious,' 'nature-gifted' performer, Billy Kersands was one of the original architects of African American minstrelsy's 'ancient oddities.'"[98] His act was renowned for "playing a slow-witted, big-mouthed, black caricature," which also emphasized large lips and his mouth by acting them out as entertainment.[99] At the same time, Kersands is an important figure in the evolution of African American performance. As Constance Valis Hill poignantly observes, while audiences convulsed over the slightest curl of Kersands's lips or the opening of his yawning chasm, they also swooned over his dancing. "Kersands was the originator of the Virginia Essence, the most graceful and elegant of all soft-shoe tap dances, which he performed to a slow, 4/4 time signature."[100] In the tradition of the African derisive song that utilized symbolic indirection, the lyrics in Kersands's verses, which he sang while dancing, contained "victories" for Black characters, even if nothing more than psychological reversals.[101] For example, his song "Essence of Virginny" required a nimble "combination of knee work and head buttoning to keep time with the music," described the *Indianapolis Freeman*, the most widely distributed "race" paper of the 1890s.[102] The dance also perfected a variation on the Irish shuffle in which African American ragtime composer Arthur Marshall (1881–1968) once described as "the performer mov[ing] forward without appearing to move his feet at all, by manipulating his toes and heels rapidly, so that his body is propelled without changing the position of his legs."[103]

In addition to his dance innovations, Kersands remixed minstrel songs with African American folk music. In "Old Aunt Jemima," a song that by 1876–77 Kersands had reportedly performed two- to three thousand times, he improvised verses as he performed, something that was rarely done on the stage at the time.[104] In 1884, the *Globe* summed up Kersands's talents as "the greatest comedian living, in his original specialties."[105] When "Mammoth, Callender Minstrel Festival," featuring Billy Kersands, was held at the Grand Opera House on May 8–10, 1884, the paper said the show was in the city, "after its glorious triumph in all the large cities."[106] Before Kersands took his final curtain call on June 30, 1915 at a theatre in Artesia, New Mexico, where he suffered a fatal heart attack after his second performance of the evening, he had made his way into the twentieth century as a *Black* minstrel performer who contributed to the expansion of the genre through dance and song. One of his final hits, "Mary's Gone Wid a Coon" (1880), came to dominate the repertoire of *Black* and White minstrels.[107] After Kersands died, fellow Black performer Salem Tuff Whitney (1875–1934) eulogized him as "the best known and best beloved minstrel America has known, regardless of color. Billy's name was a byword for minstrelsy the country over."[108]

In 1876, the *Globe* ran a report on "Coloured minstrelsy" from a correspondent based in Chicago that described Toronto's Cool Burgess as a "Canadian favourite" performing at the New Chicago Theatre in a minstrel combination named, "California Minstrels" where Burgess "perpetrated some of his eccentricities with a face as white as that of a ghost. An unregenerate public viewed the innovation without favour, and after a few weeks' run, this hybrid party withdrew. Since then, there have been several visiting bands of burnt-cork artists, and they have all done well."[109] Even as *Black* minstrelsy took the theatre world by storm, White minstrelsy did not disappear in the 1880s. On May 15, 1883, for example, "a very large house greeted the first performance of Barlow, Wilson & Co's Mammoth Minstrels," reported the *Globe*, adding, "The long and excellent programme was carried out to the satisfaction of all. The 'social session,' or musical mélange, of which the first part consisted, was first-class, the singing calling forth loud applause.... Wilson, the inimitable, kept the audience convulsed with laughter while on the stage. The gymnasts, funny skaters, and concluding burlesque, wound up an entertainment which for general excellence would be hard to excel in the minstrel line."[110]

Horace Weston (1825–90) was another Black musician, dancer, and actor who toured Britain several times before joining Haverly's *Black* troupe, along with James Bland (1854–1911), one of the most notable Black songwriters of his day. Weston, a freeborn African American from Connecticut, is often touted as one of the finest banjo players to have ever lived, spending most of his career performing with Haverly's Georgia Minstrels and becoming one of the first Black performers featured in a special role when he toured in an overseas production of *Uncle Tom's Cabin* in 1873.[111] As Stephanie Dunson writes, "Bland came to be touted as 'The World's Greatest Minstrel Man' while a member of the internationally acclaimed Haverly's Genuine Colored Minstrels."[112] Bland is credited with having written over six hundred songs such as "Carry Me Back to Old Virginny" (1878), "Oh, Dem Golden Slippers" (1879), and "Hand Me Down My Walking Cane" (1880). According to Pickering, "Bland was a huge success in Britain, achieving for himself the sobriquet idol of the halls, and although he wore black-face when appearing in minstrel shows, he managed to discard the use of...make-up for his solo performances with the banjo in the concert halls, clubs and restaurants of the metropolis."[113] These African American performers might have offered crude, if not disparaging, representations of "real" life on Southern plantations for the appeasement of White audiences, but given the employment options for Black men at the end of the Civil War, the detrimental stereotypes they peddled on stage must be weighed against the fact that ten years prior, they would not have been permitted to step foot on those same stages.

By 1871, 44 percent of the City of Toronto's total population was British-born, and 51 percent was Canadian-born, largely of British ancestry.[114] As a result, it was a city that privileged Anglo-Saxon Protestantism. As Christina Burr writes, "while the rhetoric of labour reformers typically promoted the creation of a Canadian nation that incorporated all workers regardless of race, unskilled immigrants and Chinese workers were effectively excluded as a threat to the status of Anglo-Saxon and British-Canadian workers in the workplace."[115] As emergent magazines began to publish blackface cartoons and prints, they helped erase Black people from the Canadian imagination as real people. Inspired by a transatlantic visual culture that had propagated negative depictions of Black people for centuries, these magazines stood as another manifestation of the blackface Atlantic. As Simon Featherstone writes of British minstrelsy, "[it] was not simply an imported [I]ndigenous American form, deracialized and rendered ideologically calm for the easy consumption of respectable audiences.... Rather, they illustrate an active network of transatlantic forms and performances that were energized by old complicities in slavery and emigration, new politics of emancipation, nationalism and imperialist activity."[116] Similarly, blackface in Canada was never wholly an imported American form, or a travelling British entertainment; rather, it was a transnational genre that morphed and changed based on the specificities of the local. Its meaning was intimately and complexly reworked and reinterpreted depending on the sociocultural context for which it was either created or viewed, but decentralized in that it could belong to anyone at anytime, could become politicized, or could be denied as holding any meaning at all.

The minstrel show's ability to move in and out of spaces—real and imagined—helped position the genre as "safe" for Canadians to dip their viewing toes into. While lithographic prints depicting blackface were not outwardly about Black people (blackface was not meant to be the focus of representation in a mimetic sense), it was often used as an aesthetic in political commentaries in post-Confederation Canada to defile those political leaders deemed to be harming the population identified as White, Anglo-Saxon, Protestant, and middle class.[117] Blackface was depicted as a corporeal reminder of a political system deemed detrimental to "old stock" Canadian interests. As *Black* caricature became the unifying signifier for national rights, it mirrored an American strategy that privileged working-class values and desires aired and reinforced in the minstrel show. Its racial "narrative" dovetailed with its class sources in surprising and sometimes confusing ways; theatrical displays of "Blackness" seemingly guaranteed the atmosphere of licence so central to popular entertainment in this period.[118] On August 31, 1878, thirty-five years after the Virginia Minstrels first travelled the Atlantic world formalizing blackface repertoire, J.W. Bengough created the satirical cartoon, *National Policy Minstrels*, that was published in *Grip* (see figure 5.5).[119] Bruce Retallack found a cartoon from the magazine as early as 1849 with the central image of a capering French Canadian *habitant* standing in marked contrast to the upright figure of Louis-Hippolyte Lafontaine (1807–64) depicted as standing in the background.[120] Following the 1837/1838 Rebellions, and Lord Durham's report on Canada, Lafontaine, a politician who was born Boucherville, Lower Canada, had been a supporter of *Patriotes* Papineau leading up to the Rebellions, but he switched to supporting a system of working within the existing constitutional order to achieve the political rights of French Canadians, an act that became known as "Responsible Government."[121]

By the mid-1880s, *Grip* hit a peak circulation that varied between 7,000 and 10,000 copies, and the paper was reportedly read by over 50,000 people each week.[122] As part of the expansion of mass-circulation magazines in Canada, *Grip* reached multiple publics. According to Burr, "politicians expounded their interpretations of Bengough's cartoons in official government institutions and on the stump, and intellectuals commented on his cartoons in competing periodicals. The cartoons, with the aid of the numerous public lectures, or 'chalk talks,' that Bengough conducted throughout the country,

5.5 John Wilson Bengough's political cartoon, "The National Policy Minstrels," 1886, M994X.5.273.197, The McCord Stewart Museum, Montreal.

became part of the everyday culture of work and family in Victorian Canada."[123] *National Policy Minstrels* was a commentary but as was typical of *Grip*, it used "weapons of ridicule and satire to demonize...disparate races, religions, and ethnicities. Whatever their differences from each other, all were targeted because they failed to fit the white, Protestant, Canadian-born ideal promoted by *Grip*'s editor."[124] The real National Policy was one of the first pieces of legislation passed by Canada's first parliament. It set in motion an era of industrial and cultural modernization that would have far-reaching impacts beyond politics.[125] Prime Minister John A. Macdonald promised that the National Policy would broaden nation-building efforts, including substantially increasing tariffs on a long list of manufactured goods, and introduce measures to promote railway-building and Western

European immigration.[126] By binding the Conservative Party to building an all-Canadian transcontinental railway, Macdonald added a potent nationalistic mythology to the philosophy of railways; the National Policy, western settlement, and the Pacific railway were all elements of a complex, interrelated development strategy wherein an urbanized and industrialized central Canada, flanked by rural and resource-based regions, would form the superstructure of a newly sovereign northern nation.[127] Scotland-born leader of the Liberal Party Alexander Mackenzie, Canada's second prime minister (serving from 1873 to 1878), opposed many of Macdonald's policies but what he did share with the Conservative leader was a White supremacist belief that it was the White man's cultural mandate to settle the West and build railways. "It is the mission of the Anglo-Saxon race," asserted Mackenzie in a speech in 1876, "to carry the power of Anglo-Saxon civilization over every country in the world."[128]

By the early 1880s, many social Reformers began to realize that Conservative campaign promises of prosperity for the working class under the National Policy had not occurred, and that overpopulation in cities like Toronto had resulted in factory closures and wage reductions while a handful of monopolists accumulated more wealth.[129] Bengough's writings and cartoons were transnational, appearing in journals and newspapers such as Toronto's the *Globe*, the *Montreal Star*, the *Morning Chronicle* (London), the *Public* (Chicago), the *Farmer's Advocate* (London, Ontario), the *Varsity*, and *Review of Reviews*.[130] While his cartoons were about Canada, through the purview of *Grip* he often borrowed from American politics, most notably, Thomas Nast's (1840–1902) style of political parody.[131] For over twenty years after the US Civil War, Nast's political cartoons were the most recognizable visual feature of *Harper's Weekly* (1862–86), one of the most widely circulated magazines in the US.[132] As Baird Jarman writes, though never an official organ of the Republican Party, "the *Weekly* evolved into a highly influential advocate of Republican principles during the war. By the late 1860s the periodical had established a consistent political viewpoint anchored by…Thomas Nast, who provided political cartoons and other illustrations, and George William Curtis, who supplied political editorials and other commentaries."[133]

Carl Spadoni asserts further that Bengough's ambition was to follow in Nast's footsteps, but with a Canadian perspective. "Filled with admiration for Nast's work, Bengough saw at once how caricatures could translate beliefs into graphic statements of moral conviction."[134] While he used the strokes of his pen to show public contempt and ridicule for perceived-to-be political dishonesty and mismanagement, Bengough absorbed a mentality about racialized others, using caricatures of their likeness to "prove his point," which was something he might have also borrowed from Nast. In *National Policy Minstrels*, Macdonald, as the middleman (*interlocutor*) is depicted with "Programme parti conundrums" written on the left of his tailcoat; his caption reads, "Brudder dat aint to de point." Macdonald is flanked by members of the Conservative Party who are dressed in black tailcoats, white shirts with elongated lapel collars, bowties, black dress pants and black dress shoes. The minstrels all take turns speaking to Macdonald in "black dialect," such as "Ax us an easier one" to "Gin her up." One minstrel is holding a large horn labelled "retaliation." Another says, "I give it up" while holding a fiddle and beside him, a patch on a dress shirt says, "King" with the caption, "Golly dat's a stunner!" A final *endman* is holding a tambourine with, "Wid de pertective systim whar we gwine to git a revenue without direc taxation? – dats de c'nundrum" written on it. As denoted by the cartoon's subtitle, *Brudder Tambo's Astounding Financial Conundrum*, this cartoon is a satirized depiction of the believed-to-be negative effects of the National Policy; however, by appropriating blackface and replicating the style of the Virginia Minstrels (blackface characters seated in a semicircle playing tambourine (tambo), bones, fiddle, banjo, and sometimes triangle and horn), the cartoon is also a commentary on race in Canadian federal politics.

If you consider that Bengough's audience was, like himself, White, Anglo-Saxon, and Protestant, *Grip*'s cartoons demonstrated what Alan Mendelson calls "a bias against most of the ethnic and religious groups that had immigrated to Canada.... Though Bengough did not have the terminology to call 'the Other' by that name, he used ridicule and satire" to perpetuate the view that Black people, Asians, and Jews "belonged to a lower order, with the unstated implication that these groups did not qualify for inclusion in the political nation."[135] The use of blackface served to lampoon not only a policy deemed unfavourable to working-class White men, but it was also a critique of the perceived *Americanization* of Canadian economic development. Specifically, the National Policy was seen as replicating key elements of the "American System," promoted in the early eighteenth century by Henry Clay and other Whig politicians as a system that emphasized high tariffs and infrastructure improvements; the American System had been just as partisan as the National Policy.[136]

Bengough's cartoons reveal how minstrelsy and politics were always bedfellows. From T.D. Rice to the Virginia Minstrels, White minstrelsy was, from the outset, influenced by sectional conflicts over Western expansion, Northern industrialization, and Southern plantation slavery, not to mention demographic struggles between White, Anglo-Saxon Protestants of self-proclaimed "old stock" who arrived prior to 1776, and Irish Catholics versus Black people. Considering the Whig Party aimed to identify with "rural White common people" and that the party was often lampooned as "sly political manipulators, posturing...as friends of the common man,"[137] Bengough's *National Policy Minstrels* similarly spoke to how Liberals viewed Conservatives—sly manipulators lying to the common man. The use of so-called "Black dialect" also perpetuated a racist stereotype about Black people, which was common practice in *Grip*'s cartoons. As Mendelson explains further, Black stereotypes were drawn with distorted features, the jokes used derogatory terms like "coon," or the characters were depicted either as illiterates who were naturally dishonest, cowardly, or stupid.[138]

In addition to *National Policy Minstrels*, which Bengough continued to produce through the 1880s, in another political cartoon appearing in *Grip* in 1886, titled *The Bill Board Re-Decorated*, he used seven comic panels to satirize the National Policy again. This time, the satirical cartoon parodied Macdonald's efforts to pursue political reform with Liberal politicians and Ontario Premier Sir Oliver Mowat (serving from 1872 to 1896), both of whom, as members of the Liberal Party, opposed many of Macdonald's policies (see figure 5.6). Titled, "Mackenzie and Mowat's Minstrel Combination and Several Brass Band" with a subtitle, "Organized Regardless of Expense or Consistency to Run Out John A's Greatest Show on Earth," *Bill Board Re-Decorated* was a parody of showman P.T. Barnum, whose circus was first billed as the "Greatest Show on Earth" in 1871.[139] The first panel (top left to right) featured Joseph Rymal (1821–1900), Liberal for Wentworth South (Hamilton) serving in the House of Commons from 1867 to 1882, who was a staunch opponent to most of Macdonald's

5.6 John Wilson Bengough's political cartoon "The Bill Board Re-Decorated," 1886, M994X.5.273.167, The McCord Stewart Museum, Montreal.

policies, including the National Policy and the construction of the CPR.[140] "Funny Joe Rymal, in his stump effusions," reads the caption depicting Rymal sitting over a desk that read "old jokes" next to a top hat placed on the ground. The second panel includes nine politicians sitting in a semicircle à la the Virginia Minstrels, wearing blackface and holding instruments with the *interlocutor*'s caption reading, "opening chorus 'we's all (illegible) for Ferguson," a statement that likely referred to the Liberal-Conservative political figure Charles Frederick Ferguson (1834–1909), who served in the House of Commons from 1874 to 1896. The third panel features Mackenzie and Mowat in blackface with the text, "Mackenzie & Mowat in their political double songs and dances as formerly performed by John A. and Johns Macdonald." The fourth panel (bottom left) depicts two White men staring at a sign that read, "regular annual demonstration tour [...] look at the array of talent." The print listed many other prominent Liberal figures including George Brown and more.

The fifth panel features staunch Liberal Brown in blackface, sitting on a chair holding a banjo, sticking up his left middle finger. The text in this comic reads, "the great & only G.B in his new banjo solo, 'The Exile of Erin'" while the text on Brown's elongated shoe states, "there is no standing room for me in the reform party." The sixth panel depicts six minstrels in blackface plugging their noses in a circle with *interlocutor* in the middle; the text above them reads, "Grand Cabinet Walk-Around By the Entire Company," a reference to the walkaround of the minstrel show (when a large cast, walking in circular procession to syncopated music, strutting steps, and improvised solos would take to the stage in the finale), with a statement below them that states, "He's Rank and Smells to Heaven." The seventh panel depicts businessman and Conversative cabinet minister, Richard (Dick) John Cartwright (1813–1912) in a top hat, holding a gun over a White woman lying on the ground in a dress that declares "Canada" on it; above her, the gun points toward a balloon that reads, "Protection," and next to Cartwright it states, "The Star Artist Dick Cartwright in His Own Adaptation of Forbidden Fruit," a vignette that harkens to the myth of White women's rape at the hands of foreigners. Cartwright was a tenacious foe of the National Policy, decrying the decline of property values, excessive government expenditures, and the increase in Canadian emigration to the US, all of which he argued was the direct result of the National Policy.[141]

This cartoon ultimately reveals how commonplace blackface was in the visual and popular culture of late nineteenth century Canada. Blackface was part of the Canadian common culture; just as newspapers were read by a wide public, that same public was exposed to blackface imagery even if they themselves did not attend blackface theatre productions. In the 1890s, coon songs, as they were called, would become the most popular form of minstrel music, with the word "coon" referring to the animal raccoon, whose thievery and guile were associated with Black people. It also harkened back to the first Black character of the American stage discussed in Chapter 1, Raccoon from *The Disappointment*.[142] The term was also given new meaning by the success of several African American performers who claimed the term as part of their act. First, Bowling Green, Kentucky-born

Ernest Hogan (1865–1909) wrote a song called "All Coons Look Alike to Me" in 1896, which had accompanied a Broadway musical of the same name. "All Coons Look Alike to Me" became a fighting tune in New York City, writes Stanley Lemons, because "blacks considered it to be insulting for a white person to sing or whistle it. J. Rosamond Johnson reported seeing two men thrown off a ferry boat in the middle of the river in a brawl caused by 'All Coons.' When Hogan died in 1905, he had been bitterly attacked by most of the black intelligentsia and was sorry he had ever written the thing."[143] Importantly, "a song like 'All Coons Look Alike to Me' could, quite simply, not have been written before 1848," writes David Roediger, "because human *coons* were typically *white* until that point."[144] However, *coon* had gradually emerged as a racial slur around 1848 when, as he explains further, "it first found racist use mainly on the minstrel stage" where the slur evolved from the character Zip Coon, and in the context of the many references to coon-hunting and eating coons in blackface songs.[145]

Hogan's hit was followed by the first full-length Black musical comedy, written by African American playwrights Robert Cole (1868–1911) and Billy Johnson (1858–1916), titled *A Trip to Coontown*, which debuted in New Jersey in 1897 before touring across the US and finally closing at New York's Third Avenue Theatre on April 4, 1898.[146] When the show appeared at London's Grand Opera House during the 1897–98 season it was described as "Bob Cole and Billy Johnson in their roaring, racy, rollicking musical comedy, *A trip to Coontown*, supported by a select company of colored artists."[147] Cole and Johnson's show broke new ground, not because it was the first musical to be written, produced, and performed solely by Black Americans, but because it was one of those shows most clearly affected by what Eileen Southern once described as "five kinds of stage entertainment: the ballad opera music extravaganza, the comic opera, the minstrel show, the variety show, and the touring play," and it created excitement around the potential innovations happening on the American stage.[148]

There is no doubt that Quebec City-born caricaturist and illustrator Henri Julien (1852–1908) would have heard of or seen this show when he created his satiric and folkloric series of cartoon images for the *Montreal Star* (1869–1979) in 1899, titled *Songs of the By-Town Coons*. This series stands as a historical example of how a derogatory word, originally meant to deride African Americans, could transform into a word used by African

5.7 The sheet music cover of the *Montreal Star*'s "Songs of the By-Town Coons." ca. 1889–1900. 0007098897. Bibliothèque et Archives Nationales du Québec.

Americans as a matter of describing not only a place but also modes of behaviour; however, it could, in the context of an Anglophone-Francophone culture, be co-opted to embody entirely different sets of meanings. *Songs of the By-Town Coons* depicts Sir Wilfrid Laurier's (1841–1919) Liberals, the first Francophone-led federal government, as a group of blackface minstrels (see figure 5.7). As Dominic Hardy explains, "The black/white conflict is implicitly reconfigured as both French/English and Liberal/Conservative conflicts.... The institution of parliament is seen, under the governance of a Francophone-led Liberal government, as little more than the production of a minstrel troupe, as a parody of true (English-speaking, British-Canadian, Conservative) governance."[149] In describing a depiction of Laurier's lieutenant, Lanoraie, Quebec-born Joseph Israel Tarte (1848–1907), and Halifax-born Minister of Finance William Stevens Fielding (1848–1929) singing in "Black dialect," Hardy asserts "[Tarte's] French-Canadian identity is fused with that identified in his time as 'the negro' or 'the coon' by blacking up and through the adoption of a mock Habitant voice that functions as a replacement for the caricatured 'negro' voice exemplified by Fielding's song.... Julien renewed a longstanding correspondence between the caricatural space of representation and that of the theatre, with which the form was intimately allied in both Britain and France."[150] Where Julien's *Songs of the By-Town Coons* reflected the popularization of racial caricature via the appropriation of racial physiognomies in Canadian visual culture, Bengough's *National Policy Minstrels* and *Bill Board Re-Decorated* spoke to the popularization of racial caricature via this appropriation in theatrical minstrel shows. Both depictions came at a time when a new generation of Canadian-born blackface performers hit international stages.

Most notably, London, Ontario-born George Primrose (1852–1919) teamed up with Syracuse, New York-born William H. West (1853–1902) in 1877, and toured North America initially as part of Haverly's White minstrel troupe until they left to form their own, Primrose and West's Big Minstrels.[151] Eventually Primrose and West teamed up with Lexington, Kentucky-born Milt Barlow (1843–1904) and George Wilson to form Barlow, Wilson, Primrose and West.[152] When Primrose and West rose to fame in 1877, instead of the tattered old clothes of a Jim Crow-style performance, their troupes wore satin coats, vests, breeches, silk stockings, low-cut, white satin shoes with diamond buckles, lace collards, and white wigs.[153] Primrose and West's "Big Minstrels" was one of the first shows to cast Black and White performers who took to the stage in separate parts of the show but fell under the same billing. Ultimately, just as nineteenth-century political cartoons of Irish Catholics or French Canadians are not read as neutral, depictions of White Canadians encoded with markers of a derogatory Blackness are not neutral either; they reflect a pervasive and unchecked racial discourse both informed by travelling blackface minstrel shows, domestic discourses about Otherness, and the "rightful" place for difference(s) in Canadian society.

Authentic Black performance—as developed from within and of Black community—existed in the nineteenth century. It took the form of choral singers of Negro spirituals, songs that provided hope, salvation, and inspiration to enslaved people and post-emancipation. These songs, as first performed by the Fisk Jubilee Singers, travelled the Atlantic world and beyond with the same frequency as blackface minstrelsy. Their singing was primarily for fundraising purposes, but in the process, they reimagined the possibilities for Black performance on stage. Like many other African American choirs, such as the Wilmington Jubilee Singers (1874–80) who formed out of the port city of Wilmington, North Carolina,[154] there were numerous other singing groups that formed in the 1870s and 1880s, such as the Georgia Jubilee Singers (1876– 190?), the Alabama Jubilee Singers (1876–1940s), the Tennessee Jubilee Singers (1876–91), and the New Orleans Jubilee Singers (1873–77), to name a few.[155] In Canada, the Fisk Jubilee Singers first appeared in Toronto in 1880. "The origin of this famous company of vocalists has already been noticed, and so has the cause they are labouring to promote. Fisk University has developed out of one of the schools established in the South at the close of the Civil War by Northern friends of the emancipated slaves," explained Toronto's *Globe*, adding that the school organized the band, composed of its students, to travel throughout the US to sing not only in promotion of Fisk but also to help raise funds to get the school out of debt.[156] The newspaper continued, "Starting out with eleven young vocalists, [their business manager Geo White] crossed the Ohio and made his way with some difficulty to New York, where, through the exertions of friends, a more promising career opened up for the troupe and their merits as singers began to be appreciated."[157] After making a tour of the northern states, the Fisk Jubilee Singers toured Europe, spending three years continuously travelling throughout England, Wales, Ireland, Scotland, Germany, Switzerland, the Netherlands, parts of Austria, and France; they raised over $150,000, which enabled the university to erect a new hall, enlarge the site of the institution, and advance the school's curriculum.[158]

Their style of singing was not fully appreciated by Canadian audiences initially. As an example, the *Globe* feature also noted, "The company includes four soprano, two tenor, and two bass voices and one, contralto, all of them being of a fine quality…. The pieces sung are mostly the crude… vigorous hymns in vogue amongst the plantation negroes, all of them being extremely melodious, while most of them have been well harmonised."[159] On their next tour of Toronto, Hamilton, St. Catharines, and Brantford, the Fisk Jubilee Singers performed a catalogue of Negro spirituals, many of which are still performed today, such as "Steal Away to Jesus" (c. 1862), "My Father how Long?" (c. 1865), "I'm Rolling Through an Unfriendly World" (c. 1840s–1860s), "Rocked in the Cradle of the Deep" (c. 1840), "Home, Sweet Home" (c. 1857), "Bright Sparkles in the Churchyard" (c. 1874), "Didn't My Lord Deliver Daniel" (c. 1847), "I've Been Redeemed" (c. 1880s), and "Swing Low, Sweet Chariot" (c. 1872). These songs encouraged enslaved people to flee from their bondage, have hope for a better life, and in the North they provided solace to African Americans separated from family in the South. While Toronto, Hamilton, and St. Catharines were terminal cities on the Underground Railroad, Brantford also had a history of not only slavery but Black emigration and the establishment of Black community, which is why jubilee singing was popular there.[160] In addition to Brantford, Hamilton and Halifax produced their own Jubilee choral choirs.

The O'Banyoun Jubilee Singers, founded by Reverend Josephus O'Banyoun, who was born in Brantford in 1838, comprised seven singers and an accompanist, all but one of whom were from Hamilton.[161] This group, which toured North America and Europe, were at their peak popularity during the period between 1884 to 1900.[162] In an editorial in the *Amherstburg Echo* dated November 25, 1892, the O'Banyoun Jubilee Singers were described as "[being] greeted by an audience of about 200 persons at the [Amherstburg] Town Hall, on Wednesday evening, when they appeared under the auspices of the Young Ladies' Social Club, of the A.M.E. [American Methodist Episcopal] Church." The editorial continued, "The troupe under the personal direction of Rev. J. O'Banyoun, are travelling in aid of African missions."[163] The O'Banyoun Singers also appeared in Windsor that year, giving a concert at the A.M.E. Chapel on November 21 to "an overcrowded house," as reported in the Black-operated newspaper, *Detroit Plaindealer*.[164] On September 17, 1880, in celebration of the laying of the cornerstone of the British Methodist Episcopal church on Essex Street in Guelph, the O'Banyoun Jubilee Singers performed a special concert in the City Hall.[165] Because the Fisk Jubilee Singers had influenced a whole generation of African Americans and African Canadians, the O'Banyoun Jubilee Singers' performance included Negro spirituals made famous by the Fisk singers, like "Steal Away to Jesus," "Turn Back Pharoah's Army," and "Good News – the Chariot's A'Coming."[166] As Adrienne Shadd explains, "Although initially they sang a couple of 'slave songs' or Negro spirituals

5.8 Sheet music cover for the Famous Canadian Jubilee Singers' "Plantation Lullabies," Schomburg Center for Research in Black Culture, Manuscripts, Archives and Rare Books Division, The New York Public Library. The New York Public Library Digital Collections. ca. 1890–99. https://digitalcollections.nypl.org/items/510d47df-bb3e-a3d9-e040-e00a18064a99.

as encores, they quickly realized that these songs had a powerful impact on their audience and these became the mainstay of their program."[167] The Canadian Jubilee Singers and Imperial Orchestra were another group inspired by the Fisk Jubilee Singers. Established in Hamilton in 1879 they performed before the Royal Family, touring England, Ireland, and Wales for five years during the 1880s (see figure 5.8).[168] Like the O'Banyoun Singers,

5.9 Postcard of the Original Canadian Jubilee Singers, ca. 1890, from the New York Public Library Schomburg Center for Research in Black Culture, Photographs and Prints Division. Helen Armstead-Johnson Photograph Collection.

the Canadian Jubilee Singers were a troupe that featured a male vocal quartet, a soprano soloist, and bass solos by "Boy Boss" James E. Lightfoot, who also served as orchestra director and mandolin virtuoso.[169] William and Sadie Carter, the proprietors and managers of the Canadian Jubilee Singers and Imperial Orchestra, were both from Hamilton; by the 1894–95 season, the group was kept busy with a touring schedule that included a nonstop forty-seven week tour of New York, Pennsylvania, Ohio, Indiana, and Michigan, closing July 26, 1895 in London, Ontario.[170] Importantly, the Fisk Jubilee, O'Banyoun, and the Canadian Jubilee Singers toured cities and towns across Ontario several times over in the 1880s and 1890s, but they were also extremely popular in New York, which is why a photograph of their contribution to Negro spirituals can be found in the Schomburg Center for Research in Black Culture in New York City labelled, "The Original Canadian Jubilee Singers" (see figure 5.9).

The group also spent five years touring Britain during the 1880s, dividing their time between tours of the US and Canada for the next three decades.

Their tours were covered by the *New York Clipper* (founded in 1853 by editor Frank Queen), an entertainment weekly that regularly covered sports along with theatrical news.[171] The *Clipper* published five reviews of the Canadian Jubilee Singers during their 1895 tour. "We are now in our thirty-eighth week...not missing a night since Sept. 3, 1894. We have been traveling in New York, Pennsylvania, Ohio, Indiana and Michigan, and our season closes July 25, in Detroit," the *Clipper* reported on June 1, 1895.[172] "We closed a successful season of forty-seven weeks in London, Can., July 26," the paper reported on August 3, and then on September 28, "Notes from the Canadian Jubilee Singers and Imperial Orchestra" informed *Clipper* readers that "We are having success so far, although we were compelled to cancel two dates at Warsaw, N.Y., on account of an epidemic of diphtheria."[173] The spiritual songs of African Americans and African Canadians were popular with White audiences for several reasons. First, as many of these performers were descendants of formerly enslaved people, their songs were imbued with the spirit of European music, which they would have learned during their enslavement. "Sometimes slaves were permitted in the whites' churches and exposed to white spiritual music, and versions of these songs began to be heard on the levees, plantations and riverboats. Slaves were brought from many parts of Africa, so there is no clear single musical background," asserts Angela Files.[174]

Second, the common elements of African and American spirituals—syncopation, polyrhythmic structure, pentatonic scale, and responsive rendition of text—resonated with White audiences, though they did not know what to think of Negro spiritual singing initially.[175] Stephen Talty explains further that in the antebellum American South, African Americans and Whites, enslaved persons and masters, freedmen and poor Scottish-Irish farmers, free and bond, "lived in communities more integrated than most middle-class suburban neighbourhoods today" and as a result of this close proximity, when enslaved African Americans accepted the Gospel, they consciously "entered the Western tradition. It was an irreversible decision: blacks committed their minds to the new world and began to focus much of their lives and their strategies for liberation in the church."[176] Songs like "Steal Away to Jesus," for example, were plucked directly from the African American experience on the plantation. "Come nightfall, they would steal away and either gather themselves in a prayer house or in the woods for an 'arbor mass.' If the masses were forbidden, slaves might alert one another that they were to occur that night by singing the spiritual 'Steal Away to Jesus' in the fields,"[177] explains Talty further. During some of their early appearances, many jubilee singers evoked hostility from predominantly White audiences who expected them to perform minstrel numbers, not spirituals sung on the plantation to assist those who absconded. However, skepticism and animosity quickly turned to praise and standing ovations as people came to appreciate the singers' voices.[178] As Mark Sanders explains, "That audiences immediately celebrated this 'folk' music, and in turn that this unprecedented financial success inspired similar singing groups…demonstrate the overriding influences of both economic and cultural forces in transforming a functional idiom of ritual into a consumer product better known as performance art."[179]

In Britain, Pickering notes while most reviewers were highly favourable of the African American jubilee singers "there is clear evidence of uncertainty and confusion as to how to evaluate their performances, especially among highly educated musicians and writers, with inevitable comparisons being made to blackface minstrels." Pickering writes further, "This was part of the broader pattern of vacillating, contradictory responses made by whites to black entertainers and musicians in nineteenth-century Britain…. Audience perception and pleasure was always mediated by white cultural standards, white race-thinking, and white racial stereotypes of blacks."[180] In Canada, there was a range of performances that took place from travelling circuses to minstrel shows, jubilee choral concerts, and variety acts that reached a broad-based population that included women, children, and the White working- and middle-classes, but also members of the Black community who might have shared the same space at theatre and performance hall venues with the aforementioned.[181] By the late nineteenth century, Canadian audiences would have been exposed to happy-go-lucky Uncle Toms alongside abject plantation Jim Crows; "uppity" Northern dandies and depictions of lazy Southern coons. As such, Negro spirituals were not simply another form of Black expressive culture arising out of slavery, but they were quite possibly the first genre of performance that spoke directly to the African American experience.

Jubilee choruses and orchestras might have been plucked from the Southern plantation, but their songs of freedom stood in direct opposition to *Black* minstrelsy and its reified songs of enslavement. Following an August 19, 1879 performance by the Canadian Jubilee Singers, a review published in the *Guelph Mercury* described their singing as:

> … in every respect first-class, and the pieces sang were of a sacred character, mostly plantation songs, the composition of which went to show that although the black man was a slave and in the house of bondage, the spirit was unfettered, and that he was a freeman in the highest sense of the word. Whether in the low and plaintive wail of sorrow, or in the high and jubilant song of victory, there was alike displayed a pathos and vigor enchanting. While the clear intonation in which the words were uttered made it capable for everyone to catch the words distinctly, and while enjoying the music of the song were able to appreciate the words.[182]

While jubilee singing offered the other side of the enslaved coin because performers did not wear blackface nor dress in caricature, they still performed "plantation" songs depicting life from the point of view of the enslaved as only rememberable through song, not through real-life depictions of slavery's violence and White acts of terror. As John Springhall aptly observes, "Church music or spirituals ('Let My People Go,' 'Angels, Meet Me at the Cross-roads,' 'Oh, Rock o' My Soul') did not seriously challenge minstrelsy's plantation mythology, however, but allowed whites to retain their negative caricatures of blacks by focusing on and exaggerating as alien African American styles of worship that differed greatly from more straitlaced white norms."[183] As choral singers used the stage to exercise some modicum of "freedom" in terms of expression they still did so during a period of declining Black freedoms. Thus, one of the lasting outcomes of Black performance in this era was the reframing of Black realities through entertainment. As Alison Kibler argues, there were "romantic portraits of a distinctive southern past that erased racial conflict. Such homage to a fictive southern history emerged…which attempted to redeem the Confederate tradition, and in the hundreds of popular songs that presented the South as an escape from the northern city."[184] At the same time Negro spirituals crisscrossed the Atlantic adjacent to *Black* and White minstrel troupes, all-female acts began to appear on stages across North America, embracing the burnt cork tradition of the minstrel show by putting on blackface and singing the songs of minstrelsy just as their all-male, all-White counterparts had done during the heydays of the minstrel show. The major difference, however, was that some female performers cross-dressed in male costume, some revealed their bodies in performance—something many audiences found shocking—but all women entered the theatre during its transition into what became known as vaudeville.

White women's performances in vaudeville are an important chapter in the story of racial disguise as they are the link between new and old identities, between modern culture and tradition, between the brutalities of racial hierarchies in America and the "whitewashed" histories of racial unity.[185] Whereas the minstrel show was primarily centred on the plantation, vaudeville's racialized performances emerged in the midst of political struggles over integration and Black migration following Reconstruction. As African American communities became more visible in the North, segregation and discrimination intensified; as Kibler explains further, "big-time vaudeville, with its segregated seating and the prominence of racial stereotyping in its productions, was one of the many institutions restricting African Americans' freedoms following Reconstruction."[186] As White women, Jewish women, Black women, and men took to stages across North America, the racial rules of vaudeville meant that White (mostly male) managers allowed White performers to take on a range of racial disguises, but they discouraged Black performers from trying to "look or act" like White performers. In contrast to White women who had the privilege of playing with Blackness, Black women struggled to be taken seriously, in many cases trying to break into the White ranks of leading ladies and highbrow artists.[187] The next chapter explores the development of vaudeville in the 1870s through early 1890s and the ways this integrated theatrical genre created new opportunities for White women and Black women (and men) who had been left out of the North American theatre just two generations prior. At the same time, vaudeville's large-scale productions and extended tours reinforced power relations that existed in slavery wherein White women maintained some privilege over Black women who remained largely stuck in positions of servitude. As such, vaudeville gave immigrant women, especially Jewish women from Western Europe, the ability to enter the mainstream entertainment industries as they brought their gender identity, race, and sexuality to the forefront on the stage. They also appropriated the rules of the theatre regarding *Black* minstrelsy. As Lori Harrison-Kahan explains, Jewish women complicated White identity in that "their cultural productions stage multivalent and thus highly ambivalent encounters among Jewishness, blackness and whiteness."[188] At the same time, in addition to jubilee singers, Black operatic singers challenged the minstrel show's insistence on stereotypes of Black people on plantations while an increasingly rigid colour line, both on and off the stage, upheld White supremacy and the policing of Black bodies.

6

WHITE WOMEN MINSTRELS, *DARKEST AMERICA*, AND BLACK SINGERS ON CANADIAN STAGES, 1887-97

Madame Rentz's Female Minstrels, created in 1870 by Michael Bennett (M.B.) Leavitt (1843–1935), was one of the first all-female vaudeville acts to tour Canada (see figure 6.1). Combining women in tights, minstrelsy, vaudeville, and burlesque, Madame Rentz's toured Toronto, Hamilton, and Ottawa from 1870 onward.[1] Leavitt reportedly combined the elements of the minstrel show with those of the new "girlie shows" and the result was Rentz's Female Minstrels who, by 1871, were joined by eleven other all-female minstrel companies.[2] The format of Leavitt's shows merged the three-act blackface minstrel show with aspects of Lydia Thompson's (1838–1908) all-female troupe's show, vaudeville song, and musical travesty that eventually became known exclusively as "burlesque."[3] Born in London, England, Thompson danced and performed in pantomimes in Britain and throughout Europe before becoming a leading dancer and actor in burlesque on the London stage, making such an appearance in *Robinson Crusoe* in 1875. As Gerald Lenton-Young writes of the British Blondes' first North American tour in 1868, "Although the Blondes performed burlesque as parody in the classic sense of the word, their main

6.1 Mme Rentz's Minstrels advertisement, ca. 1880, Jay T. Last Collection of Graphic Arts and Social History | Huntington Library, Art Museum, and Botanical Gardens | San Marino, CA.

attraction was the amount of figure revealed by their 'classical,' and hence respectable, costumes. Their first American show, and the first the troupe presented in Ontario, was *Ixion*."[4] Tamara Smith writes, "Critics agreed that the plot—loosely based on a Roman myth about a mortal man who seduced goddesses—was thin, but audiences loved the witty puns, the fancy costumes, the local references, the flirtatious innuendo, and the lively dancing," adding that audiences were mostly fascinated by "the almost exclusively female cast known for their shapely legs and flowing blonde hair."[5] The British Blondes toured Ontario, making appearances in Ottawa, Toronto, and Hamilton within two years of their first appearance in New York.[6] By the end of the century there were dozens of companies openly selling female sexuality. The shows featured some of the elements from the old minstrel shows like blackface, but they always included some aspect of sexual titillation or off-colour humour that was very specific to vaudeville.

Burlesque mostly offered sketches and a chorus of dancing girls (which was appealing to mostly male audiences), but the appearances of female minstrels or burlesque "girlie shows" were surrounded with controversy, especially when some managers tried to establish permanent homes for their acts.

One of the earliest Canadian examples of a burlesque comedic opera with minstrel elements appeared in an advertisement in Toronto's the *Globe* on May 11, 1870, when La Belle Hélène promoted a "Minstrel Scene" as part of their appearance at the Royal Lyceum.[7] By 1879, one Toronto critic said, "Nothing is announced as yet for next week but I hear we are to have a Red Stocking Female Minstrel Company. I hope for the sake of the new manager of this house [Toronto's Royal] that the statement is false, for it has suffered enough this season with such entertainments, no less than four blonde troupes having appeared already, one of them so bad that the newspapers called upon the police to suppress such performances."[8] In 1880, the Royal Opera House played host to Madame Rentz's Female Minstrels for a two-night engagement and its reviews point to how divided male critics were about how to interpret its sexualized display. "The performance is mostly of a musical character, and as a variety entertainment it has many attractions. The several songs in the opening part of the performance were pleasingly sung: Miss Bessie Bell proving herself a very agreeable vocalist. This miscellaneous entertainment that followed was well received," reported the *Daily Globe*, adding "There are no objectionable features in the performance, and ladies will be able to enjoy the entertainment probably as much as gentlemen."[9] Rentz's Female Minstrels combined minstrelsy, vaudeville, and burlesque, displayed their legs and bodies through snug-fitting tights, and acted out the basic minstrel show format supplemented with special attractions of their own. "In San Francisco, we had advertised that we were going to put on the can-can," recalled John E. Henshaw, who began his acting career as a prop boy with the troupe.[10] Another unique feature of all-female minstrel tropes like Rentz's was not only their ability to portray Black characters through blackface and cross-dressing, but they also stressed their unique attributes as women. The promise of a revealing glimpse at scantily clad women was the principal appeal of female minstrels to even vaudeville's increasingly racially and ethnically diverse audiences that still remained majority male.

This chapter examines the arrival of women on vaudeville stages across Canada. It probes the expanding conversations about gender, race, and ethnicity that changed the theatre. Vaudeville, after all, did not replace *Black* and White minstrelsy, jubilee, and operatic singing; rather, its acts crisscrossed the same cities, stages; sometimes actors and musicians performed across one or two or all these genres. This chapter also considers Douglas A. Jones, Jr.'s arguments that "even in his groundbreaking study of blackface minstrelsy, *Love and Theft*, [Eric] Lott hardly attends to black responses to the form, not to mention wider, concurrent black social and political formations that also framed minstrelsy's inception."[11] This chapter explores Jones Jr.'s point about concurrent Black social and political formations on the nineteenth-century stage by considering the ways Black actors, dancers, songwriters, and vaudevillians not only changed the theatre, but reimagined their identities and the parameters of their own sense of freedom. Black performers were not singularly the objects of White performers' *Black* caricature; they were innovators, even as some of their innovations created stereotypes of Blackness that remain in the popular culture today. For example, Stanley Lemons once observed that the minstrel show had been so convincing in peddling depictions of Black "character" that by the twentieth century "they were so familiar that few people had any notion that they degraded black Americans. Most people thought the caricatures were simply funny. They laughed with good humor, but their sense of humor revealed a pervasive lack of sensitivity."[12] Thus, vaudeville did not replace minstrelsy; it simply added more nuance and changed the political import of theatrical, dance, and musical forms. This chapter contends with this complexity as it relates to Canada and the late nineteenth century context of the blackface Atlantic.

In the first decades of the minstrel show, the costumes and makeup held significant racial-spatial import. Excess or oversized clothing was meant to lampoon the inability of many African Americans to find clothing of an appropriate fit and size, especially as Southern enslaved persons who absconded with the clothing of their masters and misses often fled plantations with clothing that might have been ill-fitting or oversized for their bodies. When the Virginia Minstrels hit the stage in 1843, they sat in a semicircle partly turned to the audience, partly to each other for rhythmic coordination, with Emmett playing his fiddle and Whitlock his banjo, flanked by Pelham pounding his tambourine and Brower furiously rattling the bones. They were directly caricaturing the African American reality of Northern escape versus Southern servitude using songs, skits, and comic speeches, paired with exaggerated makeup composed of skin too dark and lips too red, and clothing that was "far too large."[13] The early minstrel theatre, however, was not only a racialized domain; it was also gendered. In his examination of misogyny in vocal and choral minstrel repertoires, William Mahar asserts that American men acquired knowledge about women from "watching depictions of gender in sketches and songs performed by cross-dressed male actors and from observing the respectable and unrespectable ladies in the audience during performances and intermission promenades."[14] While men learned about women from many sources in antebellum society, the commodified minstrel show's songs about women reinforced existing attitudes about sexuality, prostitution, courtship, marriage, gender equality, and domestic responsibility.[15] From *wenches* to *Buffalo gals, yaller gals* or *yellow girls*, there were many women characters played by men in early minstrelsy, at a time when women did not regularly appear on the legitimate stage. Attending the theatre was not merely a pastime or distraction from life's challenges and troubles; instead, it was where people (primarily men who were not all literate) could learn about politics, gender roles, and race relations.

The *wench* or prima donna role encompassed both male and female traits; it was the wench's presentation of "female promiscuity and the allure of sexual freedom (at least in fantasy) that attracted interest."[16] This character continued a long-standing tradition in British theatre of the pantomime, a bifurcation of gendered characters or, as Marjorie Garber writes, "versions, of 'woman': the low comedy 'Funny Old Gal' (the Charley's Aunt or Dame role) and the romantic 'prima donna' or 'wench.'"[17] Like minstrelsy's use of blackface, the theatrical tradition of cross-dressing developed from "travesty" has existed for millennia from the ancient Greeks through to Shakespeare when mostly boys played all the female roles.[18] In early minstrelsy, the wench character served as the object of stage desire, and she may have been too active a participant—too passionate—to serve as the still, rigid, almost paralytic feminine being which was needed to ensure the formation of a successful masculine identity, an identity that needed to be established and re-established in the sentimental songs of minstrelsy.[19] Significantly, wench characters became the most popular theme in songs that underwrote early minstrelsy's immense success with urban, working-class male audiences.[20]

"Miss Lucy Long" (1842), along with "Buffalo Gals" (1844), "Cynthia Sue" (1844), and "Lucy Neal" (1848) were popular wench songs with "Lucy Long" becoming unquestionably the most popular song of minstrelsy's first decade.[21] In Boston, for example, "Lucy Long" was enacted with a different text which appeared in a sheet music edition and in a slender booklet, titled *Songs of the Virginia Minstrels* under the heading "Miss Lucy Long and Her Answer."[22] Where the wench or "The Funny Old Gal" referred to characters who performed rubber-legged acrobatics with limbs concealed in outlandish frills and furbelows, there were other characters on the minstrel stages who were sexualized. *Buffalo*, *yaller*, or *yellow gals* identified Black women of mixed lineage who were often depicted as tragic "mulattoes" of plantation slavery.[23] These "plantation girls" were depicted in songs like "Lucy Neal," which painted a sentimental portrait of a *yaller gal* as a woman victimized by a White master, a depiction that played a prominent role in cultural productions of the century like Joseph Holt Ingraham's *Octoroon* (1841), Henry Wadworth Longfellow's "Quadroon Girl" (1842), Mrs. E.D.E.N. Southworth's *Retribution* (1849), Harriet Beecher Stowe's *Uncle Tom's Cabin* (1852), and William Wells Brown's *Clotel; or The President's Daughter* (1853).[24] These melodramas explored what Saidiya Hartman calls "the pleasures and dangers of racial travesty in tales of distressed quadroons and octoroons."[25]

So popular was the wench character in theatrical performance that Montreal's Notman photographic archive also contains images of male actors costumed as women. *Mr. W. Campbell and Male* acts as a commentary on minstrelsy's categorization of women (see figure 6.2), as does *Mr. E. Shepherd in Blackface Fancy Dress* (see figure 6.3). These images reveal how female impersonators sometimes portrayed women as unattractive by wearing mismatched clothes and oversized embellished sleeves, sitting in poses with legs wide open that would have registered as masculine in the nineteenth century.[26] The minstrel show's mimicry of women, then, cannot be understood without grasping the intersections of race, gender, and class in the nineteenth century. For instance, the high-stepping gyrations of the wench character's strut

6.2 Wm. Notman & Son photograph titled "Mr. W. Campbell and Male," April 21, 1896, II-115038.1, the McCord Stewart Museum, Montreal.

often revealed "matching satin bloomers" that each wench wore beneath his skirts.²⁷ The bloomer style, which consisted of Turkish trousers worn beneath a long, wide tunic that was tied with a sash, was named the "Bloomer costume" after Amelia Bloomer (1818–94), an American feminist who, alongside suffragette Elizabeth Cody Stanton (1815–1902), had been responsible for its adoption among fellow women's rights activists in antebellum America.²⁸ As Garber notes, the minstrel show frequently lampooned "bloomers in particular, and women's

6.3 Wm. Notman & Son photograph titled "Mr. E. Shepherd in Blackface Fancy Dress," 1896, II-114528.1, the McCord Stewart Museum, Montreal.

desire to wear pants in general."[29] In its first two decades, minstrelsy's stages were thus as much about demeaning African Americans as they were about criticizing single working women, including those who worked as prostitutes, and activists who were not only demanding full citizenship rights but also leading temperance movements and dress reform.[30]

Ultimately, the minstrel show, as a homosocial, cross-dressed space, sought to thwart women's political activism by pitting women against one another. Unsurprisingly, minstrelsy's approach to the question of female equality was generally negative, "portraying marriages as getting worse the longer they last;" as well, blackface comedy stressed the hierarchical relationship implied in marriage through tropes like "the scolding wife character" who constantly criticized her husband's small faults.[31] Minstrelsy's depictions of women embodied the complex attitudes toward gender that were offered up in satires, parodies, and comic songs during the antebellum period. By the 1870s, however, the minstrel show format was waning in popularity and an emergent genre of entertainment known as vaudeville offered up something new for the stage. This new vaudeville theatre encouraged the upper classes to join with manual laborers and African Americans (although restricted to upper balconies) and White patrons to watch a variety of attractions, from Shakespeare to tumbling and juggling. But this common culture, a comingling of social groups in the theatre and of different types of acts on stage gave way to a division between high and low culture, art and popular culture.[32] As cities began to create their own culture, Susan Glenn observes that "ethnic humor, which caricatured working class and upwardly mobile Jewish, Irish, and German (called 'Dutch') immigrants, provided what was arguably the most important element in the...routines of male comics. Women comics most commonly used black/white racial references or more generalized images of exotic foreignness rather than group-specific caricatures of immigrant ethnicity."[33] By the second half of the nineteenth century, public institutions such as art museums, symphony orchestras, and foreign opera created separate, homogeneous "high culture" venues with bourgeois standards of behaviour that replaced the unruly activities that had taken place in the country's theatres and music halls.[34] Art, foreign-language opera, and classical music became separated from English-language opera, which often combined with variety acts like jugglers and blackface comedians; during vaudeville, theatrical audiences became divided into relatively homogeneous groups, with working-class men dominating the popular theatres, immigrants attending foreign-language theatres, and elite men and women patronizing expensive drama and performance halls.[35]

As White and ethnic immigrant women, Black women, and Black men began to perform on vaudeville's racialized stages in and out of blackface, White women had access to a limited range of plays, songs, and dances while Black performers were largely restricted to the *new* plantation, including forms of dialogue, song, dance, and set designs that bore little resemblance to real Southern slavery, but instead came to *represent*

slavery. As Yuval Taylor and Jake Austen write, "mixed minstrel shows arose, offering black performers in one part and white performers in another...[this] did not signify an increase in racial tolerance but rather a willingness upon the part of some black performers to perform white characterizations of black life for white audiences, just as they had done in the days of slavery."[36] By the 1890s, male-female, female-female, male-male comedy acts emerged in vaudeville, joining the minstrel show and burlesque as lowbrow performance forms that intentionally pushed limits and caused much controversy.

Vaudeville ushered in stereotypes of just about every kind of person, including immigrant comic characters who would have quelled White fears about the changing face of North America in the late nineteenth century. Sophie Tucker (1886–1966) was among the most famous of new Jewish immigrant women performers who merged elements from minstrelsy with vaudeville. At one point in her career, Tucker was also known as the "World-renowned Coon Shouter" and sometimes she was called a "Manipulator of Coon Melodies" or a "Refined Coon Shouter."[37] Other Jewish women such as Nora Bayes (1880–1928) and Fanny Brice (1891–1951), and non-Jewish women like Stella Mayhew (1874–1934) *blacked up*—or, slightly more subtly, as Lori Harrison-Kahan describes, "tanned up" at some point in their careers when they performed *coon shouting*, a style of singing that was supposedly "modeled on black song (or at least white perceptions of black song)."[38] Unlike the legitimate theatre, which referred to a performance wholly by the spoken word as a one show, one-night or two-night affair, vaudeville shows were made up of a continuous sequence of self-contained acts. Each would appear from anywhere from three to six times a day and up to seven days a week, depending on whether the theatre was part of a big-time or small-time circuit and whether it offered a full- or split-week booking.[39] Although at first Black minstrels found it difficult to play below the Mason-Dixon line (the dividing line between the slave states South and free-soil states North of it—West Virginia, Virginia, and Maryland, and Pennsylvania, Ohio, and Delaware, respectively), eventually Black minstrel troupes, unlike the dignified and high-class jubilee singers who largely avoided the Southern states, were accepted by southern White people as posing no threat to the idea of the "Negro" as an inferior race.[40] This era of late-minstrelsy, as Lynn Abbott and Doug Seroff note, "expanded professional opportunities for a broad range of African American performers and musicians," including Black women who "finally gained the minstrel, vaudeville, and burlesque stage and exerted an immediate influence as dancers, singers, and comedians."[41]

In 1890, when the state of Louisiana passed the Separate Car Act, which created "separate but equal" cars for African Americans, the statute made it illegal for any Black person—even those who had previously identified as mixed-race or Creoles of Colour—to sit in coach seats reserved for Whites. This law created the commercial conditions for the Pullman Sleeping Car Porter rail service to expand, as it replicated the master/servant relations of pre-Civil War plantation slavery. Following the landmark case *Plessy v. Ferguson* (1896), when the US Supreme Court ruled that African Americans could access the legal system "equal" to that of White Americans (but had to maintain separate institutions to facilitate these rights), White America and Black America began to live separate lives, brought together only through the visual culture and entertainment industries. Beginning in the 1890s, as Black people travelled and rode in segregated railroad cars, what was produced on stage *became*, in many instances, the only Black American narratives White audiences consumed outside of newspaper editorials about Black crime, poverty, and deprivation. At the same time, with vaudeville's mixed seating and expanded auditoriums, Black audiences had opportunities to watch Black entertainers on a more regular basis. This also created more of an appetite for Black songs and dances, even if the Black singers and dancers continued to peddle plantation-themed lyrics and grotesque bodily caricatures. In the Northern states especially, Black minstrels continued to vie with the far more dignified jubilee singers, but also with both amateur and professional non-blackface Black theater troupes; and, by the early 1890s, Black vaudeville, burlesque, circus sideshows (featuring both Black bands and Black minstrel troupes), and Negro baseball.[42] This is the context that brought *Black* minstrelsy to Canada in unprecedented numbers, along with jubilee singing and female vaudevillians who combined jokes about immigrant groups and sexualized dances. American entertainment in Canada exploded in the 1890s, leading not only to the widening of the importation of American culture, but also, as the twentieth century arrived, a cultural identity crisis that would spawn the establishment of protectionist cultural policy.

In an editorial published in the *New York Age* on February 28, 1891, William Foote, a White man who assisted Haverly for many years, was identified as someone who worked with "Negro minstrel troupes from the days of George Christy. He was for many years manager of Haverly's Mastodon minstrels.... For three years, Mr. Foote, in London, successfully controlled the Mastodons.... He made copious notes of the humorous side of the Negro character...."[43] In its 1882 appearance in Toronto, Haverly's New Mastodon Minstrels consisted of the "grand consolidation of both the old and new into one Grand Company of 80 PEOPLE."[44] Back in 1872, the *Daily Globe* had announced a performance by the Fisk Jubilee Singers at Shaftesbury Hall, Toronto's first Young Men's Christian Association (YMCA), built at Queen and James Streets. The Hall was located on the ground floor with a direct entrance from the street and had a seating capacity of about 1,700.In addition to the Toronto Philharmonic Society, which performed there until 1879, its occasional tenants included the Theodore Thomas Orchestra (1873), the Mendelssohn Quartette Club (1877), the Queen's Own Rifles Band (1878), and the Toronto String Quartette (1886–87), along with educational and temperance groups.[45] "The fact that the original company of Jubilee Singers is to give two grand concerts in Shaftesbury Hall, the first on Monday, the 18th and the second on Friday, the 22nd last, will afford no small gratification to a large number of our citizens," the *Globe* reported on October 14, 1880, adding, "Most people in Canada have heard of these sweet singers, who by their exertions have done so much for Fisk University, but they have not hitherto had an opportunity of seeing them. The present will be their visit to the Dominion, and no doubt they will receive a kindly welcome and extensive patronage."[46]

Weeks later, the Original Fisk Jubilee Singers gave another performance at Shaftesbury Hall "to a well-filled house," described the *Globe*. The newspaper then provided an in-depth editorial about their performance:

> The pieces were for the most part the sacred plantation melodies which they sang with as much verve as the slaves would have done a quarter of a century ago in Louisiana, but with more taste and artistic appreciation of their real beauties.... They are never "composed" after the manner of ordinary music, but spring into life ready-made from the white heat of religious fervour during some protracted meeting in church or

camp. But though they are the "ecstatic utterances of wholly untutored minds" they possess for the ear of even the cultivated listener a peculiar charm.... Last night's programme embraces such pieces as "Steal Away to Jesus," "Band of Gideon," "The Gospel Train," "Bright Sparkles in the Churchyard," etc.... They recognize the fact that people come to hear the plantation melodies, and the number of encores they win by singing them shows that they have a permanent hold on popular favour no less by their music than by the cause they represent. There will be another concert of the same general character, but with change of programme, in Shaftesbury Hall to-night.[47]

Where early minstrelsy challenged the abolitionist cause by focusing not only on the caricaturing of Black bodies—through dress, expressions, appearances, and adornments—but also on sentimentalizing the plantation itself (the very thing that English-speaking countries across the Atlantic were economically wedded to in the nineteenth century), jubilee singers challenged the notion of slavery itself. Rather than construct false narratives about slave life, plantation sceneries, and the believed-to-be aesthetics of slavery, the Fisk Jubilee sang from the heart the same songs that had aided in their survival. The Fisk Jubilee Singers were once described as recalling "fond memories to everyone who has dwelt in Dixie," but as Seroff rightfully notes, "nothing could have been further from the purposes of the Fisk Jubilee Singers than to recall 'fond memories' of antebellum days. Yet for decades, in fact well into the twentieth century, white audiences continued to derive sweet, distorted memories of 'old times down South' from the 'sorrow songs' of the slavery era."[48] The Fisk Jubilee Singers were civil rights activists who used the stage to protest not only unjust laws, but as W.E.B. Du Bois observed, "They [were] the music of an unhappy people, of the children of disappointment; they [told] of death and suffering and unvoiced longing toward a truer world, of misty wanderings and hidden ways. The songs [were] indeed the siftings of centuries; the music [was] far more ancient than the words, and in it we [could] trace here and there signs of development."[49]

Many Black performers during the first few decades of vaudeville had to make a deal with themselves about the roles they were playing, their potential impact on real Black people (including the opportunities they believed they were creating for Black entertainers), and the potential harm their performances would cause in the long term. As David Krasner argues, "Capitalizing on the 'coon song' craze, [Bert] Williams and [George] Walker appropriated the term 'coon' and applied it to their show…the idea of being the 'real coons' was not lost on black performers. Williams and Walker, and their friend and rival Robert 'Bob' Cole and his company, Cole and Johnson, displayed throughout their writings and actions an acute awareness of the 'real' as a cultural signifier and marketing tool."[50] At one point in the 1890s, Bahamas-born Williams (1874–1922) and Lawrence, Kansas-born Walker (c. 1872–1911) were billing themselves as "Two Real Coons." About this billing, Walker said: "We thought that as there seemed to be a great demand for blackfaces on the stage, we would do all we could to get what we felt belonged to us by the laws of nature. We finally decided that as white men with black faces were billing themselves 'coons,' Williams and Walker would do well to bill themselves as 'The Two Real Coons' and so we did."[51] By the 1900s, Williams and Walker would become the most sought-after Black performers when they starred in *In Dahomey* (1902), *Abyssinia* (1906), and *Bandanna Land* (1907). Set in Dahomey, Africa (present-day Benin), *In Dahomey* became an international success after opening at Stamford, Connecticut. It was the first in a trio of "back-to-Africa" musicals that included *Abyssinia*, about a group of African Americans travelling to Ethiopia, and *Bandanna Land*, though not about a trip to Africa was about a park of the same name for African Americans. The latter of these African-themed Black musicals would play in Toronto in 1907 and 1908, respectively.

Blackface Black performers crisscrossed stages where White men and women donned the blackface mask in pretend of Black people. This would have presented a profound crisis among the Black community. The reality of their lives was rendered invisible through their performances, which captured the public's imagination. Even Tucker offered what John Springhall has called, "a bastardized version of what were thought to be 'authentic' African American folk songs."[52] As Krasner writes further, "the real as a commercial device made it possible to break mainstream show business's color barrier. The real enticed white audiences because realism was in vogue."[53] As *coon songs* and "real coons" became popular among White audiences, it would have been something familiar to them—the idea of African Americans "selling" themselves as performers, just as they had done during slavery. "Selling blackness," as Harry J. Elam notes, "conjures images of the auction block and black bodies sold to the highest white bidder. In the arena of slavery, the auction block compelled restricted, distorted performances of blackness where any display of black agency raised concerns, and blackness became understood only in terms of white desire and black economic utility."[54] In other words, acting the part of a "coon" was marketable and commercially viable for the performer if they spoke the language that White audiences understood—that Blackness was something you could "put on" and "act out," not something to be taken seriously as a social being or political subject.

Conversely, as Black women operatic singers began to appear, performing in a style that borrowed from European opera not *Black* caricature, they challenged not only *Black* minstrels in vaudeville, but also the jubilee singers' emphasis on their past lives in slavery. The lack of historical documentation about African American civil rights and spiritual performance in the nineteenth century is one reason why Black women contraltos have been erased by history. As feminist performance scholar Peggy Phelan poignantly observes, "performance's only life is in the present. Performance cannot be saved, recorded, documented, or otherwise participate in the circulation of representations *of* representations.... Performance occurs over a time which will not be repeated. It can be performed again, but this repetition itself marks it as 'different.'"[55] While Phelan is writing about twentieth-century performance, her theories help explain why nineteenth-century Black singers who represented the Black experience through the rejection of racial caricature are lesser known today than those performers who replicated such stereotypes in minstrelsy. Soprano Elizabeth Taylor Greenfield, who toured England in the 1850s on behalf of the abolitionist movement (see figure 6.4), presented a different style of music that was, like the Fisk Jubilee Singers, a blending of European and African American folk music, but her music was not singularly of a spiritual nature. Other operatic soprano singers of the era included the Hyers Sisters (Anna Madah and Emma Louise) and Matilda Sissieretta Jones (see figure 6.5), also known as the "Black Patti" in reference to Italian opera singer Adelina Patti (1843–1919), who was one of the first woman singing sensations of the nineteenth century. Because the Fisk Jubilee Singers had challenged *Black* minstrelsy's position as the dominant form of Black expressive culture, they made room for other Black singers to exist. Because these women exist, it can be said with certainty that White audiences saw

6.4 Elizabeth Taylor Greenfield (ca. 1824–76), from the New York Public Library Schomburg Center for Research in Black Culture, Photographs and Prints Division, b11486940.

6.5 Poster featuring M. Sissieretta Jones (Black Patti), 1899, Prints and Photographs Division, Theatrical Poster Collection, Library of Congress, 2014635809.

more than one singular representation of Blackness in the nineteenth century. And yet, what remains an issue is how White audiences (i.e., elite Protestants who attended jubilee performances) interpreted these diverse performers, as working- and middle-class White people more frequently attended the concert hall, saloon, or common theatre to watch minstrel shows. For the most part, as Kira Thurman opines, "in comparison to black minstrelsy, cakewalking, and popular dance music—forms of black music-making that societies on both sides of Atlantic had deemed commercial rather than cultivated—the spiritual alone hummed with the musical promise of a civilized African American folk."[56]

The cakewalk's emergence in the 1890s, in tandem with *coon songs* at a time Megan Pugh refers to as "the nadir of American race relations," was such that "whites' racial anxiety was consuming the nation. It fueled debates in the halls of 'Redeemed' legislatures and sparked race riots in Wilmington (1898), New Orleans, and New York (both 1900).... It infused the circling movements of black cakewalkers, the image of America abroad, and the wheeling turns of 'Jim Crow.'"[57] During the spring of 1892, a rash of cakewalk extravaganzas broke out in big cities of the Northeast and Midwest. That year, the first Annual Cakewalk Jubilee was held at Madison Square Garden in New York City.[58] "By some contemporaneous accounts," write Lynn Abbott and Doug Seroff, these promoted cakewalks were spectacles of "the ridiculous, undermining and corrupting an African American tradition 'for the amusement of the white people, who look down on them, in every sense of the word, from the galleries.'"[59] The cakewalk was a dance that initially developed in African American communities as a parody of White balls; it not only functioned as a signifying critique, but became a sensation because of its groundbreaking demonstration of the grace and creativity that are foundations of African American dance.[60] The cakewalk's basic steps required dancers to kick their legs forward in a high, exaggerated march and promenade, usually in a circle, sometimes in a line.[61] The effects of the cakewalk craze did not escape Canadian listeners and composers such as Robert Nathaniel Dett (1882–1943). Born in Drummondville, Ontario (now part of Niagara Falls), Dett was one of the first Canadian-born Black composers of a new genre of music that appeared in the late nineteenth century called ragtime, a genre of music that elevated the coon song of the stage into the popular culture. Other

6.6 Sheet music cover for G.W. Adams "The Cake Winner," 1899, Library and Archives Canada, the National Library Collections, 83828508.

Canadians produced sheet versions of cakewalk songs, such as "The Cake Winner (The Most Popular Cake Walk)" (1899) by G.W. Adams, published by Toronto-based Amey & Hodgins (see figure 6.6).

The cakewalk and ragtime gained acceptance at almost the same moment as operatic recitalists such as Taylor Greenfield, who was also known as the "African Nightingale" (an homage to Swedish opera singer Jenny Lind (1820–87), known as "the Swedish Nightingale"); this was at a time when most White Americans (along with Canadians and Europeans) were unwilling to fully accept African Americans as creators and performers of classical (European) music.[62] Over a decade before the first *Black* minstrel troupe was organized, and a few years after the arrival of William Henry Lane, Taylor Greenfield made her debut as a soprano in Buffalo, New York; from 1851 to 1854 she toured the Atlantic, even making stops in Canada.[63] Born into slavery in Natchez, Mississippi around 1819, when Taylor Greenfield was legally emancipated, she emigrated to Philadelphia, and by the 1850s, she became the first Black woman to sing music professionally on any stage in Canada.[64] Also hailed as the "Black Swan" (after Irish opera singer Catherine Hayes (1818–61), also known as "the Swan of Erin" or the "Irish Swan"), Kristin Moriah explains that "[Elizabeth Taylor's] 1853 tour of England propelled her to international fame. But [h]er work frequently brought her to US-Canadian border cities and into Canada; she concertized in Toronto...and towns near Black settlements like Chatham."[65]

Significantly, the monikers attached to Taylor Greenfield aligned her with White women sopranos of a similar style. On one hand such mimetic naming would have been flattering for Taylor Greenfield because, as Arthur R. LaBrew explains, both were "the names of birds" and they were reflective of the era in which monikers were the dominant mode of distinguishing one singer from another.[66] However, as Moriah aptly notes, "in this moniker [Taylor Greenfield as the 'Black Jenny Lind'] we see race supplanting nation at the same time bird monikers were used to compare her to other white singers. Similar forms of racialized description were used for Black singers throughout the nineteenth century."[67] The Hyers Sisters are another example of race supplanting nation. At ten and twelve years of age, Anna (c. 1855–1929) and Emma Hyers (c. 1857–1901) began their careers giving recitals; their first took place at the Metropolitan Theatre in San Francisco in 1867, just two years after the end of the US Civil War, and four years after the Emancipation Proclamation.[68] Like Taylor Greenfield before them, the Hyers Sisters sang traditional European concert music, identifying themselves as Jocelyn Buckner writes, "as versatile performers capable of performing well beyond the narrow stereotypes of minstrelsy, yet their ability to also perform black musical traditions, such as spirituals, served to underscore their identity as African Americans."[69] From 1867 to 1876 the sisters performed concerts of operatic excerpts, art songs, popular ballads, and, from 1872 onward, Negro spirituals.[70] In 1876 the Hyers Sisters turned to musical theatre, creating three productions that toured throughout the US until the 1890s: Joseph Bradford's *Out of Bondage* (originally titled *Out of the Wilderness*, 1876), E.S. Getchell's *Urlina, the African Princess* (1879), and *Uncle Tom's Cabin* (1880).[71] These productions introduced audiences to Sam Lucas (1848–1916), the African American actor who would later become famous for playing Uncle Tom on film.

From 1888 to 1895, Sissieretta Jones toured the US, Canada, Europe, and the Caribbean as a soloist. She attracted international attention for her well-publicized appearances such as "Grand Negro Jubilee," which was performed at Madison Square Garden and Carnegie Hall (which opened in 1891), as well as appearances at the 1892 Pittsburgh Exposition, and the Women's Pavilion at the World's Columbian Exposition in Chicago in 1893.[72] When Sissieretta Jones headlined a concert on the main stage of Carnegie Hall in 1893 she not only became the first African American woman to appear at the prestigious New York City concert hall, but she also became a star of the stage.[73] By the mid-1890s, Sissieretta Jones had sung for audiences across the Atlantic; however, she essentially gave up on her quest for a rightful place on the mainstream opera stage that was still preserved for White singers. In 1896 she accepted an offer to appear as the principal star and figurehead of the minstrel/burlesque troupe calling itself the Black Patti Troubadours, and she went on tour along the US West Coast with Hi Henry's Minstrel Co. during the 1898–1899 season.[74] Hi (Hiram) F. Henry (1844–1920) was born in Buffalo, New York and during the 1890s, his minstrel companies also toured Canada.

Sissieretta Jones's Black Patti Troubadours toured until 1915, performing a combination of "Coon Comedy, Coon Songs, Jubilee Shouts, Cake Walks, Buck Dancers, Vaudeville, Operatic Masterpieces," alongside the likes of Black minstrel performers like Bob Cole who, after a stint with the Black Patti Troubadours in 1896, established his own production company alongside his wife, Aida (Aide) Overton Walker (1880–1914), in which he also performed *coon songs* and other comedic parts; after he departed Jones's act he co-wrote the music for *A Trip to Coontown* with Billy Johnson. In addition to Cole, Ernest Hogan also toured with Sissieretta's Black Patti Troubadours.[75] While Overton Walker did not join them on tour, she became a star in her own right, sometimes referred to as "The Queen of the Cakewalk." She also helped make the dance the most popular element of the Black theatrical stage, with her elaborate choreography and costumes drawing more White women to the dance in the 1900s.[76]

What's most significant about operatic singers like Taylor Greenfield, the Hyers Sisters, and Sissieretta Jones is they offered something entirely different on stage. They drew inspiration for their style of opera from other African American women like Flora Baston (1864–1906) dubbed "the colored Jenny Lind" and "The Double-Voiced Queen of Song" because of her soprano-baritone range, and Marie Selika Williams (1849–1937), "the third Black prima donna of the era," who became the first Black singer to perform at the White House in 1878 when she sang for President Rutherford B. Hayes—the same president who had endorsed the Compromise of 1877.[77] These Black women singers debunked many stereotypes about Black women from the wench to mammy. In the post-Reconstruction era, they demanded their civil rights in the limited spaces where they could. On April 6, 1889, the *Indianapolis Freeman* reported that Selika Williams refused to sing in an Opera House in the South because the managers refused to sell first-class seats to African Americans.[78] Similarly, after an 1893 concert in Louisville, Kentucky where Black patrons were restricted to the packed upper gallery while some of the best seats, reserved for Whites, sat empty, Sissieretta Jones told *The Louisville Commercial*, "I think people of my race ought not to be shut out in this way."[79]

One reason operatic performers have largely been forgotten by history as the likes of Jim Crow, the Virginia Minstrels, and even *Black* minstrel vaudevillians like Williams, Cole, and Hogan have been memorialized in history is because of what the minstrel mask allowed performers to do. With it, they could create a persona that fit within the wider cultural milieu where "acceptable" Blackness was equated with all that was silly, childlike, and comical while the *natural* Black performer without the burnt cork could only be taken "seriously" by White audiences when they blended European opera with African American folk music—the former being seen as *civilizing* agent. The reproducibility of minstrelsy meant that it could morph and change. Negro spiritual singers and operatic singers, on the other hand, were unique talents, not because they had received training in European musical traditions, but because they had an authentic connection to the Black church and spiritual narratives of salvation and uplift.

In the 1890s, newspapers helped foster widespread enthusiasm for a much broader spectrum of Black musical and theatrical talent. This performance resisted tones that "often pandered to popular racist sentiment" and instead was steadfast in its mission to foster Black racial and social uplift. The *Globe*, which had competition in its morning readership from the *Daily*

Mail and Empire (established in 1872 as the *Mail*), was a voice for John A. Macdonald's faction in the federal Conservative Party while, in 1887, the Macdonald Conservatives set up another Toronto newspaper, the *Empire* that, four years after Macdonald's death in 1895, would be merged with the *Mail* to become the *Mail and Empire*.[80] Meanwhile, Toronto's other newspaper, the *Evening Telegram* or *Tely* as it was also known, would become the most widely read paper in the city with its emphasis on local news.[81] Founded in 1876 by John Ross Robertson, the Toronto-born son of Scottish immigrants and a fierce defender of "British traditions," the *Tely* used "sensational practices, maverick politics, and much local news to win the support of the less sophisticated and less prosperous readers in Canada's cities," explains William Jenkins.[82] Despite their partisan differences and distribution (some were morning papers, some were evening papers) Toronto's papers were obsessed with Black minstrelsy in the 1890s, covering every angle with sensational headlines, in-depth features, and theatrical reviews.

Minstrel actor Cool Burgess was the subject of a series of articles, reviews, and advertisements in the *Telegram*, the *Globe*, and the *Toronto Leader* (1854–78), founded and published by merchant James Beaty. Other newspapers around the province and country like the *Ottawa Citizen* (1845–), *Manitoba Free Press* (1872–), *London Free Press* (1849–), and *Hamilton Herald* (1889–1936), also reported on Burgess's career.[83] When he died in 1905, the *Globe* mourned him with a headline that read, "At One Time the Most Prominent Figure in Minstrelsy." The obituary stated, "Mr. Burgess had been living quietly at Eglinton and in Toronto for eight years or more.... born in Yorkville sixty-five years ago.... Mr. Burgess travelled through the United States, with varying success, for some years, but it was not until he began his 'burnt cork' career that he discovered his true métier."[84] It continued, "The minstrel show at that time was in the heyday of its popularity, and 'Cool' Burgess soon identified himself with the most prominent organizations of the kind and acquired an enviable reputation as an endman of particular comedy powers in song, dance and story. He continued in that line for many years, rarely forsaking his black make-up." The *Globe* went on to eulogize Burgess by explaining that during his years as an entertainer he had worked with most of the prominent minstrel performers of his time, travelling the length and breadth of North America with organizations of his own, but also Canadian minstrel entertainers like

6.7 "Shoo, fly! Don't bodder me!" sheet music cover, 1869, the Historic American Sheet Music Collection, David M. Rubenstein Rare Book & Manuscript Library. Duke University, Durham, North Carolina.

George Primrose. Other obituaries noted Burgess's "Shoo, fly! Don't bodder me!" (1869) as "the most popular coon song of its decade" (see figure 6.7).[85] At the same time, in the context of Ontario's theatre scene, for some reason, 1892 saw the nostalgic return of plantation minstrel shows.

Primrose & West's minstrels appeared at Toronto's Academy of Music on King Street West on April 23, 1892 while Cleveland's Big Consolidated Minstrels appeared at the Grand Opera House for one night only on May 30, 1892.[86] A fire destroyed the Academy of Music, and after a rebuilding it opened as the city's second Academy of Music in 1889; following a remodel in 1895, the Academy of Music became known as the Princess Theatre (which closed in 1930). In a review of the latter show the next day, the *Globe* reported, "As might be expected, Cleveland's Minstrels drew a considerable audience to the Grand Opera House last night, but still not so large as the merit of this famous troupe deserved," adding that "The programme was long and varied, including besides the usual selection of quaint, humorous and pathetic plantation songs, a number of exceedingly clever attractions in the way of burlesque songs, dances, music from most extraordinary looking instruments or machines, and lastly, a marvellous exhibition of equilibristic skill by Mr. Hilton, Mr. Frank Cushman, who was introduced as the greatest living minstrel, delighted the audience with his clever mimicry of an Irishman, German, and negro."[87] That same year, an amateur minstrel troupe called the Young Liberal Club Minstrels appeared in Toronto at the Grand Opera House. After their performance, they boarded an early train for another performance at Chatham.[88] "The members will leave here by an early train and will parade with the Young Liberals band to the races in the afternoon," the *Globe* reported.[89] In a November 24, 1893 editorial in the same paper, its readers were encouraged to know who these amateur minstrels were, writing "Many know the London Young Liberal Club only by the excellent minstrel performances given occasionally by its members."[90] The Young Liberals were not merely a minstrel club—they were also doing active political work. With offices in Chatham, St. Thomas, Brockville, Hamilton, Guelph, and Stratford, the Young Liberal Club was a social and political club for the provincial and federal Liberal parties, the exclusive domain of White Anglo-Saxon Protestant men.

On February 9, 1895, an entire page was dedicated to the Ontario Federation of Liberal Club to explain its purpose and the Young Liberal movement in the province of Ontario which had, since the 1880s, continued to grow. "For several years past, clubs have been spreading rapidly in the cities and smaller centres, and it was felt that there was need for some central organization through which the formation of clubs in the country districts could be promoted and the views of the federated clubs on the public questions of the day could be presented to the political leaders and people generally," the feature explained, adding that the days' two greatest Liberal leaders—Wilfrid Laurier and Sir Oliver Mowat—were the Federation's honorary presidents. While the Young Liberals was, on one hand, the social and political club for the provincial and federal Liberal parties, it was also exclusively for White Anglo-Saxon Protestant men who felt it their mission to ensure Canada's dominant ethos remained aligned with Britain. In one printed address delivered to the Toronto Young Men's Liberal Club on January 19, 1885 titled *Loyalty*, James David Edgar (1841–99), legal editor of the *Globe*, city council alderman in St. George's Ward, and chair of the Liberal Party's parliamentary committee, said, "An Englishman is loyal to his Queen and Parliament—to the British Constitution, in which the Sovereign is the nominal head, but Parliament the real sovereign." Edgar continued, "In all speculations upon the present and future of Canada we Anglo-Saxons must not forget that a large and important element in our population is of another lineage.... To found a united nation we must have a common ground upon which we can stand with the French Canadians. Our European traditions are not theirs."[91] The 1890s was the first decade where audiences began to reminisce about the minstrel show of yesteryear. In an article reprinted in the *Globe* in 1893 (originally appearing in the *New York Herald*) the paper declared, "minstrelsy is as popular as ever, but that it must be negro minstrelsy pure and simple, not an ordinary variety show in disguise, but a good old fashioned plantation minstrel performance, with the comic old and young rural darkey of the southern home as he is, and not a collection of impossible characters that have no existence off the stage."[92] The article was written by Lew Dockstader (1856–1924), an American vaudeville actor who performed in blackface and reached the pinnacle of his career in the 1890s. "It would be a great blessing to mankind if some manager would act upon this hint and give us on the stage a real portrayal of the negro character—the real negro songs and the real mirth of one of the merriest races," the editorial added. Dockstader, who teamed up with Primrose to form Primrose and Dockstader's Minstrel Men, toured until 1904.⁹³

Such editorials reveal how sentimental vaudeville actors were for the old minstrel show, which did not cater to everyone but was instead the exclusive domain of White men performing scenes as if they were Black men and women at "home" on the plantation and "out of place" in the North. This nostalgia was also visible in Montreal where the *Gazette* and *Herald*, which became a daily newspaper in 1871, were riddled with similar nostalgic editorializing.⁹⁴ In June 1894, when *The Octoroon* appeared at the Theatre Royal, the *Gazette* reported that "Patrons of the Royal will no doubt avail themselves of the opportunity afforded this week of renewing acquaintances with an old favourite." *The Octoroon* always received a "hearty welcome. Those who have previously seen it pay their money to witness it again, and those who look upon it for the first time enjoy it equally as much as those to whom its several scenes are familiar,"⁹⁵ the paper added. The show first appeared at the Theatre Royal during the 1866 season. It was an adaptation of Dion Boucicault's (1820–90) original play based on Thomas Mayne Reid's novel, *The Quadroon* (1856) about slavery and miscegenation. Originally performed in 1859 at New York's Winter Garden Theatre, such productions were an example of the ways the conditions of the deep South had long sentimentalized the "Negro condition."⁹⁶ *The Octoroon* also appeared at Toronto's Grand Opera House in 1896, with the *Globe* noting it had been "a number of years since this piece was presented in Toronto."⁹⁷ In February 1895, a review in the *Gazette* for a performance of *In Old Kentucky* at Montreal's Academy of Music (built in 1875) was described as arriving there after much New York success. The play was described as "strength and gorgeous scenic display," and that it provided "a series of truthful pictures of Southern life" that "caught the fancy of Gotham's playgoers."⁹⁸ The main feature of the show, the newspaper proclaimed, was the "Pickaninny Band" who "played a number of brass instruments" along with the "dancing and the prankish frolic of lively colored boys." As Abbott and Seroff poignantly observe about *In Old Kentucky*, "It was a legitimate dramatic production with an almost entirely white cast. The story revolved around a group of Kentucky mountaineers—hillbillies—and it included moonshiners, revenue officers, a family feud, etc. There is nothing in the plot to indicate a place for African American performers, *In Old Kentucky* was...the vehicle which propelled the craze for 'pickaninny bands.'"[99]

In May 1895, another minstrel show called *Down in Dixie* appeared at Montreal's Theatre Royal. It also featured a "Pickaninny Brass Band," according to an advertisement in the *Herald*, which described "[a] $10,000 Cotton Compress. The Alligator Creek.... The Cottonfield Singers. The Plantation Pastimes."[100] In April 1896, as the show arrived at Toronto's Opera House, the *Globe* profiled Milt Barlow (1843–1904), who by the late nineteenth century was most known for playing the character "Old Black Joe" in touring productions of *Uncle Tom's Cabin*. "So many good stories have been written about Milt Barlow, who appears at the Toronto Opera House this week with 'Down in Dixie,' that it is almost impossible to get hold of a new one, but here is one that Milt is telling on himself," began the *Globe*'s editorial. "Some years ago, [Barlow] was travelling with a minstrel show in the south and in one of the towns they played he stopped at a hotel which had as head waiter a tall, dignified old colored man who paid a great deal of attention to Milt. It seems he took Milt for a preacher. Milt thought he would find out if the old fellow wanted to go to the show that night, and, if he did, intended to give him a pass...Milt did not give him a pass."[101]

The following day, *Down in Dixie* appeared at Toronto's Grand Opera House, and as reported by the *Globe*, "a large audience was present." In addition to its own Pickaninny Brass Band, the show was said to comprise "characters...drawn from all the classes of people that are supposed to inhabit the sunny south. There were the ruined planter, with only the memory of his wealth and station 'before the war'; the Judge, proud of himself and his position, but still prouder of his son and jealous lest his son's career should be blighted by a mesalliance; an overseer, typical of the brutal slave-driver, whose presence was more than a memory among the negroes; an old negro 'mammy' and uncle, and many others, all drawn from life."[102] That same month, Barlow brought *On the Mississippi* to Toronto, a show described as "dramatic, comic, and spectacular incidents that follow one another in rapid succession in this play carry the audience almost spell bound in amazement and delight at the passing show of life in the romantic South 'Down in Dixie.'"[103] With such sympathies for the White planter class of the South circulating Northern theatre houses (and conversely, *Black* minstrelsy's reproduction of happy, cakewalking, "negroes" both at home on the plantation's cotton fields and watermelon patches or contented in their subjugated place in the North), it is no wonder blackface continued to be the most dominant theatrical repertoire, even in vaudeville, well into the twentieth century. When Lillian Russell (born Helen Louise Leonard, 1861–1922), known at the time as "the graceful and elegant ideal of 'Anglo-Saxon' female perfection and American artistry,"[104] arrived in Toronto in 1896 in an appearance in Charles Frohman's production of Ralph Lumley's English comedy *Thoroughbred* at the Grand Opera House, the *Globe* described, "one of the incidents of the play is the appearance of the old fellow at the race-track in the disguise of a negro minstrel, a ruse which only leads to greater embarrassments than he sought to avoid."[105] Even in a performance genre that had little to do with plantation slavery or African Americans, the burnt cork mask was still a popular draw.

In April 1896, Hamilton's Grand Opera House became home to *Black* minstrels such as Field's *Darktown Brigade*.[106] Toronto's Massey Hall (erected in 1893 and completed 1894, located at 178 Victoria Street at Shuter to this day) also became a venue for live entertainment, including minstrel shows in the 1890s. As Canadian cities began to expand their infrastructure for large-scale theatrical entertainments of not only blackface but dramas and operas, *Black* and White minstrel troupes spent a lot of time touring Ontario, Quebec, and the Maritimes. The following appeared in Halifax: Reform Club Minstrels (1880); Royal Navy Minstrels (1880); Star Minstrels (1880); Faird's New Orleans Minstrels (1881); Healy's Hibernian Minstrels (1881); and Baird's Mammoth Minstrels (1883 and 1884). In New Brunswick (St. John and Fredericton): Healy's Hibernian Minstrels (1881); Baird's Mammoth Minstrels (1882 and 1884); Skiff & Gaylord's Minstrels (1882); Jerry Cohan's Irish Minstrels (1883 and 1885); Rankin's Mammoth Minstrels & Variety Combination (1884); Rankin's Minstrels (1884); Hi Henry's Minstrels (1884 and 1891);[107] Whitmore & Clark's Minstrels (1886); The Mobile Minstrels (1886); Fredericton Amateur Minstrels (1887); Barlow Bros. & Frost's Ideal Minstrels (1887); Amateur Minstrels of Saint John (1888 and 1889); Johnson & Slavin's Minstrels (1888); Gorman's Elite Minstrels (1890); Atkinson & Cook's Minstrels (1891); Cyprus Minstrels (1891 and 1894); Saint John Amateur

Athletic Club Minstrels (1892 and 1893); Amateur Snowflake Minstrels (1892 and 1893); and Arlington's New United Minstrels (1892).[108] In 1894, the Victoria Amateur Minstrels, a local company, played the Victoria Theatre on November 21 and 22.[109] According to a surviving playbill, *The Minstrel Festival* of the Victoria Amateur Minstrels also performed on the evening of May 16, 1896 an "Opening Overture" followed by songs like "The Ni—er and the Bee," and in the second part a stump speech called, "The 'New Woman,'" as performed by Mr. W.R. Higgins, and "The Alabama Cake Walk" with six characters such as "Uncle Rastus," "Aunt Liza, his wife," and "Picaninnies by Messrs. F. Richardson, E.A. Pauline, H. Howard, H. Austin and G. Goward."[110]

By 1896, Black performers were living in a state of contradiction in North America. After *Plessy v. Ferguson*, the new implemented "Jim Crow" segregation laws, long associated with T.D. Rice, also functioned as a collective racial epithet for Black people, similar to "coon" or "darkie," which dominated minstrel repertoire into the twentieth century.[111] However, as David Pilgrim explains further, "the words Jim Crow were less likely to be used to derisively describe blacks; instead, the phrase Jim Crow was a synonym for the racial caste system which operated, but not exclusively, in southern and border states between 1877 and the mid-1960s."[112] In terms of its impact on performance, the *Plessy* decision came down at the height of the all-Black minstrel musical craze, and at the moment of a historical concert at Carnegie Hall featuring African American singers Selika Williams, Flora Batson, and Sissieretta Jones, who performed there on October 12, just five months after *Plessy*.[113] In 1889, Sam T. Jack's (1852–99) *The Creole Show* departed from the minstrel show format by discarding blackface and offering a "sixteen-girl chorus and…dancing cakewalk."[114] According to Shirley Staples, *The Creole Show* was the first successful departure by African Americans from strict minstrelsy. Jack was a prominent White burlesque producer who conceived the notion of a chorus line of beautiful "Negro women." The show was a sensation, and its repeated success was largely due to its introduction of a cakewalk done in formal dress by Charlie Johnson and Dora Dean (1872–1949), an African American husband and wife duo.[115]

Most of the well-known Black performers of the decade appeared in *The Creole Show*, such as Sam Lucas (who would join Coles's *A Trip to*

Coontown tour of Boston in 1898), Billy McClain (1886–1950) and his wife Cordelia McClain (1852–1925), as well as the male impersonator Florence Hines (1890–1906), and ragtime comedian Irving Jones (1847–1932), who also specialized in coon songs.[116] Hines is particularly significant to the history of performance because when she performed her cakewalk she did so surrounded by women in a semicircle.[117] During her time, she is said to have been hailed as the Black Vesta Tilley (1864–1952), after the White English male impersonator who crossed gender and racial lines on stage. Through her performances, Hines played a Black dandy who was well-groomed, well-dressed, and a self-absorbed man—a role that broke new ground for the way it challenged the patriarchy of the theatre and the monopoly female impersonators had over racialized, gender performance.[118]

The *Creole Show* was a prelude to the extravagant lengths Al G. Field went with his all-Black production *Darkest America* (1894), which together with *Black America* (opening in Brooklyn in 1895) were two of the largest all-Black re-enactments of the Southern plantation. "Real Southern Negroes, and all Clever Entertainers at the Toronto," read the Toronto *Evening Star* (1892–1900) on May 9, in promotion of Field's *Darkest America* appearing at the city's Opera House. The *Evening Star* became a significant publication of record in Toronto, and in 1899 was recognized by progressive businessmen as a labour newspaper and voice for the Laurier government. After its debut, *Darkest America* was described in the *Colored American*, an African American newspaper, as a "delineation of Negro life, carrying the race through all their historical phases from the plantation, into the reconstruction days and finally painting our people as they are today, cultured and accomplished in social graces, holds the mirror faithfully up to nature;" minstrelsy—*Black* and *White*—would be forever changed.[119]

According to the *Evening Star*'s review of Field's *Darkest America*, "The basis of the entertainment is music, singing and dancing, and the representation of home life in the South as it actually exists in the cities and on the plantation. Wherever these people have appeared in their entertainment, press and public alike have pronounced it the most unique and pleasing thing of the kind ever presented on the stage," the newspaper declared, adding "their entertainment appeals to all classes. There is nothing of the 'Uncle Tom' character of the presentation of a down-trodden nature in the performance. It is entirely different from all other negro shows."[120] *Darkest America*, as Taylor and Austen explain, was a huge success in 1896, playing for twenty-eight weeks in fourteen different states and in Ontario and Quebec (Toronto, London, and Montreal). In addition to *Black* minstrels, Field also managed White companies. In February 1896, the *Globe* reported, "This is said to be the largest of all white minstrel companies travelling, embracing in its membership over half a hundred of the most celebrated minstrel stars and the pick of the novelties of Europe and America," adding "the company engaged this season is the strongest in merit, talent and numbers that Mr. Field has ever headed. Vocally it is said to be the strongest minstrel company travelling.... Dancing is always regarded as a prime factor in good minstrelsy, and Field's Minstrels could rest their claim for excellence on this feature alone. Wm. Rowe is undoubtedly the most graceful dancer on the minstrel stage to-day."[121] Significantly, the popularity of *Black* minstrelsy in 1896/1897 and the return of Southern plantation vignettes must be bookended with the success of the Fisk Jubilee Singers, who also launched successful tours of Ontario.

The popularity of the Fisk Jubilee Singers peaked by the mid-1890s; they would make five tours of Canada before the end of the century. In November 1884, the Original Fisk University Jubilee Singers (as they were now known) returned to Toronto to give a concert at the Horticultural Gardens and Pavilion in the afternoon on American Thanksgiving Day, and one month later they sang at Shaftesbury Hall to a large crowd.[122] Officially opened by Edward, Prince of Wales on September 11, 1860, the Horticultural Gardens and Pavilion was eventually known as Allan Gardens.[123] After a four-year absence, in October 1888 the Original Fisk Jubilee University Singers gave a concert at the Horticultural Garden and Pavilion, following a successful show at Ottawa a week prior to an immense audience that included Macdonald and Charles Dudley Warner (1829–1900), the American essayist, novelist, and co-author of *The Gilded Age: A Tale of Today* (1873).[124] At one point, the Original Fisk Jubilee Singers spent one month touring Ontario, including stops in Hamilton, Kingston, and Ottawa. In 1889, the Original Fisk Jubilee Singers performed at a Congregational church on

Spadina Avenue in the city, and at the YMCA Hall.[125] On November 24, 1891, the *Globe* featured a story about Frederick L. Loudin (1836–1904), who had become musical director in 1882 and, after a ten-year absence, was about to lead the Fisk Jubilee Singers' two-month tour of Ontario and Quebec. One of the purposes of the feature was to clear up any confusion about the multiple Fisk Jubilee Singers crisscrossing the globe since the 1880s. "I represent," Loudin said in an interview with the newspaper, "the original company of Fisk Jubilee Singers. We were first connected with Fisk University, and continued to be until 1881, when our connection ceased, on account of the many bogus companies that were on the road...travelling under our name. These companies were started during our absence in Europe, and on our return Fisk University decided it was advisable to disband the company on account of...the number of other spurious companies."[126] On January 21, 1892, the *North Ontario Times* reported on one of the last concerts given by Loudin's Fisk Jubilee Singers at the Methodist Church in Uxbridge, North Ontario, describing it as "without a doubt the best company of colored singers that ever visited Uxbridge."[127] A final *Globe* editorial on November 26, 1897 declared that the Original Fisk Jubilee Singers after "an absence of some years" would appear at the Bond Street church in downtown Toronto.[128]

When American jubilee singers headed to Canada, they faced the problem of distinguishing themselves from other jubilee singing groups who were using the "jubilee" name, like the Canadian Jubilee Singers and the Ball Jubilee Singers who performed to audiences in cities and towns including Hamilton, Toronto, Brantford, and Guelph. "Hamilton audiences are somewhat familiar with 'jubilee' singing, and there is no necessity here, of remarking upon its peculiarities," reported the *Hamilton Spectator*.[129] On November 19, 1880, at the Grand Opera House in Ottawa, under the patronage of the governor general of Canada, the Fisk Jubilee Singers performed a concert in which the *Daily Citizen* said, "Seldom has Ottawa, or any other city heard a more highly cultivated, or a sweeter voice; it was assuredly the song of a nightingale. Frantic applause greeted the lady, and it was repeated, when she sang with piquant archness, and with pretty grace, 'I Would, Would Not You?' The lady and Mr. Loudin can claim to rank among the first of concert singers, and as an accompanist on either organ or piano, Miss Ella Sheppard has few equals; her playing was perfect."¹³⁰ Jubilee singers, Canadian or American, were not always welcomed in Canadian hotels. In 1867, a Nova Scotia newspaper reporting on a performance by a group of jubilee singers noted that unlike the "hotelkeepers in Halifax and Pictou" the owner of the Norfolk House admitted jubilee singers to his hotel but "it is lamentable to know that respectable hotelkeepers in Halifax and Pictou shut their houses against these people simply because they were colored."¹³¹ The article praised one Norfolk proprietor saying he "deserves the thanks of all lovers of justice and fair play, to say nothing of common courtesy and gentlemanly behavior," but overall lamented the fact of discrimination in the province.¹³² During an 1881 tour of Montreal, the Fisk Jubilee Singers were denied entrance at two hotels, and when Loudin mentioned their names at the concert hall the following evening the audience hissed its disapproval.¹³³ The *Montreal World* subsequently wrote, "Until some law is passed which will make it perilous for a hotel to act the part of a hoodlum the country must be held dishonored by this action."¹³⁴

In Toronto, in an editorial dated September 24, 1881 and titled, "Caste in Toronto Hotels," the *Globe* denounced lodging discrimination against the Fisk Jubilee Singers. "Many citizens of Toronto retain, no doubt, pleasant recollections of the unique entertainment afforded on a former occasion by the concerts of the Fisk Jubilee Singers...will learn with indignation that they have been refused accommodation at no fewer than five of the hotels of this city," the paper lamented. The Queen's, The Walker House, The American Hotel, and the Robinson House all "flatly declined to admit them at all, while the Rossin House adopted the tactics, at least equally discreditable, of naming exorbitant terms."¹³⁵ The *Globe* then apologized to the Fisk Jubilee Singers on behalf of those who abhorred de facto segregation:

> We confess to a feeling of the deepest charging that this insult should have been offered in our fair city to body of highly respectable and Christian men and women—engaged, too, in great work of patriotism and philanthropy. We are accustomed to pride ourselves on cherishing some of the nobler traditions of our Mother Land. One of these traditions is that of a superiority to prejudices of colour or race, which glories in a just recognition of the rights of man as man everywhere,

which leads the victorious crusade for the abolition of slavery the world over, and which prompts every true Briton to extend the hand of sympathy and help the oppressed and struggling of every land. And yet when those come among us who were received and honoured by the Queen herself, as representatives of the best and noblest aspirations of a people long crushed, the hotel in our city which flaunts Her Majesty's name spurns them from its doors.... We feel sure that all cultivated and high-minded Canadians will endorse this sentiment, and earnestly and promptly disclaim any sympathy with a priggishness so offensive to all good taste and all right feeling.[136]

On October 7, 1881, the *Globe* featured another editorial on the Fisk Jubilee Singers, emphasizing the changed attitude of the city's hotels regarding their lodging. "Owing mainly to the excellent impression made by the Fisk Jubilee Singers on the music-loving people of Toronto when they were here last year, but partly also to the gratuitous advertising they have been treated to by certain hotels, they had a splendid house last night at their opening concert at the Horticultural Pavilion," the newspaper stated.[137] The audience, which represented Toronto's social elites numbered around 1,800, and the *Globe* reported, "The singers were in fine voice and spirits and sang with verve and pathos which they have never surpassed, or perhaps qualified, at any of their previous appearances in this city." The newspaper continued:

> The reception of the singers was most cordial and appreciative. Many of the numbers were enthusiastically encored, and through their powers were being taxed with some severity the performers good-naturedly responded to each recall, partly for the purpose of complying with requests for certain pieces not named on the programme.... Besides special plantation melodies such as "Steal Way to Jesus," "Good News," "I'm Rolling Through an Unfriendly World," "The Gospel Train is Coming," "Bright Sparkles in the Churchyard," etc., the programme included a beautiful part song, "O Give Me Music," finely rendered as a quartette by Messers, Loudin, Thomas, Barrett, and Payne, Mr. Loudin sang as a bass solo.[138]

Two years later the Fisk Jubilee Singers performed at the Horticultural Gardens and Pavilion for a Christmas concert described as "their last appearance before going on their European tour."[139]

This chapter aimed to demonstrate how incredibly successful jubilee singers were in remapping the boundaries of Black freedom. In the context of White women joining White men on stage as blackface minstrels, and *Black* minstrelsy's authentication of racial stereotypes, the mere presence of jubilee singers helped to broaden the possibilities for Black performers. Singers like Dett also represented some of the first diasporic influences on American music, as he borrowed from African American musical traditions while blending them into the European classical music and his own growing up in Drummondville. He also took cues from British-born Black composer Samuel Coleridge-Taylor (1875–1912) who, like Dett, sought to use music to uplift the dignity of Black people. During a second tour of North America in 1906, Coleridge-Taylor performed in Toronto.[140] As more Black composers emerged, like Texas-born Scott Joplin (1868–1917), often dubbed the "King of Ragtime," and Amherstburg, Ontario's Shelton Brooks (1886–1975), who composed several hit *coon songs* in the 1900s, sheet music increasingly became the connective force that linked music to dance, performance to people. By the early twentieth century, Canadians like Dett and Brooks who moved to the US joined the ranks of Black composers like Joplin, and many others, and together, they would transform vaudeville and help establish a popular music and dance industry. By the 1910s, new theatrical circuits that were racially integrated in terms of music composition, but racially segregated in terms of theatrical productions, dance halls, and music covers, would emerge.

CONCLUSION

This book has examined the origin story of Canada and its participation in the blackface Atlantic. My aim was to establish a historiography of the actors, dancers, playwrights, managers, songs and singers, as well as theatres, concert halls, and performance venues that all played a role in the genre's growth and development. The historical development of blackening in the theatre has always functioned as a floating signifier for Western race relations. Before the first American or Canadian minstrel actor put on "the burnt-cork mask," whether in sixteenth-century England or nineteenth-century America, mimetic dancing was a common feature in White constructions of Blackness, "often bolstering fantasies of difference and a racist stereotype of irrationality which rationalized African slavery."[1] The Atlantic world's socioeconomic investment in Black bodies can be said to have started when the first Africans came to England in 1554–55 as a result of John Lok's travels to Guinea, with the first recorded sale of enslaved Africans occurring in England in 1563.[2] By the time "blackened" characters entered the Elizabethan Tutor stage in the seventeenth century, there was collective awareness about Africans; over the next two hundred years, this developed into transnational visual culture (art, lithographic images, prints, and theatrical promotions) that created representations of the emergent slave economy of the Atlantic world, and a popular theatre industry that while we can locate the origins of in eighteenth- and nineteenth-century America, had existed in British folklore for centuries before. The idea of "blacking up" to portray Black people as out of place, comically pretentious, and downright ignorant was not created in American minstrelsy, but it was transformed and made *new* through the cross-fertilization of customs,

∾ CONCLUSION ∾

cultures, people, and places that made the "New World" quite different from anything that came before it.

Once Portuguese slave ships with captured Africans arrived on the shores of North and South America and the Caribbean in the fifteenth and sixteenth centuries, the idea of Blackness began to carry negative connotations. Despite meeting the first Indigenous Peoples who had lived on the lands for millennia, this "New World" was reimagined as new through conquest, clearing, and extermination. This is the context that gave birth to imitations of Black African dance and its distinctive gestures, as well as folk traditions traceable from at least the sixteenth century down to the antebellum period that featured dancing blackfaced figures in various guises: devils, colliers, blacksmiths, blacking polish salesmen, butts of onstage blacking episodes, blackfaced fools, and Moors.[3] What this book has argued is that theatrical performance reinforced, reified, and reintroduced real histories of slavery and of Atlantic world conquest such that audiences—both White and Black, Canadian, American, British, and beyond—in the absence of a critical discourse took these entertainments as truth since the entertainment also functioned as mere amusement. As the likes of Ira Aldridge gained fame for his performances of *Othello* in 1840s England, for example, blackface performers in America were "jumping, Jim Crow" in the minstrel show, and this new genre of theatre would come to dominate the Atlantic world. As a form of *soft power*, the theatre functioned as a pedagogical agent.

By the end of the nineteenth century, plantation slavery was so mass produced as entertainment that the public had largely forgotten the plight of over four million African Americans who had lived through slavery. In Canada, there was virtually no acknowledgement of the enslavement of Black people as central to the development of the dominion. Instead, Canadian audiences consumed the global aesthetics of slavery as part of an American entertainment culture, which became one of its most enduring commodified exports. The language from the nineteenth century used to describe Black people, like "coon" and "darkies," was as identifiable to Canadian audiences as they were to Americans, as evidenced by the many Canadians who also become famous for singing *coon songs* in the 1890s.

∽ CONCLUSION ∽

As theatrical narratives and a visual-linguistic logic became commonplace by the end of the nineteenth century, blackface was unequivocally a form of global entertainment that linked Canada with the US and Britain (and the Western world) in a blackface Atlantic where the Southern plantation was repeatedly imagined as the rightful place for Black people. At the same time, jubilee singers and concert contraltos/sopranos represented a counterpoint to the blackface Atlantic. When these acts performed in front of White audiences, who in most cases had never seen a Black person before, they were not only representing themselves but also remapping the story of Black people post-emancipation. The Canadian Jubilee Singers and the Ball Jubilee Singers challenged the American dominance over the choral stage; their acts demonstrated that Black Canadians were part of the movement toward using the stage as a protest against racial caricature, inasmuch as jubilee singers were sometimes interpreted as "people whom [Europeans] believed to be intellectually and culturally inferior—were capable of accepting and practicing European religious values and cultural traditions."[4] In some instances, they also became quasi "proof" that Black people were capable of westernization. Many Black choral singers were also criticized for emphasizing European musical arrangements, but when their lives are placed into the context of the time, such criticisms were shortsighted.

Anti-lynching activist Ida B. Wells (1862–1931) reported that during 1892, 241 Black men, women, and children across twenty-six states were lynched, and between 1882 and 1968, 4,743 lynchings were recorded, including fifty African American women between 1889 and 1918.[5] *Canada and the Blackface Atlantic* ends at a time, during the post-Reconstruction era, when Black people's struggles for voting rights, civil liberties, and freedoms were at their most restrictive. And yet, three areas of employment—sharecropping, the railroad (hotels, food service, and domestic help), and the theatre (including singing)—remained opportunities for Black people. In concluding this snapshot of the blackface Atlantic, I am reminded of Lemons's observation that "When he was being treated the worst, the Negro became the butt of the national joke, the principal comic character. In this way, popular culture's treatment of blacks reflected the society's humiliation of them.... If humor is a way of relieving social tension, then

∽ CONCLUSION ∽

making blacks into comics was one way of coping with an extreme situation. The general public tried to render one of its most fearsome problems into a funny one."[6]

Over the course of the 1890s, the "Canadianness" of blackface would become recognizable through productions at private clubs and events. These amateur shows would reflect an emergent national identity—one that was White, Anglo-Saxon, Protestant, and English-speaking. This group was the nation's ruling class, and their amateur blackface productions reflected their class and political identity. In Ontario, groups like the Young Liberals began to produce minstrel shows with greater frequency. In British Columbia, crowds of White Canadians began to gather for "Darktown" events as part of Dominion Day celebrations (today known as Canada Day, observed annually on July 1). At the same time these homegrown productions were held, vaudeville remained all the rage at Canada's legitimate theatres. As the most popular form of entertainment, it fundamentally infected North American (and European) culture with archetypes of Blackness that were not only fictitious, but so dominant Black actors realized that to embody the Blackness of vaudeville and its *coon songs* was to achieve success as actors, songwriters, and playwrights. New York's Tin Pan Alley emerged as a commercial strip that produced new music; however, the majority of this music purchased by Canadians would be produced domestically by publishing houses that arose, like the Frederick Harris Music Co. (Frederick Harris Music) based in Oakville, Ontario and founded by British-born Frederick Harris (1866–1945), and the E. Berliner Company headquartered in Montreal and founded by German-born Emile Berliner (1851–1929). Ragtime was the music these companies published. With its syncopated rhythms and fast tempos, it spawned new performance styles—from the cakewalk to burlesque—and its *coon songs* became even more recognizable by elaborate sheet music imagery that flooded the market in the early twentieth century.

This book has examined a theatrical system that no longer exists. Advancements at the end of the nineteenth century, such as New York's Theatrical Syndicate (Theatres Trust, created in 1896), which was one of the firms that took on the responsibility of booking acts as they moved across North America from Montreal to Chicago, Detroit to Toronto, more closely resembles today's theatrical network than anything that existed before it.[7] Blackface minstrelsy was America's first true global export, but it was also Canada's first imported form of global culture. Because minstrel troupes codified their songs, jokes, and one-liners, it produced a transnational humour, song repertoire, and stock characters that many of us know today. Meanwhile, many of the Black actors, singers, and dancers (in and out of blackface) have been forgotten. As blackface crisscrossed the Atlantic world it became the first form of entertainment most people knew, not just in major cities, but in towns and any place there was a theatre. For this reason, blackface minstrelsy is vitally important to Canadian, dancing, and music history. Through its people, narratives, and politics, we can gain understanding about the roots of racial production, and the wider, more elusive structure of racism that has bound us all.

APPENDICES

Appendix A

MINSTREL PERFORMERS, SONGWRITERS, AND MANAGERS

Names with no dates denote unknown birth and death dates.

Allen, Andrew Jackson "Dummy" (1788–1853)
Bailey, George F. (1818–1903)
Barlow, Milt (1843–1904)
Barnum, Phineas Taylor (P.T.) (1810–91)
Bayes, Nora (1880–1928)
Bell, Bessie
Benedict, Lew (ca. 1838–1920)
Blakeley, Thomas
Brice, Fanny (1891–1951)
Brower, Frank (1823–74)
Burgess, Colin "Cool" (1840–1905)
Burke, L.N.
Callender, Charles
Carter, Sadie
Carter, William
Christy, Edwin Pearce (1815–62)
Christy, George (1827–68)
Cohan, Jerry (1848–1917)
Cox, Robert
Cushman, Frank (1853–1907)
Delehanty, William H. (1846–80)
Demott, Garry
Diamond, John (Jack) (1823–57)
Dibdin, Charles (1745–1814)
Dixon, George Washington (1801–62)
Dockstader, Lew (1856–1924)
Duprez, Charles (1833–1902)
Durang, John (1768–1822)
Emmett, Daniel (1815–1904)
Farrell, Bob
Forrest, Edwin (1806–72)
Foster, Stephen (1826–64)
Hague, Sam (1828–1901)
Hallam, Lewis (ca. 1714–56)
Hamall, Hugh (d. 1875)
Harper, Ned (d. ca. 1861)
Hatfield, Alfred Griffin (or Griffith) (Al G. Field, Fields or A.G. Field) (1848–1921)
Haverly, J.H. Christopher (1837–1901)
Hawkins, Michael "Micah" (1777–1825)
Hayes, Catherine (1818–61)
Henry, Hi (Hiram F.) (1844–1920)
Henshaw, John E. (ca. 1853–1939)
Higgins, W.R.
Holland, George (1791–1870)
Howard, George C. (1818–87)
Howes, Nathan (1796–1878)
Hoyt, Charles Hale (1859–1900)
Jack, Sam T. (1852–99)
Kemble, Fanny (1809–93)
Kennedy, W.M.
Lavallée, Calixa (1842–91)

Leavitt, Michael Bennett "M.B." (1843–1935)
Lee, W.H. (d. 1874)
Lind, Jenny (1820–87)
Macready, William Charles (1793–1873)
Marble, Dan (1810–49)
Mayhew, Stella (1874–1934)
McAndrews, Walter James J.W. (1831–1899)
Molson, John (1763–1836)
Nichols, George
Nickinson (Morrison), Charlotte (1832–1910)
Nickinson, John (1808–64)
Pelham, Dick (1815–78)
Pell, Gilbert W. (d. 1872)
Powell, Charles (ca. 1749–1811)
Primrose, George (1852–1919)
Redmond, Patrick
Rice, Thomas Dartmouth "Daddy" (1808–60)
Ricketts, John (1769–1802)
Robinson, Hopkins (Mr. Robertson)
Rowe, William
Russell, Lillian (born Helen Louise Leonard, 1861–1922)
Scott, Mazzellah Ainsley (1820–67)
Sharpley, Sam (1831–75)
Smith, John N.
Steele, Johnny (1843–1920)
Sutherland, James (1832–88)
Sweeney, Joel Walker (1813–60)
Thompson, Denham
Thompson, Lydia (1838–1908)
Tilley, Vesta (1864–1952)
Tucker, Sophie (1886–1966)
Welch, Bob
West, William H. (1853–1902)
White, George Leonard (1838–95)
Whitlock, Billy (1813–78)
Williams, Barney (1823–76)
Wilson, George (1844–1930)
Wood, Henry

Appendix B

BLACK PERFORMERS, SONGWRITERS, AND MANAGERS

Aldridge, Ira (1807–67)
Anderson, Marian (1897–1993)
Batson, Flora (1864–1906)
Bland, James (1854–1911)
Brown, William Henry (1790–1884)
Clapp, Anthony Hannibal "Toney" (1749–1816)
Cole, Robert "Bob" (1868–1911)
Dean, Dora (1872–1949)
Dett, Robert Nathaniel (1882–1943)
Greenfield, Elizabeth Taylor (1809–76)
Hicks, Charles Barney (1840–1902)
Hines, Florence (1868–1924)
Hogan, Ernest (1865–1909)
Hyers, Anna Madah (1855–1929)
Hyers, Emma Louise (1857–1901)
Johnson, Charles E. (b. 1874)
Jones, Irving (1847–1932)
Jones, Matilda Sissieretta "Black Patti" (1868–1933)
Kersands, Billy (1842–1915)
Lane, William Henry "Master Juba" (ca. 1825–52)
Lightfoot, James Escort "Jimmie"
Loudin, Frederick L. (1836–1904)
Lucas, Sam (1848–1916)
Marshall, Arthur (1881–1968)
McClain, Billy (1886–1950)
McClain, Cordelia (1852–1922)
O'Banyoun, Josephus (1839–1905)
Sheppard, Ella (1851–1914)
Walker, Aida (Aide) Overton (1880–1914)
Walker, George (ca. 1872–1911)
Weston, Horace (1825–90)
White, Portia (1911–68)
Whitney, Salem Tuff (1875–1934)
Williams, Bert (1874–1922)
Williams, Marie Selika (1849–1937)

Appendix C

MINSTREL ACTS AND TROUPES

Amateur Minstrels of Saint John
Amateur Snowflake Minstrels
Arlington's New United Minstrels
Atkinson & Cook's Minstrels
Baird's Mammoth Minstrels
Barlow Bros. & Frost's Ideal Minstrels
Barlow, Wilson & Co's Mammoth
　Minstrels
Barlow, Wilson, Primrose and
　West's Minstrels
The Black Patti Troubadours
Bob Welch's Minstrel, Burlesque Opera
　Troupe and Brass Band
Burgess' Prendergast
Burgess and Redmond's Ethiopian
　Star Troupe
California Minstrels
Callender's All-Coloured Minstrels
The Campbell Minstrels
Carle's Ethiopian Serenaders
Charley Shay's Quincuplexal Company
Christy and Wood Minstrels
Christy's Minstrels and Brass Band
Cleveland's Big Consolidated Minstrels
Cool Burgess's Chicago Minstrels
Cooper's Negro Minstrels
Cyprus Minstrels
Duprez & Benedict's Minstrels
Duprez & Green's Minstrels
E.P. Christy's Minstrels
The Ethiopian Burlesque Minstrels
The Ethiopian Harmonists
The Ethiopian Serenaders (The Boston
　Minstrels, Dumbolton Company
　or Dumbolton's Serenaders)
Faird's New Orleans Minstrels

Fredericton Amateur Minstrels
Gorman's Elite Minstrels
Great American Slave Troupe (The
　Georgia Slave Troupe Minstrels)
Hamall's Minstrels
Haverly-Burgess Minstrels
Haverly's Genuine Colored Minstrels
Haverly's Georgia Minstrels
Haverly's Mastodon Minstrels
Haverly's Minstrels
Haverly's New Mastodon Minstrels
Haverly's United Mastodon Minstrels
Healy's Hibernian Minstrels
Hi Henry's Minstrel Co.
Hi Henry's Minstrels
Hughes and Donniker Minstrels
Jerry Cohan's Irish Minstrels
Johnson & Slavin's Minstrels
La Rue's Minstrels and Hamall's
　Serenaders
Madame Rentz's Female Minstrels
The Mobile Minstrels
The Morris Minstrels' Cork Opera
The Nightingale Ethiopian Serenaders
The New Orleans and Metropolitan
　Burlesque Opera Troupe and Brass
　Band (The New Orleans Minstrels)
The New Orleans Opera Troupe
The Original Georgia Minstrels
　(Callender's Colored Minstrels,
　Haverly's Coloured Minstrels)
Primrose and Dockstader's
　Minstrel Men
Primrose and West's Big Minstrels
Rankin's Mammoth Minstrels &
　Variety Combination

APPENDICES

Rankin's Minstrels
Reform Club Minstrels
Ricketts' Equestrian and
 Comedy Company
Rivers' Melodeon Troupe
 of Ethiopian Delineators
Royal Navy Minstrels
The Sable Harmonists
Saint John Amateur Athletic Club
 Minstrels
Skiff & Gaylord's Minstrels
Slave Troupe of Georgia Minstrels

The Snowball Minstrels
St. James Combination
Star Minstrels
Turner and Davis' Minstrels
The Victoria Amateur Minstrels
The Virginia Minstrels
White's Serenaders
Whitmore & Clark's Minstrels
Whitney's Minstrels
Wood's Minstrels
Young Liberal Club Minstrels

Appendix D

THEATRES (BY CITY)

CHICAGO, ILLINOIS
The New Chicago Theatre

FREDERICTON, NEW BRUNSWICK
Temperance Hall

GUELPH, ONTARIO
City Hall

HALIFAX, NOVA SCOTIA
City Hall
The New Grand Theatre
Academy Hall
Temperance Hall
Theatre Royal at Spring Gardens
Victoria Hall

HAMILTON, ONTARIO
The Grand Opera House
The Hamilton Royal Metropolitan

LIVERPOOL, UNITED KINGDOM
The Theatre Royal

LONDON, ONTARIO
The Grand Opera House
London's Theatre Royal
The Mechanics' Institute Hall

LONDON, UNITED KINGDOM
Royal Coburg Theatre
The Theatre Royal, Drury Lane
Vauxhall Gardens

MONTREAL, QUEBEC
The Académie de Musique
Bonaventure Hall
The Garrick Theatre Club
The Hayes Theatre
Her Majesty's Theatre
Odd Fellows Hall
Mechanics' Hall
The Montreal Theatre
Nordheimer's Hall
The Salle de Concert de l'Hôtel de Ville
The Theatre Royal

NEW ORLEANS, LOUISIANA
The Academy of Music

NEW YORK CITY, NEW YORK
The African Grove Theatre
Astor Opera House
Bowery Theatre
Carnegie Hall
The Chatham Theatre
Madison Square Garden
The Madison Square Theatre
New York's Bowery Theatre
The Park Theatre
Purdy's National Theatre
Third Avenue Theatre
Winter Garden Theatre

OTTAWA, ONTARIO
Gowan's New Opera House
The Grand Opera House
Her Majesty's Theatre
Rideau Hall

APPENDICES

QUEBEC CITY, QUEBEC
Pavillon des Patineurs

SAINT JOHN, NEW BRUNSWICK
Masonic Hall
Saint John Mechanics' Institute

SAN FRANCISCO, CALIFORNIA
The Metropolitan Theatre

TORONTO, ONTARIO
The Academy of Music (The Princess Theatre)
The Agricultural Hall
Bond Street Church
Frank's Hotel
The Grand Opera House
The Grand Theatre
The Horticultural Gardens and Pavilion (Allan Gardens)
Massey Hall
The Music Hall
Osgoode Hall
Palmer's Concert Hall
The Princes of Wales Music Hall
The Royal Lyceum
The Royal Opera House
Shaftesbury Hall
St. James' Cathedral
St. Lawrence Hall
Temperance Hall
The Toronto Lyceum
The Toronto Opera House
University College
The York Mechanics' Institute
Y.M.C.A. Hall

VICTORIA, BRITISH COLUMBIA
Colonial Theatre
Theatre Royal
The Victoria Theatre

WINNIPEG, MANITOBA
The Princess Opera House
The Rink Music Hall
Saint John's Dramatic Lyceum
Walker Theatre

Appendix E

NEWSPAPERS

Amherstburg Echo
Atlas (Toronto)
Borderer and Westmorland and Cumberland Advertiser
British Colonist (Toronto)
Canadian Illustrated News (Montreal)
Chatham Journal
Colored American (New York City)
Daily Citizen (Dalton, Georgia)
Daily Colonist (Victoria, BC)
Daily Globe (Toronto)
Daily Mail and Empire (Toronto)
Daily Telegraph (Toronto)
Detroit Plaindealer
Evening Star (Toronto)
Evening Telegram (Toronto)
Farmer's Advocate (London, ON)
The Globe
Guelph Mercury
Hamilton Herald
Hamilton Spectator
Harper's Weekly
Indianapolis Freeman
Kingston Chronicle and Gazette
Leader (Montreal)
Liberator (Boston)
London Anti-Slavery Reporter
London Free Press
Louisville Commercial (Louisville, KY)
Manitoba Free Press
Montreal Gazette
Montreal Herald
Montreal Star
Montreal Telegraph
Montreal Witness
Montreal World
Morning Chronicle (London, UK)
New York Age
New York Clipper
New York Herald
New York Tribune
North Ontario Times
North Star (Rochester, NY)
Ottawa Citizen
Provincial Freeman (Windsor, ON)
The Public (Chicago)
Review of Reviews (London, UK)
Toronto Leader
Toronto-Mirror
Toronto Patriot
True Witness and Catholic Chronicle (Montreal)
Varsity (Toronto)
Voice of the Fugitive (Windsor, ON)

Appendix F

MAGAZINES

Grip (Toronto)
Punch (London, UK)
Punch in Canada (Toronto)

NOTES

INTRODUCTION

1. Between 2016 and 2020, I conducted research at the University of Toronto's (UofT) Microfiche Collection and at the Thomas Fisher Rare Book Library, the Toronto Reference Library's Theatre Archives, the Archives of Ontario, and the City Archives of Toronto. After joining the Creative School at Toronto Metropolitan University and winning additional Social Sciences and Humanities Research Council grants, I was able to hire two graduate research assistants, Emilie Jabouin and Lucy Wowk, as well as then-undergraduate student Carianne Shakes. With the team in place, they truly did the demanding work to help me make sense of the archival work I had been doing since 2012. Between 2019 and 2021, my team conducted content analysis of playbills, transcribed newspaper clippings, and engaged in visual analysis and cataloging of images sourced from my time at the McCord Museum and UofT. This included 630 newspaper articles capturing blackface at professional theatres in Toronto and cities throughout southern Ontario, spanning 1844 to 1925 (Lucy); 483 newspaper articles on Blackness in Canada that ranged from reporting on anti-Black racism to acts of resistance, spanning 1867 to 1991, plus 168 images of blackface, spanning the 1840s to 1961 (Carianne); and eight amateur playbills, spanning 1917 to 1960 (Emilie).
2. Johnson, *Burnt Cork*, 1.
3. Patrick O'Neill dissertation work in the early 1970s also located performances of *Uncle Tom's Cabin* at Toronto's Royal Lyceum in 1853, 1854, 1856, and 1857 (with Denman Thompson as Uncle Tom), and there again in 1860. See Patrick O'Neill, "History of Theatrical."
4. Johnson, "Uncle Tom," 62.
5. Robin Winks, *Blacks in Canada*, 294.
6. Johnson and Aladejebi, *Unsettling the Great White North*.
7. Carless, "Cultural Setting," 34.
8. See "Grand Opera House on Adelaide Street, Toronto," *Historic Toronto*, March 14, 2016, https://tayloronhistory.com/2016/03/14/grand-opera-house-on-adelaide-street-toronto/.
9. Theatre scholar Robin Breon found an advertisement about the Toronto Coloured Young Men's Amateur Theatrical Society that stated the Lyceum shows were the organization's second Toronto appearance, but no record of their first performance has yet been found. Breon, "The Growth," 2. See also "Toronto

Coloured Young Men's Amateur Theatrical Society," *The JUBA Project*, https://library2.utm.utoronto.ca/otra/canadawest/content/toronto-coloured-young-mens-amateur-theatrical-society.
10 Vance, *History of Canadian*, 100. See also Thompson, "Come One," 95.
11 Francis, *National Dreams*, 30.
12 Saxton, *Rise and Fall*, 165–82; Lott, *Love and Theft*, 66–91.
13 Roediger, *Wages of Whiteness*, 140.
14 Mahar, *Behind*, 1; Springhall, *Genesis*, 57–79.
15 Nowatzki, *Representing*, 1–42; Meer, *Uncle Tom Mania*, 1–13.
16 Nowatzki, *Representing*, 6.
17 Toll, *Blacking Up*, 25–64; Lott, *Love and Theft*, 15–65; Lhamon, Jr., *Raising Cain*, 43–55.
18 Mayer, "Pantomime," 995.
19 Gilman, "Black Bodies," 237.
20 McConachie, "Cognitive Studies," 61.
21 Garber, *Vested Interests*, 41–92; McConachie, "Cognitive Studies," 64–68; Bean, "Transgressing the Gender," 245–56.
22 Kibler, *Rank Ladies*, 112–42; Glenn, *Female Spectacle*, 40–56; Staples, *Male-Female Comedy*, 92–116; Rogin, *Blackface, White Noise*, 3–44.
23 O'Neill, "History of Theatrical," 50.
24 Thurman, "Singing the Civilizing," 452.
25 Lott, *Love and Theft*, 4.
26 Jones, Jr., *Captive Stage*, 57–58.
27 Walker, *Racial Discrimination*, 9.
28 According to Williams, by 1928, 90 percent of all working Black men in Montreal were employed on the railways. See Walker, *Road to Now*, 39.
29 Rice, *Monarchs of Minstrelsy*, 72, 132.
30 Gardiner, "Burgess, Colin (Cool)." See also Thompson, *Anthems and Minstrel*, 41–42. (The author is or no relation.)
31 Thompson, *Anthems and Minstrel*, 23.
32 Thompson, 22.
33 Gilroy, *Black Atlantic*, 3.
34 Nowatzki, *Representing African Americans*, 6.
35 Nowatzki, 6.
36 Gilroy, *Black Atlantic*, 2.
37 Gilroy, 88.
38 Wood, *Blind Memory*, 143.
39 Wood, 144.
40 Cockrell, *Demons*, 62. See also Miller, "Twisting," 9.
41 Saxton, *Rise and Fall*, 167.
42 Sokol, "Singing Simpkin," 354.
43 See Chan, "Drolls," 117.
44 *Swabber* was printed in 1673 as *The Wits; or, Sport upon Sport*, now known as *The Wits II*. *The Wits* are significant to the development of comic dancing, as its dramatic and semi-dramatic features appear to have developed parallel to (making use of and in turn influencing) mid-seventeenth-century English songs. This in turn influenced the writing of theatrical music—both the popular jig and

the musical interlude, which became common by the mid-seventeenth century between acts and incorporated into the play itself. Cox was one of the first blackface-droll performers. He is described in Francis Kirkman's (1632–ca. 1680) preface to *The Wits II* as "the principal Actor, but also the Contriver and Author of most of these Farces." See Hornback, "Extravagant and Wheeling," 211 and Chan, "Drolls," 120.

45   In her book about the construction of early modern Spain, Barbara Fuchs explains that "During the eventful century between the fall of Granada and the expulsion of the Moriscos (Muslim subjects forcibly converted to Christianity) in 1609, an emerging Spain repeatedly attempted to come to terms with its own Moorishness." Fuchs, *Exotic Nation*, 1.
46   Wiles, *Shakespeare's Clown*, 44.
47   Hornback, *Racism and Early*, 47.
48   Careless, "Cultural Setting," 34.
49   Nowatzki, *Representing African Americans*, 21.
50   DuComb, *Three Centuries*, 51.
51   Valis Hill, *Tap Dancing America*, 7.
52   Lhamon, Jr., *Raising Cain*, 60.
53   Meer, *Uncle Tom Mania*, 27.
54   I elaborate on the use of the term *Black* v. "Negro" minstrelsy in Thompson, "*Black* Minstrelsy," 67–94.
55   See Toll, *Blacking Up*, 145. See also Frick, *Uncle Tom's Cabin*, 131 and Hartman, *Scenes of Objection*, 165 on the concept of transmogrification in the nineteenth century.
56   "Haverly's United Mastodon Minstrels," *National Museum of American History*, https://americanhistory.si.edu/collections/search/object/nmah_376177.
57   J.W.'s brother, Thomas Bengough (1853–1945), besides being a printer, had also been a journalist, an official reporter for the York County Courts, private secretary to Liberal Party leader Oliver Mowat (Ontario's premier from 1872 to 1896), reporter to the Canadian Senate, editor and publisher of two religious periodicals, and proprietor of Bengough's Shorthand and Business Institute. See Spadoni, *Grip*, 12–13.
58   *Grip* was also inspired by British novelist Charles Dickens's 1841 novel *Barnaby Rudge*, which features a character named "Grip" who is the companion of the "idiot Barnaby." See Burr, *Spreading the Light*, 58.

CHAPTER 1

1   Otele, "Resisting Imperial Governance," 134.
2   Hood, "America Invades," 63.
3   "Sept 13, 1814, CE: Star-Spangled Banner Yet Waves," *National Geographic*, https://education.nationalgeographic.org/resource/star-spangled-banner-yet-waves/.
4   Roediger, *Wages of Whiteness*, 45.
5   Roediger, 44.
6   Sanjek, *American Popular Music*, 159.
7   Boyko, *Blood and Daring*, 6.

NOTES TO CHAPTER 1

8 See Cockrell, *Demons of Disorder*, 52–53.
9 Forrest, *History of Morris*, 89.
10 Jones, Jr., *Captive Stage*, 56.
11 Lott, *Love and Theft*, 41.
12 Berlin, "Time," 53.
13 Johnson, "Uncle Tom," 58.
14 Miller, *Slaves to Fashion*, 82.
15 Walker, *Racial Discrimination*, 9.
16 Whitfield, *Blacks on the Border*, 9, 23.
17 Reid, *African Canadians*, 11.
18 Reid, 20.
19 The Battle of Plattsburg, also called the Battle of Lake Champlain, occurred on September 6–11, 1814. It resulted in an American victory that saved New York state from a British invasion via the Hudson River valley. The song recounts British General Sir George Prevost's (1767–1816) defeat at the hands of American soldiers. See James H. Marsh and Wes Turner, "Sir George Prevost," *Canadian Encyclopedia*, March 2, 2011, https://www.thecanadianencyclopedia.ca/en/article/sir-george-prevost.
20 Sanjek, *American Popular Music*, 159.
21 Sanjek, 159.
22 Carlin, *Birth of the Banjo*, 7.
23 Carlin, 7.
24 Carlin, 7.
25 Carlin, 7. This notion of "black dialect" refers to how Black Americans (and Caribbean people) were depicted as speaking in the popular culture of the nineteenth century into the twentieth century. For more on "Black" linguistics, see John McWhorter, *Talking Back, Talking Black: Truths About America's Lingua Franca*. New York: Bellevue Literary Press, 2017.
26 Sanjek, *American Popular Music*, 159.
27 Sanjek, 159.
28 Vance, *History of Canadian*, 81.
29 Baker, "Anti-American Ingredient," 62.
30 Vance, *History of Canadian*, 81.
31 Vance, 81.
32 Vance, 81. For example, in 1942 the musical *Yankee Doodle Dandy*, based on the life of Irish American Broadway entertainer George M. Cohan (1878–1942), featured a rousing rendition of the eponymous "Yankee Doodle." As Meagan Dwyer-Ryan explains, "In one memorable scene…little 'Georgie,' dressed in a stage Irishman costume complete with green knee britches and coat, buckled shoes, and shillelagh, reprises his father's famed 'Irish Dancing Master' act, playing the fiddle and dancing a jig. At the end of his performance, George waves an American flag." See Dwyer-Ryan, "Yankee Doodle Paddy," 58. Celebrating his transatlantic heritage as an Irish American, *Yankee Doodle Dandy* presented characters who were non-threatening and genial, and although Cohan's "buck-and-wing dancing" continued, as tap dance historian Constance Valis Hill describes, "in the long tradition of Irish blackface stage dancing," Cohan wore no such makeup when he performed the song on Broadway. See Valis Hill, *Tap Dancing America*, 31.

33 "The Star-Spangled Banner" was not officially adopted as the US national anthem until 1931.
34 "Yankee Doodle," *Digital History*, n.d., https://www.digitalhistory.uh.edu/active_learning/explorations/revolution/yankee_doodle.cfm.
35 Hodge, *Yankee Theatre*, 43.
36 Hodge, 43. Yankee is still often used to refer to all citizens of the US.
37 Miller, *Slaves to Fashion*, 8.
38 Miller, 8.
39 Whitfield, *Blacks on the Border*, 18.
40 Iroquois, Mohawk, Cayuga, and other Six Nations Peoples were relocated to Indigenous settlements across Upper Canada. See "In Defense of their Homelands," *Government of Canada*, https://www.canada.ca/en/department-national-defence/services/military-history/history-heritage/popular-books/aboriginal-people-canadian-military/defence-homelands.html.
41 Whitfield, *Blacks on the Border*, 18.
42 On September 3, 1783, the *Treaty of Paris* concluded the American Revolution, with Britain officially acknowledging the United States as a sovereign nation. This act also established the boundary between the United States and British North America (Canada).
43 Hall, "Royal Proclamation of 1763," *Canadian Encyclopedia*, February 7, 2006, https://www.thecanadianencyclopedia.ca/en/article/royal-proclamation-of-1763.
44 Jesse Robertson, "Shelburne Race Riots," *Canadian Encyclopedia*, November 24, 2014, https://www.thecanadianencyclopedia.ca/en/article/the-shelburne-race-riots.
45 Historians have typically used the word "riot" to describe eighteenth and nineteenth century acts of resistance from Black community but just as history refers to the 1837/38 conflict as a "rebellion," I have chosen in this book to refer to "race riots" as "race rebellions" so that both are seen as conflicts rather than the former as an act of civil disobedience.
46 "Timeline – Nova Scotia," *Canadian Encyclopedia*, n.d., https://www.thecanadianencyclopedia.ca/en/timeline/nova-scotia.
47 "Timeline – Nova Scotia," n.d.
48 This story is retold in Lawrence Hill's novel *The Book of Negroes* (2007) and the 2015 miniseries of the same name, co-produced by the Canadian Broadcasting Corporation and Black Entertainment Television.
49 Clarke, *Fire on the Water*, 12; Moynagh, "African-Canadian Theatre," viii.
50 Lott, *Love and Theft*, 41.
51 Jones, Jr., *Captive Stage*, 29.
52 Miller, *Slaves to Fashion*, 82.
53 Maharaj, Candice. "The Origins and Evolution of Carnival in Trinidad and Tobago." *Retrospect Journal*, n.d., https://retrospectjournal.com/2018/11/11/the-origins-and-evolution-of-carnival-in-trinidad-and-tobago-2/.
54 Berlin, "Time," 53.
55 Lott, *Love and Theft*, 48; see also Berlin, "Time," 54.
56 *The Padlock* received 54 performances in its first season, and 142 in its first nine years, thrusting the name and caricature of Mungo into eighteenth-century cultural discourse. See Carlson, "Race and Profit," 175.

NOTES TO CHAPTER 1

57 Miller, *Slaves to Fashion*, 35.
58 Based on Spanish writer Miguel de Cervantes's (1547–1616) (best-known for *Don Quixote*, 1605) short novel "The Jealous Husband" ("El celoso estremeño"), *The Padlock* centres on an old man, "Don Diego" who is obsessed with protecting the chastity of his young fiancée, "Leonora." Mungo, as Diego's enslaved servant, first appears near the end of Act 1, when he talks back to Diego in "an identifiable version of West Indian speech," marking the first time a caricatured black dialect is featured on a London stage. See Hornback, "Extravagant and Wheeling," 216.
59 Carlson, "Race and Profit," 175. The *Oroonoko* concerns a captured Angolan prince, "Oroonoko," who is taken to Surinam as a slave where he meets his love "Imoinda," who is also enslaved. Eventually Oroonoko leads an unsuccessful slave rebellion, and in his act of surrender, he kills Imoinda at her own prompting to stop her from being raped by the Governor whom he later stabs before killing himself. See Carlson, 179.
60 Diana Jaher asserts that in her portrayals of Prince Oroonoko and Imoinda, "Behn, like Southerne's colonists, objects not to slavery but to the enslavement of aristocrats…. Behn reserves most of her sympathy for the prince and wife. Unlike Southerne, she provides no vivid depiction of a nonaristocratic slave to act as corrective to her novella's elitist impulses." See Jaher, "Paradoxes of Slavery," 65.
61 Springhall, *Genesis of Mass*, 58. See also Pickering, *Blackface Minstrelsy*, 6.
62 Carlin, *Birth of the Banjo*, 7.
63 Hornback, "Extravagant and Wheeling," 217.
64 Miller, *Slaves to Fashion*, 73.
65 Gerzina, ed., *Black Victorians*, 52.
66 Miller, *Slaves to Fashion*, 75.
67 Dominique Jando, "John Bill Ricketts," *Circopedia*, n.d., http://www.circopedia.org/John_Bill_Ricketts.
68 Vance, *History of Canadian*, 70, 72.
69 Johnson, "Shield Us From," 261.
70 Brooks, "Staged Ethnicity," 204.
71 Brooks, 202.
72 Brooks, 203.
73 Brooks, 204.
74 Vance, *History of Canadian*, 70.
75 DuComb, *Haunted City*, 55–56.
76 Lemay, "American Origins," 443–47.
77 Lemay, 443.
78 Hodge, *Yankee Theatre*, 223–24.
79 *Chronicle and Gazette*, February 14, 1835, 3.
80 Hodge, *Yankee Theatre*, 226. See also Richard M. Dorson, "The Wonderful Leaps Of Sam Patch," *American Heritage*, December 1966, https://www.americanheritage.com/wonderful-leaps-sam-patch.
81 Dorson, "Wonderful Leaps."
82 Rabson, "*Disappointment* … Part I," 12.
83 Rabson, 19.

NOTES TO CHAPTER 1

84 Rabson, 19.
85 Rabson, 25.
86 Toll, *Blacking Up*, 3.
87 Cockrell, "Nineteenth-Century Popular," 165.
88 Toll, *Blacking Up*, 20.
89 Toll, 26.
90 Lott, *Love and Theft*, 77, 76.
91 Vance, *History of Canadian*, 68–69.
92 Vance, 69.
93 Sanjek, *American Popular Music*, 165.
94 Sanjek, 165.
95 Moodie, *Life*, 95–97.
96 Lenton-Young, "Variety Theatre," 172. Owned and operated by George Blanchard between 1824 and 1830 out of Montreal, there is little known of the Royal Circus other than it included two equestrians, one clown, and an actor.
97 Vance, *History of Canadian*, 76.
98 Taylor and Austen, *Darkest America*, 36.
99 Johnson, "Shield Us From," 263.
100 Lott, *Love and Theft*, 21.
101 Erin Blakemore, "Who were the Moors?" *National Geographic*, December 12, 2019, https://www.nationalgeographic.com/history/article/who-were-moors.
102 Blakemore, "Who were the Moors?"
103 John Edwards, "The Purging of Muslim Spain," *History Today*, November 11, 2017, https://www.historytoday.com/reviews/purging-muslim-spain.
104 Blakemore, "Who were the Moors?"
105 Miller, *Slaves to Fashion*, 299 (note 49). In *Othello*, antagonist Iago believes that, when compared to Cassio, a soldier in the Venetian army, Othello is "an extravagant and wheeling stranger of here and everywhere." He is also pointing to the character's supposed lack of civility. See Hornback, "Extravagant and Wheeling," 207.
106 Braxton, "Othello," 13–14.
107 Miller, *Slaves to Fashion*, 299 (note 49). If we imagine that in Shakespeare's time the port city of Venice was ethnically diverse, and that Moors represented a growing interchange between Europe, the Middle East, Asia, and Africa, Othello is meant to be read as a non-desirable figure. See Edwards, "Purging of Muslim" and Braxton, "Othello," 4.
108 See, Taylor and Austen, *Darkest America*, 36.
109 Toll, *Blacking Up*, 27.
110 Cockrell, *Demons*, 96.
111 Sanjek, *American Popular Music*, 161.
112 Cockrell, *Demons of Disorder*, 96.
113 Miller, *Slaves to Fashion*, 98.
114 Carlin, *Birth of the Banjo*, 14.
115 Sambo, a name that amused Portuguese and Spanish enslavers because it sounded like "zambo," a word for monkey, was adopted by Anglophones because it was a funny-sounding diminutive of Sam. See Strausbaugh, *Black Like You*, 297.
116 DuComb, *Haunted City*, 77

NOTES TO CHAPTER 1

117 Miller, *Slaves to Fashion*, 99.
118 Miller, 10; see also Mahar, *Behind the Burnt Cork*, 227.
119 Federic R. Sandorn, "'Jump Jim Crow!' – The Opening of an Era." *New York Times*, November 13, 1932, 8, https://www.nytimes.com/1932/11/13/archives/jump-jim-crow-the-opening-of-an-era-a-century-ago-thomas-rice.html.
120 Sandorn, "Jump Jim Crow," 8.
121 Sandorn, "Jump Jim Crow," 8.
122 *Correspondent and Advocate*, July 13, 1836, 3.
123 Carlin, *Birth of the Banjo*, 46.
124 Carlin, 9.
125 Pickering, *Blackface Minstrelsy*, 9.
126 Odell, *Annals*, 632.
127 Hornbeck, "Extravagant and Wheeling," 208.
128 Wood, "'Gimme de Kneebone Bent,'" 8.
129 Hazzard-Gordon, *Jookin'*, 18.
130 Hornbeck, "Extravagant and Wheeling," 208.
131 Taylor and Austen, *Darkest America*, 36.
132 Pickering, *Blackface Minstrelsy*, 9.
133 Hornback, "Extravagant and Wheeling," 218.
134 Hornback, 217.
135 Miller, "Twisting," 15.
136 "English-Language Theatre," *Canadian Encyclopedia*, March 16, 2006, https://www.thecanadianencyclopedia.ca/en/article/english-language-theatre.
137 Smith, "On the Margins," 44.
138 Vance, *History of Canadian*, 76.
139 Smith, *Too Soon*, 38
140 Vance, *History of Canadian*, 76.
141 Smith, "On the Margins," 47.
142 Cowan, *British Immigration*, 9. Emigration from Britain vastly exceeded immigration in the nineteenth century. Between 1815 and 1914, approximately ten million people emigrated from Britain, which amounted to about 20 percent of all European emigrants. See Amy J. Lloyd, "Emigration, Immigration and Migration in Nineteenth-Century Britain," *British Library Newspapers*. Detroit: Gale, 2007, https://www.gale.com/intl/essays/amy-j-lloyd-emigration-immigration-migration-nineteenth-century-britain.
143 Lorinc, "Ravages of Cholera," 88.
144 Cameron, "English Immigrants," 92. From 1846 to 1859, immigrants from the British Isle were primarily labourers and farmers. Carpenters ranked second in numbers, then came miners, shoemakers and tailors, house servants, blacksmiths, and masons—the workers most needed in a new country. See Cowan, *British Immigration*, 14.
145 Cowan, *British Immigration*, 14.
146 Iacovetta, *Nation of Immigrants*, 3.
147 Bowerman, "Toronto Forewarned," 72.
148 Andrew McIntosh, "Rebellions of 1837–38," *Canadian Encyclopedia*, July 15, 2013, https://www.thecanadianencyclopedia.ca/en/article/rebellions-of-1837.
149 McIntosh, "Rebellions of 1837–38."

150 Francis, *National Dreams*, 58.
151 Rhodes, *Mary Ann Shadd*, 81.
152 For more on the Blackburns' story see Karolyn Smardz Frost, *I've Got A Home in Glory Land: A Lost Tale of the Underground Railroad.* New York: Farrar, Straus, and Giroux, 2007.
153 Carless, "Cultural Setting," 18. The province of Ontario, the official name given to the largest province at Confederation in 1867, also became the centre of Canada, growing from around 100,000 inhabitants to over 2.5 million between 1812 and 1912, producing a population that was able to establish and support theatres, newspapers, and mass transportation systems.
154 Smardz-Frost, *I've Got*, 255.
155 Lawrence, "Rewriting Histories," 40.
156 Malpas, "Place and Placedness," 28.
157 Nelson, *Razing Africville*, 11.
158 Lott, *Love and Theft*, 75.
159 Runcie, "Hunting the Nigs," 196.
160 Runcie, 217. See also Kerber, "Abolitionists and Amalgamators," 34–36.
161 Roediger, *Wages of Whiteness*, 109–10.
162 Hill, *Tap Dancing America*, 12.

CHAPTER 2

1 Lenton-Young, "Variety Theatre," 176. See also *British Colonist*, June 10, 1840.
2 O'Neill, "History of Theatrical," 50.
3 Johnson, "Shield Us From," 255.
4 Also in 1840, By-Law No. 50 which served to "Regulate Theatrical Performances and other Exhibitions" provided a first-ever long list of entertainments, including "Theatres, Menageries, Exhibitions, [Various] Showmen, Mountebanks, Circus Riders, Jugglers, and other persons exhibiting any idle acts or feats for gain or profit in the City of Toronto..." and stipulated the payment of a licence fee for such entertainments. See Johnson, "Shield Us From," 274.
5 O'Neill, "History of Theatrical," 107.
6 Burr, *Spreading the Light*, 82.
7 Burr, 89.
8 Careless, "Cultural Setting," 22.
9 Hogeveen, "Evils with Which," 41.
10 Hogeveen, 42.
11 "English-Language Theatre."
12 Careless, "Cultural Setting," 34.
13 A *British Colonist* article on December 21, 1848 notes that the Royal Lyceum accommodated an audience of six hundred to seven hundred comfortably. The theatre was subsequently closed in 1850 but Nickinson leased the Royal Lyceum in 1852. After completing renovations of the premises, the theatre reopened on March 28, 1853. See Stephen Johnson, "The Royal Lyceum," *Canada West*, https://library2.utm.utoronto.ca/otra/canadawest/content/royal-lyceum-theatre.
14 Lenton-Young, "Variety Theatre," 178.

15 Lenton-Young, 178.
16 O'Neill, "History of Theatrical," 173.
17 O'Neill, 100.
18 Careless, "Cultural Setting," 30.
19 See Kimberly Boissiere and Jeremie Caribou, "Indigenous City Field Trip: Jarvis Street," https://pressbooks.library.torontomu.ca/indigenouscityfieldtrip/chapter/jarvis-street/.
20 See Adam Bunch, "Toronto's First Truly Terrible Leader – The Slave-Owning Gambling Addict Peter Russell," *Spacing*, May 28, 2013, https://spacing.ca/toronto/2013/05/28/torontos-first-truly-terrible-leader-the-slave-owning-gambling-addict-peter-russell/. Russell's most documented slavery story relates to Peggy, her husband Pompadour, a free Black man who worked for the family for wages, and their enslaved children: Jupiter, Amy, and Milly. As Adrienne Shadd observes, "Peggy and her family represented major nuisances for the Russells (Elizabeth Russell, Peter's sister). "Unable to sell Peggy, Peter Russell advertised on September 2, 1803, in the *Upper Canada Gazette*, warning readers that 'The subscriber's black servant Peggy not having his permission to absent herself from his service, the public are hereby cautioned from employing or harbouring her without the owner's leave. Whoever will do so after this notice may expect to be treated as the law directs." (See *Journey From Tollgate*, 49.)
21 In 1792, independent member of Parliament William Wilberforce (1759–1833) brought a resolution before the British House of Commons to immediately abolish the transatlantic Slave Trade. However, Minister Henry Dundas, 1st Viscount Melville (1742–1811), was one of many who argued against such proposals for abolition, stating that abolition was not practical while Britain was at war with France. Since this history gained momentum during 2020, multiple cities and municipalities have taken efforts to remove or rename streets and facilities, and remove monuments commemorating British colonizers, including slavery sympathizers like Dundas. See "Renaming Dundas-Linked City Assets," City of Toronto, https://www.toronto.ca/community-people/get-involved/community/recognition-review/renaming-dundas-street/.
22 When an enslaved Black woman named Chloe Cooley was observed being forced into a boat, bound, and gagged, near Queenston, on the shores of Lake Erie, it was reported to John Graves Simcoe, the first lieutenant-governor of Upper Canada. The incident is remembered as the driving force behind the 1793 antislavery law.
23 Shadd, *Journey From Tollgate*, 38.
24 Shadd, 38–39. A rendering of Sophia Burthen Pooley can be found at the Archives of Ontario.
25 See Elgersman, *Unyielding Spirits*, 28–30.
26 "Who was James McGill?" *McGill*, https://www.mcgill.ca/about/history/who-was-james-mcgill.
27 Macdonald was also the fourth Chancellor of McGill University, serving from 1914–1917. McGill is documented selling two enslaved Black people, named Caesar and Flora, in 1784. Three years later, he sold four enslaved people (accounts differ about whether they were Black or Indigenous). Historical records indicate that he enslaved at least five people in his own household:

NOTES TO CHAPTER 2

Marie, Marie-Louise, Jacques, Sarah, Marie-Charles (a.k.a. Charlotte, and whom some historians believe to be the same person as Sarah) and an Indigenous boy whose name is not known. McGill also profited from the trade of items produced by enslaved people in other colonies, such as molasses, rum, and tobacco. See Nathan Baker and Stanley Gordo, "James McGill," January 20, 2008, *Canadian Encyclopedia*, https://www.thecanadianencyclopedia.ca/en/article/james-mcgill.

28 "English-Language Theatre."
29 Nardocchio, *Theatre and Politics*, 8.
30 Nardocchio, 9.
31 Thompson, *Anthems and Minstrel*, 11.
32 Charpentier, "Broadway North," 50.
33 Thompson, *Anthems and Minstrel*, 13.
34 Brown, "Entertainers," 127.
35 Charpentier, "Broadway North," 50.
36 Bayne, "Origins of Black," 34. See also H. Robert Howard, "History of Odd Fellowship in Canada," *Independent Order of Odd Fellows*, https://odd-fellows.org/history/history-in-canada/. See also Graham, *Historic Montreal*, 7.
37 See "Dumbolton, James A. Biographical Overview," *The JUBA Project*, https://library2.utm.utoronto.ca/otra/minstrels/node/490619.
38 Frick, *Uncle Tom's Cabin*, 13. "Ethiopian delineators," many of them English and Irish actors, first arrived in America in the early 1800s. By 1820, they had established the singing-dancing "Negro Boy" as a dancehall character; as blackface impersonators, they performed jigs and clogs to popular songs. See Hill, *Tap Dancing America*, 8. As John Hornbeck observes, "the vestiges of early traditions of blackness, blackface, and the black mask can be located in depictions of English drama. Such examples include 'foolish black devils' that appeared in English Renaissance theatre (1558 to 1642), 'devil' plays with blackface and plays with Moors like sixteenth-century jigs." See Hornback, *Racism and Early*, 47.
39 Conroy, "History," 147–51.
40 Rice, *Monarchs of Minstrelsy*, 75. In 1853, George Christy partnered up with Henry Wood, the brother of then-New York City mayor, Fernando Wood (1812–81), to form Wood & Christy's Minstrels. The duo then went on a southern tour in 1855, appearing in Savannah, Georgia and Nashville, Tennessee. See Carlin, *Birth of the Banjo*, 90.
41 Le Camp, "Racial Considerations," 300.
42 Also known as the Molson Theatre, Theatre Royal was the first public theatre in Canada, inaugurated in 1825; it closed in 1930. "Theatre Royal," *Canadian Theatre Encyclopedia*, https://www.canadiantheatre.com/dict.pl?term=Theatre%20Royal.
43 "English-Language Theatre."
44 Ernest, *National Within*, 24.
45 Boyko, *Blood and Daring*, 24.
46 McLaren, "We Had No," 32.
47 Broyld, "Power of Proximity," 14.
48 McCorkindale, "Black Education," 347.

49 For more on Delany's time in Chatham and the role he played in the abolitionist cause, see Heike Paul, "Out of Chatham: Abolitionism on the Canadian frontier." *Atlantic Studies*, 8, no 2 (2011): 165–88.
50 Lott, *Love and Theft*, 45. The African Grove Theatre was opened by William Henry Brown (1790–1884), who is often remembered as the first known Black playwright in America. The African Grove was a response to the uncongenial atmosphere of most theatres to Black patrons who were restricted to the upper galleries at New York venues. The African Grove mounted productions of *Hamlet*, *Richard III*, and *Othello*, and as in the White theatres, hornpipes were danced and comic songs sung between the acts. See also "William A. Brown, Playwright born," *African American Registry*, https://aaregistry.org/story/william-a-brown-playwright-born/.
51 "Thomas Joiner White," *Chatham-Kent Physician Tribute*, https://ckphysiciantribute.ca/doctors/thomas-joiner-white/.
52 Rhodes, *Community on the Thames*, 2.
53 Poole, "Conspicuous Peripheries," 23.
54 Poole, 23. Chatham's other prominent residents included Toronto-born Anderson Ruffin Abbott (1837–1913), who studied at the Toronto Academy and later at Oberlin College in Ohio. In 1857, he was one of the first Black students to attend University College in Toronto, enrolling in 1858 in the Toronto School of Medicine (later affiliated with the University of Toronto). Michigan-born Amos Aray (1829–1924), who moved to Chatham in 1856 to open a medical practice, and Samuel C. Watson (1832–92), also born in Michigan, practiced medicine in the Charity Block on King and Adelaide Streets in 1858. See Eli Yarhi and Tabitha de Bruin, "Anderson Abbott," *Canadian Encyclopedia*, November 27, 2013, https://www.thecanadianencyclopedia.ca/en/article/anderson-abbott, and "Amos Aray," *Chatham-Kent Physician Tribute*, https://ckphysiciantribute.ca/doctors/amos-aray/. See also DeRamus, *Freedom by Any*, 15.
55 Shadd, *Journey From Tollgate*, 135.
56 Hepburn, "Following the North," 96.
57 Ernest, *National Within*, 26. Beginning in 1793, when the US Congress passed the first Fugitive Slave Act, it tightened the parameters of slavery by stipulating that slave owners had a right to recover their slaves in any state, and those states had the right to apprehend fugitive slaves and return them to their owners. The Act made it a crime to assist a fugitive slave, and those caught doing so anywhere in the United States faced prosecution. Free African Americans who had been living in northern states like New York, Pennsylvania, Illinois, Delaware, Ohio, Michigan, and Illinois could be sold into slavery, even if they had been born free. That same year, Upper Canada passed a gradual abolition bill, which created the perception that Canada was a haven for Black people free of not only slavery but anti-Black prejudice.
58 Boyko, *Blood and Daring*, 28. See also John P. "Remembering the Globe and George Brown: March 5: Snapshots in History," *Toronto Public Library's Local History & Genealogy*, March 7, 2017, https://torontopubliclibrary.typepad.com/local-history-genealogy/2017/03/remembering-the-globe-and-george-brown-march-5-snapshots-in-history.html.

NOTES TO CHAPTER 2

59 Frederick Douglass's Paper – August 18, 1854, *Black Abolitionist Archive*, https://libraries.udmercy.edu/archives/special-collections/. Douglass also urged his listeners to put pressure on the United States to recognize that slavery is a "soul damning crime against man and God." See Broyld, "Power of Proximity," 14. See also the *Globe*, April 5, 1851, and April 10, 1851.
60 White, *Too Good*, 97. See John Boileau, "Alexander T. Augusta," *Canadian Encyclopedia*, June 2, 2022, https://www.thecanadianencyclopedia.ca/en/article/alexander-thomas-augusta. Abbott also did quite well in real estate, and by the time of his death in 1876, he owned more than seventy-five properties. His son Anderson (1837–1913) was the first Black graduate of Toronto's King College, and in 1861, he became the first Canadian-born Black medical doctor.
61 Tubman risked her life to travel back over the border thirteen times, rescuing about seventy people. Tubman (who took up residence in St. Catharines, Canada West in 1851), along with Wilson Ruffin Abbott, Augusta, and so many other African Americans who had been living in Canada, moved back to the United States to serve in the Civil War in the 1860s, though Abbott eventually returned, settling in Chatham, Ontario.
62 Boyko, *Blood and Daring*, 28.
63 Williams, *History of Black*, 29. As an example of segregationist policy in 1850, Canada West's legislature passed a Separate School Act. Between twenty thousand and forty thousand Black people had settled among British and French-Canadian colonists, primarily in the rural areas of the southwestern and Niagara peninsulas of Canada West. Significant concentrations of African Canadians lived in municipalities along the Detroit River and Lake Erie shores such as Amherstburg, Fort Malden, Sandwich, Anderdon, Maidstone, Mersea, Gosfield Colchester, and Harrow. The southwestern shore of Lake Ontario, including the Niagara region, St. Catharines, and Hamilton, was another key area of settlement for Black immigrants. Large numbers of African Canadians had also settled further inland in towns such as London and Brantford, in and around Chatham, and as far north as Oro, on the northern shore of Lake Simcoe. See McLaren, "We Had No," 31–32.
64 Johnson, "Uncle Tom," 55–56
65 Wood, *Blind Memory*, 144.
66 Kibler, *Rank Ladies*, 113–14.
67 Cited in Vance, *History of Canadian*, 76.
68 Winans, "Early Minstrel Show," 146.
69 Snodgrass, "Missouri Compromise," 367.
70 Snodgrass, 367–68.
71 "Evolution of American," 22.
72 Frick, *Uncle Tom's Cabin*, 16.
73 Springhall, *Genesis*, 70. Throughout the 1840s, on the other hand, Northern Whig Party rhetoric stressed the benefits of temperance, self-regulation, and piety, while also adopting a hostile stance toward recent Irish immigration.
74 Lott, *Love and Theft*, 51.
75 Roediger, *Wages of Whiteness*, 140.
76 Roediger, 98.
77 Springhall, *Genesis*, 61. See also Taylor and Austen, *Darkest America*, 38.

78 Taylor and Austen, *Darkest America*, 38. Emphasis in the original. Whitlock also toured with P.T. Barnum's circus in 1839, honing his blackface act (which included playing the banjo) there.
79 Taylor and Austen, *Darkest America*, 38.
80 Saxton, *Rise and Fall*, 174.
81 Springhall, *Genesis*, 61.
82 In 1667, Virginia declared that a person could be both Christian and enslaved, thereby discouraging enslaved persons from converting to Christianity solely to gain freedom. Three years later the colony ruled that any non-Christian servant arriving in Virginia by ship was subject to lifetime enslavement. See Russell, et al., *The Color Complex: The Politics of Skin Color Among African Americans*. New York: Anchor Books, 1992, 10.
83 Nathan, "Tyrolese Family Rainer," 64.
84 Pickering, *Blackface Minstrelsy*, 15.
85 Carlin, *Birth of the Banjo*, 73.
86 Toll, *Blacking Up*, 31; see also Carlin, *Birth of the Banjo*, 73.
87 Nowatzki, *Representing*, 62.
88 Dunson, "Representations," 53.
89 Dunson, "Representations," 53. Importantly, the name "minstrel" originates from eleventh-and-twelfth-century Europe when it meant "little servant" and was typically given to a wide range of entertainers, including singers, musicians, jugglers, tumblers, magicians, and jesters. See "What was life like for a court jester?" *HistoryExtra*, November 17, 2021, https://www.historyextra.com/period/medieval/what-was-life-like-for-a-court-jester/.
90 Wood, *Blind Memory*, 148.
91 Mahar, *Behind*, 13.
92 Springhall, *Genesis*, 62.
93 Lane's contributions to performance history were mostly ignored until 1947 when dance historian Marian Hannah Winter authored an article called, "Juba and American Minstrelsy," in which she traced, recuperated, and restored the rightful place of Lane in American dance history. Prior to Winter, Edward LeRoy Rice's *Monarchs of Minstrelsy*, published in 1911 omitted Lane entirely while locating "Othello" and "Oroonoko" of the British stage as some of the first representations of blackfaced characters. The book located Charles T. White (1821–91) as the first blackface performer based on a *Boston Gazette* review of his performance of a "Mr. Graupner," singing a song called "The Negro Boy" at the Federal Theatre on December 30, 1799. See Rice, *Monarchs of Minstrelsy*, 5.
94 Alkalimat, *History of Black*, 95.
95 Lindfors, "Mislike Me Not," 1005.
96 Carlson, "Race and Profit," 184.
97 See Carlson, "New Lows," 145.
98 Winter, "Juba," 251–52.
99 Winter, 251–52.
100 Taylor and Austen, *Darkest America*, 49
101 Winter, "Juba," 252.
102 Lott, *Love and Theft*, 79. Born Phineas Taylor Barnum in Bethel, Connecticut in 1810, during his career, Barnum donned the burnt cork mask to sing "Zip Coon"

and other minstrel songs before becoming a circus magnate where he frequently hired blackface performers.
103 Roediger, *Wages of Whiteness*, 119.
104 Springhall, *Genesis*, 60.
105 "William Henry Lane," 2.
106 Toll, *Blacking Up*, 43.
107 Valis Hill, *Tap Dancing America*, 12.
108 Winter, "Juba," 251.
109 Winter. "Between the financial panics of 1837 and 1857, jig-dancing competitions proliferated in diverse settings, each with its own prospects and prohibitions," writes April Masten, adding "Both the African and Irish diasporas carried away emigrants who had danced competitively in their home countries, and by 1800 their mixing had made "Negro jigs"—a term that signified a style of dancing rather than the dancer's race—widespread among North American slaves, free blacks, and whites." See Masten, "Challenge Dancing," 607. This quote provides more context to the interconnectedness of African dance traditions and European culture, which made the blackface Atlantic what it was—a bricolage of form, styles, and folk cultures.
110 "William Henry Lane," 2. See also Masten, "Challenge Dancing," 608.
111 Dickens, *American Notes*, 101–2.
112 West, "When is the Jig," 201.
113 West, 202.
114 West, 207.
115 West, 208.
116 Johnson, "Juba's Dance," 7. Irish and African American dance traditions share commonalities. The oral traditions and expressive cultures of West Africans and the Irish that converged and collided in America can be seen in the lilting 6/8 metre of the Irish jig, which was played on the fiddle or the fife. The fusion produced Black and White fiddlers who "ragged," or syncopated, jig tunes. Similarly, the African American style of dance that angled and relaxed the torso, centred movement in the hips, and favoured flat-footed gliding, dragging, and shuffling steps, melded with the Irish American style of step dancing; upright torso minimized hip motion, and dexterous footwork favoured bounding, hopping, and shuffling. See Kealiinohomoku, Joann W. "A Comparative Study of Dance as a Constellation of Behaviors among African and United States Negroes." Congress on Research in Dance, *Dance Research Annual* 7 (1976): 1–13.
117 See also "Pell, Gilbert W, Biographical Overview," *The JUBA Project*. https://library2.utm.utoronto.ca/otra/minstrels/node/490607.
118 Pickering, *Blackface Minstrelsy*, 19.
119 Johnson, "Juba's Dance," 2. Stephen Johnson's *The JUBA Project* is an extensive database of early blackface minstrelsy in Britain from 1842–52 (see https://www.utm.utoronto.ca/~w3minstr/index.html).
120 Johnson, "Juba's Dance," 2.
121 Pickering, *Blackface Minstrelsy*, 20
122 Saddlemyer, "Introduction," 13. See also O'Neill, "History of Theatrical," 291.
123 Saddlemyer, 13.

NOTES TO CHAPTER 2

124 Breon, "The Growth," 2.
125 Johnson, "Uncle Tom," 60.
126 Taylor and Austen, *Darkest America*, 49.
127 *Uncle Tom's Cabin* first appeared as a serialized work of fiction in the *National Era* (1847–1860), a weekly abolitionist newspaper edited by Gamaliel Bailey. After a forty-week run, it was published in book form on March 20, 1852.
128 Morgan, *Uncle Tom's Cabin*, 49.
129 Lott, *Love and Theft*, 220.
130 Johnson, "Uncle Tom," 58.
131 Johnson, 60.
132 Lott, *Love and Theft*, 132.
133 Lott, 72.
134 Johnson, "Uncle Tom," 60.
135 Johnson, "Uncle Tom," 57.
136 Moynagh. "African-Canadian," viii. See also Smardz-Frost, *I've Got a Home*, 283. Some estimate that *Uncle Tom's Cabin* had hundreds of performances at the Royal Lyceum theatre.
137 Smardz-Frost, *I've Got*, 283.
138 Lenton-Young, "Variety Theatre," 178.
139 Lenton-Young, 178. See also David Gardner, "Burgess, Colin (Cool)." *Dictionary of Canadian Biography*, October 25, 2017. http://www.biographi.ca/en/bio/burgess_colin_13E.html.
140 Brown, "Pepper's Ghost." When Ottawa's Her Majesty's Theatre closed from 1870 to 1873, The Rink Music Hall (it was also called The Music Hall) hosted a succession of minstrel shows, acrobats, and illusionists, as well as the occasional comic opera and classical concert. See also Brown, "Entertainers of the Road," 125.
141 Plant, "Chronology," 310.
142 Plant, 312.
143 Brown, "Entertainers on the Road," 123.
144 See also David Gardner, "Burgess, Colin (Cool)." *Dictionary of Canadian Biography*, October 25, 2017. http://www.biographi.ca/en/bio/burgess_colin_13E.html.
145 Starkey, *In Defense*, 32.
146 Toll, *Blacking Up*, 93.
147 Thompson, "Uncle Tom's," 308. Henson carried his children on his back to escape slavery.
148 Wood, *Blind Memory*, 196.
149 Toll, *Blacking Up*, 16–18.
150 Toll, 16.
151 Robert McNamara, "The Astor Place Riot of 1849," *ThoughtCo.*, January 18, 2020, https://www.thoughtco.com/astor-place-riot-1773778.
152 McNamara, "The Astor Place Riot of 1849."
153 Roediger, *Wages of Whiteness*, 116.
154 Frick, *Uncle Tom's Cabin*, 6.

155 Lott, *Love and Theft*, 210. *Democratic Review* editor John O'Sullivan is credited with using the term "Manifest Destiny" in 1845 to describe northwestern expansion.
156 Lott, 211.
157 Lott, 211.
158 Cockrell, "Nineteenth-Century," 170–71.
159 Cockrell, 171.
160 *Treasury*, 31.
161 Lott, *Love and Theft*, 214.
162 In the case of "Camptown Races," for example, which was copyrighted and first issued by the Baltimore publisher F.D. Benteen, within a few years "[the] racetrack song had brought the [Camptown] New Jersey town so much notoriety that its citizens changed the name [to Irvington] of their town in self-defense." See *Treasury*, 63.
163 Pickering, *Blackface Minstrelsy*, 23.
164 Springhall, *Genesis*, 65.
165 Mahar, *Behind*, 27–35; See also Springhall, *Genesis*, 66.

CHAPTER 3

1 Careless, "Cultural Setting," 30.
2 Henry, *Emancipation Day*, 18. In Ontario, celebrations spread from Amherstburg on the Detroit River, to Owen Sound and Collingwood on Georgian Bay, and Niagara on the Niagara River, with larger centres such as Brantford, Toronto, Hamilton, London, and Windsor holding major celebratory days. Long-settled communities such as Buxton, Chatham, Dresden, and Sandwich hosted annual events.
3 Marquis, *Armageddon's Shadow*, 69.
4 Sutherland, "Race Relations in Halifax," 35.
5 On August 1, 1851, Black community members in Sandwich (Windsor) held their first Emancipation Day celebrations. The event featured speeches, musical and cultural performances, and a dinner organized by African American freedom seekers and abolitionists Henry and Mary Bibb, who founded the *Voice of the Fugitive*, Canada's first Black newspaper, that same year.
6 Henry, *Emancipation Day*, 62. Why would Black people defend British troops against American attacks when many of these same people were deprived of full rights of citizenship in Canada West? It is important not to interpret African Americans defending Canadian soil as outward expressions of allegiance to the British Crown. African Americans found multiple avenues to express their abhorrence for slavery in defence of their freedom, even if it meant doing so from British territory.
7 "Emancipation Day," *The Globe*, August 3, 1858.
8 Shadd, *Journey From Tollgate*, 126.
9 Shadd, 131.

10 Shadd, 134. Women who did not report an occupation were always married women who laboured inside the home, where they worked as caregivers, cooks, and cleaners.
11 Adams, "Making a Living," 16.
12 Howe, *Refugees from Slavery*, 40, 41. As an example of the anti-Blackness in London, Howe recounts a head-clerk in a hotel in the city who, in answer to inquiries about the condition of the coloured people, said the following: "N---ers are a damned nuisance. They keep men of means away from the place. This town has got the name of 'N---er Town,' and men of wealth won't come here." See Howe, 40–41.
13 Howe, 51–52.
14 Adams, "Making a Living," 9–10.
15 Sutherland, "Race Relations in Halifax," 49.
16 Bateman, "The Railway," 114.
17 Bateman, 114–15.
18 Boyko, *Blood and Daring*, 29.
19 Boyko, 29.
20 Brown, "Entertainers on the Road," 124.
21 Brown, 124–25.
22 Shadd Cary, *Plea for Emigration*, 29, 74. In her plea to African American freedom seekers to immigrate to Canada, Shadd Cary said of the British Empire "[T]here is no legal discrimination whatsoever affecting coloured immigrants in Canada, nor from any cause whatever are their privileges sought to be abridged."
23 In London, from the 1870s onward, there were no African American doctors, dentists, or pharmacists listed in censuses. See Adams, "Making a Living," 42.
24 Ryerson declared himself powerless before local trustees' decisions to exclude Black children from their schools.
25 McLaren, "We Had No," 33, 36. This idea of Canadian "powerlessness" to do anything to stop anti-Black racism and blackface minstrel shows from appearing in town took root in the nineteenth century, and in many ways continues to define Canadian anti-Black racism.
26 Broyld, "Frederick Douglass," 15.
27 Broyld, 15.
28 Broyld, 16. By the mid-1850s Chatham was a bustling frontier town on the Thames River, which flowed into the Detroit River at the United States border. It was within a few miles of Canada's largest Black settlements, including Dawn, Elgin, and Raleigh Township. See Rhodes, *Mary Ann Shadd*, 101.
29 Yee, "Gender Ideology," 57.
30 See Thompson, *Anthems and Minstrel*, 13; see also *Orpheus* I, no. 1 (July 1865), 6.
31 Le Camp, "Racial Considerations," 344.
32 Le Camp, "Racial Considerations," 344. Formed in 1838, the Mechanics' Institute was an outgrowth of the New Brunswick Philosophical Society.
33 Cited in Sutherland, "Race Relations in Halifax," 49.
34 Kilian, *Go Do Some*, 41.
35 Henry, *Emancipation Day*, 20. African Americans also settled in Salt Spring Island, British Columbia.
36 Vance, *History of Canadian*, 78.

37 "English-Language Theatre."
38 Walker, *West Indians*, 22. It was not until about 1910, however, that the Prairies (Alberta, Manitoba, and Saskatchewan) experienced their first significant Black immigration wave.
39 Boyko, *Blood and Daring*, 9.
40 Boyko, *Blood and Daring*, 27.
41 "Texas in the Union," *Globe*, January 13, 1846, 1.
42 Johnston, *Selling Themselves*, 18. The Canadian Press Association, founded in 1858, gathered together the publishers of daily and weekly newspapers, magazines, and trade papers published in the English language in Ontario. The Eastern Townships Press Association (1879), La Presse Associée de la Province de Québec (1882), and the Maritime Press Association (1888) did the same in their respective regions.
43 White, *Too Good*, 72. See also Boyko, *Blood and Daring*, 27–28. Published every other week at first, the *Globe* became a weekly in 1849, and subsequently a tri-weekly newspaper.
44 Johnston, *Selling Themselves*, 21. Many newspapermen also were investors in railroads. *Daily Colonist* editor Samuel Thompson, for instance, served as secretary-treasurer of the Toronto and Guelph Railway from 1852 to 1855. Thompson had a brief stint in politics when he served as a councillor and then as an alderman for St. George's Ward in Toronto from 1849 to 1854. See Stagg, "Samuel Thompson."
45 James Maurice Stockford Careless, "George Brown," *The Canadian Encyclopedia*, January 16, 2008, https://www.thecanadianencyclopedia.ca/en/article/george-brown.
46 Johnston, *Selling Themselves*, 22. Johnston writes further that it had been possible for newspapermen, like William Lyon Mackenzie and George Brown, to start a paper on their own resources or with limited financing because "proprietorship allowed them to express their opinions as they saw fit—which both men readily did. Then, their ability to win influence in party councils would have been proportionate to their influence with readers." See Johnston, *Selling Themselves*, 22.
47 Johnston, 23.
48 Johnston, 23.
49 "Mechanics Institute," *Globe*, December 1, 1847, 580.
50 "History of Toronto Public Library," Toronto Public Library, https://www.torontopubliclibrary.ca/about-the-library/library-history/.
51 Winks, *Blacks in Canada*, 253.
52 Francis Galton (1822–1911) would not coin the term *eugenics*, which described "the study of the agencies under social control that may improve or impair the racial qualities of future generations, either physically or mentally" until 1883, and his cousin, Charles Darwin, would not publish *On the Origin of Species* and *The Descent of Man* until 1859 and 1871. See McLaren, *Our Own*, 13–15.
53 "Compulsory Education," *Globe*, February 19, 1848, 1.
54 "Compulsory Education," *Globe*, February 26, 1848, n.p.
55 "News by the Britannia," *Globe*, July 9, 1844, 1.

NOTES TO CHAPTER 3

56 See D. J. McDougall, "Lord John Russell and the Canadian Crisis 1837–1841," *The Canadian Historical Review* 22, no. 4 (1941): 369–88.
57 Pickering, *Blackface Minstrelsy*, 1.
58 Taylor and Austen, *Darkest America*, 49, 54.
59 Hill, *Tap Dancing America*, 7.
60 DuComb, *Haunted City*, 11–12. "Most areas were a jumble of occupations and classes, of shops and homes, of immigrants and native-born Americans. Only around 1860 did Philadelphia see the beginning of concentration—a downtown area, a few manufacturing clusters, a small slum, a few blocks dominated by blacks, an occasional class and ethnic enclave—but such spatial segregation was not yet the dominant pattern." See Halttunen, *Confidence Men*, 39.
61 Roediger, *Wages of Whiteness*, 137.
62 Ernest, *National Within*, 26.
63 "Evolution of American," 7. Rooted solely in the North and with opposition to the expansion of slavery into the territories as their primary cause, the Republicans made headway quickly, winning control of the House of Representatives in 1858, just four years after the party came into existence. See also Zarefsky, *Lincoln*, 23.
64 According to Michael Rogin "the Whigs and Jacksonians both celebrated self-making, for although Andrew Jackson, the orphan who rose from the Carolina backcountry to the White House, came to personify the self-made man in national myth, the term *self-made man* was coined in 1832 by Jackson's opponent in that year's presidential election, Henry Clay." See Rogin, *Blackface*, 49–50.
65 Graber, *Dred Scott*, 18. Their suit, successful in the local trial court, was reversed by the Supreme Court of Missouri. The Missouri justices held that, as a matter of Missouri law, slave status "reattached" whenever a slave voluntarily re-entered a slave state from a free state or territory. Immediately following that defeat, Scott and his family brought a similar suit in federal court where a local federal circuit court rejected their claims, and the US Supreme Court dismissed Scott's appeal by a 7–2 vote.
66 Graber, 19.
67 Graber, 19.
68 Ernest, *Nation Within*, 26–27.
69 Lenton-Young, "Variety Theatre," 178.
70 The playbill for this appearance appears in Lenton-Young, 179.
71 Gardner, "Burgess."
72 David Gardiner, "Burgess, Colin (Cool)," *Dictionary of Canadian Biography*, http://www.biographi.ca/en/bio/burgess_colin_13E.html.
73 Rice, *Monarchs*, 138.
74 Thompson, *Anthems and Minstrel*, xx.
75 Thompson, xx.
76 The population rose from 58,000 in 1858 to 100,000 in the early 1860s, consolidating Montreal's place as Canada's other metropolis (Toronto its closest neighbour) and making it the ninth largest city in North America. See Thompson, *Anthems*, 56; also tables 2.1 and 2.2.
77 Thompson, *Anthems and Minstrel*, 52, 53.

78 Gardiner, "Burgess, Colin (Cool)."
79 Mahar, *Behind the Burnt Cork*, 1.
80 Johnson, "Shield Us From," 256.
81 Johnson, 256–58.
82 Johnson, 278.
83 Rice, *Monarchs of Minstrelsy*, 108.
84 Boyce, *Belleville*, 121.
85 Another engraving by John Henry Walker, dated ca. 1850–1885, titled *Hamall's Serenaders*, also depicts blackface characters, though it is not as grotesque as the 1875 depiction. See John Henry Walker, *Hamall's Serenaders*, ca. 1850–1885. Wood engraving relief printed on paper, 19.0 x 18.8 cm, The McCord Stewart Museum, Montreal, Quebec. https://collections.musee-mccord-stewart.ca/en/objects/21238/hamalls-serenaders.
86 Thompson, *Anthems and Minstrel*, 23.
87 Thompson, 23.
88 Plant, "Chronology," 310.
89 Thompson, *Anthems and Minstrel*, 23.
90 Nathalie Rech, "French-speaking Louisiana and Canada." *Canadian Encyclopedia*, May 3, 2019, https://www.thecanadianencyclopedia.ca/en/article/french-speaking-louisiana-and-canada.
91 Pickering, *Blackface Minstrelsy*, 120. The term "Ethiopian" did not refer to what became known as the country Ethiopia, but was a generic name attached to Blackness whether in North America, Britain, the Caribbean, or the so-called "Dark continent."
92 Cockrell, "Nineteenth-Century," 167.
93 Lott, *Love and Theft*, 104.
94 Mahar, *Behind*, 1.
95 Mahar, 201.
96 Carlin, *Birth of the Banjo*, 7.
97 Cavell, "Second Frontier," 1.
98 Furniss, "Indians, Odysseys," 197.
99 Furniss, 197.
100 See D'Amico-Cuthbert, "We Don't Have," note 15. See also *Rethinking the Great White North: Race, Nature, and the Historical Geographies of Whiteness in Canada*, edited by Andrew Baldwin, Laura Cameron, and Audrey Kobayashi (Vancouver: UBC Press, 2011); and *Race, Space, and the Law: Unmapping a White Settler Society*, edited by Sherene H. Razack (Toronto: Between the Lines, 2002).
101 Williams, *Blacks in Montreal*, 25.
102 Whitfield, *Blacks*, 3. In Nova Scotia during the mid-nineteenth century, slightly more than four thousand people of African descent resided in the province.
103 Whitfield, 84.
104 The first African in Nova Scotia, Mathieu Da Costa (c. 1589–1619), is believed to have served as an interpreter between the French and Mi'kmaq. In 1749 the imperial government supported an expedition under Edward Cornwallis to develop an English settlement to be named after Lord Halifax. Cornwallis established the town in 1749 with nearly two thousand settlers, possibly

including enslaved Black people; as the settlement grew (and to clear more land for the recruitment of even more English settlers) local officials displaced the Mi'kmaq and by 1755 had expelled and transported the Acadian population, many of whom settled in Louisiana. See Whitfield, *Blacks*, 14. See also Nelson, *Razing Africville*, 8.
105 Lawrence, "Rewriting Histories," 23–24.
106 Whitfield, *Blacks*, 84.
107 "The African Baptist and Methodist churches, along with associations such as the African Friendly Society, not only encouraged the development and sustenance of a shared identity, but also engaged in several battles to define the contours of black life in Nova Scotia," writes Whitfield. See Whitfield, 84.
108 Spray, *Blacks in New*, 62.
109 Spray, 62.
110 Harris, "Black Life," 143. Harris observes further that "when Black individuals do appear in local histories it is as footnotes to the tales of White settlers." This reality exists across the country as locating a Black subject in a Canadian archive often requires that you locate a White subject first and sift through their biography, estate wills, diary, and/or photograph albums to locate a Black person.
111 Spray, "Settlement," 68.
112 Spray, 79.
113 Johnson and Aladejebi, "Introduction," 3.
114 Razack, "Introduction," 3.
115 Lott, *Love and Theft*, 17–18.
116 Lott, 18.
117 Shadd, *Journey From Tollgate*, 58.
118 See Razack, "Introduction," 3.
119 Thompson, *Anthems*, xxviii.
120 Thompson, 54.
121 Razack, "Introduction," 1.
122 Mawani, "In Between," 52.
123 Razack, "Introduction," 2.
124 McLachlan, *Emigrant*, 33. See also Vance, *History of Canadian*, 100. McLachlan emigrated to Canada from Scotland.
125 Lott, *Love and Theft*, 4.
126 Vance, *History of Canadian*, 100.
127 Vance, 100.
128 Elliott, "Ragtime Spasms," 80.
129 Pickering, *Blackface Minstrelsy*, 147.
130 Pickering, 156.
131 Hornback, "Blackfaced Fools," 15.
132 See Boyko, *Blood and Daring*, 26.
133 Simpson, *Under the North*, 229.
134 Ronald J. Stagg, "Samuel Thompson," *Dictionary of Canadian Biography*, http://www.biographi.ca/en/bio/thompson_samuel_11E.html.
135 Stagg, "Samuel Thompson."

136 After establishing the *British Colonist*, de Cosmos embroiled himself in local politics. He was elected to the British Columbia Legislative Assembly (1871–74) as well as the House of Commons (1871–82) as representative of Victoria, eventually serving as British Columbia's second premier (1872–74). By the 1890s, the newspaper was also an outlet for local minstrel shows, such as an editorial from 1891 titled, "Little Locals" that announced, "the C.P.R. steamer Empress of India sails for Asiatic port on Sunday. The minstrel band will give an op-air concert at Campbell's corner at noon to-day." See "Little Local," *Daily Colonist*, October 10, 1891, 8. RMS Empress of India was an ocean liner built in 1890–91 by Naval Construction & Armaments Co, Barrow-in-Furness, England for Canadian Pacific Steamships. It was one of three ships specially designed to travel between Hong Kong and Canada's West Coast as part of a mail service to Britain. See *Historica Canada*, https://www.historicacanada.ca/on_this_day/empress-india-arrives-vancouver.
137 Featherstone, "Blackface Atlantic," 238.
138 Lenton-Young, "Variety Theatre," 184. See also *Toronto Globe*, June 4, 1850.
139 Lenton-Young, "Variety Theatre," 181.
140 Williams, *Marxism and Literature*, 131.
141 Frick, *Uncle Tom's Cabin*, 11.
142 Jones, Jr., *Captive Stage*, 19.
143 Toll, *Blacking Up,* 196; 228; See also Lott, *Love and Theft*, 107.

CHAPTER 4

1 Thompson, *Anthems and Minstrel*, 54.
2 Thompson, 54.
3 Boyko, *Blood and Daring*, 7.
4 Boyko, 8.
5 Harris, "Black Life," 155.
6 Marquis, *Armageddon's Shadow*, 59.
7 Richard Reid, "How black Canadians fought for liberty in the American Civil War," *Toronto Star*, January 31, 2015, https://www.thestar.com/opinion/commentary/2015/01/31/how-black-canadians-fought-for-liberty-in-the-american-civil-war.html?rf.
8 Boyko, *Blood and Daring*, 6.
9 Cited in Arenson, "Experience," 74.
10 Boyko, *Blood and Daring*, 8.
11 See "Reform Party," *Britannica*, https://www.britannica.com/topic/Reform-Party-Canada-1837.
12 Thompson, *Anthems and Minstrel*, 70.
13 Thompson, 79.
14 Marquis, *Armageddon's Shadow*, 75.
15 Weigman, *American Anatomies*, 21.
16 Springhall, *Genesis*, 71.
17 Springhall, 84.

~ NOTES TO CHAPTER 4 ~

18 Harris, *Black Life*, 148. Harris's review of the newspaper found that racist caricatures appeared on occasion in the 1860s, see n34.
19 Marquis, *Armageddon's Shadow*, 172.
20 Cited in Marquis, 86.
21 Marquis, *Armageddon's Shadow*, 84.
22 Sheehy, *Montreal*, 15.
23 Sheehy, 15.
24 Sheehy, 19. Sheehy asserts that the Ontario Bank, located on Place d'Armes in Montreal, was so strongly associated with the Confederate Secret Service that Southern bankers were thought to be employees or direct associates of the bank. John Simpson (1812–85) founded the bank in Bowmanville, Ontario in 1857. He later became one of Canada's first senators.
25 Spier and Potvin. "Calixa Lavallée," *Canadian Encyclopedia*, June 11, 2008, https://www.thecanadianencyclopedia.ca/en/article/calixa-lavallee.
26 Thompson, *Minstrels and Anthem*, 53.
27 George Brown, "American Revolution," *The Globe*, April 8, 1861, 2.
28 Boyko, *Blood and Daring*, 9.
29 J.G. Snell, "Dougall, John," *Dictionary of Canadian Biography*, http://www.biographi.ca/en/bio/dougall_john_11E.html. In 1871 Dougall left the *Montreal Witness* in the charge of his son and, with support and capital from Manhattan residents, moved to New York City where he established the *Daily Witness*, which was only briefly successful, folding in 1877; but the *New York Weekly Witness*, which he also founded in 1871, achieved considerable circulation and continued after Dougall's death.
30 Philippe Sylvain, "Clerk, George Edward," *Dictionary of Canadian Biography*, http://www.biographi.ca/en/bio/clerk_george_edward_10E.html. In 1858 the *True Witness* had 2,837 subscribers and was distributed by agents in twenty-one areas. In the following year Clerk transferred the ownership to John Gillies, who made trips to Canada West, the Maritimes, and Nova Scotia to increase the number of subscribers.
31 Maxime Dagenais, "Parti Bleu," *The Canadian Encyclopedia*, February 7, 2006, https://www.thecanadianencyclopedia.ca/en/article/parti-bleu. Cartier was the first premier of Canada East from 1858 to 1862.
32 Sheehy, *Montreal*, 30.
33 Gabrial, "Second American Revolution," 23. See also Careless, J.M.S. *Brown of The Globe, Vol. 2: Statesman of Confederation 1860–1880*. Toronto: The Macmillan Company of Canada Ltd., 1963. In his study of news coverage following the outbreak of the war, from April 1 to May 31, 1861, Gabrial found the *Gazette* published items regarding the United States in forty-eight days of news coverage, and published such items under the headlines, "Our Special American Dispatches" or "War News." See Gabrial, 24.
34 Mackey, *Done with Slavery*, 312–13. Originally founded by French printer Fleury Mesplet, who moved to Montreal from Philadelphia on the coattails of the American Revolutionary war in 1775–76, after his death the *Gazette* was reborn under the ownership of Montreal postmaster Edward Edwards.

35 Bruemmer, René. Montreal has a strong historical link to America's Confederate past," August 17, 2017, https://montrealgazette.com/news/local-news/montreal-has-a-strong-historical-link-to-americas-confederate-past.
36 Parker, George L. "LOVELL, JOHN," *Dictionary of Canadian Biography*, http://www.biographi.ca/en/bio/lovell_john_12E.html.
37 Parker, "LOVELL, JOHN."
38 Boyko, *Blood and Daring*, 8. See also *The Globe*, July 29, 1861.
39 Reid, *African Americans*, 4.
40 Some historians suggest that Hicks passed as White to manage his troupe of formerly enslaved performers. See Senelick, *Changing Room*, 277.
41 Taylor and Austen, *Darkest America*, 50.
42 de Lerma, "Hicks."
43 Johnson, *Burnt Cork*, 159.
44 Southern, "The Georgia Minstrels," 164.
45 Sampson, *Ghost Walks*, 5, 23. See also Lenton-Young, "Variety Theatre," 178.
46 Taylor and Austen, *Darkest America*, 51.
47 Pickering, *Blackface Minstrelsy*, 26.
48 Sher, *White Hoods*, 20.
49 Thompson, *Anthems and Minstrel*, 79.
50 Du Bois, *Black Reconstruction*, 188.
51 Royce, *Origins*, 2–3.
52 Many Southerners also began to do business in the expanding Northern industrialized economy; they were bolstered by the federal (Democratic) government, which had expanded during the war (including establishing the first income tax), and Northern financiers who saw great benefits from increased government spending after the war. See Riddle, "Origins," 62.
53 Du Bois, *Black Reconstruction*, 211–12.
54 Mathieu, *North*, 61.
55 Mathieu, 10. See also Holt, *Grand Trunk*, 83.
56 James Marsh, "Railway History," *The Canadian Encyclopedia*, March 25, 2009, https://www.thecanadianencyclopedia.ca/en/article/railway-history.
57 Roediger, *Wages of Whiteness*, 171–72.
58 Roediger, 172.
59 Though some Black men and women were able to succeed at barbering and hairdressing during this period.
60 Frick, *Uncle Tom's Cabin*, 16.
61 The bipartisan compromise effectively ended Reconstruction, nullifying the legislative freedoms that had been established with the passage of the Thirteenth, Fourteenth, and Fifteenth Amendments. It also included the removal of federal troops from the South, and the end of the Freedman's Bureau, which had been established for the purpose of "improvement, protection, and employment of refugee freedmen." See Bennett, Jr., *Shaping of Black America*, 252.
62 MacKenzie, "There Was No War," 364.
63 Foner cited in MacKenzie, 364.
64 Bennett, Jr., *Shaping of Black America*, 252.
65 Mathieu, *North*, 11.
66 Mathieu, 11.

∽ NOTES TO CHAPTER 4 ∽

67 These numbers are widely agreed to be unreliable and possibly underestimated. See Wayne, "Black Population," 62, and Reid, *African Canadians*, 26.
68 Sheehy, *Montreal*, 25.
69 Beckert, *Empire of Cotton*, 84.
70 Danson, "On the Existing," 7. The article was titled, "On the Existing Connection Between American Slavery and the British Cotton Manufacture."
71 Danson, 19.
72 Beckert, *Empire of Cotton*, 104. "Exports to Great Britain increased by a factor of ninety-three between 1791 and 1800, only to multiply another seven times by 1820. By 1802 the United States was already the single most important supplier of cotton to the British market, and by 1857 it would produce about as much cotton as China," he notes further. Similarly, in 1860, total sugar production was growing rapidly, total world production of sucrose stood at an estimated 1.373 million tons, or an increase of more than 233 percent from 1830. See Mintz, *Sweetness*, 73.
73 Shadd, *Journey From Tollgate*, 155.
74 *The Province of Ontario Gazetteer and Directory*, Robertson and Cook, 1869, 243. See https://archive.org/details/provinceontariooomcevgoog/page/248/mode/2up?view=theater. See also "Sharpley's Minstrels," Scott's Printing Establishment, Philadelphia, Pennsylvania, 1856 or 1857?. Library Company of Philadelphia. Afro-Americana, 2nd ed. Suppl. 2052.
75 "Amusements," *Daily Globe*, July 12, 1862.
76 Lott, *Love and Theft*, 144.
77 See Carlin, *Birth of the Banjo*, 63. See "Old Dan Tucker," which is attributed to the Virginia Minstrels but, in addition to being written by Emmett, Frank Brower is often credited as singing the song.
78 Mahar, *Behind*, 14.
79 Miller, "Twisting," 9.
80 Cockrell, "Nineteenth Century," 166. See also Jones, Jr., *Captive Stage*, 128.
81 Lott, *Love and Theft*, 134.
82 Le Camp, "Racial Considerations," 345. Vance pinpoints the Ethiopian Warblers as visiting the British-American Hotel in Kingston in September 1851 as one of the first in that city. See Vance, *History of Canadian*, 77. Located in eastern Ontario on the Tay River, southwest of Ottawa, Perth was established as a military settlement in 1816 shortly after the War of 1812.
83 See *The Franklin Repository*, May 18, 1859, 8, https://www.newspapers.com/article/the-franklin-repository-lb-lents-mamm/45680291/.
84 Lenton-Young, "Variety Theatre," 175.
85 "Perth Railway Stations," *Ontario Railway Stations*, https://ontariorailwaystations.wordpress.com/home/lanark-county/perth-railway-stations/.
86 Lenton-Young, "Variety Theatre," 178.
87 Johnson reviewed *The New York Clipper, Toronto Globe, Ottawa Citizen, Hamilton Spectator, Kingston British Whig*, and *Brantford Expositor*. See Johnson, "Uncle Tom," 58.
88 Le Camp, "Racial Considerations," 345.
89 Johnson, *Burnt Cork*, 122, 154.
90 Johnson, *Burnt Cork*, 159.

∾ NOTES TO CHAPTERS 4 AND 5 ∾

91 Reid, *African Americans*, 16.
92 Reid, *African Americans*, 16.
93 Le Camp, "Racial Considerations," 344.
94 Thompson, *Anthems and Minstrel*, 100.
95 Careless, "Cultural Setting," 30.
96 "Victoria's Victoria: Theatre Royal," http://web.uvic.ca/vv/student/theatreroyal/localtheatre.html.
97 Evans, *Frontier Theatre*, 23.
98 Evans, 16.
99 Taylor and Austen, *Darkest America*, 50, 51.
100 The Canadian National Railway (CNR) was founded 1919. From the years 1917–1923, it amalgamated five financially troubled railways: the Grand Trunk and its subsidiary, the Grand Trunk Pacific; the Intercolonial; the Canadian Northern; and the National Transcontinental. See Albert Tucker, "Canadian National Railway (CNR)," *Canadian Encyclopedia*, March 25, 2009, https://www.thecanadianencyclopedia.ca/en/article/canadian-national-railways.
101 Vance, *History of Canadian*, 78.
102 Except for Wilberforce in Ohio (1856), Fisk (1866) was one of many Black colleges and universities established in postbellum America, which also included Howard University (1867), Atlanta University (1865), Morgan (today Morgan State) (1867), Hampton Institute (today Hampton University) (1868), and Spelman Women's College (1881).

CHAPTER 5

1 Vance, *History*, 135–36.
2 See Andrew McIntosh, P.B. Waite, Ged Martin, "Charlottetown Conference," *Canadian Encyclopedia*, September 2, 2010, https://www.thecanadianencyclopedia.ca/en/article/charlottetown-conference; James H. Marsh, "Quebec Conference of 1864," *Canadian Encyclopedia*, October 9, 2013, https://www.thecanadianencyclopedia.ca/en/article/quebec-conference-of-1864-feature; Andrew McIntosh and P.B. Waite, "London Conference," *Canadian Encyclopedia*, February 7, 2006, https://www.thecanadianencyclopedia.ca/en/article/london-conference.
3 Francis, *National Dreams*, 61, 62.
4 Graybill, "Rangers, Mounties," 83.
5 Graybill, "Rangers, Mounties," 86. Sven Beckert writes that "As transportation and communication access to the southern hinterland improved dramatically in the wake of the Civil War, and as the empire of cotton moved farther into the West, growers sold their cotton directly to merchants or mill agents, or even to foreign buyers, instead of entrusting it for sale to a factor in a distant port. As a result, interior Texas cities such as Dallas, far away from the ocean, became important cotton-trading places in their own right." See *Empire of Cotton*, 318. In addition to the role the Rangers played in mythologizing Texas as a place of grit, frontiersmanship, and renegades, the state played a significant role in the expansion of plantation slavery in the years leading up to 1860.

NOTES TO CHAPTER 5

6 Daschuk, *Clearing the Plains*, 79.
7 Daschuk, 108.
8 Francis, *National Dreams*, 22. Some historians consider November 7, 1885 to be Canada's true "Independence Day" as the "Last Strike" of the CPR is what united the country; as such, it is considered one of the most important moments in Canadian history.
9 Mathieu, *North*, 8–9.
10 Mathieu, 10.
11 Francis, *National Dreams*, 22.
12 Francis, 153.
13 Francis, 153, 154.
14 Thompson, *Anthems and Minstrel*, 219.
15 Thompson, 219.
16 See Vance, *History of Canadian Culture*, 213. June 24, Saint-Jean-Baptiste Day or Fête de la Saint-Jean-Baptiste, is a national holiday in Quebec. It commemorates the Saint-Jean-Baptiste Society (1834–) which organized a gathering of all francophone communities across North America on June 24, 1880. This event was the first National Congress of French Canadians (Congrès national des Canadiens français). See Marc-André Gagnon, "Société Saint-Jean-Baptiste," *Canadian Encyclopedia*, February 7, 2006, https://www.thecanadian encyclopedia.ca/en/article/st-jean-baptiste-society.
17 Bennett Jr., *Shaping of Black*, 252.
18 The life of Portuguese-born Marie-Joseph Angélique has been documented by Williams and most notably Afua Cooper in *The Hanging of Angélique* (Toronto: HarperCollins, 2006). Owned by Mme. De Francheville of St. Paul Street, Angélique was assumed to have started a house fire on April 10, 1734 to hide her escape with Claude Thibault, a White man. Accused, tried, and convicted for destroying almost half of Montreal by fire—forty-six buildings including the convent, the church, and the hospital—authorities tragically executed Angélique.
19 The family records of one local historian reveal that when his first ancestor arrived in Montreal in the late 1840s, there were four Black families living in Montreal at that time. See Williams, *Road to Now*, 27–28. Quebec City's population grew steadily over the 1860s, but slowed dramatically over the next decade in part because the federal capital was established at Ottawa and due to a stock market crash of 1873. See Thompson, *Anthems and Minstrel*, 186.
20 Linteau, Durocher, and Robert, *Quebec*, 36.
21 Neatby, *From Old Quebec*, 7.
22 Marsh, "Railway History." See also Mathieu, *North*, 13.
23 Kilian, *Go Do*, 115, 137, 158.
24 Le Camp, "Racial Considerations," 286.
25 Vance, *History of Canadian*, 78.
26 Vance, 79–80.
27 Detre, "Canada's Campaign," 113.
28 Asian, *Chinese Labour*, 2. Several sections of the CPR were contracted entirely to the Chinese, including the ninety miles from Port Moody to Yale and the seventy miles from Lytton to Savona's Ferry. White and Chinese labourers

∽ NOTES TO CHAPTER 5 ∽

worked together on many other sections of the railroad, but the Chinese were often assigned the most dangerous tasks.
29 Dua, "Exclusion Through Inclusion," 447.
30 Dua, 461. The outright ban on Chinese immigration remained in effect until after the Second World War, when overtly racially discriminatory clauses began to be removed from Canadian immigration, citizenship, and other legislative acts. See Dua, 461–62.
31 As Jiwu Wang writes, "after a Chinese businessman returned to San Francisco from his trip to British Columbia, his optimistic report about the new country, especially his experience of being offered high wages as a cook, created much excitement among the local Chinese. Many of them, lured by the prospect of 'striking it rich' in Gold Mountain, rushed northward from California to British Columbia." See Wang, *Protestant Missions*, 10, 11.
32 See "Grand Opera House, London, Ontario" [programme, Tuesday, April 24, 1894: Hoyt's musical trifle, *A Trip to Chinatown*. University of Toronto Robarts Library Microtext Collection.] While I have not located a similar program in cities like Toronto and Hamilton, theatrical shows from Broadway rarely played one stand-alone city in Ontario, and so I can safely speculate that *A Trip to Chinatown* was seen by audiences across the region.
33 Fairfield, "Theatres," 233–34. After a fire burned down the Masonic Temple on February 23, 1900, reducing the Grand Opera House to ashes, a new Grand opened eighteen months later on September 9, 1901.
34 Dua, "Exclusion Through Inclusion," 447.
35 Razack, "Introduction," 3.
36 See Le Camp, "Racial Considerations," 300–301.
37 Le Camp, "Racial Considerations," 345.
38 Shadd, *Journey from Tollgate*, 190.
39 Frick, *Uncle Tom's Cabin*, 127. Leviticus 25:8–55 states, "And you shall consecrate the fiftieth year, and proclaim liberty throughout the land to all its inhabitants. It shall be a jubilee for you, when each of you shall return to his property and each of you shall return to his clan."
40 Du Bois, *Souls of Black Folks*, 162.
41 Tate and Bowman, *Flyer Vault*, 14.
42 Tate and Bowman, 15.
43 Careless, "Cultural Setting," 39.
44 Careless, 39.
45 Careless, "Cultural Setting," 39, 41.
46 Fairfield, "Theatres and Performance Halls," 241.
47 Brown, "Entertainers," 125; Fairfield, "Theatres and Performance Halls," 240.
48 "Vanished Hamilton: A litany of loss." *Hamilton Spectator*, February 17, 2013, www.thespec.com/news-story/2206326-vanished-hamilton-a-litany-of-loss/.
49 Fairfield, "Theatres and Performance Halls," 241.
50 Nickinson, Charlotte (Morrison), *The Canadian Biography*, https://brixton38.biographi.ca/en/bio/nickinson_charlotte_13E.html.
51 "Toronto's first theatre impresario," *Toronto Star*, May 17, 2015, https://www.thestar.com/business/toronto-s-first-theatre-impresario/article_bd4f635c-9e9c-54e7-a626-a2fd856b8cc4.html.

NOTES TO CHAPTER 5

52 See Fairfield, "Theatres and Performance Halls," 223.
53 Nickinson, Charlotte (Morrison).
54 Plant, "Chronology," 318.
55 Fairfield, "Theatres and Performance Halls," 221.
56 Careless, "Cultural Setting," 41. The Grand Theatre, which was initially owned and run by the eccentric Ambrose J. Small (who would vanish without a trace in 1919, sparking an epic, but fruitless, police search) seated 2,100 and had been Toronto's undisputed number one playhouse from 1880. See Brockhouse, "Royal Alexandra Theatre," 8.
57 Plant, "Chronology," 329.
58 The McCord's Notman Photographic Archives, acquired in stages since 1956, constitutes the majority of McCord's photographic collection with over 450,000 photographs from the Montreal studio founded in 1856 by Notman and remaining in the Notman family until it was sold in 1935 to another commercial concern, the Associated Screen News. The Associated Screen News divided the operations into the historical division, run by Charles Notman, and the commercial studio, Wm. Notman & Sons. See Longford, *Suspended Conversations*, 203.
59 Sheehy, *Montreal*, 14.
60 In 1862, Henry Wood converted a Jewish synagogue into a theatre called Wood's Minstrel Hall and it was later renamed Theatre Comique. Irish American actor and playwright Ned Harrigan (1844–1911) and Worcester, Massachusetts-born comedian Tony Hart (1855–91) managed the theatre until 1872. In 1876, Harrigan took full control of the theatre until it closed and was demolished in 1881. See "Theatre Comique," *Robert Davis Theatre Consulting Services*, http://robertdavisinc.com/comique.htm.
61 Savage, *Standing Soldiers*, 77.
62 Thompson, *Uncle*, 63.
63 Toll, *Blacking Up*, 262, 249–51.
64 Springhall, *Genesis*, 72.
65 Krasner, "Real Thing," 101.
66 Taylor and Austen, *Darkest America*, 75.
67 Toll, *Blacking Up*, 257.
68 Jones, Jr., *Captive Stage*, 52.
69 Jones, Jr., 52.
70 Glenn, *Female Spectacle*, 50.
71 Blair, "Blackface Minstrels," 61.
72 Blair, 61.
73 Pickering, *Blackface Minstrelsy*, 109.
74 Pickering, 4.
75 Southern, "The Georgia Minstrels," 164.
76 Pickering, *Blackface Minstrelsy*, 25.
77 Pickering, 25.
78 Boyko, *Blood and Daring*, 7.
79 Boyko, 7.
80 Sheehy, *Montreal*, 56.
81 Morgan, *Uncle Tom's Cabin*, 180.

NOTES TO CHAPTER 5

82. Hunter, "Toronto, Hamilton," 2. Incorporated in 1885, the Brantford, Waterloo, and Lake Erie Railway Company was granted permission for construction of a line from Berlin (renamed Kitchener in 1916) through Brantford to link with the Canada Southern Railway, continuing down to Lake Erie in 1888.
83. "Intercolonial Railway," *Government of Canada*, July 28, 2015, https://www.canada.ca/en/news/archive/2015/07/intercolonial-railway.html.
84. Tate and Bowman, *Flyer Vault*, 4.
85. Le Camp, "Racial Considerations," 345.
86. Le Camp, 346.
87. "Amusements," *Daily Globe*, December 6, 1879, n.p.
88. Frick, *Uncle Tom's Cabin*, 255, n96. See also Toll, *Blacking Up*, 145.
89. de Lerma, "Hicks."
90. Southern, "The Georgia Minstrels," 173.
91. "Haverly's United Mastadon."
92. Le Camp, "Racial Considerations," 347.
93. "City News," *Globe*, May 10, 1873, 1.
94. Tate and Bowman, "Minstrel Troupes," 5.
95. "Music and the Drama," *Globe*, March 11, 1882, 14.
96. "Music and the Drama", 29.
97. Tate and Bowman, *Flyer Vault*, 5.
98. Abbott and Seroff, *Out of Sight*, 106.
99. Springhall, *Genesis of Mass*, 73.
100. Valis Hill, *Tap Dancing America*, 18–19. "Soft-shoe" is a rhythmic form of tap dancing that does not require special shoes; instead, by tapping the feet while also sliding the feet (dancers scatter sand on the stage to enhance the sound of sliding feet) dancers generate rhythm. White American tap dancer and actor Fred Astaire made this technique famous in 1940s and 1950s Hollywood, but the technique was perfected by African American minstrel and vaudeville performers from the 1870s onward.
101. Valis Hill, *Tap Dancing America*, 18–19.
102. "Gossip of the Stage," *Freeman*, February 8, 1913. See also Abbott and Seroff, *Out of Sight*, xii. Founded by Edward Elder Cooper, a freedom-seeking formerly enslaved African American who settled in Indianapolis in 1882, in 1892 the *Indianapolis Freeman* was sold to George L. Knox.
103. Cited in Taylor and Austen, *Darkest America*, 54.
104. Toll, *Blacking Up*, 259. "Old Aunt Jemima" was commercially recorded in 1947 by the White male quartet known as the Singing Sentinels. Cited in Abbott and Seroff, *Out of Sight*, 107.
105. "Look Out," *Globe*, May 8, 1884, 6.
106. "Look Out," 6.
107. "Look Out," 6.
108. Salem Tutt Whitney, "Seen and Heard While Passing," *Freeman*, July 17, 1915. Salem Tutt and his brother, J. Homer Tutt (1882–1951) were known as "the Tutt Brothers," in American vaudeville where they worked as producers, writers, and performers until the early 1930s. They were also known as Whitney & Tutt, Tutt & Whitney, and the Whitney Brothers. See Hill and Hatch, *History of African American*, 209.

NOTES TO CHAPTER 5

109 "Chicago Affairs," *Daily Globe*, February 2, 1876, 2.
110 "Music and the Drama: Grand Opera House," *Globe*, May 15, 1883, 5.
111 "Horace Weston, 1825–90," *Library of Congress Biographies*, https://www.loc.gov/item/ihas.200038859/.
112 Dunson, "Black Misrepresentation," 56.
113 Pickering, *Blackface Minstrelsy*, 28.
114 Burr, *Spreading the Light*, 8.
115 Burr, 182.
116 Featherstone, "Blackface Atlantic," 248–49.
117 For example, in "The Origin of Landlordism," a cartoon that appeared in the October 1, 1887 issues of *Grip*, Burr suggests that Bengough declared that labourers were coming out short based on existing laws that gave landowners the right to charge rent on the use of land and the expenses of the community were thus defrayed by taxes levied on private property. To illustrate his discourse on the need for labour reform, Bengough depicted the characters in "The Origins of Landlordism" in blackface, which as Burr opines, "Bengough was not only criticizing landlordism in general, [but also] criticizing a system that was detrimental to the interests of white Anglo-Saxon working men." See Burr, *Spreading the Light*, 82.
118 Lott, *Love and Theft*, 71.
119 The cartoon was later reprinted in the 1886 book, *A Caricature History of Canadian Politics: Events from the Union of 1841, as Illustrated by Cartoons from "Grip", and Various Other Sources*.
120 Retallack, "Paddy, the Priest," 135.
121 This act effectively made LaFontaine the first prime minister of Canada in the modern sense of the term. See Jacques Monet, S.j. "Sir Louis-Hippolyte LaFontaine," *Canadian Encyclopedia*, January 20, 2008, https://www.thecanadianencyclopedia.ca/en/article/sir-louis-hippolyte-lafontaine. Lafontaine, along with fifth, Robert Baldwin (1804–58), a first-generation Irish-Canadian Protestant, and heir to the combined lands of the interrelated Baldwin, Willcox and Russell families (all of County Cork), property that comprised most of what is now downtown Toronto, is also acknowledged as one of the architects of Responsible Government. See Michael S. Cross and Robert L. Fraser, "Robert Baldwin," *Canadian Encyclopedia*, January 21, 2008, https://www.thecanadianencyclopedia.ca/en/article/robert-baldwin.
122 Burr, *Spreading the Light*, 56.
123 Burr, 56.
124 Mendelson, "*Grip* Magazine," 2.
125 The National Policy passed in advance of the 1879 Conservative budget; it would become the signature piece of legislation of Canada's first official Prime Minister, John A. Macdonald (serving from 1867 to 1873 and 1878 to 1891).
126 Harris, et al., "Protecting Infant Industries," 16. *The National Policy Minstrels* also appeared the same year the Tories won the federal election. Like the term Whig, Tory was based on a British version of traditionalism and conservatism, which upheld the social order as it evolved in the English culture; a common Tory ethos was "God, Queen, and Country." The Tories generally were also

∽ NOTES TO CHAPTER 5 ∾

monarchists and defenders of aristocracy, as opposed to the liberalism of the Whigs. See Ball, *Portrait*, 74. See also Charmley, *History of Conservative*, 103.

127 Den Otter, *Philosophy of Railways*, 205.
128 Cited in Den Otter, 206. See also Alexander Mackenzie, Speeches of the Hon. Alexander Mackenzie During His Visit to Scotland (Toronto 1876), 21–22.
129 Burr, *Spreading the Light*, 74.
130 Spadoni, "*Grip*," 13. Bengough worked as a reporter in 1872 at the *Globe*, under managing editor George Brown, before launching the first issue of *Grip* on May 24, 1873.
131 The National Policy Elephant that appeared in *Grip* on September 28, 1878 was like Nast's depiction of Republican elephant. Burr, *Spreading the Light*, 69, 70. By the early 1880s, Bengough was also caricaturing Toronto Irish personalities such as Patrick Boyle, John O' Donohoe, Edward Blake, and Catholic Archbishop John Joseph Lynch. His other works reflected criticism of the power of the Catholic Church. Terms like "wild Irish," which invoked images of both "semi-savage" Catholics and political rebels who were sometimes Protestants, were frequently used in the 1830s through 1850s. See Jenkins, "Homeland Crisis," 51; see also Roediger, *Wages of Whiteness*, 140.
132 Jarman, "Graphic Art," 156.
133 Jarman, 157.
134 Spadoni, "*Grip*," 15.
135 Mendelson, "*Grip* Magazine," 6–7. Bengough also ridiculed Asians, Irish Catholics, and Jews. See Spadoni, "*Grip*,"11–16; see also Burr, *Spreading the Light*, 72–74; 87–97.
136 Harris, et al. "Protecting Infant Industries," 16.
137 Roediger, *Wages of Whiteness*, 98. Roediger suggests further that Whigs also became "coons," especially in the speech of Democrats, who cursed Whigs in "coongress" and Whig "coonventions", Whig "coonism" and a lack of Whig "coonsistency."
138 Mendelson, "*Grip* Magazine," 10.
139 "Philip Astley and the First Circuses," *Britannia*, https://www.britannica.com/art/circus-theatrical-entertainment/Philip-Astley-and-the-first-circuses#ref888112. "The Greatest Show on Earth" was in promotion of a circus held in Brooklyn, New York that offered several attractions including the sideshow, a feature unique to American circuses. In 1872, Barnum and his partners loaded their show onto sixty-five railroad cars, giving birth to the age of the giant railroad circuses that could travel greater distances and perform in towns that had the space and population to support the large shows. Barnum's own "Greatest Show on Earth" eventually travelled on three separate trains, going distances of 160 kilometres (100 miles) or more in a single night.
140 Elwood H. Jones, "Joseph Rymal," *Dictionary of Canadian Biography*, http://www.biographi.ca/en/bio/rymal_joseph_12E.html.
141 Cecilia Morgan and Robert Craig Brown, "Cartwright, Sir Richard John," *The Dictionary of Canadian Biography*, http://www.biographi.ca/en/bio/cartwright_richard_john_14E.html.
142 Archer-Straw, *Negrophilia*, 41.
143 Lemons, "Black Stereotypes," 107.

144 Roediger, *Wages of Whiteness*, 98.
145 Roediger, 98.
146 Brooks, *Lost Sounds*, 150; see also Southern, *Music of Black*, 303.
147 See "Grand Opera House, London, Ont., programme season 1897–98," University of Toronto Robarts Library Microtext Collection.
148 Southern, "Origin and Development," 1–2.
149 Hardy, "Historical Ironies," 11, 12.
150 Hardy, 13, 14.
151 George Primrose is sometimes also named as George H. Delaney.
152 "GEORGE WILSON DIES. Retired Minstrel Show Star Was Associate of Primrose," *New York Times*, March 24, 1930, 27.
153 Lenton-Young, "Variety Theatre," 183.
154 They produced a twelve-strong (five males) choir that made their first British appearance in Liverpool on November 29, 1876. See "085: The Jubilee Singers of Wilmington, North Carolina," *Jeffery Green. Historian*, https://jeffreygreen.co.uk/085-the-jubilee-singers-of-wilmington-north-carolina/.
155 For a comprehensive list of jubilee choirs, see Sandra Jean Graham, "Spirituals and the Birth of a Black Entertainment Industry," *Biographical Dictionary of Jubilee Concert Troupes*, https://files.press.uillinois.edu/books/supplemental/p083273/web_table_4.4.html#edn.
156 "Musical and Dramatic," *Globe*, October 19, 1880, 12.
157 "Musical and Dramatic," 12.
158 "Musical and Dramatic," 12.
159 "Musical and Dramatic," 12.
160 Despite a pervasive anti-Black milieu, Brantford's Black community was significant enough to put on its own Emancipation Day celebrations. In 1903, the city "entertained a large crowd of visitors from Toronto, Hamilton, Woodstock, Guelph, and other places" at Mohawk Park, located on Lynwood by Mohawk Lake; after a street procession, Emancipation Day events ended at the Park with an afternoon of sport activities, boating on the lake, picnicking, and dancing in the pavilion. See "Colored Folk Celebrate," *Toronto Daily Star*, August 4, 1903, 5. See also Henry, *Emancipation Day*, 112.
161 Shadd, *Journey From Tollgate*, 190. Angela Files asserts that "O'Banyoun" is also spelled "O'Banyan," a surname with Irish origins; "Afro-Americans, in assuming white culture, occupation and religion, often lost touch with their African identity," she writes. See Files, "O'Banyan Jubilee Singers," 5.
162 See Amherstburg Freedom Museum. O'Banyoun Jubilee Singers. Facebook, October 20, 2018, https://m.facebook.com/AmherstburgFreedom/photos/have-you-ever-heard-of-the-obanyoun-jubilee-singers-they-gained-success-with-the/1146274212193485/.
163 Amherstburg Freedom Museum, O'Banyoun Jubilee Singers.
164 Abbott and Seroff, *Out of Sight*, 240.
165 "Flash From the Past: Jubilee Singing Was Popular in Guelph." *The Record*, April 29, 2022. https://www.therecord.com/life/local-history/2022/04/29/flash-from-the-past-jubilee-singing-was-popular-in-guelph.html. The October 21, 1896 edition of the *Guelph Mercury* provided the names of many of the O'Banyoun singers: Mrs. Waldron, Messrs. A. and J. Waldron, Miss Cromwell, who sang

NOTES TO CHAPTER 5

quartettes, the Misses Williams, who sang duets, and Miss Schofield and Mr. Mallott, who performed on the organ and violin, respectively.
166 "Flash From the Past: Jubilee Singing Was Popular in Guelph." *The Record*.
167 Shadd, *Journey From Tollgate*, 190.
168 Abbott and Seroff, *Out of Sight*, 176.
169 Abbott and Seroff, 176.
170 Shadd, *Journey From Tollgate*, 192.
171 The *New York Clipper* became a "show business" trade journal that published the activities of touring professionals and the theatre managers that book them. See Johnson, "On the Tension," 68. See also Masten, "Challenge Dancing," 623.
172 Cited in Abbott and Seroff, *Out of Sight*, 176.
173 Abbott and Seroff, *Out of Sight*, 177.
174 Files, "O'Banyan Jubilee Singers," 4.
175 Files, 4.
176 Talty, *Mulatto America*, 27, 42.
177 Talty, 45.
178 Frick, *Uncle Tom's Cabin*, 127.
179 Sanders, *Afro-Modernist Aesthetics*, 162.
180 Pickering, *Blackface Minstrelsy*, 81.
181 Johnson, "Shield Us From," 270.
182 See Cameron Shelley, "Jubilee Singers Come to Guelph," *Guelph in Postcards*, April 17, 2022, https://guelphpostcards.blogspot.com/2022/04/jubilee-singers-come-to-guelph.html. In 1862, James Innes (1833–1903) joined George Palmer as a co-owner of the *Guelph Weekly Mercury* which he ran until 1873 when he amalgamated the *Mercury* with the *Guelph Advertiser*. He ran the newspaper until 1898 when it was purchased by his nephew, James Innes McIntosh, and Francis W. Galbraith. Guelph had two newspapers before the *Evening Mercury*. The first, the *Wellington Mercury*, was founded in 1853 and published weekly by owner George Keeling; the second, the *Guelph Advertiser*, started in 1854 and was also published weekly. Prior to becoming a publisher and editor, James Innes worked as a reporter and journalist at the *Globe* and the *British Colonist*, and in Hamilton at the *Morning Banner*. He returned to the *Globe* to work in its business office when he accepted employment as editor of the *Guelph Advertiser* in 1861. In 1867, Palmer sold out to Innes and John Campbell McLagan, who added a daily edition. After McLagan dissolved the partnership in 1869, Innes operated the journal as sole publisher until 1874 when John A. Davidson, his brother-in-law and office manager, became his partner. See Nash-Chambers, Debra L. "Innes, James." *Dictionary of Canadian Biography*, http://www.biographi.ca/en/bio/innes_james_13F.html.
183 Springhall, *Genesis*, 72.
184 Kibler, *Rank Ladies*, 124.
185 Kibler, 115.
186 Kibler, 115.
187 Kibler, 116.
188 Harrison-Kahan, *White Negress*, 6

CHAPTER 6

1. Lenton-Young, "Variety Theatre," 194.
2. Lenton-Young, 194.
3. Londré and Watermeier, *History of North*, 226.
4. Lenton-Young, "Variety Theatre," 194.
5. Smith, "Fitzpoodle," 49.
6. Lenton-Young, "Variety Theatre," 195.
7. "Amusements," *Globe*, May 11, 1870, 2.
8. Cited in Lenton-Young, "Variety Theatre," 195; see also New York *Dramatic Mirror*, May 13, 1879.
9. "Musical and Dramatic," *Daily Globe*, November 2, 1880, 12.
10. Toll, *Blacking Up*, 138.
11. Jones, Jr., *Captive Stage*, 57–58.
12. Lemons, "Black Stereotypes," 102.
13. Nathan, "Performance," 35. See also Taylor and Austen, *Darkest America*, 39.
14. Mahar, *Behind*, 268.
15. Mahar, 268. Mahar pinpoints five such themes about women expressed through songs: 1) kidnapped spouses, wives, or lovers; 2) the good and bad of courtship; 3) the feminine/unfeminine woman, from the *yaller gal* to *wench*; 4) the effects of a lost innocence, urban life, and early death on men's conception of women as companions and nurturers; and 5) the sometimes contradictory and comic roles of women in public life or "polite" society.
16. Mahar, *Behind*, 311.
17. Gerber, *Vested Interests*, 276.
18. Nigel Ward, "A brief history of the pantomime—and why it's about so much more than 'blokes in dresses.'" *The Conversation*, December 16, 2016, https://theconversation.com/a-brief-history-of-the-pantomime-and-why-its-about-so-much-more-than-blokes-in-dresses-69683. Mikhail Bhaktin explains that during the Renaissance period, "European *literary* languages—French, German, English—came into being while the laughing, travestying genres of the late Middle Ages and Renaissance—novellas, Mardi Gras, *soties*, farces, and finally novels—were in the process of shaping these languages." See Bhaktin, *Dialogic Imagination*, 71.
19. Bean, "Transgressing," 248.
20. McConachie, "Cognitive Studies," 61.
21. Winans, "Early Minstrel," 150.
22. Nathan, "Performance," 39.
23. Mahar, *Behind*, 276; Senelick, *Changing Room*, 274. See also Gerber, *Vested Interests*, 276.
24. Mahar, *Behind*, 277. The word "octoroon" signifies "one-eighth (black) blood," and although octoroon women may not have had an apparent trace of African ancestry in their appearance, they were still subject to the same laws that denied rights to Black people.
25. Hartman, *Scenes of Subjection*, 28.
26. For a more detailed discussion on *wench* images in the Notman photographic archive see Thompson, "Come One, Come All," 111–12.

27 DuComb, *Haunted City*, 124. According to dress historian Gayle V. Fischer, the term "bloomers" first appeared in newspaper satires of the thin, loose-fitting trousers popular among advocates of women's dress reform in the early 1850s. See Gayle, *Pantaloons*, 79–80.
28 Wilson, *Adorned in Dreams*, 209.
29 Garber, *Vested Interest*, 227. In Britain, *Punch* even propagated a view of bloomer-wearing feminists as somehow unnatural. See Wilson, *Adorned in Dreams*, 209.
30 Bordo, *Unbearable Weight*, 157. This analysis of minstrelsy's depiction of women, however, does not quite capture the political agency of the decade which was first spurred on by the exclusion of women from the World Anti-Slavery Conference in London in 1840. Eight years later the First Women's Rights Convention, held at Seneca Falls, New York, was followed by other women's rights conventions, including one in Rochester, New York in 1848, and in 1850 the first annual National Women's Rights Convention was held in Worcester, Massachusetts. After Worchester, a Women's Rights Convention was held annually until the Civil War.
31 Mahar, *Behind*, 310.
32 Kibler, *Rank Ladies*, 5.
33 Glenn, *Female Spectacle*, 49.
34 Glenn, 49.
35 Glenn, 49.
36 Taylor and Austen, *Darkest America*, 63, 64.
37 Glenn, *Female Spectacle*, 52.
38 Harrison-Kahan, *White Negress*, 16.
39 Gebhardt, *Vaudeville Melodies*, 2.
40 Taylor and Austen, *Darkest America*, 57.
41 Abbott and Seroff, *Out of Sight*, xi.
42 Taylor and Austen, *Darkest America*, 60–61.
43 Cited in Abbot and Seroff, *Out of Sight*, 146–47.
44 "Amusements," *Globe*, January 31, 1882, 2.
45 Ruth Pincoe, "Shaftesbury Hall," *Canadian Encyclopedia*, February 7, 2006, https://www.thecanadianencyclopedia.ca/en/article/shaftesbury-hall-emc.
46 "Musical and Dramatic," *Globe*, October 14, 1880, 10.
47 "Musical and Dramatic," *Globe*, November 9, 1880, 6.
48 Seroff, "Fisk Jubilee Singers," 148.
49 Du Bois, *Souls of Black Folk*, 157.
50 Krasner, "Real Thing," 99.
51 See "George Walker, 1873–1911," *Library of Congress*, https://www.loc.gov/item/ihas.200038857/.
52 Springhall, *Genesis of Mass*, 76.
53 See Brooks, *Bodies in Dissent*, 223 and Krasner, "Real Thing," 99.
54 Cited in Krasner, "Real Thing," 104.
55 Phelan, *Unmarked*, 146.
56 Thurman, "Singing the Civilizing Mission," 470.
57 Pugh, *America Dancing*, 24.
58 Valis Hill, *Tap Dancing America*, 34.

59 Abbott and Seroff, *Out of Sight*, 205.
60 Taylor and Austen, *Darkest America*, 10–11.
61 Pugh, *America Dancing*, 11.
62 Springhall, *Rise of Mass Culture*, 70.
63 Springhall, 70.
64 Moriah, "Elizabeth Taylor Greenfield," 22.
65 Moriah, 22.
66 Labrew, *Black Swan*, 24.
67 Moriah, "Elizabeth Taylor Greenfield," 34, note 11.
68 Buckner, "Hyer Sisters' Performances," 310.
69 Buckner, 311.
70 Graham, "Hyers Sisters."
71 Graham, "Hyers."
72 Wright, "Jones [Joyner]." In 1889, Sissieretta Jones toured Jamaica, Panama, St. Kitts, and Barbados. See Abbott and Seroff, *Out of Sight*, 27–31.
73 Cited in Cooper, Michael. "Overlooked No More: Sissieretta Jones, a Soprano Who Shattered Racial Barriers." *New York Times*, August 15, 2018, https://www.nytimes.com/2018/08/15/obituaries/sissieretta-jones-overlooked.html.
74 Abbott and Seroff, *Out of Sight*, 438. See also Mike Brubaker, "Hi Henry's Minstrels and the Big Dog," TempoSenzaTempo, March 31, 2018, https://temposenzatempo.blogspot.com/2018/03/hi-henrys-minstrels-and-big-dog.html.
75 See Brubaker, "Hi Henry's Minstrels."
76 Sundquist, *To Wake the Nations*, 277.
77 Abbott and Seroff, *Out of Sight*, 40.
78 Cited in Abbott and Seroff, 41.
79 See Cooper, "Overlooked No More."
80 White, *Too Good*, 74. The *Globe* and the *Mail and Empire* would be merged in 1936 to form today's *Globe and Mail*.
81 Petrin, "Myth of Mary Mink," 107.
82 Jenkins, "Homeland Crisis," 50. The *Tely* would cease publication in 1971, but be reborn as the *Toronto Sun*, continuing the tradition of a working-class newspaper with a sensational editorial tone. Robertson started his career as a reporter and then city editor at the *Globe*, and after the *Toronto Daily Telegraph* folded in 1876 with the assistance of his former colleague, Goldwin Smith, he launched the *Tely*. See Allan Dickie, "Tely officially dead today," *Brandon Sun*, October 30, 1971, https://newspaperarchive.com/other-articles-clipping-oct-30-1971-1420966/. Robertson was elected to the House of Commons for the electoral district of Toronto East in 1896 to 1900.
83 Gardner, "Burgess."
84 "'Cool' Burgess is Dead: The Famous Minstrel Passes Away After Long Illness," *Globe*, October 21, 1905, 6.
85 Gardner, "Burgess."
86 "Music and the Drama," April 23, 1892, n.p.; "Minstrels at the Grand," May 28, 1892, 16. The Cleveland's Minstrels also appeared again at the Grand Opera House in July 1893. See "Cleveland's Minstrels," *Globe*, July 31, 1893, 8.
87 "Music and the Drama," *Globe*, May 31, 1892, 8.
88 "London Locals," *Globe*, June 10, 1892, 6.

NOTES TO CHAPTER 6

89 "London Locals," 6.
90 "London Young Liberals," *Globe* November 24, 1893, 4.
91 James David Edgar, "Loyalty: An Address Delivered to the Toronto Young Men's Liberal Club, January 19, 1885, 4, 10.
92 "Notes and Comments," *Globe*, July 4, 1893, 4.
93 Graham, "Primrose."
94 The *Montreal Herald* was a major competitor to fellow English-language papers such as the *Gazette* until it ceased publication in 1957. It was also a newspaper founded in 1811 by Scottish-descendant William Gray, a Presbyterian pro-Conservative. See T. A. Wellington, "1811: The Montreal Herald & Other Quebec Curios," *Montreal Rampage*, February 23, 2017, https://montrealrampage.com/1811-the-montreal-herald-other-quebec-curios/.
95 "Theatre Royal," *Montreal Gazette*, June 19, 1894, 5.
96 Archer-Straw, *Negrophilia*, 41.
97 "The Theatres," *Globe*, September 14, 1896, 10.
98 "In Old Kentucky," *Montreal Gazette*, February 16, 1895, 5.
99 Abbott and Seroff, *Out of Sight*, 406–407.
100 "Theatre Royal," *Montreal Daily Herald*, May 1, 1895, 4.
101 "Music and Drama," *Globe*, April 13, 1896, 4.
102 "Music and the Drama," *Globe*, April 14, 1896, 9.
103 "Music and Drama," *Evening Star*, April 1896, n.p.
104 Glenn, *Female Spectacle*, 54. Russell's starring role in Gustave Kerker's 1896 comic opera, *An American Beauty*, only confirmed her public image as the representative of "true" American womanliness.
105 "The Theatres," *Globe*, September 15, 1896, 13.
106 According to a playbill from the Hamilton Grand Opera House.
107 Hi Henry Minstrels also appeared in Hamilton, Ontario in 1888. See "Notes," *Globe*, October 27, 1888, n.p.
108 See Le Camp, "Racial Consideration," 346–49.
109 Le Camp, 268.
110 Victoria Amateur Minstrels, *The Minstrel Festival*, May 16, 1896, 2–3.
111 Pilgrim, *Understanding Jim Crow*, 41.
112 Pilgrim, 41.
113 Lewis, "Selika," pp. 1022–23.
114 Valis Hill, *Tap Dancing America*, 34.
115 Staples, *Male-Female Comedy*, 92. Dean was also known as the "Black Venus." See "Dean, Dora [Dora Dean Babbige Johnson]," *Notable Kentucky African Americans Database*, https://web.archive.org/web/20191223211607/https://nkaa.uky.edu/nkaa/items/show/1885.
116 Yuval and Taylor, *Darkest America*, 26, 64.
117 Bean, "Black Minstrelsy," 185.
118 "1890–1906 Florence Hines," *Drag King History*, https://dragkinghistory.com/1890-1906-florence-hines/.
119 Taylor and Austen, *Darkest America*, 25.
120 "The Minstrels," *Evening Star*, May 9, 1896, 3. *Darkest America* would appear again in Toronto in 1898. See "Music and Drama," *Evening Star*, May 2, 1898, n.p. See also "Queen's Theatre" Advertisement, *Montreal Star*, May 2, 1896, 8.

121 "Music and Drama," *The Globe*, February 13, 1896, 7.
122 "Fisk Jubilee Singers," *Globe*, November 4, 1884, 6. "Music and the Drama," *Globe*, December 10, 1884, 6.
123 It was named after George William Allan (1802–1901), eleventh mayor of the City of Toronto and then-president of the Toronto Horticultural Society. In 1858, Allan donated five acres from his Moss Park estate to the Society for the purpose of creating a botanical garden. After the pavilion and winter garden were destroyed by fire on June 16, 1902, the City of Toronto decided not to rebuild the pavilion concert hall. See "Allan Gardens," *Toronto Public Library*, http://static.torontopubliclibrary.ca/ve/garden_city/allan_gardens.html. The Gardens and Pavilion were once described as "having the shape of a parallelogram seventy-five feet by 120 feet, with its long axis east and west and having side walls forty-three feet high, rising to a height of fifty-five feet at the end gables of the building. Dimensions of the stage were...twenty-one feet by forty-six feet." The Horticultural Gardens and Pavilion was undoubtedly inspired by London's Crystal Palace, erected in 1851 as the first modern consumer culture exhibition. See Fairfield, "Theatres and Performance Halls," 228.
124 "Music and the Drama," *Globe*, October 31, 1888, 8.
125 "Fisk Jubilee Singers," *Globe*, January 4, 1889, 2.
126 "Fisk Jubilee Singers," *Globe*, November 24, 1891, 8.
127 Cited in Abbott and Seroff, *Out of Sight*, 83.
128 "The Original Jubilee Singers," *Globe*, November 26, 1897, 2.
129 Seroff, "Fisk Jubilee Singers," 156.
130 Seroff, 160. See also "The Fisk University Jubilee Singers – An Unparalleled Success," *Daily Citizen*, November 20, 1880, n.p.
131 Cited in Le Camp, "Racial Considerations," 267.
132 Le Camp, 267.
133 Seroff, "Fisk Jubilee Singers," 161.
134 *Weekly Louisianian*, October 29, 1881, n.p. Reprinted from *Montreal World*, n.d.
135 "Caste in Toronto Hotels," *Globe*, September 24, 1881, 8.
136 "Caste in Toronto Hotels," 8.
137 "Musical and Dramatic," *Globe*, October 7, 1881, 8.
138 "Musical and Dramatic," *Globe*, October 7, 1881, 8.
139 "Music and the Drama," *Globe*, December 1, 1883, 3.
140 Banfield, Dibble, and Laurence, "Coleridge-Taylor, Samuel."

CONCLUSION

1 Hornback, "Extravagant and Wheeling," 197–98.
2 Miller, *Slaves to Fashion*, 300, n57.
3 Hornback, "Extravagant and Wheeling," 198.
4 Thurman, "Singing the Civilizing Mission," 445.
5 Royster, *Southern Horrors*, 5.
6 Lemons, "Black Stereotypes," 104.
7 Brockhouse, *Royal Alexandra Theatre*, 66.

SELECTED BIBLIOGRAPHY

The following texts reflect the Canadian, American, and British canon on blackface minstrelsy and minstrel shows. It also aims to provide context for understanding Black performers, operatic and jubilee singers, and dancers who are too often ignored in the historiography of theatre and performance.

Abbott, Lynn, and Doug Seroff. *Out of Sight: The Rise of African American Popular Music 1889–1895.* Jackson: University Press of Mississippi, 2002.

Abbott, Lynn, and Doug Seroff. *Ragged but Right: Black Traveling Shows, 'Coon Songs,' and the Dark Pathway to Blues and Jazz.* Jackson: University Press of Mississippi, 2008.

Adams, Tracy. "Making a Living: African Canadian Workers in London, Ontario, 1861–1901." *Labour/Le Travail* 67 (2011): 9–44.

Alkalimat, Abdul. *The History of Black Studies.* London: Pluto Press, 2021.

Anae, Nicole. "'[T]hey Seemed to Recognise Us as Brethren From a Far Distant Tribe': The Influence of the Fisk Jubilee Singers among Australian and New Zealand Indigenous Communities, 1886–1936." *The Historian* 80, no. 2 (2018): 241–92. https://doi.org/10.1111/hisn.12832.

Archer-Straw, Petrine. *Negrophilia: Avant-Garde Paris and Black Culture in the 1920s.* New York: Thames and Hudson, 2000.

Arenson, Adam. "A Forgotten Generation: African Canadian History between Fugitive Slaves and World War I." In *Unsettling the Great White North: Black Canadian History,* edited by Michele A. Johnson and Funké Aladejebi, 115–39. Toronto: University of Toronto Press, 2022.

Arenson, Adam. "Experience Rather than Imagination: Researching the Return Migration of African North Americans during the American Civil War and Reconstruction." *Journal of American Ethnic History* 32, no. 2 (2013): 73–77.

Asian Heritage Society of New Brunswick. *Chinese Labour on the Canadian Pacific Railway,* July 2019. http://www.ahsnb.org/wp-content/uploads/2019/07/AHSNB-Chinese-Labour-on-the-CPR_Final.pdf.

Baker, William M. "The Anti-American Ingredient in Canadian History." *Dalhousie Review* 53, no. 1 (1973): 57–77. https://dalspace.library.dal.ca/handle/10222/59579.

Ball, Stuart. *Portrait of a Party: The Conservative Party in Britain 1918–1945.* Oxford: Oxford University Press, 2013.

Banfield, Stephen, Jeremy Dibble, and Anya Laurence. "Coleridge-Taylor, Samuel." *Grove Music Online.* October 16, 2013. London: Oxford University Press.

Bateman, Chris. "The Railway Comes to Toronto." In *25 Days That Changed Toronto*, edited by Dylan Reid and Matthew Blackett, 113–15. Toronto: Spacing Media, 2007.

Bayne, Clarence S. "The Origins of Black Theatre in Montreal." *Canadian Theatre Review* 118 (2004): 34–40.

Bean, Annemarie. "Transgressing the Gender Divide: The Female Impersonator in Nineteenth-Century Blackface Minstrelsy." In *Inside the Minstrel Mask: Readings in Nineteenth-Century Blackface Minstrelsy*, edited by Annemarie Bean, James V. Hatch, and Brooks McNamara, 245–56. Hanover and London: Wesleyan University Press, 1996.

Beckert, Sven. *Empire of Cotton: A Global Industry*. New York: Alfred A. Knopf, 2014.

Beckles, Hilary. "'War Dances:' Slave Leisure and Anti-slavery in the British-colonised Caribbean." In *Working Slavery, Pricing Freedom: Perspectives from the Caribbean, Africa, and the African Diaspora*, edited by Verene A. Shepherd, 223–43. Kingston, Jamaica: Ian Randle Publishers, 2002.

Berger, Carl. *The Sense of Power: Studies in the Ideas of Canadian Imperialism*. Toronto: University of Toronto Press, 2013.

Berlin, Ira. "From Creole to African: Atlantic Creoles and the Origins of African-American Society in Mainland North America." *The William and Mary Quarterly* 53, no. 2 (1996): 251–88.

Bhaktin, Mikhail. *The Dialogic Imagination*. Texas: The University of Texas Press, 1981.

Blackmon, Douglas A. *Slavery by Another Name: The Re-enslavement of Black Americans from the Civil War to World War II*. New York: Doubleday, 2008.

Blackwelder, Julia K. *Styling Jim Crow: African American Beauty Training during Segregation*. College Station, Texas: Texas A&M University Press, 2003.

Blair, John G. "Blackface Minstrels in Cross-Cultural Perspective." *American Studies International* 28, no. 2, Special Issue on the Impact of US Culture Abroad (1990): 52–65.

Blake, Dennis Edward. "J.W. Bengough and *Grip*: The Canadian Editorial Cartoon Comes of Age." Master's thesis, Wilfrid Laurier University, 1985.

Bogle, Donald. *Toms, Coons, Mulattoes, Mammies, and Bucks: An Interpretive History of Blacks in American Films*. 3rd ed. New York: Continuum, 2000.

Bordo, Susan. *Unbearable Weight: Feminism, Western Culture, and the Body*. Berkeley, California: The University of California Press, 1995.

Boskin, Joseph. "The Life and Death of Sambo: Overview of an Historical Hang-Up." *Journal of Popular Culture* 4, no. 3 (Winter 1971): 647–57.

Boskin, Joseph. *Sambo: The Rise and Demise of an American Jester*. New York: Oxford University Press, 1986.

Bowerman, Glyn. "Toronto Forewarned of Irish Potato Famine." In *25 Days That Changed Toronto*, edited by Dylan Reid and Matthew Blackett, 71–73. Toronto: Spacing Media, 2007.

Boyce, Gerry. *Belleville: A Popular History*. Toronto: Dundurn, 2008.

Boyko, John. *Blood and Daring: How Canada Fought the American Civil War and Forged a Nation*. Toronto: Alfred A. Knopf, 2013.

Braxton, Natalie Phyllis. "Othello: The Moor and the Metaphor." *South Atlantic Review* 55, no. 4 (1990): 1–17.

Breon, Robin. "The Growth and Development of Black Theatre in Canada: A Starting Point." In *African-Canadian Theatre: Critical Perspectives on Canadian Theatre in English*, edited by Maureen Moynagh, vol. 2, 1–9. Toronto: Playwrights Canada Press, 2005.

Brockhouse, Robert. *The Royal Alexandra Theatre: A Celebration of 100 Years*. Toronto: McArthur and Company, 2007.

Brooks, Daphne. *Bodies in Dissent: Spectacular Performance of Race and Freedom, 1850–1910*. Durham, NC: Duke University Press, 2006.

Brooks, Lynn Matluck. "Staged Ethnicity: Perspectives on the Work of John Durang." *Dance Chronicle* 24, no. 2 (2001): 193–222. https://doi.org/10.1081/DNC-100107834.

Brooks, Tim. *Lost Sounds: Blacks and the Birth of the Recording Industry, 1890–1919*. Urbana, Illinois: University of Illinois Press, 2005.

Brown, Elspeth H. "The Commodification of Aesthetic Feeling: Race, Sexuality and the 1920s Stage Model." *Feminist Studies* 40, no. 1 (2014): 65–97.

Brown, Mary M. "Entertainers on the Road." In *Early Stages: Theatre in Ontario 1800–1914*, edited by Ann Saddlemyer, 123–65. Toronto: University of Toronto Press, 1990.

Brown, Mary M. "'Pepper's Ghost is Tearing its Hair': Ottawa Theatre in the 1870s. *Theatre Research in Canada/Recherches théâtrales Au Canada* 4, no. 2 (1983). https://journals.lib.unb.ca/index.php/TRIC/article/view/7460.

Broyld, Dann T. "The Power of Proximity: Frederick Douglass and His Transnational Relations with British Canada, 1847–1861." *Afro-Americans in New York Life and History* 41, no. 2 (2020): 3–25, 27–34.

Buckner, Jocelyn L. "'Spectacular Opacities': The Hyers Sisters' Performances of Respectability and Resistance." *African American Review* 45, no. 3 (2012): 309–23.

Buckridge, Steeve O. *The Language of Dress: Resistance and Accommodation in Jamaica, 1760–1890*. Jamaica: University of the West Indies Press, 2004.

Burr, Christina. *Spreading the Light: Work and Labour Reform in Late-Nineteenth-Century Toronto*. Toronto: University of Toronto Press, 1999.

Cameron, Wendy. "English Immigrants in 1830s Upper Canada: The Petworth Emigration Scheme." In *Canadian Migration Patterns from Britain and North America*, edited by Barbara Jane Messamore, 91–100. Ottawa: University of Ottawa Press, 2004.

Canada. Royal Commission on Chinese Immigration. *Report of the Royal Commission on Chinese and Japanese Immigration*. Ottawa: S.E. Dawson, 1902. https://open.library.ubc.ca/collections/bcbooks/items/1.0348116.

Careless, J.M.S. "The Cultural Setting: Ontario Society to 1914." In *Early Stages: Theatre in Ontario 1800–1914*, edited by Ann Saddlemyer, 18–51. Toronto: University of Toronto Press, 1990.

Carlin, Bob. *The Birth of the Banjo: Joel Walker Sweeney and Early Minstrelsy*. North Carolina and London: McFarland & Company, 2007.

Carlson, Julie A. "New Lows in Eighteenth-Century Theater: The Rise of Mungo." *European Romantic Review* 18, no. 2 (2007): 139–47. https://doi.org/10.1080/10509580701297844.

Carlson, Julie A. "Race and Profit in English Theatre." In *The Cambridge Companion to British Theatre, 1730–1830*, edited by Jane Moody, 175–88. Cambridge: Cambridge University Press, 2009.

Cavell, Janice. "The Second Frontier: The North in English-Canadian Historical Writing." *Canadian Historical Review* 83, no. 3 (2002): 1–15.

Cefalu, Paul. "The Burdens of Mind Reading in Shakespeare's 'Othello': A Cognitive and Psychoanalytic Approach to Iago's Theory of Mind." *Shakespeare Quarterly* 64, no. 3 (2013): 265–94.

Chan, Mary. "Drolls, Drolleries and Mid-Seventeenth-Century Dramatic Music in England." *Royal Musical Association Research Chronicle* 1, no. 15 (1979): 117–73.

Charmley, John. *A History of Conservative Politics Since 1830*. London: Palgrave Macmillan, 2008.

Charpentier, Marc. "Broadway North: Musical Theatre in Montreal in the 1920s." PhD diss., McGill University, 1999.

Chevrefils, Yves. "John Henry Walker (1831–1899), Artisan-Graveur." *Journal of Canadian Art History/Annales d'histoire de l'art canadien* 8, no. 2 (1985): 178–225.

Clifford, Mary Louise. *From Slavery to Freetown: Black Loyalists After the American Revolution*. Jefferson, North Carolina: McFarland & Company, 1999.

Cockrell, Dale. *Demons of Disorder: Early Blackface Minstrels and Their World*. Cambridge: Cambridge University Press, 1997.

Cockrell, Dale. "Nineteenth-Century Popular Music." In *The Cambridge History of American Music*, edited by David Nicholls, 158–85. Cambridge: Cambridge University Press, 1998.

Conroy, Patricia. "A History of the Theatre in Montreal Prior to Confederation." PhD diss., McGill University, 1936.

Cooper, Afua. "Epilogue Reflections: The Challenges and Accomplishments of the Promised Land." In *The Promised Land: History and Historiography of the Black Experience in Chatham-Kent's Settlements and Beyond*, edited by Boulou Ebanda de B'béri, Nina Reid-Maroney, and Handel Kashope Wright, 193–210. Toronto: University of Toronto Press, 2014.

Cooper, Afua. "Foreword." In *Emancipation Day: Celebrating Freedom in Canada*, edited by Natasha L. Henry, 9–14. Toronto: Dundurn Press, 2010.

Cooper, Afua. "The Search for Mary Bibb, Black Woman Teacher in Nineteenth-Century Canada West." In *"We Specialize in the Wholly Impossible": A Reader in Black Women's History*, edited by Darlene Clark Hine, Wilma King, and Linda Reed, 171–85. Brooklyn, New York: Carlson Publishing, 1995.

Cowan, Helen. *British Immigration Before Confederation*, Historical Booklet no. 22. Ottawa: The Canadian Historical Association, 1978.

Cowhig, Ruth. "The Black in English Renaissance Drama and the Role of Shakespeare's *Othello*." In *The Black Presence in English Literature*, edited by David Dabydeen, 1–23. Manchester: Manchester University Press, 1985.

D'Amico-Cuthbert, Francesca. "'We Don't Have Those American Problems': Anti-Black Practices in Canada's Rap Music Marketplace, 1985–2020." *Canadian Journal of History* 56, no. 3 (2021): 320–52.

Danson, John T. "On the Existing Connection Between American Slavery and the British Cotton Manufacture." *Journal of the Statistical Society of London* 20 (1857): 1–21.

Daschuk, James W. *Clearing the Plains: Disease, Politics of Starvation, and the Loss of Aboriginal Life*. Regina: University of Regina Press, 2014.

Davis, Angela. *Women, Race and Class*. New York: Vintage Books, 1983.

Davis, Tracy C., and Stefka Mihaylova, eds. "Introduction." *Uncle Tom's Cabins: The Transnational History of America's Most Mutable Book*, 1–29. Ann Arbor, Michigan: University of Michigan Press, 2018.

de Lerma, Dominique-René. "Hicks, (Charles) Barney," *New Grove Dictionary of Music and Musicians*, September 22, 2015. https://doi-org. myaccess.library .utoronto.ca/10.1093/gmo/9781561592630.article.A2284623.

den Otter, A.A. *The Philosophy of Railways: The Transcontinental Railway Idea in British North America*. Toronto: University of Toronto Press, 1997.

DeRamus, Betty. *Freedom by Any Means: Con Games, Voodoo Schemes, True Love and Lawsuits on the Underground Railroad*. Toronto: Simon & Schuster, 2009.

Detre, Laura A. "Canada's Campaign for Immigrants and the Images in *Canada West Magazine*." *Great Plains Quarterly* 24, no. 2 (2004): 113–29.

Dickens, Charles. *American Notes for General Circulation*. London: Chapman & Hall, 1842.

Drew, Benjamin. *A North-Side View of Slavery. The Refugee: or the Narrative of Fugitive Slaves in Canada. Related by Themselves, with an Account of the History and Condition of the Colored Population of Upper Canada*. Toronto: Coles, 1972. First published 1856 by J.P. Jewett and Co. (Boston).

Dua, Enakshi. "Exclusion through Inclusion: Female Asian Migration in the Making of Canada as a White Settler Nation." *Gender, Place and Culture* 14, no. 4 (2007): 445–66.

Du Bois, W.E.B. *Black Reconstruction in America 1860–1880*. New York and London: The Free Press, 1998. First published 1935.

Du Bois, W.E.B. *The Souls of Black Folk*. Edited by Candace Ward. New York: Dover Publications, 1994. First published 1903.

DuComb, Christian. *Haunted City: Three Centuries of Racial Impersonation in Philadelphia*. Ann Arbor: University of Michigan Press, 2017.

Dunson, Stephanie. "Black Misrepresentation in Nineteenth-Century Sheet Music Illustration." In *Beyond Blackface: African Americans and the Creation of American Popular Culture, 1890–1930*, edited by W. Fitzhugh Brundage, 45–65. Chapel Hill: University of North Carolina Press, 2011.

Dwyer-Ryan, Meaghan. "'Yankee Doodle Paddy': Themes of Ethnic Acculturation in Yankee Doodle Dandy." *Journal of American Ethnic History* 30, no. 4 (2011): 57–62.

Ehlers, Nadine. *Racial Imperatives: Discipline, Performativity, and Struggles Against Subjection*. Bloomington and Indianapolis: Indiana University Press, 2012.

Eland, Ivan. "Warfare State to Welfare State: Conflict Causes Government to Expand at Home." *The Independent Review* 18, no. 2 (2013): 189–218.

Elgersman, Maureen G. *Unyielding Spirits: Black Women and Slavery in Early Canada and Jamaica*. New York: Garland Publishing, 1999.

Elliott, Robin. "Ragtime Spasms: Anxieties Over the Rise of Popular Music in Toronto." In *Post-Colonial Distances: The Study of Popular Music in Canada and Australia*, edited by Beverley Diamond, Daniel Mark Downes, Denis Crowdy, 67–90. Newcastle: Cambridge Scholars, 2008.

Ernest, John. *A National Within a Nation: Organizing African-American Communities Before the Civil War*. Chicago: Ivan R. Dee, 2011.

Evans, Chad. *Frontier Theatre: A History of Nineteenth-Century Theatrical Entertainment in the Canadian Far West and Alaska*. Victoria, British Columbia: Sono Nis Press, 1983.

Evans, Nicholas. "Ira Aldridge: Shakespeare and Minstrelsy." In *Ira Aldridge: The African Roscius*, edited by Bernth Lindfors, 157–79. Rochester: University of Rochester Press, 2007.

Fahrner, Robert. "David Garrick Presents The Padlock: An 18th-Century 'Hit.'" *Theatre Survey* 13, no.1 (1972): 52–69.

Fairfield, Robert. "Theatres and Performance Halls." In *Early Stages: Theatre in Ontario 1800–1914*, edited by Ann Saddlemyer, 214–87. Toronto: University of Toronto Press, 1990.

Featherstone, Simon. "The Blackface Atlantic: Interpreting British Minstrelsy." *Journal of Victorian Culture* 3, no. 2 (1998): 234–51. https://doi.org/10.1080/13555509809505964.

Files, Angela. "The O'Banyan Jubilee Singers of the Early British Methodist Church in Brantford." *Brantford Historical Society Quarterly* 2, no. 3 (1995): 4–5.

Fischer, Gayle., V. *Pantaloons and Power: A Nineteenth-Century Dress Reform in the United States*. Kent, Ohio: Kent State University Press, 2001.

Foggo, Cheryl. "My Home is Over Jordan." In *Remembering Chinook Country*, 151–90. Chinook Country Historical Society. Calgary: Detselig, 2005.

Foner, Eric. *Reconstruction: America's Unfinished Revolution, 1863–1877*. 2nd ed. New York: Harper Perennial, 2014.

Forbes, Camille, F. "Dancing with 'Racial Feet': Bert Williams and the Performance of Blackness." *Theatre Journal* 56, no. 4 (2004): 603–25. https://doi.org/10.1353/tj.2004.0164.

Forrest, John. *The History of Morris Dancing, 1458–1750*. Toronto: University of Toronto Press, 1999.

Foster, Cecil. *They Call Me George: The Untold Story of Black Train Porters and the Birth of Modern Canada*. Windsor: Biblioasis, 2019.

Francis, Daniel. *A History of Canadian Culture*. Don Mills, Ontario: Oxford University Press, 2009.

Francis, Daniel. *National Dreams: Myth, Memory, and Canadian History*. Vancouver: Arsenal Pulp Press, 2011. First published 1997.

Fredrickson, George M. *The Black Image in the White Mind: The Debate in African American Character and Destiny, 1814–1914*. Middletown: Wesleyan University Press, 1987.

Frick, John W. *Uncle Tom's Cabin on the American Stage and Screen*. New York: Palgrave Macmillan, 2012.

Friedberg, Anne. *Window Shopping: Cinema and the Postmodern*. Berkeley: University of California Press, 1993.

Friedlander, Alan, and Richard Allan Gerber. *Welcoming Ruin: The Civil Rights Act of 1875*. Boston: Brill, 2019.

Fuchs, Barbara. *Exotic Nation: Maurophilia and the Construction of Early Modern Spain*. Philadelphia: University of Pennsylvania Press, 2011.

Fuller, Randall. "Theaters of the American Revolution: The Valley Forge *Cato* and the Meschianza in their Transcultural Contexts." *Early American Literature* 34, no. 2 (1999): 126–46.

Furniss, Elizabeth. "Indians, Odysseys and Vast, Empty Lands: The Myth of the Frontier in the Canadian Justice System." *Anthropologica* 41, no. 2 (1999): 195–208.

Gabrial, Brian. "'The Second American Revolution': Expressions of Canadian Identity in News Coverage at the Outbreak of the United States Civil War." *Canadian Journal of Communication* 33 (2008): 21–37.

Garber, Marjorie. *Vested Interests: Cross-Dressing and Cultural Anxiety*. New York and London, UK: Routledge, 1992.

Gebhardt, Nicholas. *Vaudeville Melodies: Popular Musicians and Mass Entertainment in American Culture, 1870–1929*. Chicago and London: The University of Chicago Press, 2017.

Gerzina, Gretchen, ed. *Black Victorians/Black Victoriana*. New Brunswick, New Jersey: Rutgers University Press, 2003.

Gilman, Sander L. "Black Bodies, White Bodies: Toward an Iconography of Female Sexuality in Late Nineteenth-Century Art, Medicine, and Literature." *Critical Inquiry* 12, no. 1, "Race," Writing, and Difference (1985): 204–42.

Gilroy, Paul. *The Black Atlantic: Modernity and Double Consciousness*. Cambridge, Massachusetts: Harvard University Press, 1993.

Glenn, Susan A. *Female Spectacle: The Theatrical Roots of Modern Feminism*. Cambridge, Massachusetts: Harvard University Press, 2000.

Gottschild, Brenda Dixon. *Digging the Africanist Presence in American Performance: Dance and Other Contexts*. Westport, Connecticut: Greenwood, 1996.

Graber, Mark A. *Dred Scott and the Problem of Constitutional Evil*. Cambridge: Cambridge University Press, 2006.

Graham, Franklin. *Histrionic Montreal: Annals of the Montreal Stage with Biographical and Critical Notices of the Plays and Players of a Century*. Montreal: J. Lovell, 1902.

Graham, Sandra Jean. "Hyers Sisters." *Grove Music*, September 22, 2015. https://doi.org/10.1093/gmo/9781561592630.article.A2284679.

Graham, Sandra Jean. "Primrose, George H." *The Grove Dictionary of American Music*. New York: Oxford University Press. https://doi.org/10.1093/acref/9780195314281.001.0001.

Graybill, Andrew. "Rangers, Mounties, and the Subjugation of Indigenous Peoples, 1870–1885." *Great Plains Quarterly* 24, no. 2 (2004): 83–100.

Hall, Kim F. *Things of Darkness: Economies of Race and Gender in Early Modern England*. Ithaca: Cornell University Press, 1995.

Halttunen, Karen. *Confidence Men and Painted Women: A Study of Middle-Class Culture in America, 1830–1870*. New Haven and London: Yale University Press, 1982.

Hammond, M.O. *Simpson's Confederation Jubilee Series, 1867–1927*. Toronto: Simpson, 1927.

Hardy, Dominic. "Historical Ironies of Henri Julien (1852–1908): Researching Identity and Graphic Satire Across Languages in Quebec." *Working Papers on Design* 2 (2007): 1–25.

Harper, Phillip Brian. "Passing for What? Racial Masquerade and the Demands of Upward Mobility." *Callaloo* 21, no. 2, Emerging Male Writers: A Special Issue, Part II (1998): 381–97.

Harris, Jennifer. "Black Life in a Nineteenth-Century New Brunswick Town." *Journal of Canadian Studies/Revue d'études canadiennes* 46, no. 1 (2012): 138–66.

Harris, Richard, Ian Keay, and Frank Lewis. "Protecting Infant Industries: Canadian Manufacturing and the National Policy, 1870–1913." *Explorations in Economic History* 56 (2015): 15–31.

Harrison-Kahan, Lori. *The White Negress: Literature, Minstrelsy, and the Black-Jewish Imaginary.* New Brunswick, New Jersey: Rutgers University Press, 2011.

Hartman, Saidiya. *Scenes of Subjection: Terror, Slavery, and the Self-Making of Nineteenth-Century America.* New York and Oxford: Oxford University Press, 1997.

Hazzard-Gordon, Katrina. *Jookin': The Rise of Social Dance Formations in African-American Culture.* Philadelphia: Temple University Press, 1992.

Heike, Paul. "'Schwarze Sklaven, Weiße Sklaven': The German Reception of Harriet Beecher Stowe's Uncle Tom's Cabin." In *Uncle Tom's Cabins: The Transnational History of America's Most Mutable Book*, edited by Tracy C. Davis and Stefka Mihaylova, 192–222. Ann Arbor, Michigan: University of Michigan Press, 2018.

Henry, Natasha L. *Emancipation Day: Celebrating Freedom in Canada.* Toronto: Dundurn Press, 2010.

Hepburn, Sharon. "Following the North Star: Canada as a Haven for Nineteenth-Century American Blacks." *Michigan Historical Review* 25, no. 2 (1999): 91–126. https://doi.org/10.2307/20173830.

Hill, Constance Valis. *Tap Dancing America: A Cultural History.* London: Oxford University Press, 2009.

Hill, Errol, and James Vernon Hatch. *A History of African American Theatre.* Cambridge: Cambridge University Press, 2003.

Hobbs, Allyson. *A Chosen Exile: A History of Racial Passing in American Life.* Cambridge, Massachusetts: Harvard University Press, 2014.

Hodge, Francis. *Yankee Theatre: The Image of America on the Stage, 1825–1850.* Austin: University of Texas Press, 1964.

Hogeveen, Bryan. "'The Evils with Which We Are Called to Grapple': Élite Reformers, Eugenicists, Environmental Psychologists, and the Construction of Toronto's Working-Class Boy Problem, 1860–1930." *Labour/Le Travail* 55 (2005): 37–68.

Holt, Jeff. *The Grand Trunk in New England.* West Hill, Ontario: Railfare Books, 1986.

Hood, Sarah H. "America Invades." In *25 Days That Changed Toronto*, edited by Dylan Reid and Matthew Blackett, 60–63. Toronto: Spacing Media, 2007.

Hornback, Robert. "Blackfaced Fools, Black-Headed Birds, Fool Synonyms, and Shakespearean Allusions to Renaissance Blackface Folly." *Notes and Queries* 55, no. 2 (June 2008): 215–19. https://doi.org/10.1093/notesj/gjn031.

Hornback, Robert. "Emblems of Folly in the First 'Othello': Renaissance Blackface, Moor's Coat, and 'Muckender'." *Comparative Drama* 35, no. 1 (Spring 2001): 69–99.

Hornback, Robert. "'Extravagant and Wheeling Strangers': Early Blackface Dancing Fools, Racial Impersonation, and the Limits of Identification." *Exemplaria* 20, no. 2 (2008):197–222. https://doi.org/10.1179/175330708X311353.

Hornback, Robert. "The Folly of Racism: Enslaving Blackface and the 'Natural' Fool Tradition." *Medieval and Renaissance Drama in England*, 20 (2007): 46–84.

Hornback, Robert. *Racism and Early Blackface Comic Traditions: From the Old World to the New.* New York: Springer International Publishing, 2018.

Howe, Samuel Gridley. *The Refugees from Slavery in Canada West: Report to the Freedmen's Inquiry Commission.* Boston: Wright & Potter, 1864.

Hunter, Wayne. "The Toronto, Hamilton and Buffalo Railway." *Brantford Historical Society Quarterly* 2, no. 3 (1995): 2–3.

Huntzicker, William E. "Thomas Nast, Harper's Weekly, and the Election of 1876." In *After The War: The Press in a Changing America, 1865–1900*, edited by David B. Sachsman, 53–68. New York: Routledge, 2017.

Iacovetta, Franca, ed. *A Nation of Immigrants: Women, Workers, and Communities in Canadian History, 1840s–1960s.* Toronto: University of Toronto Press, 1998.

Jaher, Diana. "The Paradoxes of Slavery in Thomas Southerne's 'Oroonoko'." *Comparative Drama* 42, no. 1 (Spring 2008): 51–71.

Jarman, Baird. "The Graphic Art of Thomas Nast: Politics and Propriety in Postbellum Publishing." *American Periodicals: A Journal of History and Criticism* 20, no. 2 (2010): 156–89. https://doi.org/10.1353/amp.2010.0007.

Jasen, David A., and Trebor Jay Tichenor. *Rags and Ragtime: A Musical History.* New York, New York: Dover Publications, 1978.

Jenkins, William. "Homeland Crisis and Local Ethnicity: The Toronto Irish and the Cartoons of the 'Evening Telegram' 1910–1914." Special Issue: Encounters, Contests, and Communities: New Histories of Race and Ethnicity in the Canadian City, *Urban History Review/Revue d'histoire urbaine* 38, no 2 (2010): 48–63.

Johnson, Michele A., and Funké Aladejebi, eds. "Introduction." In *Unsettling the Great White North: Black Canadian History*, 3–27. Toronto: University of Toronto Press, 2022.

Johnson, Stephen. "'Getting to' Canadian Theatre History: On the Tensions Between the New History and the Nation State." *Theatre Research in Canada* 13, no. 1–2 (1992): 63–80.

Johnson, Stephen. "Introduction: The Persistence of Blackface and the Minstrel Tradition." In *Burnt Cork: Traditions and Legacies of Blackface Minstrelsy*, edited by Stephen Johnson, 1–17. Amherst and Boston: University of Massachusetts Press, 2012.

Johnson, Stephen. "Juba's Dance: An Assessment of Newly Acquired Information." In *Proceedings of the 26th Annual Conference of the Society of Dance History Scholars*, 1–16, 2003. https://www.utm.utoronto.ca/~w3minstr/featured/scholarly_analysis.html.

Johnson, Stephen. "Past the Documents, to the Dance: The Witness to Juba in 1848." In *The Performance Text*, edited by Domenico Pietropaola, 78–96. New York and Ottawa: Legas Press, 1999. https://www.utm.utoronto.ca/~w3minstr/featured/scholarly_analysis.html.

Johnson, Stephen. "'Shield Us from This Base Ridicule': The Petitions to Censor Blackface Circus Clowns, Toronto, 1840–43." In *Canadian Performance Histories and Historiographies: New Essays on Canadian Theatre*, vol. 7, edited by Heather Davis-Fisch, 254–79. Toronto: Playwrights Canada Press, 2017.

Johnson, Stephen. "Uncle Tom and the Minstrels: Seeing Black and White on Stage in Canada West prior to the American Civil War." *(Post)Colonial Stages: Critical and Creative Views on Drama, Theatre and Performance*, edited by Helen Gilbert, 55–63. Coventry: Dangaroo Press, 1999.

Johnston, Russell. *Selling Themselves: The Emergence of Canadian Advertising.* Toronto: University of Toronto Press, 2001.

Jones, Douglas A., Jr. *The Captive Stage: Performance and the Proslavery Imagination of the Antebellum North*. Ann Arbor: The University of Michigan Press, 2014.

Kalb, Deborah, ed. "The Evolution of American Elections." *Guide to US Elections 7th Edition*, 3–24. Thousand Oaks, California: CQ Press, 2016.

Kealiinohomoku, Joann W. "A Comparative Study of Dance as a Constellation of Behaviors among African and United States Negroes." Congress on Research in Dance, *Dance Research Annual* 7 (1976): 1–13.

Kerber, Linda K. "Abolitionists and Amalgamators: The New York City Race Riots of 1834." *New York History* 48, no. 1 (1967): 28–39.

Kibler, Alison M. *Rank Ladies: Gender and Cultural Hierarchy in American Vaudeville*. Chapel Hill and London: The University of North Carolina Press, 1999.

Kilian, Crawford. *Go Do Some Great Thing: The Black Pioneers of British Columbia*. Vancouver: Douglas & McIntyre, 1978.

Krasner, David. "Black 'Salome': Exoticism, Dance, and Racial Myths." In *African American Performance and Theater History: A Critical Reader*, edited by Harry J. Elam, Jr. and David Krasner, 192–211. New York: Oxford University Press, 2001.

Krasner, David. "The Real Thing." In *Beyond Blackface: African Americans and the Creation of American Popular Culture, 1890–1930*, edited by W. Fitzhugh Brundage, 99–123. Chapel Hill: University of North Carolina Press, 2011.

LaBrew, Arthur R. *The Black Swan: Elizabeth Taylor Greenfield, Songstress*. LaBrew, 1969.

Lawrence, Bonita. "Rewriting Histories of the Land: Colonization and Indigenous Resistance in Eastern Canada." In *Race, Space and the Law: Unmapping a White Settler Society*, edited by Sherene Razack, 21–46. Toronto: Between the Lines, 2002.

Le Camp, Lorraine. "Racial Considerations of Minstrel Shows and Related Images in Canada." PhD diss., Ontario Institute for Studies in Education, University of Toronto, 2005.

Lemay, Leo. "The American Origins of 'Yankee Doodle'." *The William and Mary Quarterly* 33, no. 3 (1976): 435–64.

Lemons, Stanley J. "Black Stereotypes as Reflected in Popular Culture, 1880–1920." *American Quarterly* 29, no. 1 (Spring 1977): 102–16.

Lenton-Young, Gerald. "Variety Theatre." In *Early Stages: Theatre in Ontario 1800–1914*, edited by Ann Saddlemyer, 166–213. Toronto: University of Toronto Press, 1990.

Lewis, Ellistine P. "Selika, Marie Smith (c. 1849–1937)." *Black Women in America: An Historical Encyclopedia*. Bloomington: Indiana University Press, 1994.

Lhamon, W.T., Jr. "1830, May 21 Jump Jim Crow." In *A New Literary History of America*, edited by Greil Marcus and Werner Sollors, 201–04. Cambridge: Harvard University Press, 2012.

Lhamon, W.T., Jr. *Jump Jim Crow: Lost Plays, Lyrics, and Street Prose of the First Atlantic Popular Culture*. Cambridge: Harvard University Press, 2003.

Lhamon, W.T., Jr. *Raising Cain: Blackface Performance from Jim Crow to Hip Hop*. Cambridge and London: Harvard University Press, 1998.

Lindfors, Bernth. "'Mislike Me Not for My Complexion': Ira Aldridge in Whiteface." *African American Review* 50, no. 4 (2017): 1005–12.

Linteau, Paul-André, René Durocher, and Jean-Claude Robert. *Quebec: A History 1867–1929*. Translated by Robert Chodos. Toronto: James Lorimer & Company, 1983.

Londré, Felicia Hardison, and Daniel J. Watermeier. *The History of North American Theater: The United States, Canada, and Mexico: From Pre-Columbian Times to the Present*. New York City: The Continuum International Publishing Group Inc., 1998.

Longford, Martha. *Suspended Conversations: The Afterlife of Memory in Photographic Albums*. Montreal and Kingston: McGill-Queen's University Press, 2001.

Lorinc, John. "Ravages of Cholera." In *25 Days That Changed Toronto*, edited by Dylan Reid and Matthew Blackett, 84–88. Toronto: Spacing Media, 2007.

Lott, Eric. *Black Mirror: The Cultural Contradictions of American Racism*. Cambridge, Massachusetts: Harvard University Press, 2017.

Lott, Eric. *Love and Theft: Blackface Minstrelsy and the American Working Class*. 20th Anniversary Edition. New York and Oxford: Oxford University Press, 2013. First published 1993.

MacKenzie, Scott A. "But There Was No War: The Impossibility of a United States Invasion of Canada after the Civil War." *American Review of Canadian Studies* 47, no. 4 (2017): 357–71. https://doi.org/10.1080/02722011.2017.1406965.

Mackey, Frank. *Done with Slavery: The Black Fact in Montreal 1760–1840*. Montreal: McGill-Queen's University Press, 2010.

Mahar, William J. *Behind the Burnt Cork Mask: Early Blackface Minstrelsy and Antebellum American Popular Culture*. Chicago: University of Illinois Press, 1999.

Malpas, Jeff. "Place and Placedness." In *Situatedness and Place: Multidisciplinary Perspectives on the Spatio-temporal Contingency of Human Life*, edited by Thomas Hünefeldt and Annika Schlitte, 27–39. Cham, Switzerland: Springer International Publishing, 2018.

Marquis, Greg. *In Armageddon's Shadow: The Civil War and Canada's Maritime Provinces*. Montreal and Kingston: McGill-Queen's University Press, 1998.

Masten, April F. "Challenge Dancing in Antebellum America: Sporting Men, Vulgar Women, and Blacked-Up Boys." *Journal of Social History* 48, no. 3 (2015): 605–34.

Mathieu, Sarah-Jane. *North of the Color Line: Migration and Black Resistance in Canada, 1870–1955*. Chapel Hill: University of North Carolina Press, 2010.

Mawani, Renisa. "In Between and Out of Place: Mixed-Race Identity, Liquor, and the Law in British Columbia, 1850–1913." In *Race, Space and the Law: Unmapping a White Settler Society*, edited by Sherene Razack, 47–70. Toronto: Between the Lines, 2002.

Mayer, David. "Pantomime, British." In *Oxford Encyclopedia of Theatre and Performance*, edited by Dennis Kennedy, vol. 2, 995–7. Oxford: Oxford University Press.

Maynard, Robyn. *Policing Black Lives: State Violence in Canada from Slavery to the Present*. Halifax: Fernwood Publishing, 2017.

McConachie, Bruce. "Cognitive Studies and Epistemic Competence in Cultural History." In *Performance and Cognition: Theatre Studies and the Cognitive Turn*, edited by Bruce McConachie and F. Elizabeth Hart, 52–75. London and New York: Routledge, 2006.

McCorkindale, Deirdre. "Black Education: The Complexity of Segregation in Kent County's Nineteenth-Century Schools." In *Unsettling the Great White North: Black Canadian History*, edited by Michele A. Johnson and Funké Aladejebi, 333–56. Toronto: University of Toronto Press, 2022.

McLachlan, Alexander. *The Emigrant, and Other Poems*. Toronto: Rollo & Adam, 1861.

McLaren, Angus. *Our Own Master Race: Eugenics in Canada, 1885–1945*. Toronto: McClelland & Stewart, 1990.

McLaren, Kristin. "'We Had No Desire to Be Set Apart': Forced Segregation of Black Students in Canada West Public Schools and Myths of British Egalitarianism." *Social History /Histroie Sociale* 37, no. 73 (2004): 27–50.

McLean, Albert F., Jr. *American Vaudeville as Ritual*. Lexington: University of Kentucky Press, 1965.

Meer, Sarah. *Uncle Tom Mania: Slavery, Minstrelsy and Transatlantic Culture in the 1850s*. Athens, Georgia: University of Georgia Press, 2005.

Meitzer, François. *Salome and the Dance of Writing: Portraits of Mimesis in Literature*. Chicago: University of Chicago Press, 1987.

Mendelson, Alan. "*Grip* Magazine and 'the Other': The Genteel Antisemitism of J. W. Bengough." *Histoire Sociale* 40, no. 79 (2007): 1–44.

Miller, Benjamin. "Twisting the Dandy: The Transformation of the Blackface Dandy in Early American Theatre." *The Journal of American Drama and Theatre* 27, no. 3 (2015): 1–21.

Miller, Monica. *Slaves to Fashion: Black Dandyism and the Styling of Black Diasporic Identity*. Durham: Duke University Press, 2009.

Minor, Benjamin, and Ayanna Thompson. "'Edgar I Nothing Am': Blackface in *King Lear*." In *Staged Transgression in Shakespeare's England*, edited by Rory Loughnane and Edel Semple, 166–77. London: Palgrave Macmillan, 2013.

Mintz, Sidney W. *Sweetness and Power: The Place of Sugar in Modern History*. New York: Penguin Books, 1985.

Moodie, Susanna. *Life in the Clearings Versus the Bush*. London: R. Bentley, 1853.

Moore, Paul. "Spaces In-Between: The Railway and Early Cinema in Canada." In *Rural Cinema Exhibition and Audiences in a Global Context*, edited by Daniela Treveri Gennari, Danielle Hipkins, and Catherine O'Rawe, 73–89. London: Palgrave Macmillan, 2018.

Morgan, Jo-Ann. *Uncle Tom's Cabin as Visual Culture*. Columbia and London: University of Missouri Press, 2007.

Moriah, Kristin. "'A Greater Compass of Voice': Elizabeth Taylor Greenfield and Mary Ann Shadd Cary Navigate Black Performance." *Theatre Research in Canada* 41, no. 1 (2020): 20–38. https://doi.org/10.3138/tric.41.1.20.

Morrow, Don. *A Sporting Evolution: The Montreal Amateur Athletic Association, 1881–1981*. Montreal: Montreal Amateur Athletic Association and Don Morrow, 1985.

Moynagh, Maureen. "African-Canadian Theatre: An Introduction." In *African-Canadian Theatre: Critical Perspectives on Canadian Theatre in English*, edited by Maureen Moynagh, vol. 2, vii–xxii. Toronto: Playwrights Canada Press, 2005.

Nardocchio, Elaine F. *Theatre and Politics in Modern Quebec*. Edmonton: University of Alberta Press, 1986.

Nathan, Hans. "The Performance of the Virginia Minstrels." In *Inside the Minstrel Mask: Readings in Nineteenth-Century Blackface Minstrelsy*, edited by Annemarie Bean, James V. Hatch, and Brooks McNamara, 35–42. Hanover and London: Wesleyan University Press, 1996.

Nathan, Hans. "The Tyrolese Family Rainer, and the Vogue of Singing Mountain-Troupes in Europe and America." *The Musical Quarterly* 32, no. 1 (1946): 63–79.

Neatby, Nicole. *From Old Quebec to La Belle Province: Tourism Promotion, Travel Writing, and National Identities, 1920–1967*. Montreal and Kingston: McGill-Queen's University Press, 2018.

Nelson, Jennifer. *Razing Africville: A Geography of Racism*. Toronto: University of Toronto Press, 2009.

Nicholas, Jane. "Gendering the Jubilee: Gender and Modernity in the Diamond Jubilee of Confederation Celebrations, 1927." *The Canadian Historical Review* 90, no. 2 (2009): 247–74.

Nicks, Joan, and Jeannette Sloniowski. "Entertaining Niagara Falls, Ontario: Minstrel Shows, Theatres, and Popular Pleasures." In *Covering Niagara: Studies in Local Popular Culture*, edited by Joan Nicks and Barry Keith Grant, 285–310. Waterloo: Wilfrid Laurier University Press, 2010.

Nowatzki, Robert. *Representing African Americans in Transatlantic Abolitionism and Blackface Minstrelsy*, Louisiana: Louisiana State Press, 2010.

Nussbaum, Felicity. *Limits of the Human: Fictions of Anomaly, Race, and Gender in the Long Eighteenth Century*. Cambridge: Cambridge University Press, 2003.

Odell, George. *Annals of the New York Stage, Vol. 4: 1834–1843*. New York: Columbia University Press, 1928.

Oldfield, John R. "The 'Ties of Soft Humanity': Slavery and Race in British Drama, 1760–1800." *Huntington Library Quarterly* 56 (1993): 1–14.

O'Neill, Patrick. "A History of Theatrical Activity in Toronto, Canada: From Its Beginnings to 1858." PhD diss., Louisiana State University, 1973.

Orr, Bridget. *Empire on the English Stage, 1660–1714*. Cambridge: Cambridge University Press, 2001.

Otele, Olivette. "Resisting Imperial Governance in Canada. From Trade and Religious Kinship to Black Narrative Pedagogy in Ontario." In *The Promised Land: History and Historiography of the Black Experience in Chatham-Kent's Settlements and Beyond*, edited by Boulou Ebanda de B'béri, Nina Reid-Maroney, and Handel Kashope Wright, 131–48. Toronto: University of Toronto Press, 2014.

Patrick, John J., Richard M. Pious, and Donald A. Ritchie. *The Oxford Guide to the United States Government*. New York: Oxford University Press, 2002. First published 1993.

Petrin, Guylaine. "The Myth of Mary Mink: Representation of Black Women in Toronto in the Nineteenth Century." *Ontario History* 108, no. 1 (2016): 92–110. https://id.erudit.org/iderudit/1050613ar.

Phelan, Peggy. *Unmarked: The Politics of Performance*. London and New York: Routledge, 1993.

Pickering, Michael. *Blackface Minstrelsy in Britain*. Hampshire, England: Ashgate Publishing, 2008.

Pilgrim, David. *Understanding Jim Crow: Using Racist Memorabilia to Teach Tolerance and Promote Social Justice*. Oakland, California: PM Press, 2015.

Plant, Richard. "Chronology: Theatre in Ontario to 1914." In *Early Stages: Theatre in Ontario 1800–1914*, edited by Ann Saddlemyer, 288–346. Toronto: University of Toronto Press, 1990.

Poole, Carmen. "Conspicuous Peripheries: Black Identity, Memory, and Community in Chatham, ON, 1860–1980." PhD diss., University of Toronto, 2015.

Pugh, Megan. *America Dancing: From the Cakewalk to the Moonwalk*. New Haven and London: Yale University Press, 2015.

Rabson, Carolyn. "*Disappointment* Revisited: Unweaving the Tangled Web. Part I." *American Music* 1, no. 1 (1983): 12–35.

Rabson, Carolyn. "*Disappointment* Revisited: Unweaving the Tangled Web. Part II." *American Music* 2, no. 1 (1984), 1–28.

Raimon, Eve Allegra. *The 'Tragic Mulatta' Revisited: Race and Nationalism in Nineteenth-Century Antislavery Fiction*. New Brunswick, New Jersey: Rutgers University Press, 2004.

Razack, Sherene H. "Introduction." *Canadian Journal of Law and Society/La Revue Canadienne Droit et Société* 15, no. 2 (2000): 1–8.

Razack, Sherene H. "Introduction: When Place Becomes Race." In *Race, Space and the Law: Unmapping a White Settler Society*, edited by Sherene Razack, 1–20. Toronto: Between the Lines, 2002.

Razack, Sherene H. "Making Canada White: Law and the Policing of Bodies of Colour in the 1990s." *Canadian Journal of Law and Society/La Revue Canadienne Droit et Société* 14, no. 1 (1999): 159–84.

Reid, Richard M. *African Canadians in Union Blue: Enlisting for the Cause in the Civil War*. UBC Press: Vancouver, 2014.

Reid-Maroney, Nina. "'A Contented Mind Is a Continual Feast': Tracing Intellectual Migrations through the Promised Land." In *The Promised Land: History and Historiography of the Black Experience in Chatham-Kent's Settlements and Beyond*, edited by Boulou Ebanda de B'béri, Nina Reid-Maroney, and Handel Kashope Wright, 106–28. Toronto: University of Toronto Press, 2014.

Retallack, G. Bruce. "Paddy, the Priest and the Habitant: Inflecting the Irish Cartoon Stereotype in Canada." *Canadian Journal of Irish Studies*, 28/29 (2002): 124–47.

Reynolds, Graham. *Viola Desmond's Canada: A History of Blacks and Racial Segregation in the Promised Land*. Halifax and Winnipeg: Fernwood Publishing, 2016.

Reznik, Alexandra. "A Note on Centering Black Women's Voices and Scholarship on Singer Elizabeth Taylor Greenfield." *Tulsa Studies in Women's Literature* 40, no. 2 (2021): 387–94. https://doi.org/10.1353/tsw.2021.0028.

Rhodes, Jane. *Mary Ann Shadd Cary: The Black Press and Protest in The Nineteenth Century*. Bloomington, Indiana: Indiana University Press, 1998.

Rhodes, John. *A Community on the Thames: A Pictorial History of Chatham's Business and Industry*. Published in Commemoration of the Centennial of the Chatham and District Chamber of Commerce. Chatham: Chamberlain Press, 1987.

Rice, Edward Le Roy. *Monarchs of Minstrelsy, from "Daddy" Rice to Date*. New York: Kenny Publishing Company, 1911.

Riddle, Wesley Allen. "The Origins of Black Sharecropping." *The Mississippi Quarterly* 49, no. 1 (1995–96): 53–71.

∽ SELECTED BIBLIOGRAPHY ∽

Robinson, Beverly J. "Africanisms and the Study of Folklore." In *Africanisms in American Culture*, 2nd edition, edited by Joseph E. Holloway, 356–71. Bloomington: Indiana University Press, 2005.

Roediger, David R. *The Wages of Whiteness: Race and the Making of the American Working Class*. London and New York: Verso, 2007.

Rogin, Michael. *Blackface, White Noise: Jewish Immigrants in the Hollywood Melting Pot*. Berkeley: University of California Press, 1996.

Rohr, John A. "Current Canadian Constitutionalism and the 1865 Confederation Debates." *American Review of Canadian Studies* 28, no. 4 (1998): 413–44. https://doi.org/10.1080/02722019809481612.

Rosenberg, Louis. *Canada's Jews: A Social and Economic Study of Jews in Canada in the 1930s*, edited by Morton Weinfeld, 9–44. Montreal and Kingston: McGill-Queen's University Press, 1993.

Royce, Edward. *The Origins of Southern Sharecropping*. Philadelphia: Temple University Press, 1993.

Royster, Jacqueline Jones, ed. *Southern Horrors and Other Writings: The Anti-Lynching Campaign of Ida B. Wells, 1892–1900*. Boston and New York: Bedford/St. Martin's, 2016. First published 1997.

Runcie, John. "'Hunting the Nigs' in Philadelphia: The Race Riot of August 1834." *Pennsylvania History* 39, no. 2 (1972): 187–218.

Russell, Hilary. *Loew's Yonge Street and Winter Garden Theatres: A Structural, Architectural and Social History*. Toronto: Historical Research Division, Canadian Parks Service, 1990.

Saddlemyer, Ann. "Introduction." In *Early Stages: Theatre in Ontario 1800–1914*, edited by Ann Saddlemyer, 3–17. Toronto: University of Toronto Press, 1990.

Sammond, Nicholas. *Birth of an Industry: Blackface Minstrelsy and the Rise of American Animation*. Durham, North Carolina: Duke University Press, 2015.

Sampson, Henry T. *The Ghost Walks: A Chronological History of Blacks in Show Business, 1865–1910*. Metuchen, New Jersey: Scarecrow Press, 1988.

Sanders, Mark A. *Afro-Modernist Aesthetics and the Poetry of Sterling A. Brown*. Athens, Georgia: University of Georgia Press, 1999.

Sanjek, Russell. *American Popular Music and Its Business: The First Four Hundred Years Volume II: From 1790 To 1909*. Don Mills, Ontario: Oxford University Press, 2010.

Sanjek, Russell. *American Popular Music and its Business: The First Four Hundred Years Volume III: From 1900 to 1984*. New York and Oxford: Oxford University Press, 1988.

Savage, Kirk. *Standing Soldiers, Kneeling Slaves: Race, War, and Monument in Nineteenth-Century America*. Princeton, New Jersey: Princeton University Press, 1999.

Saxton, Alexander. "Blackface Minstrelsy." In *Inside the Minstrel Mask: Readings in Nineteenth-Century Blackface Minstrelsy*, edited by Annemarie Bean, James V. Hatch, and Brooks McNamara, 67–85. Hanover and London: Wesleyan University Press, 1996.

Saxton, Alexander. *The Rise and Fall of The White Republic: Class Politics and Mass Culture in Nineteenth-Century America*. London and New York: Verso, 1990.

Schendl, Herbert. "Language Choice as a Dramatic Device in an Early Viennese Adaptation of Isaac Bickerstaff's 'The Padlock'." *AAA: Arbeiten aus Anglistik und Amerikanistik* 32, no. 1 (2007): 25–45.

Senelick, Laurence. *The Changing Room: Sex, Drag and Theatre.* New York: Routledge, 2000.

Seroff, Doug. "'A Voice in the Wilderness': The Fisk Jubilee Singers' Civil Rights Tours of 1879–1882." *Popular Music and Society* 25, no. 1–2 (2001): 131–77. https://doi.org/10.1080/03007760108591791.

Shadd, Adrienne. *The Journey from Tollgate to Parkway: African Canadians in Hamilton.* Toronto: Natural Heritage Books, 2010.

Shadd Cary, Mary Ann. *A Plea for Emigration Or, Notes of Canada West,* edited by Richard Almonte. Toronto: Mercury, 1998. First published 1852.

Sheehy, Barry. *Montreal, City of Secrets: Confederate Operations in Montreal During the American Civil War.* Montreal: Renaud-Bray, 2020.

Sher, Julian. *White Hoods: Canada's Ku Klux Klan.* Vancouver: New Star Books, 1983.

Sherwood, Marika. "Black People in Tudor England." *History Today* 33, no. 10 (Oct. 2003): 40–2.

Simpson, Donald George. *Under the North Star: Black Communities in Upper Canada Before Confederation (1876).* Trenton, New Jersey: Africa World Press, 2005.

Slout, William L., ed. *Burnt Cork and Tambourines: A Source Book of Negro Minstrelsy.* San Bernardino: The Borgo Press, 2007.

Smardz Frost, Karolyn. *I've Got a Home in Glory Land: A Lost Tale of the Underground Railroad.* New York: Farrar, Straus and Giroux, 2007.

Smith, Mary Elizabeth. "On the Margins: Eastern Canada Theatre as Post-Colonialist Discourse." *Theatre Research International* 21, no 1, (1996): 41–51.

Smith, Mary Elizabeth. *Too Soon the Curtain Fell: A History of Theatre in Saint John, 1789–1900.* Fredericton: Brunswick Press, 1981.

Smith, Shawn Michelle. *American Archives: Gender, Race, and Class in Visual Culture.* Princeton, New Jersey: Princeton University Press, 1999.

Smith, Shawn Michelle. *Photography on the Color Line: W.E.B. Du Bois, Race, and Visual Culture.* Durham and London: Duke University Press, 2004.

Smith, Tamara. "Fizpoodle and the Amazon: Gender, Burlesque, and Anglophobia in the Spirit of the Times." *Journal of American Drama and Theatre* 22, no. 2 (2010): 49–66.

Snodgrass, Mary Ellen. "Missouri Compromise of 1820." In *The Underground Railroad: An Encyclopedia of People, Paces, and Operations.* Routledge: New York, 2015.

Sokol, B.J. "Singing Simpkin and Other Bawdy Jigs: Musical Comedy on the Shakespearean Stage: Scripts, Music and Context." *Shakespeare* 10, no. 3 (2014): 353–57. https://doi.org/10.1080/17450918.2014.927912.

Sontag, Susan. *On Photography.* New York: Picador, 1977.

Southern, Eileen. *The Music of Black Americans: A History.* New York: W.W. Norton Company, 1997.

Southern, Eileen. "The Origin and Development of the Black Musical Theater: A Preliminary Report." *Black Music Research Journal* 2 (1981–82): 1–14.

Spadoni, Carl. "*Grip* and the Bengoughs as Publishers and Printers." *43rd Annual Meeting of the Bibliographical Society of Canada, University of Windsor, Windsor, Ontario, 31 May 1988*. 12–33. University of Toronto Library. https://jps.library.utoronto.ca/index.php/bsc/article/download/17697/14631/42228.

Spier, Susan, and Gilles Potvin. "Calixa Lavallée," *Canadian Encyclopedia*, June 11, 2008. https://www.thecanadianencyclopedia.ca/en/article/calixa-lavallee.

Spray, William A. *The Blacks in New Brunswick*. New Brunswick: Unipress, 1972.

Spray, William A. "The Settlement of the Black Refugees in New Brunswick, 1815–1836." *Acadiensis: Journal of the History of the Atlantic Region* 6, no. 2 (1977): 64–79.

Springhall, John. *The Genesis of Mass Culture: Show Business Live in America, 1840 to 1940*. Palgrave Macmillan: New York, 2008.

Staples, Shirley. *Male-Female Comedy Teams in American Vaudeville 1865–1932*. Ann Arbor, Michigan: UMI Research Press, 1984.

Starkey, Brando Simeo. *In Defense of Uncle Tom: Why Blacks Must Police Racial Loyalty*. New York: Cambridge University Press, 2015.

Stathis, Stephen W. *Landmark Debates in Congress: From the Declaration of Independence to the War in Iraq*. Washington, DC: CQ Press, 2009.

Stewart, Gary. "Black Codes and Broken Windows: The Legacy of Racial Hegemony in Anti-Gang Civil Injunctions." *The Yale Law Journal* 107, no. 7 (1998): 2249–79. https://doi.org/10.2307/797421.

Stouffer, Allen P. *The Light of Nature and the Law of God: Antislavery in Ontario, 1833–1877*. McGill-Queen's University Press: Montreal, 1992.

Strausbaugh, John. *Black Like You: Blackface, Whiteface, Insult and Imitation in American Popular Culture*. London: Penguin Books, 2006.

Sundquist, Eric J. *To Wake the Nations: Race in the Making of American Literature*. Cambridge, Massachusetts: Belknap Press of Harvard University Press, 1993.

Sutherland, David. "Race Relations in Halifax Nova Scotia during the Mid-Victorian Quest for Reform." *Journal of the Canadian History Association/Revue de la Société historique du Canada* 7, no. 1 (1996): 35–54. https://doi.org/10.7202/031101ar.

Talty, Stephan. *Mulatto America: At the Crossroads of Black and White Culture: A Social History*. New York: Harper Collins, 2003.

Tate, Daniel, and Rob Bowman. *The Flyer Vault: 150 Years of Toronto Concert History*. Toronto: Dundurn, 2019.

Taylor, Yuval, and Jake Austen. *Darkest America: Black Minstrelsy from Slavery to Hip-Hop*. New York: W.W. Norton & Company, 2012.

Thompson, Brian Christopher. *Anthems and Minstrel Shows: The Life and Times of Calixa Lavallée, 1842–1891*. Montreal and Kingston: McGill-Queen's University Press, 2015.

Thompson, Cheryl. "*Black* Minstrelsy on Canadian Stages: Nostalgia for Plantation Slavery in the Nineteenth and Twentieth Centuries." *Journal of the Canadian Historical Association/Revue de la Société historique du Canada* 31, no. 1 (2021): 67–94. https://doi.org/10.7202/1083628ar.

Thompson, Cheryl. "'Come One, Come All': Blackface Minstrelsy as a Canadian Tradition and Early Form of Popular Culture." In *Towards an African-Canadian Art History: Art, Memory, and Resistance*, edited by Charmaine Nelson, 95–121. Concord, Ontario: Captus Press, 2018.

Thompson, Cheryl. "The *New* Afro in a Postfeminist Media Culture: Rachel Dolezal, Beyoncé's 'Formation,' and the Politics of Choice." In *Emergent Feminisms: Complicating a Postfeminist Media Culture*, edited by Jessalynn Keller and Maureen E. Ryan, 161–75. New York and London: Routledge, 2018.

Thompson, Cheryl. *Uncle: Race, Nostalgia, and the Politics of Loyalty*. Toronto: Coach House Books, 2021.

Thompson, Cheryl. "Uncle Tom's Cabin Historic Site and Creolization: The Material and Visual Culture of Archival Memory." *African and Black Diaspora: An International Journal* 12, no. 3 (2019): 304–19. https://doi.org/10.1080/17528631.2019.1611325.

Thompson, Cheryl, and Julie Crooks. "Race, Community, and the Picturing of Identities: Photography and the Black Subject in Ontario, 1860–1900." In *Unsettling the Great White North: Black Canadian History*, edited by Michele A. Johnson and Funké Aladejebi, 433–54. Toronto: University of Toronto Press, 2022.

Thompson, David S. "Shuffling Roles: Alterations and Audiences in Shuffle Along." *Theatre Symposium* 20, no. 1 (2012): 97–108. https://doi.org/10.1353/tsy.2012.0002.

Thurman, Kira. "Singing the Civilizing Mission in the Land of Bach; Beethoven; and Brahms: The Fisk Jubilee Singers in Nineteenth-Century Germany." *Journal of World History* 27, no. 3, Special Issue: Preaching the Civilizing Mission and Modern Cultural Encounters (2016): 443–71.

Toll, Robert C. *Blacking Up: The Minstrel Show in Nineteenth-Century America*. New York: Oxford University Press, 1974.

A Treasury of Stephen Foster. New York: Random House, 1946.

Turner, Patricia. *Ceramic Uncles and Celluloid Mammies: Black Images and Their Influence on Culture*. New York: Anchor Books, 1994.

Vance, Jonathan, F. *A History of Canadian Culture*. Don Mills, Ontario: Oxford University Press, 2009.

Vaughan, Virginia Mason. *Performing Blackness on English Stages, 1500–1800*. Cambridge: Cambridge University Press, 2005.

Vermazen, Bruce. *That Moaning Saxophone: The Six Brown Brothers and the Dawning of a Musical Craze*. New York and London: Oxford University Press, 2009.

Vernon, Karina. "Introduction." In *The Black Prairie Archives: An Anthology*, edited by Karina Vernon, 1–35. Waterloo: Wilfrid Laurier Press, 2020.

Walker, James W. *Racial Discrimination in Canada: The Black Experience*. Ottawa: Canadian Historical Association Historical Booklet, 1985.

Walker, James W. *The West Indians in Canada*. Saint John, New Brunswick: Canadian Historical Association, 1984.

Wallace-Sanders, Kimberly. *Mammy: A Century of Race, Gender, and Southern Memory*. Ann Arbor: University of Michigan Press, 2008.

Wang, Jiwu. *"His Dominion" and the "Yellow Peril": Protestant Missions to the Chinese Immigrants in Canada, 1859–1967*. Waterloo, Ontario: Canadian Corporation for Studies in Religion, 2006.

Wayne, Michael. "The Black Population of Canada West on the Eve of the American Civil War: A Reassessment Based on the Manuscript Census of 1861." In *A Nation of Immigrants: Women, Workers, and Communities in Canadian History,*

1840s–1960s, edited by Franca Iacovetta, Paula Draper and Robert Ventresca, 58–82. Toronto: University of Toronto Press, 1998.

Wayward, Sarah. "Immigration, Multiculturalism and National Identity in Canada." *International Journal on Minority and Group Rights* 5, no. 1 (1997): 33–58.

West, William, N. "When Is the Jig Up—and What Is It Up To?" In *Locating the Queen's Men, 1583–1603*, edited by Helen Ostovich, Holger Schott Syme, and Andrew Griffin, 201–215. London: Imprint Routledge, 2016.

White, Randall. *Too Good to Be True: Toronto in the 1920s*. Toronto and Oxford: Dundurn Press, 1993.

White, Shane, and Graham White. *Stylin': African American Expressive Culture from Its Beginnings to the Zoot Suit*. Ithaca and London: Cornell University Press, 1998.

Whitfield, Harvey Amani. *Blacks on the Border: The Black Refugees in British North America 1815–1860*. Hanover and London: University Press of New England, 2006.

Wiegman, Robyn. *American Anatomies: Theorizing Race and Gender*. Durham, North Carolina: Duke University Press, 1995.

Wiener, Jonathan M. "Class Structure and Economic Development in the American South, 1865–1955." *The American Historical Review* 84, no. 4 (1979): 970–92.

Wiles, David. *Shakespeare's Clown: Actor and Text in the Elizabethan Playhouse*. Cambridge: Cambridge University Press, 1987.

"William Henry Lane." *Contemporary Black Biography*, 90. Gale, 2011. *Gale In Context: Biography*, https://link-gale-com.myaccess.library.utoronto.ca/apps/doc/K1606005297/BIC?u=utoronto_main&sid=summon&xid=6e467f62.

Williams, Dorothy. *The Road to Now: A History of Blacks in Montreal*. Montreal: Véhicule Press, 1997.

Williams, Raymond. *Marxism and Literature*. Oxford: Oxford University Press, 1977.

Wilson, Elizabeth. *Adorned in Dreams: Fashion and Modernity*. Berkeley: University of California Press, 2003.

Winans, Robert B. "Early Minstrel Show Music, 1843–1852." In *Inside the Minstrel Mask: Readings in Nineteenth-Century Blackface Minstrelsy*, edited by Annemarie Bean, James V. Hatch, and Brooks McNamara, 141–62. Hanover and London: Wesleyan University Press, 1996.

Winks, Robin. *The Blacks in Canada: A History*. 2nd ed. Montreal and Kingston: McGill-Queen's University Press, 1997. First published 1971.

Winter, Mariam Hannah. "Juba and American Minstrelsy." In *Moving History/Dancing Cultures: A Dance History Reader*, edited by Ann Dils and Anne Cooper Albright, 250–55. Middleton, Connecticut: Wesleyan University Press, 2001.

Wittke, Carl. *Tambo and Bones: A History of the American Minstrel Stage*. Durham, North Carolina: Duke University Press, 1930.

Wood, Marcus. *Blind Memory: Visual Representations of Slavery in England and America, 1780–1865*. Manchester: Manchester University Press, 2000.

Wood, Peter. "'Gimme de Kneebone Bent': African Body Language and the Evolution of American Dance Forms." In *The Black Tradition in American Modern Dance*, edited by Gerald E. Myers, 8. Durham, North Carolina: American Dance Festival, 1988.

Wright, Josephine. "Jones [Joyner], (Matilda) Sissieretta [Black Patti]." *Grove Music Online*, October 16, 2013. https://doi-org.myaccess.library.utoronto.ca/10.1093/gmo/9781561592630.article.A2249930.

Yee, Shirley J. "Gender Ideology and Black Women as Community-Builders in Ontario, 1850– 70." *Canadian Historical Review* 75 (1994): 53–73.

Young, Gerald-Lenton. "Variety Theatre." In *Early Stages: Theatre in Ontario 1800–1914*, edited by Ann Saddlemyer, 166–213. Toronto: University of Toronto Press, 1990.

Zarefsky, David. *Lincoln, Douglas, and Slavery: In the Crucible of Public Debate.* Chicago: University of Chicago Press, 1993.

INDEX

abolition: groups, 18, 20, 27, 64–65, 67, 124–26, 196, 198; in the press, 88, 97–99; newspapers, 54, 58, 65–67, 88, 93, 95, 130, 162, 176, 213; societies in America, 64–65, 76, 89; societies in Canada, 67, 124–25, 158

Abyssinia, 197. *See also* Walker, George; Williams, Bert

Academy of Music of New Orleans, 105

Act to Limit Slavery in Upper Canada (1793), 61

Aldridge, Ira, 18–19, 76–78, 81, 87, 122, 220

Allen, Andrew Jackson "Dummy," 30

American Circus, 9, 15–16, 38–39, 42–46, 51, 56–57, 62–64, 69, 72, 80, 83–84, 98, 102, 104, 108, 135–38, 154, 159, 169, 180, 194, 241, 243, 248–49, 267, 283

American Civil War (1861–65), 12, 20–21, 31, 72, 75, 87, 89, 93, 101, 103–4, 109, 111, 113, 117–24, 126–34, 138, 142, 144, 149, 152, 155, 157, 164, 167, 175, 194, 202, 247, 257, 261, 271; "Appeal to Canadians", 120; Canadian soldiers in, 93, 104, 120, 121–22, 124–25; economic investment in, 118, 122, 124, 126, 134, 258; neutrality in, 120, 124; political performance during, 122; and political revolution in Canada, 121

American political parties: Democratic, 7, 71, 101, 131–32, 259; Republican, 101, 119, 132, 167, 254, 267; Whig, 101, 169, 247, 254, 260, 266–67

American Revolutionary War (1775–83), 11, 15, 29, 31–34, 38, 40, 41, 53, 60–61, 120, 125–26, 239, 258

Astor Place Rebellion (Shakespeare Riot) (1849), 85, 250; conflict between popular culture and high culture, 85, 192

Bandana Land (1907), 197; *See also* Walker, George; Williams, Bert

Bengough, John Wilson (J.W.), 22, 165–70, 174, 237, 266–67. *See also* political cartoons

Black America, 213

"Black dandy", 32, 45, 47, 69–70, 105, 135–36, 213. *See also* Zip Coon

Black Loyalists: in Amherst, 89; in Amherstburg, 89; in Birchtown, 33–34; in Boyd Block, 67; in Brantford, 176; in Chatham, 65–67, 89, 202, 246–47, 251–52; in Dawn Settlement (1841), 29, 65; in Elgin Settlement at Buxton, 29, 65, 67, 94, 251; in Halifax, 11, 29, 89, 110–11; in Hamilton, 90; in James Charity Block, 67; in Murray Block, 67; in Oro Township, 29; in Sandwich, 65, 88–89, 247, 251; in Shelburne, 33–34; in "Colored Village," St. Catharines, 65; in Wilberforce Settlement, 29, 65

The Black-a-moor Wash'd White, 38

Bland, James, 163; "Carry Me Back to Old Virginny" (1878), 163; "Hand Me Down My Walking Cane" (1880), 163; "Oh, Dem Golden Slippers" (1879), 163

INDEX

British Blondes, 184–85; in *Ixion*, 185. See also Thompson, Lydia
British North America (BNA) Act, 141
Brown, George, 67–68, 96–98, 121, 125, 171, 246, 253, 258, 267. see also *The Globe*
Burgess, Colin "Cool," 5, 12, 20, 83–84, 95, 102–5, 107, 113, 116, 135, 137, 163, 205, 207, 236, 250, 254–55, 272; performing "Shoo, fly! Don't bodder me!," 207
burlesque: at the minstrel show 80, 87, 104, 160, 163, 193, 207; Black representation in 82, 104, 108, 194, 212; Ethiopian Burlesque Troupe, 95, 135; music of, 222; female performance of, 22–23, 184–86, 194, 203, 212; developing North American theatre 59; in Toronto 64, 152, 186; Shakespearean, 8

California Gold Rush, 86, 95, 112, 147
"The Cake Winner," 201. See also dance: cakewalk
Callender, Charles, 4, 21, 139, 159–62
Canadian Jubilee Singers and Imperial Orchestra, 9–10, 177–79, 181, 215, 221
Canadian railway companies: Canadian Pacific Railroad (CPR), 6, 62–63, 114, 139, 142–43, 146–48, 158, 170, 262; during Confederation, 142–43; Grand Trunk Railway, 20, 62, 92, 261; Great Western Railway, 19, 92, 130; Intercolonial Railway, 158, 265; Lake Erie Railway Company, 158, 265; Ontario, Simcoe & Huron Union Railroad (Northern Railway of Canada), 92; Toronto, Hamilton and Buffalo Railway Company, 158. See also Pullman, George
Caribbean celebrations: Crop Over, 35; Jonkonnu (John Canoe), 35; J'ouvert, 35
Charlottetown Conference, 141
Chinese immigration: ban on, 145, 147, 263; Chinese Head Tax, 147; Chinese Tax Act, 147; and railroad labour, 6, 144, 147–48, 262–63

Christy, Edwin Pearce, 8, 72, 74–75
Civil War. See American Civil War
clown: American circus, 39, 44, 45, 108; blackface, 16–17, 42–43, 45, 57, 59, 72, 98, 115, 133; English pantomime, 43, 80, 82, 108, 115
"Coal Black Rose" (1829), 45–47, 69, 135. See also Dixon, George Washington
Cole, Robert "Bob," 172, 197, 203–4, 212
colonization of Indigenous land, 6, 11, 26, 32–33, 53–54, 101, 109–10, 112–13, 142–43. 146, 239
Compromise of 1820, 102
Compromise of 1850, 85
Compromise of 1877, 132–33, 204
Confederate sympathizers, 20, 118, 122, 124, 126, 134, 152, 157–58, 258; in the Maritimes 120, 122, 157. See American Civil War
Confederation, Canadian, 21–22, 53, 96, 105, 117, 121, 140–43, 145–46, 148, 243
Conservative Party (Canada), 97, 121, 125, 151, 167–70, 173, 205
"coon," 41, 169, 171–73, 180, 197–98, 212, 220, 267; shouting, 193; singers, 156; songs, 21, 41, 171, 197, 200, 203, 207, 213, 218, 220, 222; *Zip Coon*, 45–47, 49–50, 54, 59, 69, 105, 136, 172, 248
The Creole Show, 212–13. See also dance: cakewalk; Lucas, Sam
cutting contests, 79. See also Diamond, John; Lane, William Henry

dance: buck and wing, 39, 203, 238; cakewalk, 200–201, 203, 211–13, 222; callithumpians, 27; English clog dancing, 29, 39, 44, 128, 245; hornpipe, 16, 29, 39, 42, 44, 100, 246; moorish dance, 17, 78; mummers, 27; tap dance, 100, 162, 238, 265
Darkest America; 21, 23, 184, 213–14
"darkie," 47, 69, 71, 155, 212, 220
Davis, Jefferson, 119, 126
Diamond, John, 4, 18–19, 78–79, 81. See also jigging
The Disappointment; or the Force of Credulity (1767), 40–41, 47, 50, 171. See also raccoon

INDEX

Dixon, George Washington, 16, 44–47, 49–51, 135–36
Douglass, Frederick, 65–68, 94, 247
Dred Scott v. Sanford, 101–2, 254
Du Bois, W.E.B., 9, 149,196, 259, 263, 271; "sorrow songs", 9, 149, 196; *Souls of Black Folk,* 263, 271

Emancipation Day, 88–90, 94, 109, 251, 268
Emancipation Proclamation, 126, 202
endmen, 19, 59, 69, 102, 106, 154, 168, 205. *See also* minstrel show; Tambo and Bones
Ethiopian Serenaders, 19, 63, 71–72, 75, 81, 83, 87, 95
European folk performance: blackening, 16–17, 23, 27, 44, 103, 115, 119, 219–20; commedia dell'arte, 8, 43, 80, 108; drolls, 17, 29, 237; fool, 8, 32, 41, 50, 63, 115, 220; foolish black devils, 17, 245; harlequin, 8, 39, 43, 108; moors, 17, 27, 38, 43–44, 50, 108, 220, 237, 241, 245; pantomime, 8, 39, 43, 80, 108, 184, 188, 270.

female impersonation: Aunt Dinah, 105; Aunt Liza, 212; buffalo gals, 188–89; cross-dressing, 8, 28, 39, 100, 182, 186, 188, 191; Dame, 8, 188; Funny Ol' Gal, 188–89; Mammy, 106, 204, 210; plantation girls; 189, the scolding wife, 191; wench or prima donna; 8, 188–190, 204, 270; wench songs, 189; yaller gals,188–89, 270; yellow girls,188–89. *See also* minstrel characters
Fisk Jubilee Singers (1871), 9–10, 139–40, 149, 175–78, 195–96, 198, 214–15, 216–17, 218. *See also* jubilee
Foster, Stephen, 6, 56, 86–87, 115; "Backside of Albany" ("The Siege of Plattsburg"), 30, 109; "Camptown Races"(1850), 6, 251; "Massa in de Cold", 5–6, 115; "My Old Kentucky Home, Good Night" (1853), 6, 87; "Oh! Susanna" (1848), 6, 86; "Old Folks at Home," 6, 87; "Old Uncle Ned" (1848), 6, 86

Fourteenth Amendment to the United States Constitution, 118, 259
Fraser Canyon Gold Rush, 6, 96, 114, 116, 140, 146–47
free Black populations; employment of, 21, 67, 93–94, 129, 131, 146, 164, 236, 259; sharecropping, 129–30, 138, 221
Freedman's Bureau, 132, 259. *See also* abolition
Fredericton Temperance Hall, 149, 158
Fugitive Slave Act, 67–68, 75, 85, 91, 116, 246

The Globe: American Civil War coverage, 126; circulation and influence, 88, 96–97, 253; discussion of abolition, 96–99, 125; discussion of politics, 97, 204–5, 208; on Emancipation Day, 89; establishment of, 96; eulogies, 205; on minstrelsy, 163, 208; on the Fisk Jubilee Singers, 175, 195, 215–17; political cartoons of, 167; theatrical promotion, 60, 135, 158, 160, 162, 186, 205, 207, 209–11, 214. *See also* Brown, George
Greenfield, Elizabeth Taylor, 9, 23, 198–99, 201–3, 272
Grip, 22, 165–69, 237, 266–67, 276, 286, 291. *See also* political cartoons
Guelph City Hall, 176

Hague, Sam, 123, 128, 137, 139, 157
Halifax (NS) performance halls: Academy Hall, 4; City Hall, 158, New Grand Theatre, 43, 51; Temperance Hall, 51; Theatre Royal at Spring Gardens, 64
Hamilton (ON) performance halls: Grand Opera House, 151–52, 211, 237; Hamilton Royal Metropolitan, 83–84, 151
Harper, Ned, 49; *See also* burlesque
Harper's Ferry Raid/Chatham Convention, 66
Hayes, Rutherford, 132, 204
Haverly, J.H. Christopher, 21, 103, 135, 139, 159–60, 163, 174, 195

297

Haverly's United Mastodon Minstrels, 4, 21, 158–59, 195
homegrown Canadian blackface, 5, 20, 12, 83, 88, 95–96, 113, 116–17, 205, 222
Hyers Sisters, 23, 198, 202–3, 272

immigration: building the railroad, 6, 114, 147–48, 262–63; during the Cholera Outbreak (1832) 52, 242; during the Great Potato Famine (1845–52): 52, 100; policy in Britain, 52
In Dahomey (1902), 197. *See also* Walker, George; Williams, Bert
Inkle and Yarico (1787), 38
interlocutor, 19, 168, 170–71. *See also* minstrel show

jigging, 16–17, 29, 39, 78–80, 100, 236, 238, 245, 249. *See also* cutting contests; Diamond, John; Lane, William Henry
Jim Crow: beginnings, 47; character, 15, 48–49, 51, 70, 102, 105–6, 135; costume, 174; cultural influence, 50, 54, 59, 204; dance, 39, 50, 69, 136, 200; in Canada, 57–58, 84, 108, 180; in "Jump Jim Crow", 16, 47, 51, 135, 220, 242; relationship with Zip Coon, 49–50, 54, 69, 136; and segregation, 23, 212. *See* Rice, Thomas "Daddy"
Jones, Matilda Sissieretta "Black Patti," 9, 23, 198–99, 203–4, 212, 272, 293
Josiah Henson, 65, 82–84, 250; *The Life of Josiah Henson, Formerly a Slave, Now an Inhabitant of Canada* (1849), 82, 84. *See also* tom shows
jubilee, 150, 181, 198. *See also* Canadian Jubilee Singers, Fisk Jubilee Singers
Julien, Henri, 172, 174; *see also* political cartoons; "Songs of the By-Town Coons"

Kansas–Nebraska Act of 1885, 101
Kersands, Billy, 160–61, 162 ; effect on black minstrelsy, 217–19; "Essence of Virginny," 162; "Mary's Gone with a Coon", 161–62; "Old Aunt Jemima", 161–62; use of improvisation and African folk music, 162; Virginia Essence, 162. *See also* Original Georgia Minstrels

Lane, William Henry, 18–19, 76, 78–82, 87, 100, 122, 201, 249; performance innovations, 56, 76, 79–80, 100, 248; juba (dance), 18, 76, 79–80; understanding by white audiences, 78, 80
Laurier, Wilfrid, 173, 208, 213
Lavallée, Calixa, 11–12, 20, 95, 103–7, 113, 116, 124, 144–45, 258; *See also* "O Canada"
Liberal Party, 97, 121, 167, 169, 171, 173, 207–8, 237
Lincoln, Abraham, 101, 119, 122, 124, 126, 132, 152, 155
London Conference, 142, 261
London (ON) performance Halls: Grand Opera House 148, 150, 172, 263, 268; Mechanics' Institute Hall, 150; Theatre Royal, 83, 150
London, England performance Halls: Royal Coburg Theatre, 77; The Theatre Royal, Drury Lane, 36; Vauxhall Gardens, 81
Lower Canada, 11, 25, 33, 35, 40, 43, 52–53, 60–61, 107, 165
Lucas, Sam, 202, 212

Macdonald, John A., 121, 142–43, 1 66–70, 205, 214, 244, 266
Madame Rentz's Female Minstrels, 23, 184–86. *See also* women in minstrelsy
Maritimes Emancipation Freedom Festivals, 89, 111
Metropolitan Theatre, 202
migration of Black populations: "The Blacks in Canada" (1971), 4; fleeing the transatlantic slave trade, 9, 11, 18, 53, 61, 64, 66–68, 70, 113, 116, 176, 246; in the Maritimes, 11, 33, 109–11; in Victoria and Vancouver Island, 96, 146; "A Plea for Emigration, or Notes on Canada West", 93, 252; post-Reconstruction, 182; post-War of 1812, 28; in Quebec, 145; and the Revolutionary War, 32; *The Refugees from*

INDEX

Slavery in Canada West, 91; White aggression towards, 91, 94, 146

minstrel characters: Old Black Joe, 210; Old Dan Tucker, 135, 260; "piccaninnies," 212; Pickaninny Brass Band, 209–10; Uncle Rastus, 212. *See also* female impersonation

minstrel show: and abolition, 18; American, 22, 44, 55, 102, 165, 220; audiences of, 85, 129, 156–57, 200; Black 21, 23, 155–56; Blackface, 28, 48, 55, 58, 95, 104–5, 118, 144, 146, 148, 174; characters, 105, 107; costumes and makeup of, 43, 49, 75–76, 82, 100, 104–5, 128, 157, 163–64, 187–90; disseminating Black culture, 10, 28, 108, 113, 123, 147; in Canada, 59, 68, 83, 96, 133, 135–36, 165, 180, 222, 250, 252; in the Maritimes, 95, 138; in Montreal, 63, 147, 210; repertoire of, 16, 19, 23, 44, 75–76, 87, 103, 107–8, 147, 154, 162, 165, 188, 211–12, 223; representation of Black populations, 76, 83–85, 95, 113, 183, 187, 193; representations of women, 188–91; reviews, 160; songs of, 80, 87, 188; structure of, 17, 19, 38, 69, 106, 184, 186, 192, 212; themes of, 9, 118, 182; 120; in Toronto, 102, 117, 152, 211; in Western Canada, 5, 19, 148, 257

Montreal (PQ) performance halls: Academie de Musique, 62; Bonaventure Hall, 62; Garrick Theatre Club, 63; Hayes Theatre, 62; Her Majesty's Theatre, 62; Mechanics' Hall 62–63, 122; Montreal Theatre, 62; Nordheimer's Hall, 62; Odd Fellows Hall, 63; Salle de Concert de l'Hôtel de Ville, 62; Theatre Royal, 62–64, 103, 210, 273

Mungo, 36–38, 41, 51, 77–78, 238–39. *See also The Padlock*

"My Long Tail Blue" (1827), 45, 49, 135–36. *See also* Dixon, George Washington

Nast, Thomas, 167–68, 267. *See also* political cartoons

National Policy Minstrels, 22, 165, 166–71, 174, 266–67

Negro Election Day, 28, 34–35, 111

Negro spirituals, 9, 149–50, 174–76, 178–81, 202; and White audiences, 150, 180

New Chicago Theatre, 163

New Orleans Minstrels, 12. *See also* burlesque

New York's Five Points neighbourhood, 78, 80, 100. *See also* Diamond, John; Lane, William Henry

New York City performance halls: African Grove Theatre, 66, 246; Astor Opera House, 85; Bowery Theatre, 55, 71, 78; Carnegie Hall, 203, 212; Chatham Theatre, 45, 55, 78; Madison Square Garden 200, 203; Madison Square Theatre, 147; Park Theatre, 55; Purdy's National Theatre, 92; Third Avenue Theatre, 172; Winter Garden Theatre, 209

North American Convention of Colored Freemen, 68

North-West Mounted Police (the Royal Canadian Mounted Police), 5–6, 112, 115, 142, 148

nostalgia: for Black servitude and the plantation, 16, 18–19, 64, 95, 138, 149, 156–57, 207–9; for minstrel shows of the past, 87, 209

Notman, William, 152, 264; photos of Confederate community, 152; photos of female impersonation 189–91, 270; photos of minstrelsy, 152

O'Banyoun, Josephus, 10, 176, 268

O'Banyoun Jubilee Singers 10, 176–78, 268–69. *See also* Canadian Jubilee Singers

O Canada (Chant National), 12, 144. *See also* Lavallée, Calixa

olio, 57, 59, 117; *See also* minstrel show

Original Georgia Minstrels, 127–28, 158–61

Oroonoko: or, the Royal Slave (1695), 36, 38, 240, 248

Ottawa, Ontario Performance Halls: Gowan's New Opera House, 150; Grand Opera House, 215; Her

299

INDEX

Majesty's Theatre, 83, 150, 250; Rideau Hall, 150; Rink Music Hall, 150, 250
Out of Bondage (originally titled *Out of the Wilderness*) (1876), 202. See also Hyers Sisters

The Padlock, a Comic Opera, in Two Acts, 36–38, 239–40; See also Mungo
Papineau, Louis-Joseph, 53, 165; see also Patriotes
Patriotes, 53, 165
Pavillon des Patineurs 144
Pinkster, 28, 34, 111
"plantation girl" melodramas: *Clotel; or The President's Daughter* (1853), 189; *Octoroon* (1841), 189, 209; "Quadroon Girl" (1842), 189; *The Quadroon* (1856), 209. See also *Uncle Tom's Cabin* (novel); female impersonation: wench
Plessy v. Ferguson (1896), 194, 212
political cartoons: *Bill Board Re-Decorated*, 22, 169–70; *National Policy Minstrels*, 22, 165–66, 168–69, 174, 266; representation of Black people, 164, 168–69, 174; *Theatre Comique*, 152. See also Bengough, John Wilson; Julien, Henri; Nast, Thomas
Provincial Freeman 65, 88, 130. See also Shadd Cary, Mary Ann
Pullman, George, 178; railway porters, 11, 131, 133, 139, 194, sleeping cars, 11, 20, 130–31, 133, 139, 194
Punch, 22, 50, 271
Punch in Canada, 22

Quebec Conference, 121, 142, 261

Raccoon, 41, 47. See also *The Disappointment*
ragtime, 162, 200–201, 213, 218, 222, 179; rhythm and syncopation, 86, 171, 179, 222, 249
rebellions of 1837–38, 52, 89, 99, 104, 126, 165, 242
Reconstruction, 129–30, 132, 145, 149, 155, 182, 213, 259; post-Reconstruction, 155, 204, 221

Reform Party, 58, 96–97, 121, 125, 167, 171, 211, 257
Report on the Affairs of British North America (1839), 53, 99
Rice, Thomas Dartmouth "Daddy," 16, 47–51, 84, 135–36, 169, 212, 236, 245, 248, 254–55; in New York's Seventh Ward, 16
Robinson Crusoe; or Harlequin Friday, 39, 184
romanticizing the South: *Down in Dixie*, 210; *In Old Kentucky*, 209–10, 273; *On the Mississippi*, 210. See also Pickaninny Brass Band
Royal Proclamation (1763), 33, 239

Saint John (NB) performance halls: Mechanics' Institute, 95, 137, 149, 158, 252; Saint John Dramatic Lyceum, 51
Sambo, 47, 50, 241. See also Dixon, George Washington
segregation: in Canadian schools, 94, 247; de facto 141, 145, 216; Jim Crow, 23, 212; spatial, 100, 116, 254; through "separate but equal" legislation, 68, 194; through the Common Schools Act of 1850, 93–94; through the Separate Car Act, 194
Shadd Cary, Mary Ann, 65, 88, 93, 120–21
Shakespeare, William: plays, 43–44, 64, 146; theatre of 8, 17, 60, 77, 81, 85, 188, 192, 237, 241
Shelburne ordinance "forbidding Negro Dances & Negro Frolicks", 35
The Slave (1816), 38
Songs of the By-Town Coons, 172–74
St. Antoine (Little Burgundy), 11, 62
stump speech, 59, 75, 170, 212. See also minstrel show

Tambo and Bones, 22, 59, 69, 101–2, 106, 168, 188
Tragedy of Othello, the Moor of Venice, 43–44, 77–78, 84, 220, 241, 246, 248. See also Shakespeare, William
Theatre Royal Liverpool, 157

∽ INDEX ∽

Thirteenth Amendment to the Constitution, 123, 129, 259
Thompson, Lydia, 184. *See also* British Blondes; burlesque
tom shows: *Life Among the Happy*, 84; Uncle Tom, 82, 84, 180, 202, 213, 235, 238, 247, 250, 260; *Uncle Tom's Cabin* (show; 1852, 1880), 18, 82–84, 163, 202, 210, 235, 250. *See also* Uncle Tom's Cabin (novel)
Toronto: anti-blackface petitions and protests in, 9, 18, 56–58, 81, 89, 104–5, 135; class divisions in, 58–59; Toronto Coloured Young Men's Amateur Theatrical Society, 5, 81, 235; degeneration in the 19th century, 58–59
Toronto (ON) performance halls: Academy of Music (The Princess Theatre), 207; Agricultural Hall, 151; Bond Street Church, 215; Frank's Hotel, 31; Grand Opera House, 150–52, 158, 160, 162, 207, 209–11, 235, 263, 266, 272; Grand Theatre, 152, 264; Horticultural Gardens and Pavilion (Allan Gardens), 151, 214, 218, 274; Massey Hall, 211; Music Hall, 149, 151, 158; Osgoode Hall, 53; Palmer's Concert Hall, 151; Princes of Wales Music Hall, 151; Royal Lyceum, 5, 60, 81, 83–84, 103, 151, 186, 235, 243, 250; Royal Opera House, 150, 152, 158, 161, 186; Shaftesbury Hall, 195–96, 214, 271; St. James Cathedral, 53, 90; St. Lawrence Hall, 53, 68, 83, 90, 125, 151, 160; Temperance Hall, 151; Toronto Lyceum; 59; Toronto Opera House, 210; University College, 53, 246; York Mechanics' Institute, 98; Y.M.C.A Hall, 195
transatlantic slave trade; 7, 14, 15, 27–29, 36, 61, 86, 244
traveling circuses: Barnum's Menagerie and Museum, 84; George F. Bailey circus tour, 136; L.B. Lent's Mammoth National Circus, 137; Royal Circus (1826), 241
Trip to Coontown, 172, 203. *See also* Cole, Robert "Bob"; Johnson, Billy

The Triumph of Love; or, Happy Reconciliation (1795), 37
Tyrolese Minstrels (Rainer Family), 72. *See also* Virginia Minstrels

Uncle Tom's Cabin (novel), 4, 12, 82, 115, 189, 250
Underground Railroad, 66, 110, 114, 176, 243
Upper Canada, 3, 11, 25, 29, 31, 33, 40, 42, 52, 60–61, 65, 83, 94, 110, 145, 239, 244, 246
Urlina, the African Princess (1879), 202. *See also* Hyers Sisters

vaudeville, 9, 22–23, 62, 182, 184–87, 192–94, 196, 198, 203, 208–9, 211, 218, 222, 265; the Jewish blackface performer in, 9, 22, 182–83
Victoria (BC) performance halls: Colonial Theatre, 96; Theatre Royal, 138; Victoria Theatre, 146, 212
Victoria Hall, 95
Virginia Minstrels, 17, 19, 38, 56, 71–73, 75, 87, 107, 117, 135, 165, 168–70, 187, 189, 204, 260
visual culture surrounding black populations, 12, 23, 134, 145–46, 154–55, 164, 174, 194, 219

War of 1812, 11, 15, 23, 25, 26, 28, 29–31, 41, 58, 60, 66, 83, 109, 111, 120, 152, 260
Walker, George, 197
Welch, Bob; 136. *See also* burlesque
western expansion: empty land myth, 149; European identity in the Canadian West, 143–44; "fill in the middle" settlement, 147; manifest destiny, 86, 251; minstrel shows in western Canada 19, 96. *See also* Canadian railway companies; Fraser Canyon Gold Rush; North-west Mounted Police
white supremacy: the Ku Klux Klan, 128–29,132, 289; "Lost Cause" Movement, 132, 157–58; "White Man's Burden," 8

301

Williams, Bert: 197, 204

Winnipeg (MB) performance halls: Princess Opera House, 160; Walker Theatre, 160

women in minstrelsy: Black, 182, 192, 194; challenging the patriarchy, 231; "Girlie Shows," 184, 186; female minstrel troupes, 23, 184, 186; onstage sexuality, 183, 185, 188; race cross-dressing, 28, 39, 157

Yankee: Sam Patch (the Yankee Leaper), 40; Uncle Sam, 152; Yankee Doodle Dandy 31, 40–41, 238–39; *Yankee Story*, 40

www.ingramcontent.com/pod-product-compliance
Lightning Source LLC
Chambersburg PA
CBHW052132070526
44585CB00017B/1796